MORTGAGE LENDING

Fundamentals and Practices

MORTGAGE

FUNDAMENTALS

Second Edition

Sponsored by
Mortgage Bankers Association of America
Chicago, Illinois

LENDING

AND PRACTICES

WILLIS R. BRYANT

McGRAW-HILL BOOK COMPANY
New York   San Francisco   Toronto   London   1962

THIS BOOK IS DEDICATED to all young men and young women who are pursuing or who plan to pursue a career in mortgage banking in all or any one of its many phases or in related activities.

MORTGAGE LENDING

Copyright © 1956, 1962, by McGraw-Hill, Inc.
All Rights Reserved. Printed in the United States of America.
This book, or parts thereof, may not be reproduced
in any form without permission of the publishers.

Library of Congress Catalog Card Number 61-18258

8 9 10 11 12–MAMM–7 5 4 3 2

ISBN 07-008609-5

Preface

The first edition of this book was written as the result of a belief that young men and young women interested in developing skill in the art of mortgage lending were in need of a textbook containing an integrated statement of basic fundamentals and general principles.

In order to attain this objective, the book provided information regarding procedures; it also provided an appraisal of the social significance of mortgage lending, and contained an account of the ways in which the activities of the lenders have been enhanced and circumscribed by law.

This second and revised edition continues to emphasize these basic fundamentals. It also incorporates recent developments in the mortgage lending industry and in related activities as well as the essential updating of statistics and related data.

Material in this book is suitable for use not only by students and instructors but also by men and women presently engaged in any phase of the business of mortgage banking.

The first edition of this book has been in use in a large number of universities and colleges throughout the nation, in the Mortgage Bankers Association School of Mortgage Banking, in other trade association educational programs, in university extension programs, and in mortgage banking and institutional investor firms in all segments of the financial community during the past five years.

This book is the product of the author's experience as a lending officer in a major commercial bank, as president and part owner of a mortgage banking firm, as a teacher in extension programs of the University of California, as a teacher in the MBA School of Mortgage Banking at Stanford University, and as a teacher of home mortgage lending under the auspices of the American Institute of Banking.

For an advanced study and analysis of mortgage lending and related building and financing subjects, the author suggests that students make full use of the Bibliography and Suggested Reading list at the end of each chapter and the very complete Glossary of Terms Most Frequently Used in Mortgage Lending, pages 395 to 408.

Willis R. Bryant

Acknowledgments

The compilation and presentation of a textbook such as this requires a great deal of study and research in the field of mortgage lending and related activities, as well as extensive advice, counsel, suggestions, data, and plans of business associates and others, if the product is to be complete.

The author wishes to express his appreciation to Leroy Lewis, National Educational Director, American Institute of Banking, Section American Bankers Association, New York, for permission to use portions of Chapters 11 and 12 and portions of the Glossary of the textbook *Home Mortgage Lending*, published by the American Institute of Banking, 1953. These two chapters and the Glossary were written by the author.

The author would also like to acknowledge and thank the following for their assistance, timely advice, and contributions:

S. J. Baughman, President, Federal National Mortgage Association, Washington, D.C.

Bouvier's Law Dictionary, J. B. Lippincott Company, Philadelphia. (Glossary of Terms)

Ralph E. Bruneau, Vice-president, Valley National Bank, Phoenix, Arizona. (Chapter 8)

Homer V. Cherrington, Professor Emeritus of Finance, Northwestern University and Ohio University.

Duncan B. Campbell, Campbell-Farnow School of Real Estate, Inc., San Francisco.

John Coplen and Maurice Paquette, Loan Guaranty Division, Veterans Administration, San Francisco.

Cyclopedic Law Dictionary, Callaghan and Company, Chicago. (Glossary of Terms)

George Gummerson, Vice-president, Title Insurance & Trust Company, Los Angeles. (Glossary of Terms)

Joseph R. Jones, Vice-president, Security First National Bank of Los Angeles. (Chapter 4)

Land Title Guarantee and Trust Company, Cleveland, Ohio. (Chapter 7)

vi

Richard C. Larson, President, C. A. Larson Investment Company, Beverly Hills, California. (Chapter 11)

Gault W. Lynn, Assistant Vice-president, Federal Reserve Bank of San Francisco.

Frank J. McCabe, Jr., Executive Vice-president, Mortgage Bankers Association of America, Chicago.

Robert Macduff, formerly District Director, Federal Housing Administration San Francisco.

Samuel E. Neel, General Counsel, Mortgage Bankers Association of America, Washington, D.C. (Chapter 7)

Thomas L. Nims, formerly Secretary, Savings and Mortgage Division, American Bankers Association, New York.

Linden L. D. Stark, Vice-president, Crocker-Anglo National Bank, San Francisco. (Chapter 8)

V. R. Steffensen, President, First Security Bank of Idaho, Boise, Idaho. (Chapter 9)

D. Clair Sutherland, Senior Vice-president, Bank of America, N.T. & S.A., San Francisco. (Chapter 1)

Roy F. Taylor, President, Puget Sound Mutual Savings Bank, Seattle, Washington. (Chapter 9)

James G. Wasson, Director, Loan Administration, Mortgage Bankers Association of America, Chicago. (Chapters 11 and 12)

Paul F. Wendt, Professor of Finance, School of Business Administration, University of California, Berkeley, California.

Urban K. Wilde, Manager, Mortgage Loan Department, Coldwell, Banker and Company, Los Angeles. (Chapter 8)

L. E. Woodford, Vice-president, Federal Home Loan Bank of San Francisco.

Contents

1 The Fundamental Aspects of Mortgage Lending

PURPOSES

1. To describe the basic economic reality that underlies mortgage lending, mortgage financing, and the mortgage market
2. To discuss the importance of mortgage lending
3. To discuss briefly some fundamental aspects of mortgage lending
4. To trace the development and growth of this industry
5. To review the procedures and practices that were responsible for mortgage lending difficulties in the past
6. To describe the measures taken to correct these difficulties, thus improving mortgage lending procedures in their entirety
7. To describe the activity of the government in mortgage lending during the past thirty years
8. To estimate the importance of mortgage lending to lenders and to the national economy

Basic Economic Reality That Underlies Mortgage Lending, Mortgage Financing, and the Mortgage Market

A study of mortgage lending, mortgage financing, and the mortgage market would be very incomplete without a detailed examination of the basic economic reality that underlies the mortgage market and the mortgage banking industry and their relation to other money market activities that exist in the entire nation.

Basic Sources of Funds

Two basic questions are involved: (1) Where does the money come from? (2) Why and how does this money find its way into the mortgage market? Stated technically, we are interested in the supply of mortgage funds and the demand for these funds and in the problems involved in matching demand with supply.

1

The basic source of funds for the mortgage market is personal savings. These savings are the difference between the take-home pay of the more than 55 million spending units in the economy and the amount spent by those families and individuals for goods and services. Such savings fluctuate widely in line with changes in the fortunes and desires of each individual.

There are some complicated factors that affect these savings. Income minus spending equals savings. From this it can be seen that the volume of savings may be affected in four ways: by increased income, by reduced income, by increased spending, or by reduced spending. Under these circumstances it is no surprise that savings may fluctuate widely.

Savings are a residual and are thus dependent on the many factors that govern the flow of income to individuals and the many factors that govern their spending decisions. The general health of the economy, manifested especially in the level of employment and wages, determines the level of income, while this factor and others besides, notably the desire to maintain a certain standard of living, determine the level of consumer spending. The bulk of savings is only the unplanned result of these diverse pressures. As a result, we see consumers saving at very different rates at different points of the business cycle, despite a general tendency to save between 4 and 8 per cent of income (see Table 1). For instance, savings amounted to about 20 per cent of income during the war years of 1942 to 1945, when consumers would or could not spend all their vastly inflated incomes, while consumers actually spent more than they earned in an effort to maintain customary living standards in the Great Depression years of 1930 to 1934.

Economic Effects Resulting from Methods by Which Savings Are Accrued

In addition to the variability resulting from the residual nature of savings, there are other economic effects resulting from the methods by which savings are accrued. Saving in any period is equal to the change in net worth in that period. Consequently, an individual may save by adding to his liquid assets, or he may save by paying off his indebtedness. Again, he may accumulate voluntary savings, which fluctuate in regard to amount and to time or frequency of accumulation (according to the free decision of the saver), or he may make contractual savings, which require fixed payments at fixed intervals, as opposed to voluntary savings. Contractual savings would include fixed commitments, namely, scheduled repayments of homeowner and installment debt, plus net insurance and pension payments. Consumers now tend to commit around one-fifth of their current income in advance for purposes of debt repayment or asset accumulation. Thus, contractual savings reduce the amount of income available to individuals for discretionary spending, and thus tend to curb an inflationary spiral in an

TABLE 1 TRENDS IN PERSONAL SAVINGS, 1935–1960
(In billions of dollars)

Item	Average year				1955	1956	1957	1958	1959	1960
	1935–1939	1940–1944	1945–1949	1950–1954						
Personal income before taxes............	$68.8	$123.1	$192.3	$267.3	$310.2	$332.9	$351.4	$360.3	$383.3	$402.2
Less personal taxes............	2.5	9.7	20.2	30.7	35.8	40.0	42.6	42.4	46.0	50.4
Disposable personal income............	66.3	113.4	172.0	236.6	274.4	292.9	308.8	317.9	337.3	351.8
Less consumption expenditures............	63.6	90.8	158.7	219.0	256.9	269.9	285.2	293.5	313.8	328.9
Equals personal savings............	2.7	22.6	13.3	17.6	17.5	23.0	23.6	24.4	23.4	22.9
Personal savings as per cent of disposable income............	44.2	19.9	7.7	7.4	6.4	7.9	7.6	7.7	6.9	6.5

SOURCES: *Survey of Current Business; Federal Reserve Bulletin.*

3

upturn of the economy and to hamper a deflationary movement in a recession.

Obviously, the payment of fixed sums at stated times, whether for the purpose of adding to assets or for the purpose of debt repayment, imparts a certain stability, or rigidity, to the economy, which is especially noticeable today in view of the rapidly increasing importance of contractual savings. A measure of their importance can be seen from the size of consumers' fixed commitments, which have increased fivefold since 1939 while take-home pay was rising fourfold. As far as savings institutions are concerned, the fact that a growing share of savings is contractual in nature adds to the stability of the incoming flow of funds, but it also presents problems at times in finding worthy uses for the unending flow. Finally, let us note that so far as the economy as a whole is concerned, contractual savings have important implications for the business cycle. They tend to put a brake on inflation in a boom. On the other hand, they have a deflationary impact in a business downturn.

How Savings Funds Are Allocated

In order to answer the second question of how these funds are allocated between the mortgage market and all other uses, it is necessary to examine the basic factors determining the demand for mortgage funds.

Analysis of the Housing Market

The vast majority of mortgages are held on residential property. Therefore, analysis of the demand for mortgage funds should begin with an analysis of the housing market which of course depends on the number of households. Households are constantly being formed and extinguished, but it is the net change in their numbers, that is, "net household formations," which is relevant to the demand for new dwelling units. Households are formed when individuals living in existing households split off to form separate units, either by marriage or by individuals moving into separate apartments or homes. On the other hand, households are extinguished by death or through the redoubling of persons previously maintaining separate households.

Major Factors Affecting Households

There are two major factors affecting the number of households. The first is the demographic factor, that is, the number and age distribution of the population, which directly affects the number of persons coming of marriageable age, the death rate, and the number of people in the age groups from which households are customarily formed. The second is the level of real income, which affects the marriage age and the extent to which young and old may live apart.

The importance of the demographic factor in the household-formation age group should be obvious. In many respects, however, the second factor, income, is just as crucial. High income stimulates migration, it encourages marriage, and it promotes undoubling by making it possible for many marginal individuals and families to maintain separate households. Thus, the sustained period of high income which the nation has enjoyed since World War II has been responsible for eliminating the backlog of deferred marriages, for lowering the marriage age, and for increasing the number of so-called "nonnormal" households, which in the recent past have comprised up to 50 per cent of net household formations. Because these sources have been tapped during the postwar period, continued high income is not likely to accelerate the rate of household formation, but a sharp drop in income could reduce the rate through marriage deferrals and could cause many "nonnormal" households to evaporate through redoubling.

The demand for dwelling units may also be affected by a number of other factors. These include the relative prices of housing and other goods, changes in taste, credit availability, and the public's asset position. However, in most cases these effects are indirect. Such factors bear more directly on the type and quality of accommodation demanded than on the decision to seek separate quarters. In fact, these factors also appear to be secondary in importance to income in regard to the quality of units, their space, condition, style, and convenience. For instance, average value per unit may be expected to rise as real income rises, giving income a significance for loan opportunities apart from its effect on the number of households. It should be remembered, however, that there is a limit to this growth; as a person's real income rises, the proportion which he spends on housing tends to decline, partly because of the competition of other goods for the consumer's dollar and partly because of the competition of social attractions outside the home.

The number of new household formations largely determines the total change in demand for dwelling units, and thus the basic demand for mortgage funds. There are various ways of utilizing the existing stock of housing, however, and so the number of newly constructed units may differ from net household formations. The market can adjust to a change in the number of households through the expansion or absorption of vacancies, the number of demolitions, and the creation of additional units through conversion of existing houses, as well as through new construction. The amount of new building required can be expressed as equal to the net increase in households, plus net change in vacancies, plus demolitions, less net conversions.

Factors Affecting Demolitions and Conversions

Demolitions are affected by many factors, some being noneconomic in nature, such as the effect of urban renewal and highway building programs. Conversions are to some extent a substitute for new starts. They were particularly important during the Great Depression, World War II, and the immediate postwar years when new construction was down, either because of depressed demand or because materials were in short supply. These conditions are not likely to be duplicated in the foreseeable future. Hence we can concentrate on the influence on total demand from new construction and changes in vacancy rates.

Preference for New Construction

New construction may take place in the face of rising vacancies, but if new construction is to exceed household formations, it can do so only because new houses are preferred to vacant existing units. There are several apparent reasons for this preference for new construction.

One factor is comparative terms; in recent years permissible down payments and length of amortization period have been more stringent on older houses, and thus it has been easier to gain access to new housing. A second factor is comparative price; in the seller's market of the postwar period, used-house prices long failed to reflect the age of the structure, and so here again there arose a preference for new construction. A third factor is the change in the public's taste for housing; this too favors new construction, since a shift has apparently occurred in favor of new suburban single-family dwellings as against older urban multiunit dwellings.

All these factors mentioned affect in some way the potential demand for mortgage funds. However, the most important source of mortgage demand is from the new construction covering homes and other types of properties even though the number of transactions involving used houses is larger. New-house transactions have a greater significance for the volume of lending than transactions involving older houses since they do not involve outstanding loans, while the exchange of existing houses frequently involves the cancellation of existing loans. Residential mortgage volume also is affected by changes in the general level of real estate prices, by any trend toward larger and more expensive dwellings, and by the rate of prepayments under prosperous conditions.

Factors That Influence the Allocation of Savings

What factors influence the allocation of savings between mortgages and other alternative uses for funds, such as the securities of corporations and government agencies? For example, what forces in 1960 determined that mortgage debt would exceed both corporate debt and public debt? The allocation of funds among these alternative uses of savings depends to a certain extent upon the capital demands of industry and government just as it depends upon the underlying demand for mortgage funds. But other factors also influence the direction of flow of savings. Those factors are influenced both by monetary policy and by institutional developments arising in the mortgage market.

The general monetary controls wielded by the Federal Reserve System, its open market operation, reserve requirements, and the discount rate would not ordinarily tend to affect directly the allocation of funds. Specific controls, however, such as Regulation X a few years ago, would obviously have an important effect, similar to the traditional mortgage lending requirements instituted by lenders. These requirements would govern down payments, amortization periods, and the financial qualifications of loan applicants, such as present income, prospective income, and liquid assets. When such requirements are strict, on the part of lenders, Federal agencies, or both, effective mortgage demand would be diminished and available funds would tend to flow into other channels. The reverse would, of course, hold true in periods of easier requirements. We may note here the vast increase in demand for mortgage funds resulting from the historical shift in down-payment requirements. Prior to World War I, equity funds constituted about one-half of the funds used for new residential construction, but in recent years this proportion had fallen to one-quarter.

Investment Policies of Investors

The allocation of funds is strongly dependent on comparative interest rates, since investors will always seek investments yielding the most attractive return, when confronted with outlets of comparable quality and safety. This factor would account for the postwar shift of funds from government securities into mortgages and also for the 1956–1957 shift of funds away from the government-supported end of the housing market. The allocation of funds is also influenced by the relative marketability of assets, although this factor is more important for commercial banks than for other investors. The degree of risk also plays an important role. Since every institution wishes to operate within a certain ratio of risk assets to capital funds, this policy more or less sets a limit to the acquisition of securities other than government securities or government-guaranteed mortgages. Finally, traditional ratios in the composition of assets also affect the investment policies of institutions, especially when such proportions are prescribed by law; for instance, the percentage of mortgages to total assets that individual banks and other institutional lenders may hold in certain states.

Financial Intermediaries Have Organized the Mortgage Market

Now, with numerous individuals in the economy looking for outlets for their savings, and with numerous individuals and corporate and governmental treasurers looking for sources of long-term financing, a well-organized market has developed to bring the two groups together. Financial intermediaries of all types have organized this market, in order to see that long-term savings are allocated to the long-term investments most urgently desired by the economy. In fulfilling this function, these financial intermediaries have an important impact on the economy. They contribute to an increase in economic efficiency by quickly channeling funds from those who want to save into the hands of those who want to invest. Furthermore, their decisions to increase or decrease the liquidity of funds can exert a powerful deflationary or inflationary influence.

The major institutions fulfilling this necessary intermediary role in the economy are mortgage bankers, as such (loan correspondents), commercial banks, mutual savings banks, life insurance companies, and savings and loan associations. Some indication of their importance is given by the data on mortgage debt held by such intermediaries at the present time (see Table 2). At the end of 1960 they held the vast bulk of the mortgage debt, which represents a fifty-fold rise in debt financing since the 1890s. Noticeable shifts have occurred, however, in the relative importance of these intermediaries in mortgage financing over the past half century. Commercial banks have increased their share, as have life insurance companies, savings and loan associations, and mutual savings banks. But more noticeable than these increases in mortgage investments has been the steep drop in the importance of individuals in mortgage financing—a drop in market penetration from 60 per cent at the turn of the century to about 10 per cent today. Obviously the large institutional investors now dominate the field.

The Increasing Importance of Commercial Banks in Mortgage Financing and Its Effect upon the Mortgage Market

Let us consider now the increasing role played by commercial banks in mortgage financing. One factor has already been mentioned: the substantial decline in importance of individuals in the financing field. But in addition, the relatively rapid growth of commercial bank resources also has been important in this regard, especially since commercial banks have over a period of time been placing a larger proportion of their total resources in mortgage loans.

There are several reasons for the increasing importance of mortgages in commercial bank portfolios. First, there has been a progressive liberalization of legal restrictions on real estate lending by national banks. Prior to 1916, these banks were prohibited altogether from making loans on urban real estate; in that year they were granted such authority, but the maximum maturity allowable was only twelve months. Gradually, the maximum maturity was extended, and naturally each of these changes encouraged more active participation by national banks in the real estate market.

The Federal Housing Administration Program

A second factor favoring increased mortgage-to-total-asset ratios by commercial banks and all other investors has been the development of Federal Housing Administration programs.

Federally underwritten loans have been exempt from restrictions imposed on commercial banks with respect to maximum loan-to-value ratios and maximum maturities. Moreover, the FHA-insured or VA-guaranteed mortgage is more marketable than the conventional mortgage, an important consideration to commercial banks.

The increasing importance of mortgages in commercial bank portfolios may also reflect the tremendous liquidity of banks and all other financial institutions at the end of World War II, liquidity resting in large part on the policy of the Federal Reserve System of pegging the price of government securities. This liquidity permitted the banks to take advantage of the opportunities offered by the very strong postwar mortgage market.

In the years 1946 to 1948, commercial banks were more active in the mortgage market than during any previous period in their history. By doubling their holdings of nonfarm mortgage debt in this period, they increased their share of outstanding nonfarm mortgage debt from 14 to 20 per cent. This rapid increase suggests that factors influencing the composition of bank assets may frequently be more important in determining the amount of banks' mortgage financing than changes in total bank resources, especially since commercial bank assets declined in this period while the assets of other financial intermediaries were increasing.

One factor in this shift in asset composition was a rise in time deposits in the face of falling total deposits, and the size of time deposits naturally is a key determinant in a bank's mortgage lending policy. Another factor was the excess liquidity afforded by the $90 billion of price-supported government obligations held at that time, which could easily be transformed into less liquid mortgage funds. Moreover, at that time mortgages were an attractive investment from the point of yield, whereas the longest-term government bonds yielded less than $2\frac{1}{2}$ per cent, the interest rate on federally underwritten mortgages was from 4 to $4\frac{1}{2}$ per cent.

Commercial banks have maintained an important position in the mortgage market since that early postwar boom, again doubling their total mortgage portfolio holdings; but their share of the market has declined, in line with their decreasing liquidity and the declining attractiveness of mortgage yields. Moreover, changes in the holdings of commercial banks apparently have fluctuated more than changes in the holdings of other mortgage lenders. Because of their liquidity requirements, the mortgage investment goals of commercial banks apparently shift more markedly and more quickly than those of other savings institutions. Commercial banks also act as a residual source of mortgage financing, with their holdings tending to increase most rapidly when the demand for mortgage funds exceeds the capacity of other savings institutions. The best example of this is the development of the mortgage warehousing phenomenon in recent years which is described in Chapters 1 and 10 of this book.

Influence of the Federal Government on the Mortgage Market

This discussion of the institutions dominating our mortgage market would be far from complete without some mention of the tremendous influence exerted by the Federal government during recent decades. Certainly, the government programs deserve great credit for increasing the aggregate demand for housing by aiding the flow of credit available to borrowers at low interest rates and by promoting the use of monthly amortization.

The Federal government moved to meet these problems in the mid-1930s. In 1934, with the creation of the Federal Housing Administration, the emphasis shifted from relief to recovery. A plan of insuring loans for repairs to real property, at first considered purely temporary, also became a part of the permanent plan.

The National Housing Act of 1934,[1] which established the Federal Housing Administration, also provided for privately owned national mortgage associations (mortgage banker loan correspondents) in order to create a secondary mortgage market on a national scale. It was not until 1938, however, that legislation was passed aiming at government sponsorship of such a secondary market. In that year the Federal National Mortgage Association was set up with Reconstruction Finance Corporation capital. And FNMA has since become a real influence in urban residential financing.

The Servicemen's Readjustment Act of 1944[2]

The other major innovation of the Federal government in this field was the introduction of the VA loan. Under the Servicemen's Readjustment Act of 1944, the Veterans Administration agreed to guarantee mortgage loans made by private lenders to veterans for the purchase of homes. This and other housing legislation has been amended frequently since that time, but

[1] See Chap. 9, "The Federal Housing Administration Program."
[2] See Chap. 10, "The Veterans Administration Loan Program."

the basic principle has remained intact and has been a constant stimulus to low- and middle-income housing.

In actuality, new nonfarm starts financed by government programs increased by more than half between 1953 and 1955, then fell even more steeply between 1955 and 1957, and in 1958 started up again. During all this time conventionally financed loans remained at a relatively stable level. The problem has centered around the rigidities introduced into the market by politically oriented housing legislation, rigidities affecting mostly the interest-rate structure, and thus the orderly flow of funds into mortgages. During the recent period of rising bond yields the fixed nominal interest rate on government-backed mortgages, in conjunction with the uncertainty of discounts, placed such instruments at a competitive disadvantage in comparison with conventional mortgages. Moreover, the minimum equities required apparently were not high enough to be acceptable to some lenders.

The Mortgage Market, Mortgage Lending, and Mortgage Financing

This, then, is the general shape of our mortgage market. Into that market flows a large segment of individuals' savings, to be funneled into the mortgage lending stream, a stream whose dimensions are set primarily by population and income factors. At the center of the market stand the financial intermediaries, who keep the savings stream flowing smoothly into mortgage and other channels. In the background stand the Federal agencies, which help keep the main channel open for the smoothest possible flow of savings into mortgage investments. The channel has its hazards, as has been noted, but it contributes substantially, now as in the past, to the nation's mainstream of economic activity.

In view of the drastic changes that have taken place and continue to take place in the mortgage market over a generation, leading mortgage lenders and economists are of the opinion that there is no possibility that this market, which now plays a major role in the general money market, will ever escape from the impact of monetary policy or from competition in this general money market.

Included in this volume is a review of housing legislation innovations and new departures in mortgage financing made and planned to be made by the new political administration under the leadership of John F. Kennedy, who was inaugurated President of the United States early in the year 1961.

Importance of Mortgage Lending

In 1945 the total real estate mortgage debt in the nation amounted to approximately $37 billion; at the end of 1960 it had risen to over $206 billion. Over $157 billion of this latter total was in the loan portfolios of life insurance companies, commercial banks, savings and loan associations, and mutual savings banks; approximately $49 billion was held by individuals, government agencies, and others (Table 2).

TABLE 2

COMPARATIVE REPORT OF MORTGAGES ON ONE- TO FOUR-FAMILY RESIDENCES, MULTIFAMILY, COMMERCIAL, INDUSTRIAL, AND FARM PROPERTIES

(In millions of dollars)

	12/31/45	12/31/52	12/31/54	12/31/55	12/31/60
Savings and loan associations.......	$5,376	$18,440	$26,142	$31,461	$60,084
Insurance companies...............	5,934	19,560	23,881	27,172	38,789
Mutual savings banks *.............	4,200	11,310	14,951	17,399	26,881
Commercial banks.................	4,251	14,810	17,397	19,707	27,158
Subtotal......................	19,761	64,120	82,371	95,739	152,912
Estimated total of farm loans held by above institutions..............	2,341	3,590	4,085	3,600	4,684
Total.......................	22,102	67,710	86,456	99,339	157,596
Government agencies, individuals, and others........................	11,927	19,300	22,959	25,195	40,804
Subtotal......................	34,029	87,010	109,415	124,534	
Estimated total of farm loans held by government agencies, individuals, and others....................	2,341	3,590	4,085	5,400	8,400
Grand total....................	36,370	90,600	113,500	129,934	206,800

FARM MORTGAGE LOANS

(In thousands of dollars)

	12/31/52	12/31/54	12/31/55	12/31/60
Federal Land Banks and Federal farm mortgage corporations............	$1,095,257	$1,280,000	$1,480,000	$2,538,000
Life insurance companies..............	1,701,611	2,046,000	2,273,000	2,984,000
Commercial banks..................	1,033,043	1,158,000	1,297,000	1,648,000
Farmers Home Administration.........	257,936	271,000	278,000	482,000
Others, including individuals, banks, etc..	3,090,128	3,415,000	3,738,000	5,478,000
Total farm mortgage debt...........	7,177,975	8,170,000	9,066,000	13,130,000

* Do not carry farm loans.

SOURCES: Federal Reserve Bank of San Francisco, Research Department; *Federal Home Loan Bank Review*, Washington; *Institute of Life Insurance Fact Book*, New York, 1960; American Bankers Association, Savings and Mortgage Division, New York.

The financial condition of the country is directly affected by the manner in which mortgage lenders invest such funds and by the way they adjust their lending policies to meet almost daily changes in the real estate market and the mortgage market. There are wide variations in mortgage investment policies of lenders. Some are extremely conservative; others are very liberal. Some invest in mortgage loans on homes only; others invest in mortgages on all types of properties except homes; still others restrict their mortgage investments to one or two types of properties only.

Because of the tremendous flow of funds into the mortgage market on a daily basis, it follows that the underlying soundness of mortgage lending policies of institutional investors, particularly, has a profound effect upon the economic and financial condition of the country. These policies are described in some detail in Chapter 2.

Mortgage lending activities contribute to the development and growth of the communities in which we live and for that reason have a major effect upon our economic life. If mortgage lending activities are not carried on wisely, the result could be financial trouble for borrowers and lenders, economic and social losses, and a complete disruption in our present manner of living. Unsound mortgage lending could even help to bring on another Great Depression.

During the entire period from around 1930 to the present time it has been necessary for those who were responsible for the investment policies of mortgage lenders to adjust their policies to the new trends in mortgage lending and the mortgage market. Without a comprehensive knowledge of the principles and practices which govern sound mortgage financing, mortgage lenders during this period would not have been in a position to cope with the thousands of problems which have arisen daily in the expansion and growth of lending operations. And in order to facilitate the work of lending, it has been necessary to devise additional programs both for the training of college students and for improvements in the qualifications of old and new employees within lending institutions.

Certain Basic Economic and Physical Characteristics Have an Important Bearing upon Mortgage Lending

There are certain economic and physical characteristics of real estate itself that are of basic importance in mortgage lending and have a direct bearing upon lending policies and operations, namely, the following:[3]

1. Properties are fixed in their location. Both land and the completed structures remain in the same locations indefinitely.

2. Properties have comparatively long lives, and the existing supply has an important bearing upon the market at all times.

3. Any property, regardless of type, is a complex product which requires a large volume of various types of labor at the site.

4. Building activities and property values are subject to extreme fluctuations.

[3] *Home Mortgage Lending*, chap. 1, American Institute of Banking, Section American Bankers Association, New York, 1953.

Classification of Mortgages by Property Types an Essential Part of Operations

For the purpose of increased efficiency in operations, mortgage debt is usually divided by lenders into ten classifications according to types of properties, together with the number and dollar amount of each type, namely:

1. Dwellings (one- to four-family)
2. Flats (including stores with flats above, also duplexes)
3. Apartments
4. Stores and office buildings
5. Industrial buildings
6. Hotels (including summer resorts)
7. Unimproved land—industrial
8. Unimproved land—residential and business
9. Farms
10. Others (special-purpose, such as churches, theaters, lodge halls, fraternity houses, garages, golf courses, service and gasoline stations, general markets, bowling alleys, etc.)

This portfolio information is always kept readily available, as it is a necessary part of portfolio analysis and is used in determining lending policies.

This book will be concerned mainly with one- to four-family dwellings. The basic fundamentals of mortgage lending which cover homes, however, are also applicable to loans on all the other types of properties listed above. Until a few years ago studies covering mortgage lending and related activities classified loans on real estate, other than farms, as "urban mortgages." There were three classifications in this group according to type of property mortgaged, namely, commercial, multifamily or apartment, and one- to four-family homes. Because of the great expansion in construction of properties not in this urban mortgage category, this classification has in general been replaced by the term "nonfarm mortgage debt." A large portion of this nonfarm mortgage indebtedness consists of loans on single-family dwellings. It is estimated that 75 per cent of the present noncorporate mortgage indebtedness in the nation is represented by mortgage loans on homes.

Availability of Statistical Information on Mortgage Lending and the Building Industry

Comprehensive statistical data covering mortgage lending, the existing supply of dwelling units, new housing starts, vacancies, family formations, and other market factors have been developed by lenders, government bureaus, and trade associations throughout recent years.

Government bureaus include the Housing and Home Finance Agency, the Federal National Mortgage Association, the Federal Deposit Insurance Corporation, the Federal Housing Administration, the Veterans Administration, the Federal Home Loan Bank System, the Federal Reserve System, and the U.S. Department of Labor.

Trade Associations include the Mortgage Bankers Association of America, the American Bankers Association, the Institute of Life Insurance, the United States Savings and Loan League, the National Savings and Loan League, the Associated Home Builders, the National Association of Real Estate Boards, and others.[4]

The Building Industry Is Subject to Extreme Changes in Activities

Building activities and property values are subject to extreme fluctuations. Neighborhoods are also subject to great changes in conditions, including fluctuations in value and appeal. Values and rents also rise and fall, and a constant study of real estate market behavior is imperative if the mortgage lending industry is to operate efficiently. There has been a rising market since 1934, but the past history of mortgage lending indicates that a falling market in the future is possible. Many leading mortgage lenders and economists believe that there will never be a repetition of the debacle of 1932 because of the many safeguards which have been developed since the beginning of the Great Depression for the protection of the borrower and the lender. The validity of this forecast will have to await the verdict of history.

One of the controlling factors now used to determine the soundness of mortgage credit extended is the ability of the borrower to repay the loan. This requires exhaustive analysis of the borrower which, surprising as it may seem, has been developed only in recent years. The development in importance of the borrower in a mortgage loan transaction will be discussed in detail in later chapters.

Basic Method Used in Financing Purchases of Property

The customary practice in mortgage lending calls for paying a minor portion of the purchase price in cash and borrowing the rest. The cash investment of the typical purchaser during the past few years has been relatively small, especially since the inception of the FHA program in 1934 and more particularly since the VA home loan program was established in 1944. The 100 per cent financing of VA home loans has been a highly debated subject, and the more conservative lenders have strenuously opposed such liberal financing. During the past few years the amount

---

[4] See listing of trade associations, guilds, and institutes directly related to mortgage financing in Appendix A.

of loan permissible on conventional loans, based on loan-to-value ratio, has been progressively increased.

Throughout our history very few individuals have had sufficient savings to purchase property without borrowed funds. By means of long-term credit, which has been developed on an extensive scale only since the Great Depression, a borrower can purchase a home and live in it or purchase other types of properties while paying off the mortgage indebtedness on a monthly basis. Prior to the Great Depression these borrowings were for short periods only.

Provisions Covering Repayment of the Loan

When an individual buys a residential property or any other type of property and borrows funds to complete the purchase, the repayment of the loan is guaranteed in part by the pledge of the property purchased. This pledge is made by the use of a legal instrument known as a "mortgage." In many states it now takes the form and name of a "deed of trust." This instrument gives the lender certain rights in the property, which he may use in order to protect the loan in case the borrower defaults on some covenant of the mortgage, or deed of trust. Such a mortgage or deed of trust, signed by the borrower, is given as the collateral for the note, which is also signed by the borrower.[5]

The first mortgage or deed of trust is one by which the lender establishes certain claims against the owner's right in the property, claims which are prior to those arising from any other type of mortgage. Any claims of the government, however, usually have a prior claim over the first mortgage. The second mortgage gives the lender who holds this mortgage a claim against the owner that is subordinate to the rights of the holder of the first mortgage. In those rare instances in which a third mortgage is used, the claims of the third mortgagee are subordinate to the rights of the holder of the second mortgage.

Mortgage loan obligations are classified according to provisions for repayment as follows: (1) flat loan, (2) fully amortized, (3) partially amortized, (4) direct reduction, and (5) demand mortgage.

1. A flat loan requires no principal payment during the term of the mortgage. It is usually a short-term loan in which the borrower has a large equity which would warrant no reduction of principal for a considerable period.

2. A fully amortized mortgage is one which is repaid in specified amounts during the term of the mortgage with the result that the full amount is repaid at the end of the period for which the loan was arranged. Both FHA and VA home loans are fully amortized. These payments are nearly always

---

[5] Both terms, mortgage and deed of trust, refer to the pledge of the property as security for the loan (see Glossary of Terms).

on a monthly basis. A fully amortized loan is also known as a "level-pay-ment" mortgage.

3. A partially amortized mortgage calls for payment of a portion of principal, 40 per cent, 50 per cent, or 60 per cent, for instance, during the term of the loan. Some conventional loans are made with such repayment provisions.

4. A direct-reduction mortgage is one that provides for crediting all principal payments (which are usually for large amounts) directly to the reduction of the outstanding balance at stated intervals. Direct-reduction mortgages are used primarily for farm loans, and the terms call for the interest and principal payment on an annual or semiannual or quarterly basis usually at times when crops are harvested.

5. A demand mortgage is one in which the borrower agrees to pay the full amount on demand. A demand mortgage or deed of trust is usually written for one year, and the borrower has a small loan in comparison to the value of the property.

Combinations of all forms of the above mortgage amortization plans are frequently used. This is particularly true of conventional loans made by institutional lenders on all types of properties.

Provision for charging a small penalty, if the loan is paid in full prior to its maturity, is usually incorporated in every type of mortgage or deed of trust contract. The FHA will not permit a borrower to pay off more than 15 per cent of the principal during any one year without a penalty, but if the entire loan is paid off, a penalty of 1 per cent of the original amount of the loan is charged. Without penalty, a veteran may pay as much of the principal as he desires at any time when he makes use of a VA loan. Many commercial banks allow a loan to be paid off without a penalty and without a time restriction.

Mortgage Lending Activities Prior to the Great Depression

Shortly after World War I, there was a significant increase in industrial productivity in the United States. This development resulted in an expansion of opportunities for employment of large numbers of workers, many of whom found that, with the help of mortgage lenders, they could finance the purchase of their own homes. The result was an increase in both building activity and in mortgage lending operations.[6]

In the late 1920s the Great Depression got under way. Both consumer and business purchases dropped, and as a consequence there was a sharp curtailment of production and hence business activity in general. Employment and income dropped, and by 1932 the economy was in a critical situation. From 1932 to 1936 there was a general disposition on the part of

[6] For a more comprehensive study of the growth of mortgage lending and related activities, refer to Bibliography and Suggested Reading at the end of this chapter.

business enterprise to get in as liquid condition as possible through use of the Federal Reserve System, the Reconstruction Finance Corporation, the Federal Home Loan Bank System, the Home Owners' Loan Corporation, and such all-but-forgotten experiments as the NRA and the WPA. The Federal government attempted to allay fear and restore some measure of confidence in the future of the country.

Mortgage loans had proved to be one of the most stable and dependable revenue-producing assets of banks, life insurance companies, savings and loan associations, individuals, and others for over one hundred years. However, in the year 1925, there began a slow rise in the rate of foreclosure of mortgage loans, and by 1932 it had reached proportions that were alarming.

Real estate activity had commenced to slacken some two or three years before the general stock market crash which occurred late in 1929. Mortgage interest rates were high during the 1920s, following World War I. Many buyers of real estate who could not raise enough money on first mortgages arranged for second and in some cases even third mortgages to be placed against their properties. When general business conditions became severe, holders of flat first mortgages wanted installment payments upon renewal of the one-year loan, holders of second mortgages wanted their notes paid or exacted high charges for renewals or extensions. Rents dropped, collections were difficult, and defaults in payments increased very rapidly. Foreclosures rose sharply.

One of the causes of trouble during the Great Depression was the short-term flat loan. It is estimated that only 12 per cent of all mortgage loans in the portfolios of institutional investors prior to that time were on an amortized basis; little if any attention was paid to the collection of the principal payment of these loans. Such short-term loans called for frequent renewal with additional expense involved and in the early 1930s when the real estate market started falling rapidly, many borrowers were unable either to pay off the called loan or bear the expense of renewal. This, as well as the low loan-value ratio required by law, forced many borrowers to take second mortgages on their property at high interest rates. As a result, a great many holders of second mortgages became owners of properties on which the borrowers could not take care of their obligations.

Also, prior to the Great Depression most borrowers were required to pay property taxes direct, and most lenders failed to keep adequate records of the payment of taxes. It was found that on numerous loans in default at that time there was an accumulation of three or four years' unpaid taxes together with heavy penalties covering such nonpayments.[7]

Another cause of trouble was that lenders failed to analyze the financial position of borrowers or of their ability to repay their obligations. It is only in recent years that borrower risk ratings have been established.

[7] Result of survey conducted by the author during the Great Depression.

The operations of most mortgage lenders were also restricted geographically and the risks under the circumstances were localized. There was no nationwide market for mortgage loans, and consequently when the Great Depression occurred, mortgage lenders in all parts of the country found themselves holding mortgages which were frozen assets.

As a result of the many painful lessons learned during that period, great improvements have been made in all phases of mortgage lending operations. Techniques have been developed for assembling and analyzing all the necessary information covering the property, the neighborhood, and the borrower, as well as their relation to one another and to the terms of the mortgage contract. In addition to this, operational procedures covering mortgage lending have been greatly improved.

Action Taken to Solve Mortgage Lending Difficulties during the Great Depression

Up until 1929, mortgages, while recognized as satisfactory investments for savings banks, life insurance companies, savings and loan associations, and individuals, were not considered especially desirable for commercial banks because of their lack of liquidity. Mortgages were largely local investments and had no national market. Because of this lack of a secondary market, mortgage investments became frozen with the coming of the Great Depression. Deposits in banks and accounts in savings and loan associations were withdrawn more rapidly than mortgage loans could be liquidated, and institutions as well as individuals were unable to meet their obligations on demand, although they often held valuable assets that eventually would pay out in full.

The Creation of the Federal Home Loan Bank System

The Federal Home Loan Bank System was created, by authority of the Federal Home Loan Bank Act approved July 22, 1932, to provide a credit reserve for thrift and home-financing institutions. The types of institutions eligible for membership in the Federal Home Loan Banks were savings and loan, building and loan, homestead associations, mutual savings banks, cooperative banks, and insurance companies.

Federal savings and loan associations, as provided for in the Home Owners Act of 1933, may make insured or guaranteed loans up to maximum percentages of appraised value permitted by FHA and VA. Conventional home loans may be made up to 80 per cent of appraisal, and under well-defined limitations up to 90 per cent of value for low-cost housing. The percentage of loans compared to their total assets is usually high, being close to 85 per cent. However, they may borrow from the Federal Home

Loan Bank against their collateral (65 per cent on conventional loans, 90 per cent on FHA and VA loans). Borrowing may be for short periods or for as long as ten years.

The Creation of the Home Owners' Loan Corporation

The distress of individuals and financial institutions became a matter of public concern, which reached a climax with the bank holiday of 1933 immediately following the inauguration of Franklin D. Roosevelt as President of the United States. In 1933, 1934, and 1935 several important laws for the relief of borrowers and for the protection of financial institutions were passed by Congress. One of the first created the Home Owners' Loan Corporation, an agency established by congressional action in 1933. Its purpose was to grant long-term mortgage loans at low interest rates to distressed homeowners who were unable to obtain refinancing through normal channels, and to help stabilize the mortgage market. Another purpose was to furnish relief to mortgage lenders who held mortgages which were frozen. Refinancing of frozen loans by the HOLC saved many mortgage lenders from bankruptcy or other serious financial troubles. The HOLC ceased its lending activities in 1936 and wound up its affairs in May, 1951.

Moratorium Laws

In 1933 and the following year most states passed moratorium laws which, generally speaking, permitted a debtor to file a petition in court which under certain circumstances operated as a stay of foreclosure of his real property. In addition, specific laws were passed tightening up foreclosure proceedings, giving additional rights to redeem after foreclosure, and definitely limiting deficiency judgments and the means of obtaining them.

The National Housing Act of 1934[8]

The most revolutionary change in the methods of making home mortgage loans occurred in 1934 when the National Housing Act was passed by Congress and the FHA was created to encourage improvement in housing standards and conditions and to provide a system of mutual mortgage insurance.

There is no question that this act accomplished its early purposes, although many institutional lenders were slow to express approval of the plan. Some were suspicious of the government's entrance into the field of private enterprise. Others did not like the idea that the government was going to insure loans. Still others feared Federal control of mortgage rates. By and large, lenders saw more benefits than harm in the FHA plan and decided to support the FHA program along the lines of its original concept.

[8] See listing of major housing acts in Appendix B.

From the standpoint of the borrower, the principal changes that took place when the FHA plan went into effect were these:

1. The borrower was enabled to obtain a long-term home mortgage loan with a high ratio of loan to value.

2. The borrower's financing costs were lessened by eliminating the need for frequent renewals of a short-term mortgage and by doing away with the occasion for a second mortgage, which usually bore a high rate of interest and which in many other ways had proved to be distressing.

3. The plan of a fixed monthly payment to include principal, interest, taxes, insurance, and other such costs helped the borrower to budget his expenses and often enabled him to take better care of his housing obligations.

4. A careful analysis of the prospective borrower's ability to service the debt was instituted.

5. Minimum housing construction standards were developed.

From the standpoint of lenders, these changes took place:

1. Real estate mortgages became more and more liquid as FHA loans entered their portfolios in increasing percentages, because these loans were readily marketable.

2. Banks, insurance companies, and other institutional lenders were enabled to grant such loans at a higher percentage of loan to value than was permitted by state or national laws covering conventional loans.

3. Many banks began to employ larger percentages of time deposits in making mortgage loans, because a substantial portion of those loans now carried government insurance and could in a sense be classified as "non-risk" assets.

The early FHA Title II loans carried an interest rate of 5½ per cent plus ½ of 1 per cent servicing fee for the lender, plus ½ of 1 per cent for mortgage insurance premium, making a total carrying cost to the borrower of 6½ per cent per annum. During the succeeding years the government canceled the authorization to charge a servicing fee and reduced the interest rate on several occasions but did not restore any of its rate reductions until May 2, 1953, when the rate of 4¼ per cent was increased to 4½ per cent on single-family dwellings, plus ½ of 1 per cent mortgage insurance charge, which remains unchanged. The FHA Title VI rate of 4 per cent (a war measure) ran from May, 1946, until March, 1950; until the latter date, the FHA Title II rate was 4½ per cent. The FHA Title II interest rate was progressively increased to 5¾ per cent in 1960 and in early 1961 was reduced to 5½ per cent and shortly thereafter to 5¼ per cent.

The Federal Savings and Loan Insurance Corporation

Title IV of the National Housing Act created the Federal Savings and Loan Insurance Corporation to provide for safety of accounts in savings and loan associations, the principal source of home mortgage credit. This corporation is equivalent to the Federal Deposit Insurance Corporation in the banking field.

The Reconstruction Finance Mortgage Company

The RFC Mortgage Company was organized in 1935 as a subsidiary of the RFC to aid in the maintenance of a market for mortgages, particularly those insured under Titles I, II, and VI of the National Housing Act and VA loans.

It continued to function through April, 1948, when the last of the mortgages committed for purchase prior to July 1, 1947, were purchased or the commitments expired. The company's dissolution was ordered on June 30, 1947, by Public Law 132, 80th Congress. The company operated for about ten years after the establishment of FNMA, and the mortgage purchasing activities of the RFC Mortgage Company were not in any way competitive with those of FNMA.

The Creation of the Federal National Mortgage Association and Its Effect upon the Mortgage Market[9],[10]

The Federal National Mortgage Association was organized by the RFC on February 10, 1938, under the provisions of the National Housing Act. This association, commonly known as "Fannie Mae," was basically a standby organization to give relief in time of emergency. At one time grouped with other agencies to form the Federal Loan Agency, it was transferred to the U.S. Department of Commerce in 1942, and on September 7, 1950, under Reorganization Plan 22 was made a part of the HHFA. Over a period of years it was authorized to purchase or commit for purchase FHA and VA loans. Funds for mortgage purchases were obtained by FNMA by borrowing from the United States Treasury. When the RFC Mortgage Company went out of existence on June 30, 1947, its holdings and commitments for veterans' loans totaled $134 million. For the next year until July 1, 1948, there was no government secondary market for VA loans as FNMA was not active in the market. This seriously cut into the VA home loan program.

As the open-market price for VA loans had been below par for most of the period from 1947 to the end of 1953 it was quite natural that FNMA did a tremendous business whenever it had government funds at its disposal and offered 100 cents on the dollar for loans priced elsewhere at approximately 95 cents on the dollar. While there were many institutional lenders which, to serve their communities, did sell loans to FNMA, never-

[9] See *Background and History of the Federal National Mortgage Association,* p. 8, footnotes 9 and 13.

[10] See *Background and History of the Federal National Mortgage Association,* October 31, 1959.

theless most FNMA purchases were undoubtedly from mortgage bankers (loan correspondents) and other such lenders who did a large volume of business making VA loans and selling them as quickly as possible at par to FNMA.

It should be stated that, because there is no central mortgage bank, private-enterprise secondary markets have never been very satisfactory. The RFC Mortgage Company and FNMA furnished funds for FHA Title VI loans on war housing, and FNMA furnished funds for FHA Title IX loans for defense areas. FNMA's last purchase of Title IX loans under the initial 1951 authorization occurred in August, 1957.

The new FNMA, chartered under the provisions of the Housing Act of 1954, started its activity with funds provided by government subscription of $93 million of preferred stock available from accumulated funds of the former FNMA. The rechartered FNMA, among its several duties, will manage and liquidate the former FNMA portfolio.[11]

Under the present setup, sellers of mortgages to this agency must purchase nonrefundable (but transferable) capital stock of the new FNMA in an amount of 2 per cent of their sales to that corporation. With respect to the sale of debentures and short-term discount notes FNMA may issue (with the approval of the Secretary of the Treasury), and have outstanding at any one time, obligations which in the aggregate do not exceed 10 times the sum of the Association's capital, surplus, and reserves, and undistributed earnings in connection with its secondary market operations.

Prices paid for mortgages in the secondary market operations are required by law to be established from time to time within the range of market prices for the particular class of mortgages involved, as determined by FNMA.

On April 18, 1960, the Association inaugurated a new method of meeting a portion of its secondary market operations financing requirements through the issuance of short-term discount notes similar to commercial paper. The notes are tailored to meet the individual needs of corporate, institutional, and other investors seeking short-term obligations at published rates with a maturity range of 30 to 270 days. This form of financing provides FNMA with a greater degree of operational flexibility and serves as a supplement to FNMA's debenture borrowing program.

Soldiers' and Sailors' Civil Relief Act of 1940

While describing Federal action to aid mortgage debtors and lenders, the Soldiers' and Sailors' Civil Relief Act of 1940 should be mentioned,

[11] For a comprehensive coverage of this subject, see *Background and History of the Federal National Mortgage Association,* October 31, 1959, pp. 18–20, footnote 32, pp. 15 and 27–28, footnote 49, p. 28, footnote 51; pp. 1, 2, and 4 of *FNMA Semiannual Report* to HHFA, dated June 30, 1960.

although the act came six years after the other relief measures, previously mentioned, were passed. Its enactment was not due to the Great Depression but was based on strengthening the national defense and suspending enforcement of certain civil liabilities of those who entered into the Armed Forces of the United States. The act protected the families of men and women in the military service against foreclosure or the need to make principal payments on their obligations, or to fulfill certain other contracts in individual situations except by direction of a court after a hearing to determine the ability of the defendant to comply with the terms of the contract. This program worked out very satisfactorily, as there was complete cooperation shown by both such borrowers and lenders.

The Servicemen's Readjustment Act of 1944

In preparation for the termination of hostilities and in anticipation of the needs of the home-coming veterans, Congress passed the Servicemen's Readjustment Act of 1944. In addition to provisions for hospitalization, unemployment, and education, there was a sincere desire to aid veterans in acquiring the homes they would need at the end of the war. The original guaranty by the United States government on loans to veterans to acquire homes was $2,000. The 4 per cent rate was satisfactory because of the tremendous sums of money which were accumulated during the war years and were available for the mortgage market. On December 28, 1945, the amount of the guaranty was raised from $2,000 to $4,000, not to exceed 50 per cent of each individual loan, and on April 20, 1950, was raised to $7,500, not to exceed 60 per cent of each loan. The immediate effect of each increase in the guaranty plus the great and steady demand for homes and the paying of premiums for shelter was a rise in the price of homes. This legislation helped to bring about an upward movement of prices in general and thus probably contributed to an increase in the cost of housing for the group for whose benefit the legislation was passed.

Combination FHA and VA (Section 505) Loans to Veterans

During 1948 and 1949 in particular, the Section 505 loan became the most popular form of meeting veterans' needs for mortgages. This form was a combination of an FHA loan (usually 80 per cent of the total) and a VA secondary loan for the balance. This gave the lenders about 4.4 per cent as against 4 per cent per annum on the straight VA loan. However, the cost of processing these loans was quite high. Two of the steps taken by Congress to induce lenders to return to the 4 per cent VA loan activity were embodied in the Housing Act of 1950 when the 505 (a) loan was terminated and when provision was made for the VA to make direct government loans to veterans in those outlying areas where private funds were not available. This direct lending has so far had little, if any, effect on the mortgage market.

Housing Starts and Mortgage Loan Totals after World War II

By December 31, 1960, the VA had guaranteed over 5⅘ million loans, totaling more than $50 billion. Institutional lenders and others made many VA loans during the years 1945, 1946, and 1947. These lenders were satisfied with a return of 4 per cent per annum, for there had been a huge accumulation of savings and a small demand for loans during the war. But as those idle funds were invested, the market tightened, and many institutions discontinued making long-term 4 per cent mortgage loans to veterans. From 1948 to 1952 there was a scarcity of 4 per cent private mortgage money, except for late 1949 and 1950 when the insurance companies were selling their government bonds to the Federal Reserve banks at a premium and reinvesting in guaranteed and insured mortgages. During this time, the government supplied mortgage money for VA loans through the medium of FNMA.

It is important that housing starts and mortgage loan totals for the period after World War II be reviewed; building activity has a direct effect on the supply of, and demand for, houses and a corresponding effect on the availability of funds for mortgage lending. From 1933, when there were only 93,000 housing starts, there was a steady, although modest, increase in the number of new homes built, up to and including 1941 when the Japanese attacked Pearl Harbor. The housing starts for 1941 amounted to 715,200. After war was declared, the government issued restrictions and set up a system of priorities which practically stopped all construction except that which was necessary to the war effort. As a consequence, housing starts dropped sharply to a low of 169,000 in 1944 and showed no increase until the war came to an end in 1945. The next fifteen years showed these increases:

1946	670,000	1954	1,220,400
1947	849,000	1955	1,328,900
1948	931,000	1956	1,118,000
1949	1,025,100	1957	1,041,900
1950	1,395,100	1958	1,209,400
1951	1,091,300	1959	1,378,500
1952	1,131,400	1959	1,531,300 (new series)*
1953	1,103,800	1960	1,274,000 (new series)

* See *Construction Reports—Housing Starts*, U.S. Department of Commerce and Bureau of Census, Washington.

SOURCE: Federal Reserve Bank of San Francisco, Research Department.

New Series for Housing Starts

The new series for housing starts is designed as a comprehensive measure of the number of new housing units on which construction is started in the entire United States each month.

A housing start consists of the start of construction on a new housing unit, when located within a new building which is intended primarily as a housekeeping residential building designed for nontransient occupancy. A housing unit is defined as a single room or group of rooms intended for occupancy as separate living quarters by a family, by a group of unrelated persons living together, or by a person living alone. A housekeeping residential building is a building consisting primarily of housing units. Housing starts, as here defined, excludes the start of construction on group quarters such as dormitories, fraternity houses, nurses' homes, rooming houses and on transient hotel accommodations, motels, tourist cabins and courts, etc. The definition includes both farm and nonfarm housing, both year-round and seasonal housing, housing of all values and all levels of quality, prefabricated housing, shell houses, houses built of secondhand materials, and both permanent and temporary units. Both privately owned and publicly owned housing are included. It excludes the production of mobile homes (or house trailers) which is not classified as construction. Conversion of existing dwellings is not included.

Meanwhile the total holdings of mortgage loans by institutional investors followed somewhat the same course as that of housing construction, reaching a low of $16,800,000,000 in 1936 and gradually climbing to $21,000,000,000 in 1945. The rapid growth of mortgage investment from 1946 to 1960 is disclosed by the following figures covering the holdings of institutional investors:

1946	$25,056,000,000	1954	$ 85,787,000,000
1947	32,021,000,000	1955	99,339,000,000
1948	37,707,000,000	1956	111,207,000,000
1949	42,743,000,000	1957	119,741,000,000
1950	51,636,000,000	1958	131,475,000,000
1951	59,410,000,000	1959	145,427,000,000
1952	67,600,000,000	1960	157,596,000,000
1953	75,056,000,000		

SOURCE: Federal Reserve Bank of San Francisco, Research Department.

Net Increase in Outstanding Mortgage Debt[12]

The net increase in the outstanding residential mortgage debt in 1960 was 19 per cent less than the record net increase of $15.2 billion in 1959. Of the $12.3 billion net increase in outstanding residential mortgage debt

[12] SOURCE: *Housing Legislation of 1961*, Appendix, Committee on Banking and Currency.

in 1960, $11.1 billion was in the one- to four-family mortgage segment and $1.2 billion in the multifamily segment.

At the end of 1960 the total outstanding residential mortgage debt was $160.5 billion. About 88 per cent of the total, or $142 billion, was secured by mortgages on one- to four-family properties; the outstanding multifamily mortgage debt was $18.5 billion at the year end.

Most of the increase in the outstanding mortgage debt in 1960 was in conventional loans which increased by $9.3 billion to a total of $98.2 billion, equal to 61 per cent of the residential mortgage debt. The FHA-insured segment increased by $3.3 billion to a total of $32.6 billion, or 20 per cent of the residential mortgage debt total at the end of the year. There was a slight decrease in the VA-guaranteed portion of the debt, which declined by $0.3 billion in 1960, the third consecutive year in which there was a slight decline. At the end of 1960, the VA outstanding mortgage debt was $29.7 billion, which was 19 per cent of the outstanding residential mortgage debt.

Creation of the Housing and Home Finance Agency

A review of the historical development of mortgage financing should include mention of the creation of the Housing and Home Finance Agency by the President's Reorganization Plan 3 of 1947. This brought together under one head the Home Loan Bank Board, the FHA, the Public Housing Administration, and the National Housing Council. Later on the FNMA was placed under the same authority. The VA Loan Guaranty Division became an "ex officio" member of this agency.

Our Managed Economy and Its Effect upon Mortgage Lending

Many economists are of the opinion that throughout the period beginning in 1933 the United States shifted in the direction of a "managed economy." Whether it was well or poorly managed depends upon the economic beliefs and political thinking of each individual. Whatever one's views on this issue, it is difficult to avoid the conclusion that inflationary tendencies were accentuated by many of the things the government did. Throughout this period one of the most important problems with which the government had to contend was what could be done to prevent further deterioration in the purchasing power of the dollar. Congress passed measures with the hope that it could prevent inflation from getting out of hand. These economic-political developments make an interesting study. They have given mortgage lenders many difficult financing problems to solve because of the profound effect these developments have had upon the mortgage market and the national economy.

Almost every year since 1944 has witnessed the passage by Congress of new legislation designed to improve conditions in the housing and home-financing industry and the mortgage market. Most of the measures contained items beneficial to the welfare of the nation, but some of these measures were undoubtedly inflationary (see Appendix B, List of Major Housing Acts).

Inflationary Aspects of Home-financing Measures

The inflationary results of some of the home-financing measures enacted by Congress from 1944 to 1947 plus the overliberal policies of many mortgage lenders in 1946 and 1947 became the concern of President Truman and those in control of numerous agencies of the United States government. The President appealed to the bankers to help combat inflation. During the closing months of 1947 and the early months of 1948, the Open Market Committee of the Federal Reserve System lowered its support price on government bonds, interest on short-term treasury obligations went up, the Federal Reserve Board raised its discount rate twice by a total of ½ of 1 per cent per annum and increased the reserve requirements of member banks. Institutional lenders that were making 100 per cent loans at 4 per cent interest under Section 501 of the Servicemen's Readjustment Act discontinued this practice. For the time being loans to veterans were limited to those arising under the previously described Section 505 of the Servicemen's Readjustment Act. That the money market had tightened was rather generally recognized. Congress empowered the Administrator of Veteran Affairs, with the consent of the Secretary of the Treasury, to increase the rate for VA 501 loans from 4 per cent to 4½ per cent. In any case the increase to 4½ per cent came too late to stimulate the VA home-loan market. This was true throughout the nation and especially in the Far West and Southwest.

The Government-bond Market Has a Direct Effect upon the Mortgage Market

The major types of mortgage lenders deal in United States government securities as well as in mortgages to an important extent. These lenders are faced with the problem of allocating their long-term investments between these two and other forms of long-term credit in such a way as to secure a high rate of return, minimize the risk of capital loss, and retain as high a degree of liquidity as is consistent with these goals. They are therefore influenced in their lending policy by the course of government-bond yields. When government-bond yields rise, government bonds become more attractive to these lenders than they were previously, and these lenders may proceed more cautiously in their commitments to buy mortgage paper. This hesitancy in commitments may show up as a slowdown in actual mortgage lending a few months later.

Conversely, if government-bond yields fall below a level which is competitive with prevailing mortgage yields, lenders are encouraged to increase their mortgage commitments, and even to sell government bonds in order to obtain funds for mortgage lending. The government-bond yield should be compared, not with the effective rate of interest on mortgage loans, but with the interest minus the cost of servicing a mortgage loan. This servicing fee is usually ½ of 1 per cent. Changes in government-bond yields have exercised a significant effect on the mortgage market in the last few years.

Action of the Open Market Committte

During 1948, 1949, and 1950, particularly the latter two years, insurance companies and mutual savings banks sold large blocks of long-term government bonds to the Open Market Committee, mostly at par or at a premium, and placed the proceeds in real estate mortgages. This operation was quite profitable and possibly gave an artificial stimulus to the veterans' loan market.

In March, 1951, the Open Market Committee of the Federal Reserve System and the Treasury Department entered into an agreement which provided that the Federal Reserve System would withdraw its support of government-bond prices.

The influence of government-bond yields on mortgage lending has therefore been especially noteworthy since the "unpegging" of the government-bond market in 1951. Before 1951, the Federal Reserve System stood committed to support government-bond prices at the levels which had prevailed for the preceding decade, and in this way to keep government-bond yields at a very low level. After March, 1951, the Federal Reserve System no longer was committed in this way, and government-bond yields were free to rise or to fall, as the market (and the policy of the Treasury and the Federal Reserve System) dictated.

Activity of FHA and VA Lending Only a Part of the Entire Mortgage Lending Industry

In this discussion, emphasis has been placed on FHA and VA loans because the great changes during the past twenty-five years in our mortgage pattern have undoubtedly taken place in the field of government-insured and -guaranteed loans. However, conventional lending by no means disappeared; conventional mortgages continue to represent a substantial part of the holdings of institutional lenders.[13] One important change in bank conventional lending took place some twenty years ago, namely, the trend from ten-year fully amortized conventional home loans which replaced one- to four-year conventional home loans to twenty-year fully amortized loans on owner-occupied single-family dwellings. Life insurance companies and savings and loan associations were also permitted to make long-term conventional loans on homes and other types of properties.

Restraint of Mortgage Credit—Regulation X

Credit extended on real estate, especially residential properties, expanded rapidly after World War II, and was exerting strong inflationary pressure in mid-1950, when it became necessary for the United States to embark on a major defense program. The economy was operating close to capacity and there was little prospect that the program could be carried out without diverting resources from other uses. Excessive credit to finance construction would have led to greater competition with defense requirements for manpower and materials, bidding up costs and prices, and increasing inflationary pressures throughout the economy.

The Defense Production Act of 1950

In this setting, temporary authority to regulate certain real estate credit was granted to the President of the United States by the Defense Production Act of September, 1950. The President was authorized to regulate the terms on which (1) real estate loans could be made, insured, or guaranteed by Federal agencies and (2) credit not so insured or guaranteed could be extended in connection with the construction or major improvement of real property.

The President delegated authority for regulating government-aided lending to the HHFA Administrator, and authority for restricting other kinds of real estate credit to the Board of Governors of the Federal Reserve System.

In mid-fall, 1950, the Federal Reserve Board issued Regulation X[14] for real estate credit. The HHFA Administrator concurred in the Board's regulation and applied similar restraints to federally aided loans. Regulation X, like Regulation W for consumer credit, applied to the terms on which individual loans could be made. It specified the maximum amount that

[13] FHA loans outstanding as of 12-31-60, approximately $26,700,000; VA loans outstanding as of 12-31-60, approximately, $29,700,000; conventional loans outstanding as of 12-31-60, approximately, $85,400,000. Source: Federal Reserve Bank of San Francisco, Research Department.

[14] *The Federal Reserve System: Purposes and Functions,* chap. 4, Board of Governors of the Federal Reserve System, Washington, 1954.

could be borrowed, the maximum length of time the loan could run, and the minimum periodic amounts that had to be paid to amortize the principal amount of the loan.

An amendment to the Defense Production Act in June, 1952, continued authority for real estate credit regulation until mid-1953, but required that the regulation be relaxed earlier if the estimated number of dwelling units started in each of three successive months was below an annual rate (seasonally adjusted) of 1.2 million. Estimates for the next three months were all below the specified rate and, accordingly, the Board suspended regulation of credit terms in mid-September, 1952.

Action taken under Regulation X and parallel regulation of government-aided loans were the first attempts in this country, and probably anywhere in the world, to restrain an inflationary rise in real estate credit through comprehensive regulation of mortgage terms. The experiment was too brief, however, to permit judgment concerning the effectiveness of such regulation.

The Federal Open Market Committee

This Committee[15] comprises the seven members of the Board of Governors of the Federal Reserve System and five presidents of District Federal Reserve banks. The president of the Federal Reserve Bank of New York is always a member of the Committee. From the other eleven District Federal Reserve banks five presidents are elected on a rotating basis. It has responsibility for deciding on changes to be made in the Federal Reserve System's portfolio of government securities—in other words, when and how much to buy or sell in the open market and under what conditions. The Reserve banks, in their operations in the open market, are required by law to carry out the decisions of the Open Market Committee.

The Federal Open Market Committee meets in Washington every three weeks and reviews the national business and credit situation with the help of its staff, which is drawn from the staffs of the Board of Governors and the Reserve banks. In meetings of the Committee, representatives of the Reserve banks bring to the council table their special knowledge of regional conditions. Decisions about open-market policy are made in the light of a full discussion of national and regional factors.

Purchases and sales of securities for the Federal Open Market Committee are effected in the name of the System Open Market Account, participations in which are allocated among the twelve Federal Reserve banks in accordance with the ratio of each Reserve bank's total assets to the total assets for all Reserve banks combined. All transactions are supervised by the manager of the account, who is an officer of the Federal Reserve Bank of

[15] *Ibid.,* chap. 5.

New York. Such transactions are required to be in accordance with instructions issued by the Committee.

Housing Starts in 1951

Despite this unsettled condition of the mortgage market and despite the government's effort to restrict housing starts in 1951 to a total of 800,000, the final total for that year showed about 1,100,000,[16] a record which up to that time had been surpassed only once in the entire history of the country—in 1950 when 1,395,000 units had been built.[17]

Mortgage Funds Tend to Flow into the More Rapidly Growing Areas of the Nation

In a country as large as the United States, certain areas have an oversupply of certain materials and commodities, while there is an undersupply in other areas. There is a concentration of manufacturing such as the automotive industry, close to the source of raw materials. Money follows somewhat the same general pattern; there is great accumulated wealth in New York and New England, while in many areas throughout the nation, particularly in the West, Southeast, and Southwest, investment funds available from those sources are not in sufficient supply to meet the demand. Tremendous amounts of mortgage investment funds are therefore obtained from these Eastern investors, made up primarily of commercial banks, mutual savings banks, and life insurance companies.

The Laws of Supply and Demand and Their Application to Mortgage Fund Investments

The afore-mentioned uneven distribution of commodities has been overcome to some extent by transportation and price adjustments which take care of the cost of moving a particular commodity from one point to another. For example, an automobile delivered in Seattle is priced higher by the amount of freight charges than the same automobile delivered at Detroit, Michigan. Those same laws of supply and demand and of trade and commerce apply to funds concentrated in financial centers and invested in mortgages in distant parts of the country. As an illustration, life insurance companies for many years and mutual savings banks in recent years have made loans in California, Oregon, Washington, Texas, and other Western, Southwestern, and Southeastern states. The rates on these loans were sufficiently high to justify paying an agent a proper servicing fee. In the case of

[16] Federal Reserve Bank of San Francisco, Research Department.
[17] See housing-start statistics earlier in this chapter.

VA and FHA loans, that fee has usually been ½ of 1 per cent per annum of the principal of the loan. An insurance company investing in a VA 4¾ per cent loan in these areas would, therefore, receive a gross return at the rate of 4¼ per cent interest per annum, out of which would have to be taken the insurance company's own cost of operation estimated at another ¼ of 1 per cent; hence the net return on this type of investment would not exceed 4 per cent interest.

FHA and VA Interest Rates until May, 1953, Not Competitive

Many private groups claimed that the problem of maldistribution of money and mortgages could be readily solved by allowing a higher rate of interest in the areas of scarcity of funds, but most private institutions believed that a uniform rate across the nation on FHA and VA loans would accomplish the same result with less confusion and that the law of supply and demand would operate to reduce the rate below the allowable maximum in areas of accumulated capital. The interest rate increase on both FHA and VA loans, effective in early May, 1953, did not prove a solution to this problem.

Expansion of Mutual Savings Banks Investments

Prior to 1949 mutual savings banks in Massachusetts were denied the right to buy FHA or VA loans except those made within the state or in contiguous states; savings banks in New York were under similar restrictions until 1950. At present such institutions may buy FHA and VA loans in any state of the nation. Mutual savings banks buying out-of-state loans are subject to the same costs as insurance companies and must pay about the same costs of maintaining their own office operations.[18] Therefore, it is quite natural that a savings bank in New York might be willing to make a VA loan over its counter without paying a servicing fee while at the same time it would refuse to buy a VA loan in other states because it would show a lower net yield after servicing.

Rental Housing Activity

During its entire history the FHA has encouraged both the construction of homes for owner occupancy and rental housing (see Figure 30, Chapter 9). Prior to World War II, loans on rental units on which FHA insurance was obtained were principally made under Section 207 of the National Housing Act and reached a maximum volume of about $100 million for

[18] *The Annotated Laws of Massachusetts,* chap. 168, sec. 50 (a), June 2, 1949; "Banking Law," *McKinney's Consolidated Laws of New York,* sec. 235, par. 20, July 1, 1950.

each of the years 1938 and 1939. Section 608 was approved in May, 1942, but the greatest activity under the provision was not reached until the postwar years of 1947 to 1950, when some $3 billion of loans on multiple-family units were insured. Section 803 (the Wherry Act) was added in 1949, and a fairly large volume of loans on rental units at military posts has been insured under this section. Section 213 (co-operative housing) came into being with the Sparkman Bill of 1950 but has not proved to be a very important factor. Sections 903 and 908 (known as "Title IX") for programmed housing in defense areas, were authorized in September, 1951. Most of Title IX projects have been indirectly financed by FNMA.

To test the marketability of Title IX loans, a mortgage lender had to find the answer to the question "Could these houses be readily sold or rented if the defense project in that vicinity was removed?" Most Title IX financing had been arranged on an interim financing basis through banks and other private lenders which held a "takeout" commitment from FNMA to purchase the resultant long-term loans. As FNMA funds were exhausted early in 1952, Congress, when it passed the Housing Act of 1952, provided an additional $900 million fund for buying Title IX loans.[19]

Development of Discount Market and Method of Operation

At no time throughout a period of many years had the pattern of mortgage financing been more complex than from 1952 to 1961. The greatest confusion existed in the financing of VA loans. Because the rate on such loans remained at 4 per cent until May 5, 1953, an unusual type of discount market developed. Such a discount market operates in the following fashion: The builder is approved by the VA as a nonsupervised lender. He then, as a builder-lender, makes loans of his own funds to veterans and sells the resultant loans to a third party. So long as he, as a builder-lender, does not require the veteran to pay more than 1 per cent flat for processing costs under the local allowable VA schedule, he is permitted to sell his loans at whatever price he can get.

It was expected that the complexities in the pattern of mortgage financing would be reduced to some extent by the increase in the FHA Title II interest rate and the VA rate increase on veteran 501 loans. It was the hope of many mortgage lenders that as a result of increases a par market on both FHA and VA loans would develop. However, in part because of the builder-lender program described in the preceding paragraph, it was impossible to sell these particular loans at par even as late as 1961, and there was little hope at that time for a par market for a long time to come.

[19] See *Background and History of the Federal National Mortgage Association,* October 31, 1959, footnote 43, which describes the "set-aside program for the purchase of defense, disaster, and military housing mortgages."

The Housing Act of 1953 was a miscellany of amendments to the National Housing Act, the Servicemen's Readjustment Act, and related legislation. It also authorized the FNMA program of selling and purchasing mortgages on a "one-for-one program."[20]

The vital part of the new bill was that which repealed legislation covering the selling price of FHA and VA mortgages. The discount market and the builder-lender program covering VA 501 loans were given approval.

On July 8, 1953, the VA issued *Loan Guaranty Information Bulletin* 131 on the subject of fees and charges. It permitted the originating lender to pass back to the builder or other seller the amount of any commitment or warehousing fee or charge, as well as the amount of any discount which might be involved in the sale of a guaranteed or insured VA mortgage.

This new legislation meant continuation of both the discount market on FHA and VA loans and the builder-lender program. As the new legislation did not permit an institutional lender with such loans in its own portfolio to pass the discount back to the builder, there apparently was no other way by which the VA home loan program could be sustained except by builder-lender operations, even though builder-lenders would have preferred to get out of the lending business altogether.

Home-building and Mortgage Lending Activity during 1954

Home builders for the sixth straight year started more than a million homes in 1954. The total for the year 1954, which was 1,215,600 dwelling units, exceeded both the 1952 total of 1,130,000 units and the 1953 total of 1,103,800 units. It is important to note that the 1953 total of 1,103,800 was reached despite a shortage of mortgage money and some fears of a possible recession. The total dwelling starts for the year 1954 were therefore up to that time the second largest since the record year of 1950, when 1,400,000 homes were started.

The 1953 and 1954 achievements offset to some extent forecasts that the nation had caught up with postwar shortages and that needs for new housing in the future would not run more than 750,000 units each year. However, there is no doubt that at the end of the year 1953 there were more dwelling units unsold than in any of the previous five years. This probably had the effect of stabilizing prices on homes.

The biggest problem which confronted the home-building industry in 1953 was the shortage of mortgage money, which reached crisis proportions in some areas of the nation.

In September, 1953, this situation began to improve, and easier money reduced the yields on securities which compete with mortgages for the invest-

[20] See *Background and History of the Federal National Mortgage Association,* October 31, 1959, footnote 45.

ing dollar. The gap between the demand for and the supply of mortgage funds continued to be a problem, and solutions were being sought at both business and government levels. Building prices had remained fairly stable, despite the pressure of rising costs of labor and land development. The selling price of new homes remained fairly steady, while the selling price of existing homes showed a slight falling off in both demand and price.

The VA issued new regulations regarding collection of fees and charges. The only fees and charges that were controlled were charges made against the veteran purchaser. Charges made on collections from others such as the builder or real estate agent were no longer subject to control. This clarified both FHA and VA lending procedures.

The Voluntary Credit Extension Program

Title VI of the Housing Act of 1954 covered the operations of the Voluntary Credit Extension program. This program was offered by the Life Insurance Association of America and the American Life Convention for the formation of national and regional committees to assist in placing FHA and VA loans in remote areas, in small communities, and for special purposes. The plan called for the creation of a national committee composed of representatives of all types of mortgage lending institutions including mortgage companies and builders and realtors who would supervise the activities of similarly composed regional committees.

Assuming a marketable rate of interest would be maintained, it was expected that this organization would help to broaden the distribution of funds for FHA and VA mortgages for hard-to-place cases, including loans to racial minorities. The National Voluntary Home Mortgage Credit Committee consists of the HHFA Administrator as chairman, two representatives of each type of private financing institution, two representatives of residential builders, and two representatives of real estate boards; all members serve on a voluntary basis. It also provides that one representative each from the VA, the Federal Reserve Board, and the Home Loan Bank Board may serve as advisers. This program has been successful and was extended an additional four years by the Housing Act of 1961. The basic function is to facilitate the flow of funds for FHA and VA mortgages to areas with shortages of local capital for such loans or inadequate facilities for access thereto, wherever consistent with sound underwriting principles.

Home-building and mortgage lending activities in the nation for 1954 continued at a rate which made it another boom year in dwelling construction. This activity in private-home building resulted in part from the change in the mortgage market during late 1953 and 1954. With the general easing of money conditions in early 1954 the mortgage market began a recovery, and both FHA and VA 4½ per cent interest rate loans with some equity slowly approached par.

A large supply of mortgage money became available in early 1954 on VA-guaranteed loans on the basis of nothing down with thirty years maturity. In May, 1954, nearly 25 per cent of VA-guaranteed loans closed were made without a down payment.[21]

Continuation of the Housing Boom

The housing boom continued during 1955.

Mortgage funds on a nationwide basis since World War II have been in adequate supply for all legitimate and conservative needs at fair rates of interest. However, there have been periods of months, and sometimes as long as a year or two, when investors were unwilling to place their funds in mortgages because unduly low rates of interest were set by law or because the other terms of financing sought by builders or home buyers were considered unsound by the lending groups.

Beginning in April, 1955, the supply of funds available for making conservative loans was adequate, but not for investment in thirty-year no-down-payment VA loans.

Most of the few insurance companies heretofore buying no-down-payment loans discontinued this practice, and mutual savings banks of New York likewise curtailed their purchases. The same insurance companies and mutual savings banks were seeking seasoned FHA and VA loans where the borrowers had reasonable equities in their homes.

In late July, 1955, the government tightened its credit terms on home purchases in a precautionary move to head off any inflationary trend. The FHA and the VA announced a 2 per cent increase in minimum cash payments and a five-year reduction in the thirty-year maximum repayment period. Veterans who had heretofore been able in many instances to buy a house without a down payment, supported by a VA loan, were required to make a down payment of at least 2 per cent of the purchase price in cash, plus payment of the closing costs in cash. Former servicemen had been able to buy homes with no money down and with repayment over a thirty-year period since April, 1953. For FHA-insured loans, minimum down payments were increased 2 per cent, and maturities were reduced to twenty-five years.

This tightening of mortgage procedures was the second step announced within a few months designed to stabilize the mortgage market. In April, both the FHA and the VA announced that closing costs, such as fees, title searches, and the like, would have to be paid in cash. Before then, home

[21] Federal Reserve Bank of San Francisco, Research Department.

buyers had been permitted in some cases to add these settlement charges to their mortgage loans.

On the other hand, most mortgage lenders welcomed the tightening of mortgage terms on both FHA and VA loans, as it meant a curbing of some of the more marginal building projects. It also meant a general tightening of mortgage credit covering purchases of homes with an FHA or VA loan and consequently would have a stabilizing effect upon the mortgage market. Even so, lenders expected that the prospect for housing starts for the year 1955 would be well over 1,200,000 in number. The figure actually reached was 1,329,000.

A very important bill passed by Congress was the long-pending measure granting national banks the privilege of making fully amortized loans of twenty-year maturity up to two-thirds of value. The new law also permitted farm and residential construction loans with nine-month maturity. The previous law restricted national banks to 60 per cent of value. This action by Congress met with approval throughout the nation. It placed national banks in a more competitive position with life insurance companies, savings and loan associations, and mutual savings banks. Those states which restricted mortgage loans of state-chartered commercial banks to 60 per cent of appraisal value followed suit. This had a beneficial effect upon state banks that compete for mortgage loans with other types of institutional investors.

Mortgage Credit Becomes More Restricted

Progressive tightening of credit characterized the money markets during 1956. No form of credit escaped the rise in price due to the heavy borrowing demands of individuals, firms, corporations, municipalities, and the state and Federal government.

Throughout the year upward changes in rates came with great frequency, climaxing during the last quarter with FHA's increase in the allowable interest rate from 4½ per cent to 5 per cent and with the Federal Reserve Board's action amending Regulation Q to permit a maximum of 3 per cent per annum to be paid by banks on savings accounts as against the former limitation of 2½ per cent. Shortly after this amendment was passed most banks throughout the nation announced that the 3 per cent interest would be paid on savings deposits starting January 1, 1957. At that time most savings and loan associations, both Federal- and state-chartered, announced that interest on deposits would be increased. This increase ranged from ½ of 1 per cent to 1 per cent.

While these and other moves came with a measure of suddenness toward the year end, they were no surprise to students of economics or to astute mortgage lenders generally, who for some time had been pointing out the inevitable effects of borrowing faster than loanable wealth was being created. In the long run, the events of the year 1956, as far as money and credit were concerned, proved beneficial to the nation. The interest rates charged borrowers were actually quite reasonable, and the increased rates paid to savings depositors proved an added incentive to building up savings accounts, thus creating more loanable funds.

Savings deposits during 1956 grew at a lesser rate than during the previous year. Mutual savings banks and life insurance companies continued to purchase FHA and VA loans throughout the nation and generally at large discounts. In order to maintain a relatively constant percentage of mortgage loans to deposits, private repurchasable capital, and reserves, it was necessary for prudent mortgage lenders to be quite selective in extending mortgage credit and to encourage operative builders to dispose of most of their resultant loans in such secondary markets as were available to them.

FHA Lowers Down Payment and Increases Interest Rate

Following the passage of the Housing Act of 1957 on July 31, the Federal Housing Commissioner formalized by regulation the lower down-payment schedule on FHA loans authorized by the act. At the same time the permissible interest rate was raised to 5½ per cent per annum. In compliance with the mandates of Congress the FHA Commissioner issued instructions designed to place limits on charges, fees, and discounts related to insured mortgages through their various stages of origination, purchase, and sale in the primary markets.

This triple action did not produce the results sought by Congress, nor did it please builders and lenders. The interest rate increase should have placed FHA loans in a better position to compete with corporate bonds and other types of investment offerings. The lowering of down payments when lenders were trying to spread available dollars among as many borrowers as possible added pressure for more credit than could be expected from institutions already heavily invested in mortgage loans.

The inadequate interest rate and the little- or no-down-payment pattern had injured the investment standing of VA loans, and heavy discounts on such loans in the investment markets made this form of financing very costly to most builders.

In the field of mortgage credit 1957 was a difficult year for borrower and lender alike, particularly for those whose business had been dependent upon loans insured or guaranteed by the United States government. The VA home-loan program might have stopped entirely if it had not been for remaining obligations of institutions previously committed to purchase loans developed from tract operations, which in many instances had slowed down because of sales resistance. The FHA although not too well prepared to absorb the expected increase by reason of added VA applications was handicapped by instructions from Congress to place limitations on lenders' fees and charges. This action of course prevented a free market and went a long way to offset the favorable action in August of raising the FHA interest from 5 per cent to 5½ per cent.

During 1956 and 1957 the home-building industry and the mortgage lending industry experienced certain readjustments brought about in large part by the excesses of 1955 and previous years.

Notwithstanding the constant threat of legislation and the possibility of a recession deeper than existed in 1957 there seemed to be more favorable factors than unfavorable ones in the outlook for home construction during 1958. On the encouraging side there was no substantial inventory of unsold houses. A good demand for homes to meet the needs of newly created families and to replace obsolete residences existed.

Less competition for mortgage loans for plant expansion was expected. During 1956 and 1957 this financing placed a heavy strain on the supply of long-term credit. The restraint on mortgage credit at the time allowed thrift institutions to build up their liquid resources sufficient to provide ample funds for new mortgage loans without distorting their traditional investment patterns.

On the unfavorable side, rising costs of both land and improvements priced many houses beyond the reach of prospective buyers. Higher-priced homes engendered requests for larger individual loans, thus preventing a spread of the available mortgage funds to a wider number of mortgagors. Increased unemployment was also an important factor in retarding sales.

At that time, while only the most optimistic would predict a housing boom for 1958, it seemed reasonable to expect that 1958 would exceed the 1957 housing starts by at least 10 per cent, and such an increase could prove helpful in bolstering up other parts of the economy.

Changes in Federal Legislation Affecting Housing and Home Financing

Changes in Federal legislation affecting housing and home financing have become annual occurrences for many years. Usually the major changes are enacted into law during July or August after debates and committee hearings in both houses of Congress. In 1958 an Emergency Housing Bill was passed on March 19, in record time, and became law on April 1, when signed by the President of the United States. The act had many features which were not in accord with the views of the administration. (See list of housing acts in Appendix B.)

There is no doubt that easy credit terms tend to stimulate sales. The danger faced is that of inflation which was almost certain to follow the extension of loose credit, the widening of direct government lending, and the resumption of deficit financing. In any event the supply of mortgage funds for 1958 appeared to be ample. This condition had been brought about by a decline in home building for the previous two years, by a substantial growth in savings deposits during 1957, and by repayments from the steadily increasing total of mortgage loans outstanding.

The elimination of discount controls as provided in the Emergency Act permitted an easier flow of FHA and VA mortgages in the secondary markets although that activity was of greater interest to brokers and investors in "discount" loans than to lenders who continued to adhere to a program of investing only in loans where owners had reasonable equities in their properties.

While legislators passed liberal laws to aid home construction and while lenders were prepared to finance all needed housing, there remained the question of whether or not the public was in a buying frame of mind. Builders for the most part were proceeding cautiously.

Veterans Administration Program

The interest rate on VA loans was taken out of the Housing Act of 1959 and signed by the President of the United States as a separate bill (H.R. 2256). The interest rate was raised from $4\frac{3}{4}$ per cent to $5\frac{1}{4}$ per cent.

One hundred million dollars was authorized for direct loans to veterans where private funds were not available.

The Money Markets during the Year 1959

During the year 1959 the money markets entered their tightest phase in many years, with interest rates at a high level. A 5 per cent rate placed on an issue of four-year ten-month Treasury notes was the highest paid for a similar issue in thirty years. These increased rates meant higher costs to borrowers on new loans.

The tightness in the mortgage market evoked demands for relief which received strong support from congressional spokesmen.

However, the administration was opposed to expansionist policies, and stressed a continuing vigorous attack on inflation, which in respect to government programs was taken to mean not instituting special measures for easy credit and not putting government money into direct lending and subsidy operations.

The year 1960 began in the midst of a period of business expansion which had been only temporarily interrupted by a serious steel strike. It came after a year in which demands for credit, especially for mortgage installment loans, and Federal government financing had been exceptionally high. Although the volume of funds made available during the year was the largest on record, it could not accommodate all the demand that pressed upon it. In view of this pressure the Federal Reserve had found it advisable to exert its own counterpressure against further expansion. As a consequence, 1960 began with the financial markets in a state of extreme tightness and with interest rates at a thirty-year high.

VA Mortgage Guaranty and Loan Operation Extended

On June 29, and 30, 1960, respectively, the House and Senate passed H.R. 7903 extending both the VA home-loan guaranty program and the VA direct-lending program for another two years. The amount of the direct-lending program was continued at $150 million a year. In June of 1961 the VA loan guaranty program was extended to 1967 for veterans of World War II and to 1975 for veterans of the Korean conflict. The direct lending program for veteran home loans was also extended.

FHA Loans May Be Sold to Individuals

On July 13, 1960, the FHA Commissioner announced the issuance of new regulations under which FHA loans insured under Section 203 (b) may be sold to individuals. This action was considered to be one of the most progressive steps taken since the inception of FHA and opened up an entirely new source for investment in FHA Loans.

Trend of Interest Rates on Mortgage Loans

Starting in late 1948, the trend in interest rates moved in an upward direction, and by the middle of 1959 all types of new debt securities were at the highest point reached since the early 1930s. By comparison with interest rates of thirty years past, these interest rates were not inordinately high. On the contrary they were actually on the low side. At most times prior to the Great Depression, interest rates were higher than they are now, and they have been higher in previous periods when capital has been in great demand. It is the low interest rate phase from the mid 1930s to 1948 that is unique in interest-rate history rather than the present ascent to moderately high levels.

Mortgage Interest Rates and Security Yields

During the late 1950s a profound change had been taking place in which mortgage yields were being geared to other investment yields in a manner not previously encountered. In view of the history of finance these problems of adjustment, however, are readily understandable.

Prior to the end of World War II mortgage investments were very little affected by monetary policy, and the mortgage interest rate was not seriously involved in institutional investment policies. It moved with considerable independence of outside influences. The growth of the relative importance of the mortgage debt was accompanied by growth in the participation by institutional investors in mortgage lending. In 1925 only 59 per cent of the mortgage debt was held by financial institutions, while by 1960 the mortgages held by institutional investors were approximately 76 per cent of the total mortgage debt. Table 3 shows the major changes in representative interest rates and securities yields for the years 1946 to 1960. Times are selected to show the greatest changes during this period. This is very valuable and informative data which gives a comprehensive picture of interest rates and securities yields of all investment sources.

Real Estate Investment Trusts

An important development in mortgage credit took place in the late 1960s when the Internal Revenue Code was amended to put real estate investment trusts on a par, taxwise, with other types of investment funds. The adaptability of the trust as a medium for pooling savings for investment in mortgages was immediately recognized. The trusts are required to operate in conformity with the applicable rules of the Internal Revenue Service, of the Securities and Exchange Commission, and, if insured and guaranteed mortgage are involved, of the FHA and VA.

The New Era in the Mortgage Market

In the space of a generation, investment in mortgages, and particularly home mortgage lending, has added enormously to its weight in the economy and also has been transformed from an operation dominated by local institutional lenders and individuals to one of national institutional character. The transformation goes much further, because both the character of the institutions themselves and the environment in which they work have changed significantly.

In view of the drastic changes that have taken place in the mortgage market over a generation, leading mortgage lenders and economists are of the opinion that there is no possibility that this market will ever escape from the impacts of monetary policy or from competition in the general money market.

A new era in the mortgage market is here. The problem is to learn how to make it a means for meeting the housing and other real estate financing needs of the nation. A major step in this program would be for the government to adapt its mortgage interest-rate policies to reality. The very essence

TABLE 3 REPRESENTATIVE INTEREST RATES AND SECURITIES YIELDS, 1946–1960

Investment medium	Mid-1946	Mid-1953	Mid-1957	Late 1957	Mid-1958	Late 1959	Mid-1960	End 1960
I. Short-term credit:								
U.S. government, 90-day bills	0.38	2.11	3.29	3.53	0.83	4.50	2.30	2.30
U.S. government, 9–12 months, certificates and notes	0.83	2.46	3.55	4.02	0.98	4.99	3.03	2.85
Prime commercial paper, 4–6 months	0.75	2.75	3.79	4.10	1.50	4.88	3.40	3.50
Prime bankers' acceptances, 90-day	0.50	1.88	3.36	3.83	1.13	4.47	3.13	3.00
Brokers' collateral loans ("call money")	1.00	3.25	4.50	4.50	3.50	4.75	4.50	4.50
Prime short-term business loans (N.Y.)	1.84	3.39	4.12	4.62	3.70	5.00	5.00	4.75
Short-term municipal bonds, high-grade, 1-year	0.50	1.70	2.40	2.60	0.75	2.85	2.00	1.50
Federal Reserve discount rate	1.00	2.00	3.00	3.50	1.75	4.00	3.50	3.00
II. Medium-term credit:								
U.S. government, 3- to 5-year notes and bonds	1.15	2.92	3.77	3.99	2.25	4.95	3.70	3.75
Medium-term municipal bonds, high-grade, 5-year	0.70	2.10	2.90	3.10	1.70	3.00	2.75	2.55
Medium-term corporate bonds, high-grade, 5-year	1.32	2.75	3.50	3.90	2.90	4.00	3.85	3.50
Term loans to business, prime	2.00	3.50	4.50	5.00	4.25	5.00	5.00	4.50
III. Long-term credit:								
U.S. government, long-term bonds	2.16	3.29	3.58	3.73	3.19	4.25	3.85	3.75
Municipal bonds, long-term, Aaa Moody's	1.04	2.64	3.19	3.43	2.74	3.50	3.30	3.15
Corporate bonds, long-term, Aaa Moody's	2.49	3.40	3.91	4.12	3.57	4.60	4.40	4.35
Corporate bonds, long-term, Baa Moody's	3.03	3.86	4.63	5.09	4.55	5.30	5.22	5.10
Mortgage loans, FHA-insured	4	4½	5	5¼	5¼	5¾	5¾	5¾
Mortgage loans, residential, conventional	4½–5	5–5½	5½–6	6	6–6½	6½	6–6½	6
IV. Savings institutions:								
Commercial bank savings account	1	1½	3	3	3	3	3	3
Mutual savings bank accounts	1½	2½	3	3	3	3	3–3½	3
Savings and loan association accounts	2½	3	3½	4	3	4–4½	4½	4–4½
U.S. savings bonds, Series E, to maturity	2.90	3	3¼	3¼	3¼	3¾	3¾	3¾
V. Stocks:								
Industrial preferred, high-grade Moody's	3.43	4.24	4.60	4.68	4.15	4.67	4.44	4.50
Common stocks, Dow-Jones 30 industrial	3.38	5.90	4.56	5.29	4.50	3.13	3.47	3.45
Common stocks, Moody's 200 composite	3.97	5.49	4.05	4.68	4.15	3.34	3.60	3.50

SOURCE: Adapted by permission from David F. Jordon and Herbert E. Dougall, Investments, 7th ed., Prentice-Hall, Inc., Englewood Cliffs, N.J., 1960.

of an effective relationship between the mortgage market and other investments with which they compete is a freely moving interest rate in the government insured and guaranteed mortgage loan programs. In this new era, mortgage interest rates may be expected to move in close conformity with movements in interest rates generally. It is further evident that the mortgage market must learn to live with the wide range of yield movements and the more direct and intensive competition to which its matured position in the economy has exposed it.

Mortgage Financing Developments Resulting from Innovations Initiated by the New Political Administration

Shortly after John F. Kennedy was inaugurated as President of the United States, he ordered FHA to reduce the maximum permissive interest rates on mortgages insured under Section 203 (one- to four-family houses), Section 213 (sales-type cooperatives), Section 220 (urban renewal houses), Section 221 (housing for displaced families), Section 222 (houses for servicemen), Section 809 (houses for civilians at military establishments), and Section 232 (nursing homes).

The change in rate was effective (from $5\frac{3}{4}$ per cent to $5\frac{1}{2}$ per cent) for all mortgages for which applications for insurance were received on or after February 2, 1961.

Coincident with this move, FNMA raised the prices offered for FHA and VA mortgages by $\frac{1}{2}$ percentage point. FNMA estimated to have available at that time about $850 million for secondary market purchases. Current sales by FNMA were adding to availability more rapidly than purchases were subtracting from it.

Effect of Change of Interest Rate

This move, one of the first in the President's program for economic stimulation, had a disturbing effect upon the mortgage market. Discounts generally dropped two points.

The Emergency Program

Along with the change in FHA interest rates and FNMA prices, other elements in a housing program figured prominently among the steps announced in the President's economic message of February 2, 1961. Following the proposals stated in the message, HHFA spurred its regional directors to speed up urban renewal projects. On the college housing program, the Community Facilities Administration authorized the approval of construction advances prior to final execution of the loan agreement and moved to hasten the processing of pending cases.

The CFA also reduced the interest rate from 4⅜ per cent to 4¼ per cent for loans for community facilities, made cities of any size eligible for loans, made eligible for financing any type of public works not already receiving Federal aid, and took steps to accelerate its whole operation. The Public Housing Administration likewise endeavored to expedite its operation.

Robert C. Weaver Confirmed as HHFA Administrator

Robert C. Weaver was confirmed as HHFA Administrator without a roll-call vote. His interest in housing is broad, and his activities have been largely in the area of public housing and in dealing with the problems of racial discrimination in the housing market. It was believed that he would avoid extremism and give a competent well-balanced administration.

Housing Program to Develop Slowly

The delays in organizing the housing agencies by the new political administration inescapably spelled delay in the development of the administration's housing program. Although no housing legislation had been requested by the President of the United States in connection with his emergency proposals, a special message dealing with amendments and innovations in the housing statutes was expected at a later date.

Pending Housing Bills and Proposals

At this time numerous housing bills were in the process of being submitted to Congress, covering college facilities, community facilities, urban affairs, housing for the elderly, veterans' housing, public housing, and many other subjects.

The Housing Message

On March 9, 1961, the long-heralded housing message was delivered by the President of the United States, John F. Kennedy. The key to the administration policy was in the following words:

There is no longer an enormous backlog of economic demand which can be released simply by supplying ample credit. Credit devices must now be used selectively to encourage private industry to build and finance housing in the lower price ranges to meet the unfilled demands for moderate income families. It is these families who offer the largest and the most immediate potential housing market, along with those of still lower incomes who must rely on low rent public housing.

The message proposed numerous special aids for special sectors of this assumed demand, much of it involving an undertermined amount of subsidy in terms of outright grants or submarket rates of interest. The main proposals were briefly as follows:

1. Housing for Moderate-income Families

Extend "on a temporary and experimental basis" the present FHA insurance and no-down-payment forty-year mortgages (Section 221 of the FHA statute) to include any family and amend the statute "to make these mortgages more attractive to private investors." Provide a "new program of long-term low interest-rate loans for rental and cooperative housing, financed by the special assistance fund of FNMA, and processed and supervised by the FHA." Occupancy to be limited by an income test.

2. Helping Low-income Families

Authorizing an additional 100,000 public housing units, and making revisions in the statute giving local authorities greater scope in determining the character of the housing and the occupancy thereof.

3. Housing for the Elderly

Increase the direct loan program for elderly housing from $50 million to $100 million. Reserve 50,000 housing units for elderly persons and families.

4. Improving Our Cities

Allow communities wide discretion in determining renewal areas.

5. Residential Rehabilitation Conservation

Provide "new authorization for FHA to insure a wide variety of loans for home improvement purposes."

6. Metropolitan Development

Provide an increase of the Federal share of planning grants to two-thirds and increase the authorization from $20 million to $100 million.

7. Land Reserve

Direct HHFA and the Department of the Interior jointly to develop a long-range program and policy for dealing with open space and orderly development of urban land.

8. Community Facilities and Urban Transportation

Authorize an additional $50 million for loans for public facilities.

9. Rural Housing

Extend the present direct loan program for farm housing for an additional five years.

10. Veterans' Housing

Extend the operative period of the VA and direct loan program and expand direct loan authority above the present $150 million to the extent experience should demonstrate that guaranteed loans are still difficult for veterans to obtain at officially fixed interest rates.

11. A New Department of Housing and Urban Affairs

In view of all the existing and government activities affecting urban life, the President of the United States recommended and would shortly offer a suggested proposal for the establishment in the executive branch of a new Cabinet-rank Department of Housing and Urban Affairs.

The proposals in this message were then translated into statutory language. Virtually every one of the proposals was controversial.

Neal J. Hardy Confirmed as Commissioner of the Federal Housing Administration

On March 6, 1961, the nomination of Neal J. Hardy was favorably reported without dissent by the Senate Banking and Currency Committee, and the following day the Senate unanimously confirmed the appointment. There were numerous problems confronting the FHA—problems of meeting rising operating expenses with its own income and of improving delays in processing time. Equally serious were the current delays in issuing debentures in payment of foreclosed loans.

Joseph P. McMurray Confirmed as Chairman of the Federal Home Loan Bank Board

The confirmation of Joseph P. McMurray was made on March 2, 1961, for the unexpired term of former Chairman Albert Robertson and for a new four-year term beginning June 30, 1961. Mr. McMurray was immediately directed by the President of the United States to proceed to California to discuss interest rates and dividend payments with local savings and loan associations.

Phillip N. Brownstein Promoted to Chief Benefits Director, Veterans Administration

Phillip N. Brownstein joined the VA Loan Service in 1946 and has been active in VA housing since that time. He holds VA's highest accolade, the exceptional service award. In his new post he will be in charge of the entire benefit program except for insurance and medical hospital activities. Assistant Director of VA Loan Service, John Dervan, has succeeded Phillip Brownstein, but only until a permanent successor is selected, as John Dervan has stated that he prefers to remain in the second spot in this activity.

Introduction of the 1961 Housing Bill

This bill, which was considered the most complex housing bill that has been proposed in recent years, was sent to the Congress in April, 1961.

The bill followed closely the lines of policy laid down in the March 9, 1961, message of the President of the United States, John F. Kennedy. It was introduced on March 29 by Senator John J. Sparkman as S. 1478 and by Representative Albert M. Rains as H.R. 6028. It was a document of nine separate titles, the principal features of which were outlined previously in some detail in this chapter.

Hearings on the 57-page housing bill (S. 1478) were concluded in eight working days, two of which were taken up by government witnesses, and under the circumstances, a thorough discussion of the complex measure was impossible.

Mortgage Bankers Association of America General Counsel, Samuel E. Neel, was the last nongovernment witness. His testimony stressed the undesirability of the forty-year, no-down-payment mortgages, arising particularly because of the added risk to which the borrower was exposed from the reduction in the supply of mortgage funds returning to the market through amortization payments. The testimony also expressed opposition to the proposal to pay FHA mortgage claims in cash instead of debentures as unwisely removing responsibility from the private lending institutions.

Without waiting for the Senate to conclude its work, Representative Albert M. Rains' Subcommittee of the House Banking and Currency Committee began hearings on the housing measure (H.R. 6028, identical with S. 1478) on April 24. The subcommittee developed for its own consideration a number of proposals not included in the administration bill.

The Cabinet Post Question

As repeatedly promised, the President of the United States sent to Congress on April 18, 1961, his proposal for establishing a new executive department to be called the Department of Urban Affairs and Housing. The Cabinet proposal caused much concern among those who considered that private credit provides the predominant means for maintaining home construction and improvement in housing standards. In the new department, the private credit function, as exemplified in FHA, is distinctly given a place secondary to subsidized urban renewal and housing operations.

The proposal included a new statement of national policy replacing the Housing Act of 1949, in which the objective was a "decent home in a suitable living environment" and major dependence was on private enterprise for attaining this objective. In the new statement, top position is given to the purpose of "sound development and redevelopment of our cities" with the "provision of decent homes in suitable living environment" lost far down in the verbiage, and private enterprise is not mentioned at all.

FHA Interest Rate Again Lowered

On May 27, 1961, the President of the United States ordered the Federal Housing Administration to reduce the interest ceiling on FHA-insured loans from $5\frac{1}{2}$ per cent to $5\frac{1}{4}$ per cent interest, effective May 29, 1961.

In two other credit-rating actions, the President of the United States announced that FNMA would increase purchases in the secondary markets, and instructed the Federal Home Loan Bank Board to advance money at lower interest rates and thus encourage reduction in the mortgage interest rates charged by savings and loan associations.

The charge of $\frac{1}{2}$ of 1 per cent on FHA loans was also under study. This charge adds $\frac{1}{2}$ of 1 per cent to the actual rate paid by home purchasers, and makes this total payment $5\frac{3}{4}$ per cent even though the FHA interest ceiling has been reduced to $5\frac{1}{4}$ per cent.

Many builders and mortgage lenders predicted that the $\frac{1}{4}$ of 1 per cent reduction in the FHA interest rate would impart little stimulus to home buying. Most observers were of the opinion that the reduction was "too insignificant" to spur demand for dwellings at a time when unemployment was extensive.

INTEREST-RATE CEILINGS UNDER FHA PROGRAMS—HOME
MORTGAGE PROGRAMS

Title, section, and program	Statutory maximum		Regulatory maximum	
	Date	Rate, %	Rate	Rate, %
Title II:				
Sec. 203: Sales housing...	June 27, 1934	5 to 6	Nov. 27, 1934	5 and $5\frac{1}{2}$
			June 24, 1935	5
			Aug. 1, 1939	$4\frac{1}{2}$
			Apr. 24, 1950	$4\frac{1}{4}$
			May 2, 1953	$4\frac{1}{2}$
			Dec. 3, 1956	5
			Aug. 5, 1957	$5\frac{1}{4}$
			Sept. 23, 1959	$5\frac{3}{4}$
			Feb. 2, 1959	$5\frac{1}{2}$

VA Program—Prescribed Maximum Interest Rates and Statutory Ceiling

	VA interest rate, %			VA interest rate, %	
	Pre-scribed maxi-mum	Statu-tory ceiling		Pre-scribed maxi-mum	Statu-tory ceiling
1934–August 1939......	...	...	December 1956–August		
August 1939–1944......	...	...	1957.................	4½	4½
1944–August 1948......	4	4	August 1957–April 1958...	4½	4½
August 1948–April 1950.	4	4½	April 1958–July 1959.....	4¾	4¾
April 1950–May 1953...	4	4½	July 1959–September 1959	5¼	5¼
May 1953–December			September 1959..........	5¼	5¼
1956................	4½	4½			

The Housing Act of 1961 was passed by Congress on June 28, 1961. This housing act was more comprehensive in subject matter, more liberal in its terms, more extensive in the use of government funds, and more far-reaching in its possible effect on the relationship between government and private mortgage finance and building than any housing measure heretofore enacted. (For details covering the Housing Act see Appendix B.)

The progressive development of the mortgage lending industry, as described in this chapter, is a tribute to the private-enterprise system in overcoming housing shortages and in financing the building requirements of the nation despite wars, strikes, scarcities of materials, manpower shortages, priorities, and legislation. By the same token our government must also be given credit for much of the good which has been accomplished.

Some of the major needs of the mortgage lending industry today, in the opinion of the author, are the following:

1. Elimination of the builder-lender program and discontinuance of unnatural discount practices

2. Establishment of a central mortgage bank which could control the mortgage market on the basis of supply and demand

3. Making mortgage funds available on a satisfactory basis to the fast-growing areas of the nation

4. Adoption of more uniform methods of operation among the leading mortgage lenders in the country

5. Education of personnel within the mortgage lending industry

6. Adoption of highly efficient mortgage loan-collection and portfolio management techniques

7. Improvement in both customer relations and public relations

8. Elimination of much of the "red tape" in both VA and FHA operations and regulations

9. Flexible interest rates on both FHA and VA loans

10. Expansion of mortgage lending studies in universities, colleges, and related educational institutions as well as trade associations in order adequately to train young men and women in this highly important and interesting profession

SUMMARY

In 1945 the total mortgage indebtedness in the United States was approximately $37 billion, while at the end of 1960 this figure had risen to over $206 billion. Over $157 billion of this total was held in the loan portfolios of institutional investors, while approximately $49 billion of mortgage loans was held by individuals, government agencies, and others.

The mortgage lending industry and all other related real estate operations as well are an important part of the social, economic, and governmental life of the nation. The proper investment of funds available for mortgage investment has been the responsibility of mortgage lenders, and it has been necessary for these lenders to adjust lending policies to meet almost daily changes in the real estate market. If mortgage lending activities are not carried on wisely, the result could be trouble for borrowers and lenders, economic and social losses, and a complete disruption in our manner of life.

The study of mortgage lending embraces financing in all its phases, covering all types of building activity, including homes, farms, hotels, business buildings, apartments, industrial properties, subdivision developments, shopping centers, and many other types of properties.

The basic physical and economic characteristics of real estate are that properties are fixed in location and have comparatively long lives; and the supply has an important bearing on the loan market at all times. A property, regardless of type, is a complex product, and its construction requires a great deal of labor at the site. Building activities and property values as well as neighborhoods are subject to great fluctuations in value.

The customary practice in mortgage lending calls for paying a minor part of the purchase price in cash and borrowing the larger portion. The cash investment during the past few years has been relatively small, especially since the inception of the FHA program in 1934 and since the VA home-loan program was established in 1945.

When an individual purchases a property and borrows the funds to complete the purchase, the repayment of the loan is guaranteed by the pledge of the property purchased. This pledge is made by the use of a legal instrument known as a mortgage, or deed of trust.

The difficulties experienced by both borrowers and lenders in the early 1930s included rigid restrictions on the loan-value ratio, short-term mortgages, the failure of lenders to keep informed of tax payments on mortgaged properties, and lack of systematic portfolio management and loan-servicing procedures.

Some of the measures taken in recent years to improve the quality of mortgage loans include:

1. Introduction of higher-percentage, long-term amortized loans

2. Recognition of the borrower as an important safeguard against mortgage risk

3. Determination of the soundness of a loan by assembling and evaluating all the required information on location, property, and borrower, instead of relying primarily on the loan-value ratio or on the property itself

4. Creation by Congress of the Federal Home Loan Bank System to provide a reserve banking system for residential mortgage lending institutions

5. Creation by Congress of the FHA, which insures mortgages and has so standardized and graded them that they now have a national market

In 1933, 1934, and 1935, several important laws were passed by Congress for the relief of borrowers and for the protection of lending institutions.

The most revolutionary change in the pattern of making home mortgage loans occurred in 1934 when the National Housing Act was passed and the FHA was created.

Real estate loan portfolios became more liquid as FHA loans were added to portfolios, and lenders generally increased the percentage of loans to time deposits, as FHA loans were considered practically "nonrisk" assets.

The Servicemen's Readjustment Act of 1944 created the VA loan program. Most large mortgage lenders supported this program enthusiastically until it was felt that the 4 per cent rate was inadequate.

In 1947 the HHFA was created; it brought together under one agency the activities of the Home Loan Bank Board, the FHA, PHA, the National Housing Council, and later the Federal National Mortgage Association.

The biggest problem which confronted the home-building industry in 1953 was the shortage of mortgage money. As a result, the discount operation on both FHA and VA loans and the builder-lender program developed.

In late December, 1953, the President's Advisory Committee on Government Housing Policies and Programs submitted its report. The report dealt with all phases of housing and home finance in which the government is active. It contained many excellent recommendations, a majority of which were incorporated in the Housing Act of 1954.

Home-building and mortgage lending activities in the nation for 1954 continued at a rate which made it another boom year in dwelling construction.

The housing boom continued during 1955. Many believed that a surplus of housing was being created, while others believed that the rate of residential construction could still be increased.

Builders during early 1955 were gambling both on the public demand for single-family dwellings and on the supply of mortgage money that would be available. Conservative lenders at that time recommended that immediate steps be taken to tighten up on down payments and amortization periods for both FHA and VA loans.

At no time during the past twenty-five years had the pattern of mortgage financing been more complex than it was in 1952 through 1961. Many lenders were of the opinion that a more realistic rate on both FHA and VA loans would be the solution to most of the lending problems which existed. Such an increase was made in May, 1953, but it was not until February and March of 1954 that these rate increases began to have a satisfactory effect upon the mortgage market; and at that time the market value of both VA and FHA 4½ per cent interest rate, with a reasonable down payment, reached par.

The Housing Act of 1955 was passed by Congress in late July, 1955, and was signed by the President a few days later. It tended to liberalize some of the provisions of the Housing Act of 1954. Congress also passed a law which permitted national banks to make mortgage loans based on 66⅔ per cent of the appraised value of the property. This ratio was previously 60 per cent. In late 1959 this ratio was increased to 75 per cent.

Progressive tightening of credit characterized the money markets during 1956. Throughout the year upward changes in interest rates came with great frequency, and the Federal Reserve Board's action amending Regulation Q permitted banks to pay 3 per cent interest per annum on savings accounts as against the former limitation of 2½ per cent.

In the field of mortgage credit, 1957 was a difficult year for borrower and lender alike, particularly for those whose business had been dependent upon FHA-insured and VA-guaranteed loans. In 1958 the elimination of discount controls as provided in the Emergency Housing Bill permitted an easier flow of FHA and VA mortgages in the secondary market.

During 1959 the money markets entered their tightest phase in many years, with interest rates at a high level. In July, 1960, new regulations were issued under which FHA loans insured under Section 203 (b) may be sold to individuals, which action opened up an entirely new source for investment in FHA loans.

Another important development in mortgage credit took place in late 1960 when the Internal Revenue Code was amended to put real estate investment trusts on a par, taxwise, with other types of investment funds.

In view of the drastic changes that had taken place in the mortgage market over a generation it became apparent that there was no possibility that this market would ever escape from impacts of monetary policy or from competition in the general money market.

Shortly after being inaugurated President of the United States, in early 1961, John F. Kennedy ordered the FHA interest rate reduced from $5\frac{3}{4}$ per cent to $5\frac{1}{2}$ per cent, and shortly thereafter ordered this rate again reduced to $5\frac{1}{4}$ per cent.

On March 9, 1961, the Housing Message was delivered to Congress by the President. It proposed special aids for special sectors, including "Housing for Moderate Income Families," "Housing for the Elderly," "Improvement of Cities," "Residential Rehabilitation Conservation," "Land Reserve," "Community Facilities and Urban Transportation," "Rural Housing," and "Veterans Housing." It also recommended the establishment in the executive branch of a Cabinet-rank Department of Housing and Urban Affairs. The Housing Act of 1961 was passed by Congress on June 28, 1961.

QUESTIONS

1. Why is mortgage lending now recognized as one of the major financial activities in the United States, and why does this industry, together with all other real estate operations, play an important part in the economic life of the nation?
2. Name several basic activities that the study of mortgage lending embraces.
3. Name four physical and economic characteristics of real estate.
4. Is the need for housing influenced more by number and composition of families than by total population? Explain.
5. Discuss any one of the controlling factors in determining the soundness of mortgage credit.
6. The practice of making loans on mortgage security is one of the major functions of what three types of large lenders?
7. Mortgage debt is usually divided into ten classifications according to type of property mortgaged. Name these ten classifications.
8. Why has the cash investment in a property usually been small in relation to the amount borrowed during the past few years?
9. Explain why the 100 per cent financing of VA home loans has been a debatable subject.
10. What type of legal instrument does the borrower use to guarantee repayment of a loan?
11. Is it true that the law governing mortgage loans is voluminous and years of study and experience are necessary to enable one to become familiar with it in any detail? Explain.
12. Describe the various provisions for repayment of the loan.
13. Name five causes of trouble with mortgage loans during the Great Depression.
14. Name some of the risks which are inherent in a mortgage loan.
15. Why did mortgages become frozen during the Great Depression?
16. What was one of the early relief measures passed by Congress?

17. Name the five types of institutions eligible for membership in the Federal Home Loan Bank System.

18. Savings and loan associations may make mortgage loans up to what percentage of the appraised value of the security?

19. The most revolutionary change in the pattern of making home loans occurred in 1934 by the passage of what act and the creation of what agency?

20. When was the Servicemen's Readjustment Act passed and what was the purpose of the act?

21. List the principal changes for the borrower which took place when the FHA program went into effect.

22. Describe the advantage of FHA loans to lenders.

23. Explain the purpose of the Soldiers' and Sailors' Civil Relief Act of 1940.

24. What was the original amount of guaranty on a VA home loan? What amount was it increased to? What is the amount now?

25. Describe the most popular method of meeting veteran's needs for mortgages during 1948 and 1949.

26. The HHFA established in 1947 brought together under one head what governmental agencies?

27. In your opinion did we have a "managed economy" during the period prior to 1953? Explain.

28. Explain what have been important domestic problems with respect to the national economy during the past few years.

29. In 1947 how did the government endeavor to combat inflation?

30. Name some inflationary aspects of the housing acts of 1948, 1949, and 1950.

31. The great change in the pattern of mortgage lending during the past several years has taken place in what type of loans?

32. Are mutual savings banks in New York and Massachusetts now permitted to purchase VA and FHA loans in any state in the nation?

33. In your opinion is the pattern of mortgage financing in a very complex condition today? Explain.

34. Briefly describe the builder-lender method of financing VA home loans.

35. Name some of the reasons for the great increase in the selling prices of homes and other properties from 1946 to 1961.

36. Describe the basic provisions of the Housing Acts of 1956, 1957, 1958, 1959, housing legislation passed in the year 1960, and the Housing Act of 1961.

37. Briefly describe the mortgage market during the years 1956 through 1961.

38. On what date were the VA Mortgage Guaranty and Loan operations extended and for how long?

39. Describe the movement of mortgage interest rates during the past ten years, and explain how mortgage yields are now geared more closely to other investment yields than ever before in history.

40. Briefly explain the development of Real Estate Investment Trust legislation during the year 1960.

ASSIGNMENTS[22]

1. Estimate the types of institutions that hold the major number of mortgage loans in the community in which you live. If you work in a city and live in a suburb, also estimate the above in the city where you are engaged in business.
2. Estimate the mortgage debt in both cities. How has the mortgage debt changed since 1925?
3. Describe the VA home-loan activity in both cities since the inception of the Servicemen's Readjustment Act of 1944.
4. Obtain mortgage or deed-of-trust forms of various types from some lender and study these forms carefully.
5. Obtain note forms of various types and study these forms carefully.
6. Set up a statistical report covering the population of the community in which you live for the years 1925 to the present time.

BIBLIOGRAPHY AND SUGGESTED READING

California Land Security and Development, University of California Press, Berkeley, Calif., 1961.

Colean, Miles L., *The Impact of Government on Real Estate Finance in the United States,* chaps. 3, 4, 6–8, National Bureau of Economic Research, Inc., New York, 1950.

The Federal Reserve System: Purposes and Functions, Board of Governors of the Federal Reserve System, Washington, 1954.

Fisher, Ernest M., *Urban Real Estate Markets: Characteristics and Financing,* chap. 4, National Bureau of Economic Research, Inc., New York, 1951.

Home Mortgage Lending, chap. 1, American Institute of Banking, Section American Bankers Association, New York, 1946.

Klaman, Saul B., *The Post War Rise of Mortgage Companies,* National Bureau of Economic Research, Inc., New York, 1959.

McMichael, Stanley L., *How to Finance Real Estate,* chaps. 1, 39, Prentice-Hall, Inc., Englewood Cliffs, N.J., 1951.

Marcus, William A., "Changes in the Pattern of Mortgage Lending," lecture, Western Mortgage Banking Seminar, Stanford University, Stanford, Calif., Aug. 21, 1953.

Pease, Robert H., and Homer V. Cherrington (eds.), *Mortgage Banking,* chap. 1, McGraw-Hill Book Company, Inc., New York, 1953.

Weimer, Arthur M., and Homer Hoyt, *Principles of Urban Real Estate,* The Ronald Press Company, New York, 1949.

[22] Sources of information for these assignments: title companies, FHA and VA district offices, chambers of commerce, and local mortgage lenders.

2

Sources of Funds for

Mortgage Lending

PURPOSES

1. To discuss the major and minor sources of funds for mortgage lending
2. To describe briefly the methods of operations of institutional lenders and noninstitutional lenders
3. To explain the types of loans made by these lenders and their basic lending policies
4. To describe the scope of operations of mortgage bankers
5. To describe the legislation and regulations which control the mortgage lending operations of these various types of lenders
6. To discuss the importance of sound mortgage lending policies and the need for liquid portfolios

Institutional Lenders Dominate the Mortgage Lending Market

The mortgage lending market is dominated by institutional lenders who make a great majority of the loans on all types of real estate properties. The major institutional lenders, as well as the major sources of funds for mortgage lending, are life insurance companies, commercial banks doing a savings business, mutual savings banks, and savings and loan associations. The large majority of the life insurance companies and mutual savings banks invest their funds through mortgage bankers operating throughout every state in the country. These mortgage bankers are appointed by life insurance companies and mutual savings banks as their loan correspondents. Mortgage bankers make mortgage loans in their respective cities and areas and, when completed, deliver these loans to the life insurance companies and mutual savings banks for which they act as correspondents. The assets of these institutions are thus invested in mortgage loans on homes, stores, apartments, office buildings, and industrial plants in all parts of the country.

In general, life insurance companies make conventional loans on all types of properties and supply most of the demand for loans on properties where large loans are required, such as large commercial properties, industrial properties, shopping centers, and hotels. They also invest large amounts of their funds in mortgages insured by the FHA and by the VA. Commercial banks doing a savings business, as well as mutual savings banks, invest mostly in mortgages on single-family dwellings and do a great deal of business in FHA-insured loans. Some also have invested large amounts of funds in VA-guaranteed loans. Savings and loan associations confine themselves almost exclusively to one- to four-family-home loans and finance such investments by means of the conventional loan in which they are permitted to make a comparatively high loan based on a percentage of the appraisal value of the property. These conventional loans also call for an interest rate which is usually above the normal market rate.

Noninstitutional Lenders Consist of a Wide Variety of Organizations

Noninstitutional lenders consist of a wide variety of organizations and individuals, many of whom specialize in certain types of properties. These noninstitutional lenders provide the minor sources of funds for mortgage lending. Such lenders include individuals, trust departments of banks, title companies in some areas, mortgage investment companies, universities, colleges, and other types of endowed institutions, pension funds of various kinds, real estate brokers, executors of estates, and others. A considerable amount of this business is originated and handled by mortgage bankers.

These lenders follow no uniform lending practices and in general are not subject to national or state laws or the requirements of other regulatory bodies. As a result of this freedom, noninstitutional lenders can take greater risks in their investments such as making extremely high loans with respect to percentage of appraisal value; they do not typically use the technical credit analysis procedures which have been developed by institutional lenders. As greater risks are taken, such investors receive relatively high interest rates. Noninstitutional lenders are also the main sources of funds for second- and third-mortgage financing.

Government Sources of Funds for Mortgage Lending

The VA

On April 20, 1950, Congress enacted legislation to permit the VA to make direct loans to veterans in those areas where funds were not available from private lenders.[1] All areas in which these loans could be made had to

[1] National Housing Act of 1950, Public Law 475, 81st Cong., secs. 512, 513.

be designated as such by the VA. As of December 31, 1960, approximately 177,104 in number and $1,463,000,000 in amount of direct loans had been made. This activity has had little effect upon the VA home loan mortgage market as it is a small proportion of the total volume of such financing.

The Federal Home Loan Bank System Now Operates Mainly for the Benefit of Savings and Loan Associations

The Federal Home Loan Bank System was created by the authority of the Federal Home Loan Bank Act approved July 22, 1932, to provide credit for thrift and home-financing institutions. As now constituted, it operates mainly for the benefit of savings and loan associations. Lending institutions that qualify for membership purchase capital stock in the nearest district bank and are given the privilege of obtaining funds either on a secured or to a limited extent on a nonsecured basis. The Home Loan Banks have authority to secure additional funds through sales of securities and may also serve as depositories for member associations. There are now eleven established districts of the Federal Home Loan Bank System with a central bank in each district (refer to detailed explanation in Glossary of Terms).

There is also a miscellaneous group of government agencies which are indirectly concerned with some form of mortgage financing such as the Farmers Home Administration and the Federal Farm Loan Bank System. The operations of such agencies are covered in detail in the *United States Government Organization Manual* published by the Division of the Federal Register, National Archives Establishment, Washington 25, D.C.

Mortgage lending operations of life insurance companies, savings and loan associations, commercial banks, mutual savings banks, mortgage bankers, as well as individuals, are covered in some detail in the following paragraphs of this chapter.

Methods of Borrowing Funds

When an individual wishes to purchase a home, or some other type of property that has great appeal to him not only from a price or investment standpoint but from every other standpoint, and he does not have sufficient funds to pay for this property in cash, he must borrow the money. In most cases he will have located this property through a real estate broker, who in turn suggests the lender or mortgage banker to contact in order to borrow the necessary funds. In case the lender agrees to make the loan after a complete investigation of both the property and the prospective borrower has been made, the funds will be advanced by the lender through its mortgage loan correspondent if the lender is a life insurance company or mutual savings bank, or by its own mortgage department if the lender is a savings and loan association or a local commercial bank. Prior to the completion of the transaction, however, certain procedures would be required, such as the sales agreement, title search, property appraisal, credit analysis of borrower, and many others. Many loans are not made by the lender originally contacted for the loan. There is a wide variation in the amount of loan that can be made by each type of lender, as well as the terms that can be given for each loan.

Life Insurance Companies Are a Major Source of Mortgage Funds

These companies have been active in the mortgage lending field for over 100 years. In 1850 forty life insurance companies had assets of about $7 million. At the end of 1960 there were over 1,400 such companies with assets of over $119 billion.

Ninety-five per cent of the assets are represented by debt instruments, such as government bonds, public utility bonds, railroad bonds, and first mortgages. A very small percentage was invested in preferred and common stock. As of the end of 1960, the major investments of life insurance companies were as follows[2]:

Industrial and miscellaneous bonds........	$26.7 billion	22.4% of assets
Public utility bonds....................	16.7 billion	14.0% of assets
U.S. government securities..............	6.4 billion	5.4% of assets
Mortgages on real estate................	41.7 billion	34.9% of assets
Railroad bonds........................	3.6 billion	3.1% of assets

Operations are governed by the laws of the state in which the company is incorporated, as well as by the laws of all other states in which they operate. This has the effect of having these companies abide by the most stringent laws in all states where operating.

Life insurance companies incorporated in California, for example, are restricted in mortgage loans to 75 per cent of appraisal value or sales price, whichever is lower on home loans, and 66⅔ per cent on loans on all other types of properties. Although there is no restriction in term of years, company policy usually holds the term to not more than twenty-five years. Life insurance companies incorporated in other states in general have similar restrictions. Some states, however, permit a higher percentage of loan to value.

The interest rates charged by life insurance companies prior to the year 1953 ran from 4 to 5 per cent, but during the year 1953 these rates

[2] *Life Insurance Fact Book, 1961*, Institute of Life Insurance, New York.

were increased. By 1960 they had advanced to about 6 to 6½ per cent for the average residential loan. The rate of interest is affected by the age of the property, quality of construction, qualifications of the borrower, amount and term of loan, as well as the neighborhood.

In nearly all states the maximum loan permissible is 75 per cent of the sale price, but most life insurance companies will not lend over 75 per cent of the appraised value of the property. On multiple-unit dwellings a large equity by the owner is required.

On large loans covering shopping centers and other types of commercial properties, most insurance companies prefer "national" tenants whenever possible. Some will not even consider such a loan unless a substantial part of the income is from tenants of good financial standing.

On residential properties the maximum amount of a loan by most companies is $25,000, but some will lend up to $30,000. In most states there are limitations governing the maximum amount that may be loaned on a single-family residence.

It is obvious that a loan written for a term of six months to one year would have no prepayment penalty charged. On long-term loans a borrower may in most cases pay 20 per cent of the original amount of the loan per year without penalty. All loans in life insurance portfolios are assignable and can be reconveyed.

Life insurance companies are concerned with the net yield of their investment, and mortgage loans must show a satisfactory yield in order to attract the funds of these institutions.

A few insurance companies make construction loans and this activity is on the increase. Such loans are generally made by mortgage bankers or commercial banks. When the building is completed, the mortgage banker then closes a long-term loan on the property and delivers this final loan to the insurance company or mutual savings banks or other outlets.

The average charge for processing a loan is 1 per cent of the amount of the loan, plus the costs of title search, recording of papers, cost of appraisals, and all other out-of-pocket expenses. The mortgage banker acting as mortgage loan correspondent handles all details for his insurance company or mutual savings banks or other investors both in making the loan and in collecting the payments, taxes, and insurance premiums on the loan in the entire fifteen, twenty, or twenty-five years that it remains outstanding. For this work, called "servicing the loan," or "loan administration, collection, and servicing," the mortgage banker is paid ½ of 1 per cent based on the outstanding principal balance by the owner of the mortgage. Some commercial banks have become very active in this business and especially in the home-loan market. This activity is steadily and progressively on the increase.

Loans made by life insurance companies are mostly in the following categories:

1. Purchase money—for occupancy or investment
2. Construction loans or improvement loans
3. Refinancing existing indebtedness
4. Consolidation of mortgages
5. Achieving a lower interest rate or longer term
6. Provision of additional funds

Appraisal Policies of Life Insurance Companies

Most life insurance companies tend to adjust the market value of a property in making appraisals for mortgage lending purposes to a conservative value estimate. This is slightly below the current sales price in most instances. Many insurance companies are prohibited by law from lending on a leasehold interest. In establishing land value the comparable-sales method of pricing other properties in the area is used. These companies are also very strict about the neighborhoods in which they will make mortgage loans. Many areas are eliminated by them as not satisfactory. Improvements, such as patios, fences, barbecues, swimming pools, sprinkler systems, are not accepted in setting the value of the property. The average house in a neighborhood will be given a better appraisal than the largest house in order to set a pattern for the area. Also, most insurance companies do not like to make a loan on an old house unless it is in exceptionally good condition. Tract homes sometimes get a lower value factor than do individual homes in established neighborhoods. Insurance companies are reluctant to lend on two-bedroom homes, and prefer three-bedroom homes with at least 1½ baths.

In estimating the amount an applicant should pay for a home, insurance companies figure that the applicant should not pay for the home over twice the amount of his annual income. For example, if his annual income is $5,000, he should not pay more than $10,000 for his home. They require that the monthly payment on the loan should not exceed 20 per cent of the borrower's net take-home pay. The monthly payment on a loan includes the funds to cover taxes and insurance, and in the case of an FHA loan, the mortgage insurance premium. Where the husband and wife both work, the income of the wife is negligible because of the possibility that she may stop working at any time. In figuring the annual income of an applicant, a credit for the bonus he receives at the end of each year will not be acceptable unless this bonus has been a regular payment for a number of years.

Some insurance companies as well as other types of conservative lenders are more strict about granting loans to borrowers whose incomes are subject to weather conditions and therefore irregular. Such workers include those who are employed in the canning industry, fruit picking, and the like. Applicants who work on a commission basis must substantiate their income by a record of several years' earnings as well as establish that this income is likely to continue. All applicants who are self-employed must submit financial statements, as well as a copy of their income tax reports for two or three previous years.

An American Title Association title insurance policy is always required, and the title insurance company handling the transaction must be acceptable to the insurance company.

Commercial Banks Play a Vital Role in Mortgage Lending

There are approximately 14,000 banks in the United States, slightly under 9,300 organized under state laws and about 4,700 under the National Bank Act. Practically all these invest in mortgage loans. Banks, therefore, are a strong factor in the mortgage lending field.

Funds to Be Loaned Depend on Type of Security, Type of Loan, and Interest Rate

The funds to be loaned by banks and other institutional lenders are affected by the type of property, and an adequate appraisal of that property must be made, as the property is the underlying security for the loan. It naturally should follow that a prudent lender would see to it that he makes only sound appraisals and sound loans on good properties to borrowers who measure up to the required standards. This also means that both the borrower and the lender must be protected. In other words, sound mortgage lending policies must be maintained by banks at all times. Banks are known for both conservative appraisals and conservative lending policies.

Determination of General Lending Policies of Banks

The mortgage lending policy of individual banks is usually determined by the president, the board of directors, the executive committee, and the vice-president in charge of the mortgage loan and savings departments.

One of the most important objectives is safety of the investment, which includes liquidity. These officers must decide the percentage of mortgage loans which can be made against savings deposits,[3] the types of loans to be made, the interest accrual average which should be maintained, and whether to seek loans or be restrictive in seeking loans.

The major function of a bank in mortgage lending is to invest the funds of others entrusted to it and to obtain a reasonable return on the investment based on a conservative lending program. The demands and needs of both

---

[3] National banks are restricted to 60 per cent of time deposits on mortgage loans.

the community and its depositors must be anticipated. Thoroughly adequate reserves must be maintained, including short-term investments, government bonds, and cash.

Mortgage Financing Practices Are Not Uniform throughout the Nation

Mortgage financing practices by banks are not uniform throughout the country, and mortgage laws covering banks differ in each of the fifty states. The Federal legislation to which attention was given in the previous chapter has bridged state lines and helped banks form their present pattern of mortgage financing. Differences in state laws have had in many instances a profound influence upon the practices of banks and upon the volume of mortgages held by banks and other types of lending institutions. They exert a profound influence upon real estate operators, builders, brokers, and life insurance company loan agents.

Limitations Covering Mortgage Lending by Banks

Basic control of mortgage lending by banks lies in the limitations imposed by Federal statutes on national banks and by the laws of the various states on state-chartered commercial banks and in the regulations and decisions of the appropriate supervisory authorities, such as the Federal Reserve System, the VA, and the FHA.

Up until the end of July, 1955, conventional mortgage loans made by national banks were restricted to 60 per cent of the appraised value of the property. At that time Congress passed a law which permitted national banks to make conventional loans up to 66⅔ per cent of the appraised value and extended the term on fully amortized loans to twenty years. The new law also permitted farm and residential construction loans with 9 months' maturity. Nearly all states which restrict state-chartered banks to loans of 60 per cent of the appraised value of the property took similar action. This ratio of amount of loan to appraised value for national banks was increased to 75 per cent by Public Law 86-251, 86th Congress, and dated September 9, 1959.

Lending Policies Change from Day to Day

The mortgage lending policies of banks and other institutional lenders should never be thought of as having been established for an indefinite period but rather as changeable, in order to conform with changing conditions in the real estate and mortgage market. A lending policy adapted to a depressed real estate market would be unsound in a period of rising costs and prices, and a policy adjusted to excellent market conditions could be harmful if carried into a period of depression. Lending policies must take into account major changes which occur frequently in the real estate and mortgage market and must be adjusted to them. FHA and VA changes in regulations, policies, and procedures have a direct effect upon the mortgage lending policies of lenders. Changes which occur are affected by, and are in turn a part of, the changes that occur in general economic and business conditions. A study of the history of mortgage lending reveals that the real estate and mortgage markets have been subject to violent fluctuations varying from the peak of booms to the depths of depressions.

Each large mortgage lender has specialists in different phases of operations. For example, in a large banking institution there is an officer in charge of the FHA operations, another in charge of VA loan operations, another in charge of title and escrow operations, another in charge of delinquent-loan collection and servicing operations, another in charge of appraisals, and so on. Also, in most banks there is a real estate or mortgage loan committee which passes on all loan applications. Over-all lending policies of banks are usually established by the president, board of directors, and the officer in charge of the mortgage loan department.

The Real Estate Broker an Important Adjunct to Mortgage Lending Operations

The real estate broker, who brings the buyer and seller together and who fits very definitely into this mortgage pattern, not only must know FHA and VA loan operations but should also be part banker, part title man, part appraiser, part lawyer, and must also know all the fundamentals of real estate and mortgage lending operations. He should know the best source at the moment for a mortgage loan. He should understand mortgages, deeds of trust, contracts of sale, loan terms, including amortized and straight loans. In addition to this, he should have an understanding of the building business, know economics, and be a keen student of human nature. Such men have had an interest in improvements in mortgage lending operations that have taken place during the past decade and have also had much to do with the industrial and business development of all sections of the nation.

Importance of Liquidity and Marketability of Loans in a Bank Portfolio

Interest earned and collected represents the major income of banks in a mortgage loan. In making such investments, liquidity and marketability are of paramount importance, and it follows that sound mortgage lending policies must be maintained. Many mortgage financing opportunities are brought to banks and other lenders by real estate brokers and operators. By the same token banks and other lenders are a source of a great deal of business for real estate brokers and real estate operators. Literally thousands of potential buyers, as well as sellers, are sent to brokers and other realty operators by banks during any given year.

In any sound lending institution the element of risk must be recognized as a part of each loan made, and it is, therefore, figured in over-all operating expenses. Reserves for possible losses are required of banks by the Federal Reserve System, as well as by state and national banking laws.

Improvements in Mortgage Loan Financing Operations by Banks

Improvements in the mortgage loan financing operations have been put into effect by all banks engaged in mortgage lending during the past 30 years. One of the major improvements was that the borrower became recognized as one of the most important safeguards against the risks of loss. Prior to this time, the property itself was practically the only security for the loan. Improved methods in analyzing the borrower's ability to pay were adopted. Care was taken to see that the borrower did not overextend himself in the purchase of the property. Both the borrower and the lender got greater protection. Great improvements in appraisals and valuations were made. National and state banking laws were amended to permit longer-term loans. Real estate brokers and operators have contributed greatly to these improvements in the fundamentals of mortgage financing by cooperating in every respect with borrowers and lenders.

Improvements in Mortgage Lending Practices Have Meant More Liquid and Healthier Loan Portfolios

As a result of the progressive improvements in mortgage lending practices since the Great Depression, the mortgage loan portfolios of most banks as well as other types of prudent lenders today are probably stronger, more liquid, and healthier than ever before. Today these lenders are undoubtedly better prepared for a possible serious recession or depression than at any time in history, because they have profited by the many lessons, such as described, which they learned during and since the Great Depression. Laws governing mortgage lending have been broadened and improved. Today their operations and procedures are handled on a very scientific basis. This is also true of all other phases of this industry. All basic fundamentals of mortgage lending have been improved to such an extent that such investments are protected as fully as possible.

Responsibility of Institutional Lenders with Respect to Time Deposits

Lenders entrusted with the investment of funds belonging to others have a great responsibility. It is to invest these funds as safely as possible, using all the knowledge gained through experience and the experience of others to ensure a safe return of principal and a fair rate of interest for the use of these funds. A strict adherence to those basic fundamentals of mortgage lending which will adequately protect the seller, the lender, and the borrower is essential for our national economy and prosperity.

Interest Rates Charged by Banks on Mortgage Loans

On conventional loans the interest rate during 1952 to 1955 varied from 5 to 6 per cent, dependent upon the property, the term of the loan, the strength of the borrower, and the location of the property. By 1960 this rate had increased progressively to 6 to 6½ per cent. The 6½ per cent rate or more was charged primarily in outlying areas.

In some banks the prepayment of the loan is allowed without penalty.

The amount of funds available for investment is a strong factor in determining a loan policy. During the period of low interest rates many banks restricted mortgage loans to the banks' own depositors only.

Appraisal Policies of Banks Are Conservative

These policies are determined by the bank management, but are usually very conservative. The appraisal reflects long-term economic value and never approaches peak values reached in boom periods.

Conservative appraisals by banks have been maintained for many years and even before the Great Depression of the 1930s. Appraisals by banks usually run from 5 to 20 per cent below the estimated reproduction cost or market value, whichever is lower.

Mutual Savings Banks Are Large Investors in Mortgage Loans[4]

Mutual savings banks are located mainly in the Eastern states. Five are located in the Pacific Northwest and four in states in the Middle West.

These banks have no capital stock, but are mutual in character, as the depositors share in the earnings of the bank after allowance for expenses, reserves, and contributions to surplus or guaranty fund.

The interest rate paid on savings accounts is never established in advance. Earnings are determined at the end of each period, which may be quarterly, semiannually, or annually. At this time the Board of Trustees determines the rate that will be paid for the period. The interest earned is then credited to the accounts of the various depositors.

A mutual savings bank operates under the laws of the state in which it was chartered. There are 515 such banks operating in seventeen states and the Virgin Islands, and 312 are located in the states of New York and Massachusetts.

As is the case with most other types of banks, savings withdrawals are paid on demand. The right is reserved, however, to require notice of withdrawal ranging from a period of one week to six months.

[4] See "Mutual Savings Banking," *Annual Report,* May, 1961. Also, "Activities of Trade Associations" in Appendix A.

If state laws permit, mutual savings banks are eligible for membership in the Federal Reserve System and in the Federal Deposit Insurance Corporation, as well as in the Federal Home Loan Bank System.

Very few such banks have become members of the Federal Reserve System, or of the Federal Home Loan Bank System, mainly because these systems do not provide any particular advantages to them. Most mutual savings banks, however, have membership in the Federal Deposit Insurance Corporation. Their national organization is known as the National Association of Mutual Savings Banks, New York City.

Mutual savings banks make conventional, FHA, and VA loans. On conventional loans, the maximum amount which may be loaned is 75 per cent of the appraisal of the property. These banks have concentrated their operations in the residential field and about 90 per cent of each portfolio consists of loans on one- to four-family dwellings.

As of December 31, 1960, these banks had about $26,935,000,000 invested in mortgage loans. This amounts to 74 per cent of time deposits, which were approximately $36,343,000,000 at the end of 1960 (see Table 4).

Only life insurance companies, savings and loan associations, and commercial banks carry more mortgage loans. This is true even though they operate in only seventeen states. Legislation in 1949 permitted these banks to invest in many other states than where located; consequently their investment activities have a great bearing on the mortgage market.

Practically all loans made by mutual savings banks are on an amortized basis, and payments are required monthly. Like other types of lenders, their operations in VA loans during the past few years have been restricted, as the interest rate which can be obtained on conventional loans is at least ½ to 1 per cent higher. For this same reason, investments in FHA loans have also been restricted. Like all other prudent lenders, their lending practices and management policies are conservative.

Mutual savings banks acquire new loans in large metropolitan areas directly from the borrowers or through brokers. As these banks may make construction loans, they make many loans of this character. Their interstate lending is done through mortgage bankers who are appointed as mortgage loan correspondents for the mutual savings bank.

Savings and Loan Associations Are Very Active in the Mortgage Market[5]

Savings and loan associations are thrift and home-financing institutions founded on the basis of mutual cooperative enterprise. In addition to mak-

[5] For a detailed and very comprehensive coverage of savings and loan association operations, activities, and procedures, see *Mortgage Lending* by Lawrence V. Conway, American Savings and Loan Institute Press, Chicago, Ill., 1960.

ing mortgage loans, they also sell United States savings bonds, traveler's checks, and money orders and provide Christmas club accounts and rent safe-deposit boxes.

The ownership is in the hands of savers and investors, who are holders of share accounts which correspond closely, except in a legal sense, to those savings deposits in banks. In a few states, most notably California, Ohio, and Texas, stock companies are common among associations. Savings in such companies are generally creditor obligations, of similar legal status to time deposits in commercial banks. The lending policies are determined by the board of directors composed of local business and professional men, who usually carry accounts with the particular company. Regulations of the Federal Savings and Loan System require that conventional loans generally be limited to an area within 50 miles of the office.

The principal function of a savings and loan association is to gather savings of as many people as possible, and to lend these savings safely to other people for the purpose of building, buying, making improvements, and refinancing. Loans are to a great extent restricted to amortized first-mortgage loans on dwellings. Another function is to obtain repayment of these loans so that the funds may be returned to the original saver. These associations operate either with a Federal charter or with a charter obtained from state authorities.

Federal savings and loan associations are chartered by the Federal Home Loan Bank under authority of the Home Owners' Loan Act of 1933.[6] All shareholders' investments are insured up to $10,000 by the Federal Savings and Loan Insurance Corporation.

Investments are largely limited by Federal statutes to share loans, property improvement loans, and first mortgages on improved real estate. Surplus funds may be invested only in obligations of the United States or the Federal Home Loan Bank.

A Federal association may usually lend a member up to 90 per cent of its account upon pledge of the share with or without amortization. On most conventional mortgage loans the property must be located within 50 miles of the association's office. There is no specific limitation for any one loan, but all loans in excess of $35,000 plus other types of loans may not exceed 20 per cent of assets.[7]

The appraisal report covering the property must be signed by at least two qualified persons selected by the board of directors.

These associations may make amortized conventional loans on homes or combination homes and business properties up to a maximum of 90 per cent of their appraisal but on loans on other types of properties are restricted to

---

[6] *The Federal Home Loan Bank Review 1932–1952*, Federal Home Loan Bank, 1952.
[7] *Rules and Regulations for Savings and Loan System*, Home Loan Bank Board, Washington.

60 per cent of the appraisal. Few loans are made on commercial, multiunit, or unimproved properties.

The maximum term permitted on a mortgage loan is 25 years except on FHA and VA loans, on which these associations are subject to current regulations in the same manner as other lenders.

Most associations rarely go over 70 per cent of the appraisal or over fifteen years for the term of a loan, and many limit themselves to seven-, eight-, nine-, and ten-year loans.

Interest rates vary as to area and size and type of loan, but in 1952 and 1953 were from 5½ to 6½ per cent. From that period the interest rate moved upward from 6½ to 7½ per cent. Loan fees also vary among these associations and run up to 1 per cent or more of the full amount of the loan. There is usually a penalty of some sort if a loan is paid off before maturity, and all associations charge two or three months' interest in each such case.

Most associations vary as to systems of appraisal used. Like other lenders, they attach a great deal of importance to the neighborhood and the age of the property.

These associations are very active in the medium- and low-priced-home field, and type of employment is not considered as important a factor as with other types of lenders. On home loans the monthly payment is generally held to 20 per cent of the net take-home pay. They are very active in the construction loan field, and each contractor is checked very carefully as to credit and ability. Lien and completion bonds are required in some cases.

During the year 1960, savings and loan associations continued to be the main source of home mortgage funds. They made 42 per cent of the mortgages of $20,000 and under recorded in 1960, about the same proportion as in the preceding year. Close to 60 per cent of the $11.1 billion net increase in one- to four-family mortgage debt was represented by the net increase in mortgage holdings of savings and loan associations. Portfolio increases of mutual savings banks and life insurance companies each amounted to about 13 per cent of the net increase in one- to four-family mortgage debt. The commercial banks during this same period showed only a negligible increase in the holdings of this type of mortgage. The balance of the net increase was reflected largely in the holdings of "individuals and others," and government agencies, principally FNMA, in FHA and VA mortgages.

The Scope of Operations of Mortgage Bankers

Mortgage bankers operate primarily as the mortgage loan correspondents of life insurance companies, mutual savings banks, pension funds, and other financial institutions. They may furnish mortgage loans to these institutions from only one metropolitan area, one state, or sometimes in several states.

These mortgage bankers are one of the prime sources for mortgage loans in the country. They make loans on homes, on income property, and under FHA and VA. Many of these mortgage bankers have sizable capital funds of their own and are consistent lending sources in the mortgage market. Many of these companies engage in additional business operations such as handling property rentals, leases, management of properties, and also act as insurance agents. Some also operate as real estate brokers.

These companies are usually organized under state laws, and their operations therefore vary to some extent in the various states. They are subject to minimum supervision and have a wide latitude of powers. It should be noted, however, that the investors who have mortgage bankers as loan correspondents carefully watch the operations of such companies and require audit reports and financial statements, at least annually. Many obtain their funds for operations from commercial banks, by obtaining lines of credit and by arranging for advances from banks against mortgage documents while such loans are in the process of being sold to the ultimate purchaser of the paper. These banks also analyze the financial statements and audit reports of such companies. These companies are usually free of lending limitations such as are placed on institutional lenders and, except for inspections by an examiner in conformity with state laws, assume entire responsibility and make all decisions about their mortgage lending operations and their collection and portfolio administration covering these loans. Some companies serve only as intermediaries and resell the loans as soon as they are made. They are also good sources of construction loans, which are made with their own funds or with the funds of the companies they represent and prior to sale are converted to long-term conventional mortgage loans.[8]

The Role of Individual Investors in the Mortgage Lending Market

Many years ago, before institutional lending developed to its present extent, the bulk of mortgage lending was done by individuals. The amount of mortgage lending by this type of investor continues to be surprisingly large. The funds loaned represent surplus of the particular individual investor, many of whom prefer this type of investment to stocks, bonds, and other outlets for surplus funds. In most cases, each loan is for a small amount and usually on a one- to four-family dwelling.

Individuals obtain mortgage loans through title companies, mortgage bankers, real estate brokers, by advertising, or through others who deal in real estate operations. Many such loans are not acceptable to a prudent lender, and the individual investor is compensated by a higher interest rate. Many of the lenders arrange to have a bank, mortgage banker, or title company

[8] Saul B. Klaman, *The Postwar Rise of Mortgage Companies*, National Bureau of Economic Research, Inc., New York, 1959.

handle loan collections and servicing of their loans for a fee. Others who only hold three or four such loans handle their own collections. Some individual investors with high credit standing also borrow funds from banks in order to increase their mortgage holdings. This is especially true of individuals who deal mainly in second mortgages, on which the rate in most cases is much higher than on a first mortgage. There is far more risk involved in the handling of second mortgages.

TABLE 4   TIME DEPOSITS, PRIVATE REPURCHASABLE CAPITAL, POLICY RESERVES, PERCENTAGES OF MORTGAGE LOANS TO DEPOSITS

(In millions of dollars)

	12/31/49	12/31/52	12/31/54	12/31/55	12/31/60
Savings and loan associations:					
Private repurchasable capital..	$12,460	$19,210	$27,259	$32,142	$62,154
Mortgage loans*.............	11,700	18,440	26,142	31,408	60,084
Per cent....................	94.0	96.0	95.9	97.7	96.7
Insurance companies:					
Policy reserves...............	$51,460	$62,579	$71,100	$79,359	$98,473
Mortgage loans..............	12,894	21,250	25,927	29,445	41,771
Per cent....................	25.0	33.9	36.5	39.1	42.4
Mutual savings banks:					
Time deposits...............	$19,273	$22,590	$26,302	$28,129	$36,343
Mortgage loans*.............	6,578	11,380	15,007	17,457	26,935
Per cent....................	34.1	50.4	57.1	62.1	74.1
Commercial banks:					
Time deposits...............	$36,328	$41,010	$47,209	$48,715	$71,641
Mortgage loans..............	11,550	15,870	18,555	21,004	28,806
Per cent....................	31.8	38.7	39.3	43.1	40.2
Total....................	$119,521	$147,560	$171,870	$184,345	$268,611
Loans....................	42,722	66,940	85,631	99,314	157,596
Per cent.................	35.7	45.4	49.8	53.9	58.7

* Do not carry farm loans.

SOURCES: Federal Reserve Bank of San Francisco, research department; American Bankers Association, savings and mortgage division, New York.

COMMENTS: The above statistics reveal the mortgage loan investments of institutional lenders as well as the percentage of such loans to assets for the years 1949 through 1960. These figures reflect the great growth of the mortgage loan investments of these investors.

An individual investor can take greater risks in mortgage lending than an institutional investor, because an individual is not bound by the regulations of governmental agencies or state regulatory bodies except in those cases where the individual makes FHA loans as a supervised lender, or VA loans as a nonsupervised lender. In late 1960, FHA issued regulations permitting individual investors to purchase FHA loans. This action was undoubtedly a very important and progressive move which would broaden the sources of funds for FHA loans.

The major problem which confronts the average individual investor is in establishing the value of the property on which he will make a loan. In many cases an appraiser is employed to set a value on the property, while in other cases the individual himself establishes the value. He not only must be certain as to what the property is worth but must use his own judgment in deciding whether the established value is correct. There are so many hazards and pitfalls in establishing values of properties that a cautious individual investor will always use the service of an appraiser who is a member of the American Institute of Real Estate Appraisers or the Society of Residential Appraisers. All such appraisers are very reliable and are able to give the individual investor an accurate market value of each property. The maximum term of loans made by individual investors is usually ten years, while most such loans have a maturity of from five to ten years.[9]

TABLE 5

THE SOURCES OF NEW FUNDS

(In billions of dollars)

1953–1959 actual; 1960 and 1961, Preliminary and Estimated

Sources of funds	1953	1954	1955	1956	1957	1958	1959	1960P	1961E
Financial institutions	11.5	12.4	14.0	12.4	12.1	14.5	16.3	15.2	15.8
Life insurance companies.....	4.7	5.0	5.3	5.0	4.7	4.9	4.9	5.2	5.3
Savings and loan associations.	3.7	4.2	5.7	4.9	4.9	6.3	8.4	7.0	7.2
Mutual savings banks........	1.8	2.0	2.1	2.0	1.7	2.4	1.5	1.6	1.8
Fire and casualty companies..	1.3	1.2	0.9	0.5	0.8	0.9	1.5	1.4	1.5
Commercial banks............	4.1	10.2	4.8	4.4	5.1	15.2	4.2	9.3	8.1
Corporations and corp. pension funds	4.0	2.0	12.9	1.1	4.7	3.4	11.5	4.8	8.6
Corporations...............	2.3	0.1	11.0	−1.1	2.1	0.7	8.3	1.5	5.1
Corporate pension funds.....	1.7	1.9	1.9	2.2	2.6	2.7	3.2	3.3	3.5
U.S. government, states, and localities.................	5.1	4.1	4.5	5.5	5.5	1.3	4.7	4.1	3.8
U.S. investment accounts.....	2.4	1.3	2.1	2.3	1.3	−0.9	−0.7	1.4	0.6
Federal loan agencies........	0.2	−0.1	0.6	0.9	1.6	0.6	2.5	1.7	1.5
States and localities........	2.5	2.9	1.8	2.3	2.6	1.6	2.9	1.0	1.7
Federal Reserve banks.........	1.2	−1.0	−0.1	0.1	−0.7	2.1	0.3	0.7	0.6
Individuals and others	6.0	2.4	10.0	8.6	6.8	4.1	19.2	3.8	4.2
Foreigners.................	0.6	0.6	1.3	0.5	*	*	4.5	1.1	1.3
Individuals and others (residual)...................	5.4	1.8	8.7	8.2	6.8	4.1	14.7	2.7	2.9
Total supply.............	31.9	30.1	46.1	32.2	33.5	40.6	56.2	37.9P	41.1E

[9] For a more complete coverage of this subject, refer to Bibliography and Suggested Reading at the end of this chapter.

TABLE 5 *(Continued)*
THE DEMAND FOR NEW FUNDS
(In billions of dollars)
1953–1959 actual; 1960 and 1961, Preliminary and Estimated

Demand	1953	1954	1955	1956	1957	1958	1959	1960P	1961E
Business..................	7.2	9.8	19.2	18.4	16.3	14.1	19.0	17.0	14.5
Commercial and farm mortgages.................	2.3	2.8	3.6	3.8	3.5	5.2	6.0	4.5	4.8
Corporate bonds..........	4.8	3.8	4.2	4.7	7.1	5.9	4.1	5.0	4.0
Corporate stocks (excluding investment companies)...	1.9	1.8	1.9	2.5	2.7	2.1	2.4	1.8	2.7
Business credit (including trade credit)...........	−1.8	1.4	9.5	7.4	3.0	0.9	6.5	5.7	3.0
Individuals...............	13.4	12.6	19.9	14.0	11.9	13.1	21.7	17.5	14.8
Residential mortgages.....	7.6	9.6	12.6	10.8	8.6	10.1	13.2	10.9	11.1
Consumer credit..........	3.9	1.1	6.4	3.6	2.8	0.3	6.4	3.9	1.3
Other uses...............	1.9	1.9	0.9	−0.4	0.5	2.7	2.1	2.7	2.4
Government...............	7.8	3.5	3.5	−3.5	0.4	7.5	10.1	−0.6	6.8
U.S. governments.........	7.8	3.5	2.0	−4.1	−1.7	8.0	7.9	−0.6	6.0
Federal agency issue.......	*	*	1.5	0.6	2.1	−0.5	2.2	*	0.8
State and local............	3.5	4.2	3.5	3.3	4.9	5.9	5.4	4.0	5.0
Total demand..........	31.9	30.1	46.1	32.2	33.5	40.6	56.2	37.9P	41.1E

NOTE: Because of rounding, components may not add to totals shown.
* Less than $50 million.
P, preliminary; E, estimated.
SOURCES: William C. Freund, Associate Professor of Finance, Graduate School of Business Administration, New York University, New York; Life Insurance Association of America, New York.

Mortgage Holdings of Various Types of Investors

A comparative report showing the amount of mortgage loans held by various types of institutional lenders as well as the percentage of loans to total assets or deposits is shown in Table 4. These statistics should be studied carefully by those who wish to be informed regarding the portfolios of the respective lenders.

Table 5 shows "Sources of New Funds" and "Demand for New Funds." This table should also be carefully studied and analyzed.

SUMMARY

The mortgage market is dominated by institutional lenders, who make a great majority of the loans on all types of real estate properties.

The major lenders are life insurance companies, savings and loan associations, commercial banks doing a savings business, and mutual savings banks.

Life insurance companies are among the major sources of funds covering homes, apartment houses, commercial buildings, shopping centers, hotels, and industrial properties, while mutual savings banks, savings and loan associations, and commercial banks confine their mortgage investment mainly to one- to four-family dwellings.

While savings and loan associations are quite restrictive covering VA and FHA loans, the other three large investors do a considerable amount of business in both VA and FHA loans. Some lenders confine their lending to conventional loans only. Mortgage bankers (loan correspondents) throughout the country have occupied a significant role in helping large numbers of individuals and institutions to finance the purchase of real estate. Acting as mortgage loan correspondents for life insurance companies and other financial institutions, these mortgage bankers develop a major share of the home, apartment, store, and industrial financing in the country.

The lending policies of all these investors are very changeable, as they must conform to the frequent changes which occur in the real estate and mortgage market.

One of the major improvements made in mortgage lending operations during the past twenty-five years has been recognition of the borrower as an important line of defense against the risks of loss which are inherent in every mortgage loan. Prior to this, the property itself was practically the only security for the loan. Greatly improved borrower relations have also been developed.

There is a wide variation in the amount of loan compared to appraisal which can be made by different types of lenders covering conventional loans. Until the end of July, 1955, commercial banks were restricted to 60 per cent of the appraisal, which was lower than any of the others. At that time Congress passed a law which increased this ratio to 66⅔ per cent. And in September 1959 this ratio was increased to 75 per cent. This action placed these banks in an even more competitive position in the mortgage market.

QUESTIONS

1. Explain why an individual may take greater risks in mortgage lending than institutional lenders.
2. Name the type of institutional lender which previous to 1959 had the lowest loan-to-value ratio.
3. Describe how mutual savings banks in large metropolitan areas acquire new loans.
4. Explain how the Secretary of the Treasury sets the pattern for new offerings or refundings of all types of government bonds.
5. Give the date the Federal Home Loan Bank Act was passed and explain its major purpose.
6. Explain private repurchasable capital in savings and loan association operations.

7. Describe how banking plays a vital role in the free enterprise system.
8. Give reasons why organizations with large endowment funds, such as universities, colleges, or foundations of rich families, invest considerable funds in the mortgage market.
9. State the authority that permits savings and loan associations to make both FHA and VA home loans.
10. Explain the difference between a savings and loan association and a building and loan association.
11. Name two minor sources of funds for mortgage lending.
12. Do life insurance companies usually charge a prepayment penalty for pay-off of the mortgage loan before maturity?
13. Explain why mortgage funds to be loaned depend to a great extent upon the type of security, type of loan, interest rate, and strength of borrower.
14. What type of lender makes the largest portion of loans on stores and hotels?
15. Explain why all Federal savings and loan associations are members of the Federal Home Loan Bank System.
16. Explain why the laws governing mortgage financing are not uniform throughout the fifty states.
17. Many large life insurance companies invest a considerable amount of funds in loans of $50,000 or more on eligible properties. Give reasons.
18. Explain why some large banks in the Southwest and on the Pacific Coast have sold some loans to Eastern investors during the past few years.
19. Give the year the first savings and loan association in the United States was organized.
20. Are mortgage investments of life insurance companies governed by the laws of the state in which they operate, or by the laws of the state in which incorporated?
21. Explain the purpose of the Federal Savings and Loan Insurance Corporation.
22. Explain how some banks are permitted to invest in mortgage loans by the trust department of the bank.
23. Explain why life insurance companies are strong factors in the mortgage lending field.
24. Describe how some individual investors handle the collection and servicing of their own loans.
25. Give some reasons why the amount of mortgage lending made by individuals continues to be surprisingly large.
26. Individuals obtain mortgage loans from what sources?
27. Explain in detail the role of mortgage bankers in the mortgage lending industry.
28. Explain why there are wide fluctuations in the mortgage financing market.
29. Explain how the Federal Reserve Board and the Federal Reserve banks buy government bonds as an investment just like a life insurance company, bank, or other type of investor.
30. Explain why mortgage lending policies of prudent lenders are not static and permanent but changeable.

31. What is the significance to mortgage investors of yields on United States government bonds?
32. Are mutual savings banks eligible for membership in the Federal Reserve System? In the Federal Deposit Insurance Corporation? In the Federal Home Loan Bank System?
33. Explain why in good times or bad the risk of loss in a mortgage loan transaction can never be completely eliminated.
34. Explain why liquidity of the mortgage loan portfolio is of great importance.
35. Explain how the basic control of mortgage lending by both state-chartered and national banks is exercised.

ASSIGNMENTS

1. Select a typical mortgage company in the city where you are employed or reside, and write a concise report regarding the methods of operations of that company.
2. Explain how the large life insurance companies in your locality operate in mortgage financing.
3. Analyze the activity of the individual investor in the mortgage loan market in your home town.
4. Describe the manner in which banks in the city where you reside handle mortgage lending operations.
5. Briefly describe the mortgage lending activity of savings and loan associations in the area where you reside.

BIBLIOGRAPHY AND SUGGESTED READING

Behrens, Carl F., *Commercial Bank Activities in Urban Mortgage Financing,* National Bureau of Economic Research, Inc., New York, 1952.

Combined Financing Statements, 1960, Federal Home Loan Bank Board, Washington.

Conway, Lawrence V., *Mortgage Lending,* American Savings and Loan Institute Press, Chicago, 1960.

Edwards, Edward E., *Urban Real Estate Financing by Savings and Loan Associations,* National Bureau of Economic Research, Inc., New York, 1952.

Klaman, Saul B., *The Volume of Mortgage Debt in the Post War Decade, Tech. Paper* 13, National Bureau of Economic Research, Inc., New York, 1958.

Life Insurance Fact Book, pp. 62–92, Institute of Life Insurance, New York, 1960.

Lintner, John, *Mutual Savings Banks in the Savings and Mortgage Markets,* chaps. 2–4, 8, 9, Harvard University, Graduate School of Business Administration, Division of Research, Cambridge, Mass., 1948.

McMichael, Stanley L., *How to Finance Real Estate,* chaps. 12–15, Prentice-Hall, Inc., Englewood Cliffs, N.J., 1952.

Pease, Robert H., and Homer V. Cherrington (eds.), *Mortgage Banking,* chaps. 12, 13, 18, McGraw-Hill Book Company, Inc., New York, 1953

Saulnier, R. J., *Urban Mortgage Lending by Life Insurance Companies,* chaps. 1–5, National Bureau of Economic Research, Inc., New York, 1950.

Savings Banking, chaps, 3, 4, 9, 10, 16, 20, American Institute of Banking, Section American Bankers Association, New York, 1946.

Savings and Home Financing Chart Book, 1960, Federal Home Loan Bank Board, Washington.

Savings and Loan Fact Book, 1960, United States Savings and Loan League, Chicago, Ill.

Source Book, 1960, Federal Home Loan Bank Board, Washington.

3 Organization and Control of Mortgage Lending Operations[1]

PURPOSES

1. To explain the objectives of the management and administrative control of the mortgage loan portfolio
2. To discuss the operations of such a program
3. To outline the functional procedures of executive management and each division of the department
4. To outline the legal limitations covering mortgage loan investments
5. To explain the importance of a systematic analysis of the mortgage loan portfolio

The purpose of a mortgage lender's investment in mortgage loans is to earn net income. The purpose is achieved with maximum success if mortgage loans are repaid according to contract, if losses are avoided, and if the expenses of managing the portfolio are properly controlled. To see that these conditions are fulfilled is the objective of the executive management and the loan administration program. Lenders now commonly recognize the fact that constant supervision is necessary in order to maintain the mortgage loan portfolio in sound condition. The cost of such supervision is justified if it results in a reduction of defaults and an avoidance of losses, and if satisfactory customer relations are maintained.

Control of Mortgage Lending of Institutional Lenders Varies Widely

Basic control of mortgage lending lies in the following:

1. In the limitations imposed by Federal statutes on national banks, and by laws of the various states on state-chartered commercial and savings banks

2. In the regulations and decisions of the appropriate supervisory authorities, such as the FHA, VA, Federal National Mortgage Association, Federal Reserve bank, and Federal Home Loan Bank Board

[1] Subjects covered in this chapter represent mainly an analysis and study by the author of organization and control of mortgage lending operations of several types of mortgage lenders including the institutions with which he has been associated.

3. In the regulations of the Federal Savings and Loan System under a Federal charter covering savings and loan associations

4. Under the insurance commissioner of each state, who carries out the laws passed by the state legislature covering insurance companies

5. Under the building and loan commissioner of each state covering state-chartered savings and loan associations

The regulations of these bodies vary widely.

The mortgage lending policy of any lender must conform to daily conditions in the real estate and mortgage market and, therefore, will be one of constant change. The lending policy adopted for use in a falling market would never be satisfactory during a rising market. There have been tremendous changes in the real estate and mortgage market during the past 25 years. Even today we are facing many new problems in mortgage lending because of the condition of the market. The market must be watched at all times because of the fluctuations that occur. Any changes of administration in Washington could not only have a marked effect upon the entire mortgage market but cause the changing of lending policies of all types of mortgage investors.

All officers engaged in the investment and production phase of mortgage lending must understand the economic and sometimes political activities which provide support for the real estate and mortgage market. To be kept informed about the economic background and economic activities of the locality where the mortgage lender is located, these officers generally analyze prevailing wages in the area, unemployment, salaries, dividends, profits, trend of savings accounts, bank clearings, department-store sales, and industry payrolls. Changes in population and changes in the composition of families are also studied. Attention must be given to mortgage recordings in public offices or reports of recordings in publications covering deeds, mortgages, foreclosures, etc. Studies are also made concerning vacancies in the area according to types of properties. It is also important to maintain daily information regarding the amount of new construction in the areas as well as changes in construction costs. Maps are available in some large cities which show the extent of occupancy and of vacancies in different types of properties. Armed with the foregoing information, executive management can formulate investment and lending policies and can decide whether loans should be sought aggressively and what portion of available funds should be invested in the various types of loans and the various types of properties.

Functions Involved in Mortgage Lending Operations

In order to understand the functions involved in the organization, management, administration, and control of mortgage lending operations, it is necessary that each part of the entire operation of the mortgage loan department be carefully outlined and analyzed. By use of the functional chart (Figure 1) the basic divisions and functions of this department can be identified. Regardless of the size of the portfolio, or the types of loans in the portfolio, each one of these basic functions must be maintained if the department is to operate efficiently and if the objectives of mortgage lending operations are to be achieved. There are many variations of functional charts—each must be set up to meet the needs of each particular lender.

Officer in Charge of the Mortgage Loan Department

This officer is responsible for the efficient operation of every phase of the department. This includes *lending policies, personnel,* and *all operating procedures.* In some commercial banks doing a savings business, he is also in charge of the savings operations, as funds for investment in mortgage loans are savings deposits. In most banks this officer is also a member of the *commercial loan committee.* This is a very important assignment, as many commercial loans are made to borrowers who also have mortgage loans with the bank. After consultation with the board of directors, the president, and the executive committee, this officer sets the investment policy for the lender, including the types of loans in which funds should be invested, such as conventional, FHA, VA, home, business-property, subdivision, and all other types. He works directly under the president in the operation of the department. Usually in large lending institutions the executive committee approves all mortgage loans over $10,000. Some companies require executive-committee approval on loans only in excess of $25,000. A few companies set this requirement at $50,000. When a quick decision is required, large loans are made with the consent of the *president.* Later the approval of the executive committee is obtained. The officer in charge of the mortgage loan department consults his executive assistants in operating the department. All general operations listed in the functional chart are usually supervised by executive assistants, who must have sufficient authority to make decisions regarding the operations of their respective divisions; otherwise very inefficient procedures could result. *It is necessary for these officers to anticipate as much as possible the information which the officer in charge of the department will desire concerning any particular phase of operations and control.* They should also be prepared at all times to suggest satisfactory solutions to existing problems.

The officer in charge of the department, the president, and the board of directors, as well as the executive committee, must have sufficient information to enable them to set the policies for converting available funds into earning assests. Decisions must be made not only as to the manner in which the funds should be invested but also as to how much should be

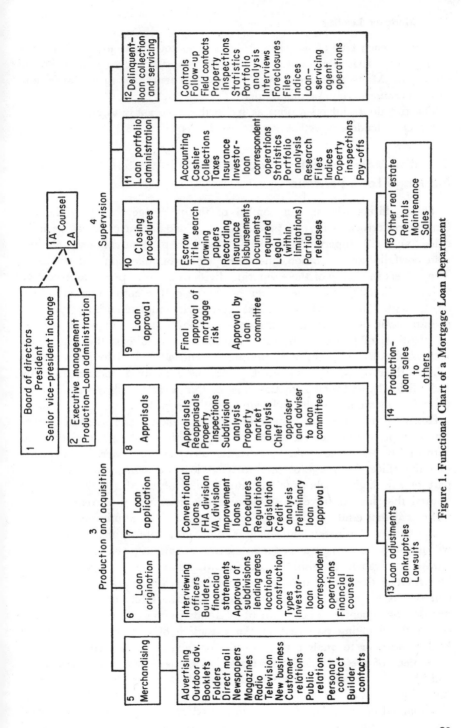

Figure 1. Functional Chart of a Mortgage Loan Department

invested in each type of securities. In order to know the result of the investment policy, it is necessary that this officer watch earnings and cost of operations. Many other items require careful attention if successful investment operations are to be maintained.

The functions and operations as set forth above apply to all other types of mortgage lenders as well as commercial banks.

Executive Management, Control, and Administration of the Mortgage Loan Portfolio

Those officers who are in control of the mortgage loan portfolio are directly concerned with (1) production and acquisition of loans, as indicated, and (2) supervision, which includes loan approval, loan closing, loan portfolio administration, and delinquent-loan collection and servicing. The officers in charge of these separate divisions usually operate as executive assistants directly under the officer in charge of the entire mortgage loan department. They must be given and must merit complete authority over the operations of these particular divisions but naturally are required to refer all questions of policy to the officer in charge and discuss these questions with him. Adequate control of production and administration of the portfolio is their operating responsibility. All divisions must operate smoothly and efficiently, and their activities must be thoroughly synchronized in order to achieve maximum results and keep operating costs low.

Executive assistants are responsible for formulating and suggesting general loan-production and lending policies, which are then considered and approved by the higher policy-making authority of the lender. It is essential that the officer in charge of the mortgage loan department be an integral part of this higher policy-making authority. Only in this way can he be assured that his executive assistants are kept informed of current developments and that established policies are being effectively administered.

The aim of the investment policy is to obtain a return, or income, which will not only be as high as possible but also as safe as possible. Safety must always be given first consideration. Following safety of the principal, most important is the net yield or return obtainable. There are many different opinions as to proper investment policies and the safety of certain investments. Consequently the investment of funds in mortgage loans follows a constantly changing pattern and the executive officers of each mortgage lender endeavor to analyze these needs for their particular company. The investment of these funds in mortgage loans, the repayment of the loans, and the reinvestment of these funds as well as the additional savings is generally known as the fund-conversion program.

A manual of operations is an important adjunct to success in the over-all management and administration of the mortgage loan department operations. Such a manual should not only outline the basic lending policies and objectives of the lender but should also outline in some detail the procedures of each division of the mortgage loan department. Schedules of charges covering processing fees, construction-loan fees, reconveyance fees, interest rates, and other charges should also be included in the manual.

If mortgage loans are made on a sound basis in conformity with a well-considered policy and are properly serviced, not only the lender but also the individual borrowers and the community as a whole will benefit. This is undoubtedly the objective of all prudent lenders.

Basic Operations of a Mortgage Loan Department

Most mortgage loan departments perform the following services:
1. *Production and acquisition of the loan*
   a. Merchandising
   b. Origination
   c. Loan application
   d. Appraisal
2. *Supervision of the loan*
   a. Loan approval
   b. Loan closing
   c. Loan portfolio administration
   d. Delinquent-loan collection and servicing
3. *Other operations*
   a. Loan sales to others
   b. Loan adjustments
   c. Other Real Estate

Production and Acquisition of Loans

The first four divisions of the functional chart (Figure 1) are set up under the subheading of "Production and Acquisition" and cover merchandising, loan origination, loan application, and appraisals. Practically all the divisions operate within the mortgage loan department. However, in large institutions all advertising operations are usually handled by the separate advertising department, which handles the entire advertising for the company as a whole, and development of new business is controlled by a separate new-business department.

Customer Relations, Public Relations, Personal Contact, Builder Contact

Customer relations, personal contacts, and contacts with investors and builders regarding mortgage lending, however, are handled by an officer or officers in the mortgage loan department. Large lenders usually have one or more officers in constant contact with the public, with investors, and with builders who require financing for future construction. By financing such builders the lender in turn is able to obtain the ultimate loans on the properties. In companies which operate branch offices, the manager of each branch and his assistants maintain these contacts with potential customers.

Loan Origination

A very important part of the general operations of a large mortage loan department includes not only lending policies but also a constant study of pending legislation in Congress and proper interpretation of both FHA and VA regulations.

The loan-origination division consists of officers and other members of the staff who meet prospective borrowers either in the office of the lender or in the field. Most interviews are at the offices of the lender. All officers, as well as branch managers in branch operations, are initial interviewers. This includes the officer in charge of the entire mortgage loan department.

Interviews cover all types of loans and preliminary informal discussions are held covering the pending transactions.

If a large-scale building operation is involved, the builder's financial statement must be submitted and analyzed. Also, in such cases the area where the project is to be located must be approved. Types of construction must also be approved. A well-trained interviewing officer should always know the lending policies of his own institution covering the above points.

Many contacts for financial guidance and counsel are made at the office of the lender. Trained officers who have a knowledge of the mortgage market and related subjects handle such interviews.

Loan Application

After the preliminary interview has been completed, the actual handling of the loan application is the function of each of the officers in charge of the divisions set forth in the functional chart (Figure 1) under "Loan Application."

In large operations a separate officer is in charge of the FHA division, the VA division, and the conventional-loan division. The procedures covering both FHA and VA loans are quite complicated, and the officers in charge of these particular divisions must be expertly trained. They must fully understand existing FHA and VA regulations covering the processing of such loan applications, including the presentation of such applications to the FHA or VA as well as the actual closing of such loans. In comparatively small companies, particularly mortgage bankers, acting as loan correspondents, only one or two officers are required to handle all the functions previously described, and also to appraise the properties and prepare the loan submissions to the investors. In order to perform these functions efficiently and effectively, such officers must be highly intelligent and have outstanding ability and skill in this work and a complete knowledge of the mortgage lending profession, which usually is the result of many years of experience, careful training, and education.

Appraisals

One of the most important sections of a mortgage lending department is an adequate appraisal division staffed by efficient appraisers under the direction of an expert chief appraiser.

There are many purposes involved in appraisal of properties, the most important of which undoubtedly is to determine that the value of the property is adequate at the time the loan is made. This estimate of value is required by law in all states which limit the amount of the ratio of the loan to the estimated value of the property.

Values of properties are subject to frequent changes, and it is the duty of the chief appraiser to estimate the relative course of the future value of each property. He is charged with the responsibility of properly training his assistants so that there will be a uniform method of valuation.

Other functions of appraising include reappraisals and property inspections as well as analysis of subdivisions, and all areas in which the lender makes mortgage loans, and approval of the type of property on which a loan is being considered.

This chief appraiser is not only an adviser on property values to the officer in charge of the mortgage loan department but in many companies is also an adviser to the loan committee. In some companies he is a member of the loan committee; in others, he plays a major role in executive management, control, and administration of mortgage lending operations.

It is now recognized by many leading mortgage lenders that before a member of the staff can assume the duties and responsibilities of management, control, and administration, he must have had adequate training and experience in appraisal operations and procedures.

Supervision (Maintenance)

Under this title in the functional chart (Figure 1) there are listed "Loan Approval," "Closing Procedures," "Loan Portfolio Administration," and "Delinquent-loan Collection and Servicing." Actual supervision and administration of the loan portfolio begins with the written approval of the loan application and closing procedures. The entire operation of the basic divisions of the department constitutes a cycle in which the funds of the lender are converted into mortgage loans, which subsequently are reconverted into cash and again become available for investment. This operation is generally termed the fund-conversion program. A break in this cycle occurs when it is necessary to complete foreclosure on loans that are not paid according to terms, or where a serious default in one of the covenants of the mortgage has occurred. Also, there is a type of cycle in which a lender sells the loan to another investor after it has been processed and closed. The funds received on sale of such loans are usually promptly reinvested.

Loan Approval

Final approval of all loans is ordinarily made by the loan committee, which by some lenders is called the finance committee. This committee generally consists of the officer in charge of the mortgage loan department and two or three executive assistants. In some companies certain members of the board of directors serve on the finance committee.

On conventional loans the preliminary approval of the mortgage loan application is made by one of these executive assistants. On both VA and FHA loan applications preliminary approval of the application is usually made by the respective officers in charge of these divisions. Final approval of such loans is given by the loan committee. These procedures are also followed by investors in handling loan correspondent submissions.

In the branch-office operations of any type of mortgage lender each branch manager is given a loan limit and is authorized to make loans up to that amount without approval of the loan committee. Managers must have knowledge of conditions in their particular areas and must at all times know the lending policies which are established by the executives at the main office.

Closing Procedures

In the functional chart both loan-approval functions and closing procedures are placed under "Supervision" rather than "Production and Acquisition," as it is felt that the actual acquisition functions have ceased when preliminary approval of the loan has been given. Approval of each loan application is usually given verbally well in advance of the actual written loan approval. This is especially true on the smaller loans being placed in the portfolio.

Closing procedures are highly technical, and officers with knowledge of titles to properties and related subjects handle these operations. All documents required by the lender in the transaction, such as the note and mortgage, are drawn up by this division, the title search is analyzed, the loan disbursements are made, and the documents are recorded by most companies through a title company. Many mortgage banking firms use the services of a highly skilled escrow attorney to perform these services.

When these functions are completed, the loan becomes a part of the portfolio.

Loan Portfolio Administration

In the loan supervision operations and after the loan is a part of the portfolio, most of the routine contacts of borrowers are made through the loan collection division. Favorable customer relations depend to a large extent on the quality of the service provided. A close-working relationship should always be maintained between the various operating divisions of the mortgage loan department. Such a relationship promotes more pleasant employee relations and improves the efficiency of the mortgage loan department operations. Quite frequently it is necessary for an executive assistant to handle the duties of another executive assistant during absences from the office or for other reasons.

No longer is it the generally accepted policy that once a mortgage loan is put on the books it can be forgotten. Lenders now recognize the fact that if a mortgage loan portfolio is to be maintained in sound condition, it must be constantly supervised.

Loan portfolio administration may be described as the core of this supervision program. It must operate efficiently if these functions are to be effectively performed. As previously stated, customer relations in particular must at all times be given careful consideration inasmuch as some borrowers have no contact with the lender except through the loan portfolio administration division.

Delinquent-loan Collection and Servicing

In the operation and maintenance of the delinquent-loan collection and servicing division, the officer in charge of the entire mortgage loan department should periodically be informed of the delinquent loans in the portfolio, the trend of delinquencies, and any changes in the portfolio condition which might require special attention. The officer in charge of the delinquent-loan collection and servicing division should recommend and approve all foreclosure action, as well as the handling of all other difficult loan cases. Operating procedures, personnel problems, and statistical reports should be reviewed periodically with the officer in charge of the mortgage loan department. Unless he is continuously informed of operations and operating problems, he will not be in a position to supervise properly the over-all operations of the mortgage loan department.

Loan Sales to Others

Contacts with purchasers of loans as well as preliminary negotiations concerning sale of mortgage loans in the portfolio are usually made by the officer in charge of the mortgage loan department. The actual contract settlements and the delivery of all documents involved are handled by trained officers within the department.

Loan Adjustments

In large mortgage lending companies this division is usually not a direct part of the mortgage loan department but is an entirely separate operating division which handles bankruptcies, lawsuits, accounts of deceased borrowers, and various other problems of both the commercial loan and the mortgage loan departments. In life insurance companies the office of the general counsel usually handles such cases.

Other Real Estate

Most lenders maintain a separate division covering these operations. Some lenders call this the real estate management department. The control of the handling of acquired properties, as well as the sale of such properties, is directly under the supervision of the officer in charge of the mortgage loan department. Usually a committee consisting of the head of the mortgage loan department, the officer in charge of the Other Real Estate division, the chief appraiser, and a member of the loan committee approve each transaction.

Importance of Portfolio Analysis

The major objectives of analysis of the mortgage loan portfolio are:
1. To determine the characteristics of the portfolio, as well as loan trends
2. To determine net income
3. To determine efficiency of operations
4. To ascertain weakness or strains in the mortgage lending operations which might be developing
5. To obtain an objective view of the entire operation of the department

Information Needed for Study

In order to obtain this information the following statistics should be analyzed: loan types, such as FHA, VA, and conventional loans; loans by dollar amount; volume of loans by geographic areas; interest accruals; maturities; paid-off loans; delinquencies; loan-value ratios; amount of the average loan in the portfolio; foreclosures completed during a given period.

Frequent analyses of the operations of each particular division are made and discussed with the executive assistants in charge in order to ascertain activities and problems.

With the above information the officer in charge of the mortgage loan department is able to ascertain the effectiveness of each integral part of the operations of the department. The analysis also serves as a guide to reserve policy, as in any mortgage loan portfolio, no matter how healthy, some losses are unavoidable. This information is also needed in order to set up the asset valuation of the mortgage loan portfolio.

Counsel

Mortgage lending operations cannot be adequately maintained without the use of counsel. Some lenders, such as large life insurance companies, have a general counsel, as well as a complete legal department within their own organizations. Others use the services of outside legal firms, many of whom are engaged on a retainer basis.

The lending of money on real estate security involves legal principles and practices which differ materially from those applicable where money is loaned with marketable collateral as security. The lender on real estate security must ascertain that the borrower has a good legal title to the real estate to be pledged as security. Real estate and the pledging of it as security is governed by the laws of the state in which the security is situated. Statutes vary from state to state. Hence, legal counsel is not only required during the processing and closing of a loan but usually throughout the life of each loan. This is a field of law, including escrow and loan-closing operations, which is rapidly expanding throughout the entire nation.

SUMMARY

If the basic functions covering mortgage lending are to be clearly understood, it is necessary that the relations of the various divisions of the mortgage loan department be known.

By means of a functional chart (Figure 1) the basic divisions of a typical large mortgage loan department are identified. Regardless of the size of the department, however, the functions must be maintained if the proper major objectives of mortgage lending are to be achieved. There are many variations of functional charts, and each one must be set up to meet the needs of each particular lender.

The officer in charge of the mortgage loan department is responsible for the efficient operation of every phase of the department. This includes lending policies, personnel, and all operating procedures. He sets the investment policy after consultation with the board of directors, the president, and the executive committee.

The officer in charge of each division as set forth in the functional chart is directly concerned with executive management, control, and administration of the mortgage loan portfolio. The purpose of the lender's investment in mortgage loans is to earn net income. This purpose can be achieved with maximum success only if payments on loans are made in accordance with the terms, if losses are avoided, and if expenses of operating the department are properly controlled.

Control of mortgage lending is circumscribed by Federal statutes, state laws, government regulations covering FHA and VA loans, and rulings of the Federal Savings and Loan Commissioner, the insurance commissioner, and the building and loan commissioner.

The mortgage lending policy of any lender must conform to daily conditions in the real estate and mortgage market. There have been tremendous changes in the market during the past several years.

Basic operations of most mortgage loan departments consist of the following: acquisition of the loan, which covers merchandising, origination, loan application, and appraisal; supervision of the loan, which covers loan approval, loan closing, loan portfolio administration, and delinquent-loan collection and servicing; operations which cover loan sales to others, loan adjustments, and Other Real Estate.

All these operations and functions are essential in mortgage lending, and the officers in charge of each separate operation must be thoroughly trained and skilled in order to handle their duties efficiently.

Mortgage lending operations cannot be adequately maintained without use of counsel, as the lending of money on real estate involves legal practices and principles which differ materially from those applicable where money is loaned with marketable collateral as security.

QUESTIONS

1. Explain why it is necessary that the executive officers watch earnings and costs of operations.
2. An important part of a manual of operations covering a mortgage loan department is the functional chart. For what reasons?
3. Why is constant supervision of the loan portfolio necessary?
4. Net income can only be achieved if what objectives are maintained?
5. What operating division handles bankruptcies, lawsuits, and accounts of deceased borrowers?
6. Are the laws pertaining to mortgage loans of state-chartered commercial and savings banks generally less restrictive than national banking laws?

7. Name the most nearly riskless investments.
8. Name four major responsibilities of executive management regarding mortgage investments.
9. The officer in charge of the mortgage loan department is responsible for what operating phases of the department?
10. Following safety of principal and interest, what is the deciding factor in the selection of a mortgage loan as an investment?
11. List the basic operations of a mortgage loan department.
12. What are primary reserves of a mortgage lender?
13. Explain how the amortization payments regularly received on mortgage loans are then available for reinvestment. This is a part of what program?
14. Explain how analysis of the portfolio also reveals to some extent the effectiveness of the loan administration program.
15. Name some of the reasons why legal counsel must be used in mortgage lending operations.
16. What is the purpose of a mortgage lender's investment in mortgage loans?
17. Explain why mortgage loans do not qualify as reserves.
18. Define weekly record of runoff of the mortgage loan portfolio.
19. Describe how portfolio analysis can reveal weakness or strains which might be developing in the loan portfolio.
20. Name the most important purpose of an appraisal of the property.
21. Explain the basic controls of mortgage lending.
22. Explain why a manual of operations is essential in a mortgage loan department.
23. What officer or officers make the final approval of all mortgage loans?
24. Why is portfolio analysis necessary?
25. In loan origination and application operations explain why all officers are initial interviewers.
26. Why are the mortgage lending policies of any lender those of almost constant change?
27. Explain why loan-closing procedures are highly technical and officers with a knowledge of titles to properties and related subjects should handle these operations.
28. Describe how executive management arrives at the asset valuation of the portfolio.
29. Give reasons why all officers engaged in the operational phases of mortgage lending should understand the economic activities which provide support for the real estate and mortgage market.
30. Explain why most large lenders maintain a separate division covering real estate management or Other Real Estate operations.
31. Can the cost of handling mortgage loans be measured with a fair degree of accuracy?
32. Give some of the advantages of financing speculative builders.
33. Name the purpose served by the maintenance of adequate primary and secondary reserves.
34. Briefly describe how real estate brokers provide loans for lenders.
35. List the functions included in supervision of the loan portfolio.

ASSIGNMENTS

1. Set up a functional chart covering the mortgage lending operations of a company of your own selection in the city where you reside.
2. Bring to class a concise report of the regulations which control the lending operations of the type of company selected by you.
3. Describe the various types of mortgage lenders in your community.

BIBLIOGRAPHY AND SUGGESTED READING

Home Mortgage Lending, chap. 15, American Institute of Banking, Section American Bankers Association, New York, 1946.

McMichael, Stanley L., *How to Finance Real Estate,* chaps. 17, 40, Prentice-Hall, Inc., Englewood Cliffs, N.J., 1949.

Pease, Robert H., and Homer V. Cherrington (eds.), *Mortgage Banking,* chap. 3, McGraw-Hill Book Company, Inc., New York, 1953.

Present Day Banking, chaps. 2, 9, American Bankers Association, New York, 1947.

4   Loan-application Procedures

PURPOSES

1. To describe the content of a typical application form covering a conventional loan
2. To discuss methods of processing an application for a mortgage loan
3. To describe the types of properties on which mortgage loans are made
4. To explain the importance of giving accurate information to the applicant regarding closing charges, including fees, cost of title search, tax accruals, notary fees, and recording fees
5. To discuss construction loans, including construction loans to operative builders
6. To explain the importance to the lender of complete and accurate credit information covering the borrower

What Is the Loan Application?

The mortgage loan application is the key to the loan transaction. It should give in detail all pertinent information regarding the applicant, the property, and the type of loan desired. A statement covering applicants assets and liabilities and also a statement of income and expense should be a part of the application. All the information submitted must be completely accurate, as must all other information which is contained in considerable detail in the application. Otherwise it is not possible for the lender to analyze the proposed transaction properly.

Importance of the Loan Application

An application for a home loan is usually the largest financial undertaking in the life of the average homeowner, and great care must be exercised in analyzing the financial aspects of the transaction in order to make sure the home buyer is not overextending himself. A prudent lender will always make a careful study of every aspect of the transaction in order to be certain that the borrower is qualified to purchase the home at the price asked, that he will be able to make the payments required on the loan, that the property is in good condition and well constructed, and that all conditions in connection with the loan are sound. These same rigid requirements are necessary for applications covering a mortgage loan on any other type of real estate. Loan applications covering properties other than home loans are generally far more technical and require a much greater amount of detailed information and supporting exhibits.

It is important that the lender be genuinely interested in this applicant and that the interviewer in processing the application be able to obtain all the necessary information for judging the soundness of the proposed loan. Each applicant is a different type of personality, and in each case the handling of the transaction might be varied to some extent in order to handle properly the deal under consideration and treat effectively the personality involved. For the past several years new and younger borrowers have applied for and have been granted home loans. The down payment required on a home loan has frequently been small, and as a result of this a thorough analysis of the ability of the borrower to repay the loan is made. There are many other factors which also must be analyzed. These younger borrowers have required and have been given complete information regarding mortgage loans and the responsibilities entailed.

Contents of the Application for a Conventional Loan

There are seven major items in the average form of application for a conventional loan, namely:
1. Formal request for loan and statement of the applicant
2. Description and location of the property
3. Description of improvements
4. Encumbrances, mortgages, or other liens against the property
5. Credit information covering the potential borrowers—financial statement
6. Signature and summary statements
7. Loan approval or disapproval by loan committee

Statement of the Applicant and Formal Request for Loan

One of the most important parts of an application is to have the complete name of the applicant and his wife, if married, at the top of the application form in the space provided. This is also a requirement covering corporations and partnerships on loan applications on commercial and industrial properties. The name or names should always be as they would appear on the note and mortgage. After this information, the following basic information should be recorded on the application form:

1. Amount of loan desired.
2. Rate of payment and term of loan.
3. Interest rate requested.
4. Proposed use of funds.
5. Statement of ownership of the property—list of any others claiming interest and the nature of such claims.
6. Street address of the property.
7. City and county in which property is located.
8. Legal description. This requirement is mandatory.
9. Occupancy by owner, tenant (show rentals), others, nature of occupancy.
10. List of any encumbrances on the property, unpaid balances, terms of payment, rate of interest, owned by, present status (show any default).
11. Any improvement bonds or assessments, unpaid balances, terms of payment, present status.
12. Whether property homesteaded.
13. Any judgments or mechanics' liens.
14. Any condemnation action.

All the above information is of vital importance, and if the information submitted is completely accurate, it will aid the lender materially in processing the application. Surprisingly enough in a majority of cases the applicant for a loan has available only a meager portion of this information. In many cases even the street address of the property is not known by the applicant. In far too many cases covering existing structures the applicant has no knowledge of any loans on the property or the amount of the property taxes.

In the case of homes being built in subdivisions for occupancy when completed, the builder supplies in detail all necessary information regarding the property. If the lender also handled the interim financing, all information covering the property, the maximum loan which can be made, as well as interest rate, term, and type of loan, will have been set up previously by the lender. In such cases if the applicant for a loan on such a property measures up to all requirements, the loan can be quickly made.

Description of the Property

In all cases the applicant should furnish the complete legal description of the property and also the street address. The Preliminary Title Report which gives this information in detail is in nearly all cases attached to the loan application. The size of the lot should be given, and the type of building which is on the property, or to be constructed, should be described. If the building is more than five years old, a termite-inspection report should generally be required. In most areas the cost of corrective measures covering infestation is borne by the seller, while preventive work is borne by the buyer. A sales agreement should always contain a clause regarding separate responsibilities of the buyer and seller with respect to this problem.

The required information about the property is set forth below:

1. Complete legal description
2. Street address
3. Size of lot
4. Type of buildings
5. When purchased—cost
6. Improvements made since purchase—cost
7. Improvements to be made—type
    a. Method of construction
    b. Contract?
    c. Cost plus?
    d. Amount, $
    e. Estimated cost, $
8. Amount of taxes
9. Inspection made for pest infestation
    a. Date
    b. Was infestation eliminated?

Credit Information about the Borrower

An important concern of the lender is whether the borrower will be able to keep up the payments required by the contract. There are many other factors which must be taken into consideration, but the quality of most home loans and all other types of loans is judged by the probability that they will be repaid in accordance with the terms of the mortgage agreement.

Some of the credit information required is the following:

1. Occupation
    a. Employed by
    b. Number of years
2. Previous employment
    a. Number of years
3. Securities (stocks or mortgages owned)
    a. List each one—give value, any encumbrance, when due
4. Real estate owned—list each parcel
    a. Owner's value

      b. Liens
        (1) Amount
        (2) Terms of payment
        (3) Holder
      c. Gross annual income
      d. Gross annual expense
  5. Life insurance—cash value
      a. Loans thereon
      b. Beneficiary
  6. Bank accounts in detail—where carried
  7. Other assets—describe
  8. Other liabilities—describe
      a. Amount
      b. Secured by
      c. Payable
      d. Any delinquencies
  9. Borrower's income
      a. Salary
      b. Securities
      c. Properties
      d. Other
10. Expenses
      a. Interest
      b. Taxes
      c. Assessments
      d. Upkeep of properties
      e. Living expenses
      f. Monthly installments on other debts, including consumer debt, store accounts, etc.
      g. Number of persons supported from income
      h. Any suits, judgments, or litigation
      i. General remarks

Some lenders have a separate form covering the financial statement of the potential borrower.

The Appraisal Report

A few commercial banks have the appraisal report incorporated in the loan-application form covering a conventional-loan application (Figure 2). On home-loan applications particularly it is their opinion that this procedure will streamline operations considerably. Even though the appraisal report must contain minute details regarding the property and neighborhood, these

TYPE OF LOAN   **YOUR STATE TRUST COMPANY**   Application Number...1234...

Conventional   Willow-Glen   OFFICE   Loan Number...

APPLICATION FOR CITY REAL ESTATE LOAN

January 31 ...19 61

DOAKES, Elmer K.   DOAKES, Mary
(Applicant's full name)   (Full name of Wife or Husband)

We ...hereby apply to AMERICAN TRUST COMPANY, hereinafter referred to as "Bank" for a loan

of $...12,000.00... for...20...year..., with interest at the rate of ...6...per cent per annum, payable in monthly installments of

$...86.04...inclusive ~~exclusive~~ of interest, the said loan to be secured by a Deed of Trust on the following described real estate in the

City of ...Your Town..., County of ...Your County..., California.

DESCRIPTION AND LOCATION OF PROPERTY: Lot No...123...Block No...23...Tract...Fern... | Description verified with title report

Lot on the...S/E...Line of...Santa Fe...Street, distant...75...feet
N/E...of...Ramona...Street; thence...60'...feet by...120...
feet deep. Assessor's Lot No...123...Block No...23...House No...1234 Santa Fe... | Authorized Officer

IMPROVEMENTS—Consists of (type of construction, number of stories and rooms)

Completion expected 2-28-61

Statement of Income and Expenses

	Income	Expenses
Taxes		
Ins.		
Water		
Elect.		
Fuel		
Power		
Scav.		
Mgr.		
Janitor		

Built...1960-61...by...Swenston...City Zone...Yes...
(Year)
Street Pavement...Yes...Sidewalk...Yes...Sewer...Yes...
Annual Taxes $...244.00...Occupied by...New Construction...Monthly rental $...******...
If street or other assessment is not fully paid, in what form is the lien?...Paid...Bal. Due $...
Is property being sold on contract?...No...To whom?...

ENCUMBRANCES, MORTGAGES OR OTHER LIENS AGAINST THE PROPERTY:

NAME OF HOLDER	Original Amount	Balance Due	Rate of Interest
First Construction Loan - Your State Trust Company	$	$9,800.00	%
Second			
Third			

When was property acquired by you?...Now being purchased...Purchase Price $...20,000.00...Secondary loan?...None...
(Year)
When and what were last improvements made?...New Construction...Cost $...

Present Insurance: Fire $...20,000.00...Is Extended Coverage included?...Yes...Earthquake $...No...
For what purpose is loan to be used?...Complete the purchase price - $20,000.00...

If property is offered for sale, sale price will be $...If a building loan, actual cost will be $...

And the undersigned hereby agrees: to furnish at his own expense such a policy of title insurance as shall be acceptable to the Bank; to pay notarial and Bank fees, costs of recording and releasing; and the undersigned further agrees to permit the title papers and abstracts to remain with the Bank during the existence of the loan; to execute loan papers in form satisfactory to the Bank; to insure the property against loss or damage by fire, earthquake, and/or any other risks which in the opinion of the Bank should be insured against, in an amount, and with companies, acceptable to the Bank, the policies therefor to be delivered immediately to the Bank and to be payable, in case of loss, to the Bank.

The undersigned hereby agrees that, if the loan hereby applied for, or any part thereof, is to be used in the construction of a building or other improvements on the above described property, the disbursement of this loan shall be made in accordance with Building Loan Requirements of this Bank; and,

The undersigned further agrees that no work will be done or materials placed on the above property until after the Deed of Trust securing this loan shall have been placed of record.

The acceptance of this application for a loan shall in no way constitute a contract or agreement on the part of the Bank, and it is understood and agreed that the money herein applied for shall not be subject to the order of the undersigned until the Deed of Trust is recorded and becomes a first lien upon the property herein described, and until all other requirements of the Bank have been complied with, until which time the undersigned hereby expressly waives any claims or rights to such sum.

Has application for loan been filed elsewhere?...No...Where?...Declined?...Granted $...

THE STATEMENTS MADE ABOVE AND ON THE REVERSE HEREOF ARE SUBMITTED FOR THE PURPOSE OF OBTAINING CREDIT AND ARE CERTIFIED TO BE TRUE AND CORRECT.

Property may be inspected on...Any Day..., 19...

If vacant, key may be obtained at...
Seller on premises

Application taken and $...120.00...Fee received
by...F. B. Fritz

Sign here...(Sgd.) Elmer K. Doakes
Sign here...(Sgd.) Mary Doakes
Present Address...1625 Main Street
Phone...Willow 6-5525
Address to be used after loan closed}...
Phone...

Figure 2

CREDIT INFORMATION REQUIRED

Applicant must fill out in detail

A—EMPLOYMENT: _____ Self __X__ Other

    1. Name of Employer ..... Daylight Lines
    2. Address of Employer ... 666 Missouri Street
    3. Type of Business .... Motor Transportation
    4. Position held .... General Manager
    5. No. of years in present employment ... 10 years
    6. Annual Salary or Income $ 11,000.00
    7. Other Income $ .. Dividends $500.00
B—DEPENDENTS: No. 2 Ages 38 and 8
C—NET WORTH $ .. 20,000.00
D—OTHER INFORMATION:

BANKING BUSINESS

Commercial Account carried at .... Willow-Glen .... $ 7,400.00
             Bank   Branch   Ave. Bal.

Savings Account carried at .... Willow-Glen .... $ 8,000.00
             Bank   Branch   Ave. Bal.

Safe Deposit Box at .... Willow-Glen
             Bank   Branch

Commercial Loans .... None
             Bank   Branch   Balance

Life Insurance in force .. $15,000.00

Loans on Policies .... None

If not now a client of this bank, will give the following business

Applicant's Age .. 41 .... Race .. White

FOR BANK USE

	Cost	Current Market Value	Bank Appraisal
Land	$	$	$ 4,000.00
Improvements	$	$	$ 16,000.00
Proposed Impts.	$	$	$
Totals . . .	$	$	$ 20,000.00

APPRAISER'S REPORT

CLASSIFICATION 1 — 2 — 3 — 4 — 5 — 6 — 7 — 8 — 9 — 10

I hereby certify that I have made a very thorough examination of the property described herein and report as follows:

Fern Tract: Surroundings old and new. UNDER CONSTRUCTION: one story and basement frame dwelling of 6 rooms and dinette (3 bedrooms). Stuccoed front, terrazzo steps, oak floors, pine trim, sheetrock interior, fireplace, 2 tiled baths, shower over tubs, central gas furnace, 2-car garage in basement. Contains approximately 1600 sq. ft. Course of construction. Front white coated, decorating started.

Photos taken 1-31-61

                         John Brown
                              Appraiser

                       APPRAISAL REVIEWED

Date .... 2-4 .... 19 61   William Black
                              Chief Appraiser

COMMITTEE'S DECISION

                           2-4 .... 19 61

A loan is hereby approved for .. 20 .. years .. to be secured by a Deed of Trust on terms and conditions as follows:

                       Carl E. Ward
                                        Manager

$ 12,000.00
    { $ 86.04 .... monthly installments

inclusive
  of interest .. 6 ....% payable monthly.
Fire Insurance (including Extended Coverage) required
             $ 12,000.00

Earthquake Insurance required $ .. No
Advised .. 2-4 1961
F.H.A. Conditional Commitment
F.H.A. Firm Commitment #.......... $ .... Received .... Submitted ....
F.H.A. Rejection

    C   John Smith
    O
    M   Harold Jones
    I
    T   Edward Holmes
    T
    E
    E

Figure 2. (Continued)

data cannot be given completely on such a form. A typical report would be along the following lines:

Bank Appraisal

Land...................... $ 4,000.00
Improvements.............   16,000.00
Total.................... $20,000.00

FERN TRACT: Surroundings old and new. UNDER CONSTRUCTION: 1-story-and-basement frame dwelling of 6 rooms and dinette (3-bedroom). Stuccoed front, terrazzo steps, oak floors, pine trim; sheet-rock interior; fireplace; 2 tiled baths, shower over tubs; central gas furnace; 2-car garage in the basement. Contains approximately 1,600 sq. ft. COURSE OF CONSTRUCTION: Front white-coated, decorating started.

All mortgage lenders, with few exceptions, throughout the nation require that far more comprehensive and detailed information be reported on both the loan application and the appraisal report than is described in Figure 2.

Such a type of application is shown in Figure 3, and the appraisal report covering this particular property is shown in Figure 4.

This described transaction covers a conventional home-loan application and an appraisal report for a loan submission made by a mortgage banking firm (loan correspondent). Although the loan application is on the form of the mortgage banking firm, the appraisal report is made on the investor's appraisal form. On loan submissions covering commercial, industrial, and other types of properties, both the loan application form and the appraisal form used are the investor's forms. Many institutional investors require that both the loan application and the appraisal report on conventional home-loan submissions also be made on the forms of the investor.

Practically all mortgage lenders use separate loan application and appraisal report forms, and this procedure in the handling of loan applications and loan submissions is generally accepted as a more efficient operation than the combined loan application and appraisal report form.

The appraisal report is considered by all mortgage lenders to be a very confidential document, and consequently should be used in that manner and should not be made a part of the loan application form.

Summary Statement by Borrower

An applicant should certify in the space provided on the form that the information submitted is correct and that it is submitted for the purpose of obtaining credit. This certification is of great legal importance, and should be a mandatory requirement. In addition to signing the application, the applicant should give his home address and telephone number, as well as business address and telephone number.

RESIDENTIAL

BRYANT-JOHNSON MORTGAGE COMPANY
Suite 467, Russ Building, 235 Montgomery Street, San Francisco 4
YUkon 1-5242

REAL ESTATE LOAN APPLICATION

TERMS
The undersigned ("Applicant", jointly and severally if more than one) hereby applies to BRYANT-JOHNSON MORTGAGE COMPANY ("Lender") for a................................loan as follows:
Principal sum $...18,000.00.....Term...25....Yrs.........Interest Rate...6....% per annum.
Monthly payments, including interest and principal $....116.10........... Lender may collect a monthly reserve for taxes and fire insurance (insurance agent of borrower's choice).
Further privilege to make additional principal payments under following conditions:
Privilege to repay up to 20 percent of the original loan in any one loan year without penalty. After two years loan may be paid in full with penalty of three months interest.

SECURITY
The loan shall be secured by a first deed of trust or (at option of Lender) a first mortgage lien upon the property in the CITY of...Belmont..............
COUNTY of....San Mateo.................STATE of...California................
ADDRESS OF PROPERTY...#10 Wildwood Lane, Belmont, California...........
Title to be vested in....DONALD A. OLSON and FRANCELLA B. OLSON................
Legal description...Lot 12 and a portion of Lot 13, Block I, of "Monticello Belmont, California" which map is filed of record in Book 5T of Maps, pages 25 and 26, recorded May 15, 1958 in office of the County Recorder of San Mateo County, California.
....Lot Size...70 ft. x 170 ft. approximately

DESCRIPTION Description of the property...7½ room frame dwelling - 1,749 square feet.....
....
....
....
Chattel mortgage (if required) on....None............

PROPOSED CONSTRUCTION
Land cost $..................Date of purchase..............................
Building cost $...............Other improvements $............Total $...........

EXISTING CONSTRUCTION
Cash ☒
Date purchased...February 1960.Age of building....New...yrs. Purchase price $..26,950.00..Trade ☐
Improvements since purchase...Cost $...........

TAXES
Not yet assessed
Actual....................................   Building $..................
Estimated....................Year.................Assessed Value: Land .. $..................
                                        Special Assessments ....$..................

INSURANCE
Existing ... $...........................   Extended Coverage ....
Recommended $.......................   Earthquake.....   ....
                                            Flood ....
Will have fire and extended coverage   Personal Property
in excess of loan amount   (required if chattel mortgage given)..............
                                            Other.................

OCCUPANCY
Vacant...................................Occupants Name.....................
Occupied...Owner......................Owner or purchaser.....................
                            Rented................., if rented monthly rent...........

EXISTING LOAN
Construction loan only by builder
Held by..........................Address...............................
Original Amount $..............Date of loan.................Maturity...............
Unpaid balance $..........Interest rate...........%. Payment $.............per............
Can loan be paid in full now...........Is loan delinquent in any manner.............

GENERAL
Is there any existing contract or indebtedness for repairs or additions...None.........
Funds from this loan will be used for:..Completion of purchase price............
Will there be a second lien....No....if so, amount $....None.....how repayable..None....

Figure 3

EMPLOYMENT STATUS.

Applicant: DONALD A. OLSON _____ (age) 38 | Co-Applicant: FRANCELLA B. OLSON _____ (age) 35
(a) Employer's name. Maybank Corporation of America
(b) Employer's address. Boston, Massachusetts
(c) Type of business. Hotel Chain
(d) Position occupied. Engineer
(e) Name and title of superior. John F. Bryant, Vice President
(f) Number of years in present employment. 10 years
(g) Prior to employment. Mordkin Company, Chicago

Co-Applicant: FRANCELLA B. OLSON (age) 35
(a) Housewife
(b)
(c)
(d)
(e)
(f)
(g)

FAMILY STATUS.
Number of years married 14
Ages of dependents 6
other than spouse 11

ANNUAL INCOME.
Base pay of applicant . . . . $ 12,000.00
Base pay of wife . Housewife . . . . $
Annual overtime or other employment
earnings . . . . $
Net income from real estate . . . . . $
Income from other sources (list sources and
amounts) . . . . $
Stocks and Bonds $ 500.00
$
$
TOTAL INCOME . . . . $ 12,500.00

LIFE INSURANCE (on applicant). Plus Company Policy
(1) Total in force, $ 32,000.00 Cash value, $ 30,000.00
(2) Less amount of loans on policies . . . . $ ---
(3) Net cash surrender value . . . . . . $ 30,000.00

SETTLEMENT REQUIREMENTS
Purchase Price or
Construction Cost (including land) . . . . $ 26,950.00
Approximate cost of closing . . . . . . $ 300.00
TOTAL . . . . $ 27,250.00
Less amount of loan applied for . . . . . $ 18,000.00
Investment required by Mortgagor . . . . . $ 9,250.00
Less amount already paid . . . . $ 2,500.00
Balance of funds to be paid . . . . $ 6,750.00
Source of these funds:
First National Bank of Boston
(Proceeds of sale of present home)

FINANCIAL STATEMENT

ASSETS	AMOUNT	LIABILITIES (Household)	AMOUNT
Cash in following Banks:		Accounts payable (except installment accounts)	100.00
First National Bank of Boston	3,200.00	Installment account payable, automobile	
		Monthly payment . . . . $	
Earnest Money Deposit on Purchase	2,500.00	Other installment accounts payable	
Estimated Resale Value of Real Estate Owned	25,000.00	Monthly payment . . . . $	
Accounts and Notes Receivable—Good		Notes payable balance due	
Stocks and Bonds (At Market Values)	8,500.00	Repayment terms for . . . . months	
Mortgages and Trust Deeds		Monthly payment . . . . $	
Furniture and Household Goods	1,000.00	Indebtedness on real estate	6,250.00
Automobile (At Market Value) . (2)	3,000.00	Other liabilities	
Other Assets (Itemize) Jewelry	1,000.00	Mortgage & Tax payts. monthly	96.00
Salary (month)	1,000.00	Life Insurance	40.00
		Salary - Deduct Taxes	500.00
		TOTAL LIABILITIES	6,986.00
		Subtract Total Liabilities from Total Assets	45,200.00
TOTAL ASSETS TOTAL	45,200.00	DIFFERENCE (NET WORTH)	38,214.00

REAL ESTATE OWNED (Address)	Value	Loan Balance	Annual Gross Income	Annual Expense Inc. Loan Charges	Annual Net Income
45 Winston Road	$25,000.00	$6,250.00	Home		
Natick, Massachusetts					

Have sold house and accepted down payment of $2,500.00. Should close within 10 days.

To induce lender to make this loan, applicant declares all the information given herein to be true and complete to the best of his knowledge. Applicant states that he or she knows of no adverse interest or claim affecting the Title to the subject property, except as herein expressly set out. Applicant agrees to furnish to lender, at applicants expense, the following:
1. Credit Report by a standard agency.
2. ATA Policy of Title Insurance in an amount, and from, a company acceptable to the lender, such policy showing the lender's deed of trust or mortgage to be a first lien.
3. Photographs.
4. Termite Inspection (when required).
5. Survey and such recording or notary fees as lender may deem necessary.

Applicant herewith authorizes Bryant-Johnson Mortgage Company to order any of the above and expressly agrees to promptly reimburse them for same, irrespective of approval or rejection by lender of this loan application.

Applicant agrees to pay to Bryant-Johnson Mortgage Co. a loan commitment fee of $180.00 upon receiving approval of the loan upon the terms and conditions herein applied for.

Date February 10, 1960

Telephone Number CEDAR 5-1234

Mail address 45 Winston Road,
Natick, Massachusetts
or
Maybank Corporation
315 Montgomery Street
San Francisco
Telephone Number - YUkon 1-3232

(Signed) DONALD A. OLSON
(Applicant sign here)

(Signed) FRANCELLA B. OLSON
(Applicant sign here)

Figure 3. (Continued)

NORTHWESTERN LIFE INSURANCE COMPANY
SEATTLE, WASHINGTON
APPRAISAL REPORT

February 10, 1960

Property Address __#10 Wildwood Lane, Belmont, California__

Borrower __DONALD A. OLSON and FRANCELLA B. OLSON__ Existing Construction __X__ Proposed____

N

W   See Plot Attached   E

S

Legal Description

__See attached sheet__

__(Metes and Bounds description)__

LAND and UTILITIES

Size of Land __Irregular__   Level __X__   Easements – Location and Use

Total Area __12,000 sq.ft.__   Slope _____   None

Street Surface	Sidewalks	Water Supply System	Sewage Disposal System	Electricity
Hard Surface	Yes	Yes	Yes	Yes

CONSTRUCTION

Building Dimensions
1,749 sq.ft. plus garage 536 sq.ft.

Total Square Feet
2,285 sq.ft.

Size of Basement
None

Finished ___ ___
        yes no

Age and Condition	Architectural Appearance	Alignment
New Excellent	Excellent	Satisfactory

Walls and Finish	Type of Construction	Heating System and Fuel
Sheet Rock Painted	Double construction	Central Heat Forced air

Roof Wood shingle	Woodwork Painted	Floors Concrete	Number of Fireplaces 2

Size of Garage   Sq. feet __536__   Carport ____No____

In Basement __No__   Detached __No__   Attached __Yes__

INTERIOR LIVING AREA

No. of Bedrooms __4__   Size of Bedrooms __12' x 15'__ , __12' x 13'__ , __12' x 13'__, __11' x 12'__

_____ , _____ No. of Full Baths __2__   No. of Half Baths __None__

Total No. of Rooms __7½__ Family Room __No__   Utility Room __8' x 9'__

Kitchen __Yes__ Recreation Room __No__   Misc. Rooms __None__

Dining Area __Yes__ Den __No__   _____   _____

Dining Room __No__ Living Room __14' x 16'__   _____   _____

GROUND APPEARANCE			MISCELLANEOUS EXTRAS		
Patio Good	Pool None	Landscaping Good	Carpet No	Dishwasher Yes	Refrigerator No
			Drapes No		

Figure 4

GENERAL

Consistency with neighborhood_____(average_____; better__X__; sub-average_____)

Sale and rental value of typical properties in neighborhood $25,000 to $30,000   Blocks to:
No rentals - sales are from

Transportation_2 blocks_; Shopping center_3 blocks___; Schools__4 blocks_____

ESTIMATE OF VALUE

REPLACEMENT ESTIMATE: (including required repairs)

House...1,749 square feet at $11.75 .... $ 20,500.00

Garage .... $ 2,500.00

Other Improvements.. $_____

Total... $ 23,000.00

Replacement valuation of improvements .... $ 23,000.00

Land Value... $ 4,000.00

REPLACEMENT ESTIMATE .... $ 27,000.00

Reasonable sale value of property on usual terms.............................. $ 27,000.00

Monthly rental value (in good condition)......................$Est. $235.00 to $250.00 per month

City___Belmont_____State__California__Date_February 10,_____19 60____

I have read the application. I have satisfied myself that the legal description contained in this application is correct. I have satisfied myself as to the rights of the parties in possession who state that they are_not yet occupied but will be owner occupied on or about February 20, 1960.

In my opinion this property has a value as follows:

Land ....$ 4,000.00

Buildings..............................$ 23,000.00

Other Improvements ....$ 27,000.00

Total............$_____

and I recommend a loan of .... $ 18,000.00

See notes attached re Land Value

Kitchen equipment includes built-in oven, dishwasher (all "Westinghouse") and a

"Waste King" garbage disposal. Sash is aluminum, entry hall floor is polished Mexican

Terrazo. Walls to wainscott and floors in baths are ceramic tile. Fixtures are

"Kohler" and are colored. Large masonry fireplace in living room and brick Bar-B-Que

in kitchen.

(Signed) RAYMOND S. ROYAL
Appraiser
February 10, 1960

Figure 4. (Continued)

Approval or Disapproval of the Loan

Space is provided at the end of a typical conventional-loan application form for the approval or disapproval of the loan application by the loan committee or the authorized loan officer. Interest rate, monthly payment, and term of loan are set forth above the signature of the loan officer or signatures of the loan committee.

Variations in Methods of Filing Application

The written application, as previously described, has many advantages. Some applications are received by telephone, others by mail, a few are transmitted verbally. In the latter cases very little information is available for the lender. All available information in each such case is immediately transcribed on the loan application form and the missing data are obtained later.

VA and FHA applications will be reviewed in chapters which follow. A farm-loan application will also be described.

Types of Properties on Which Loans are Made

Although a majority of loans are made on one- to four-family dwellings, the following additional types of properties are found in most mortgage loan portfolios and classified as follows:

1. Dwellings (one- to four-family)
2. Flats (with stores below)
3. Apartments
4. Stores and office buildings
5. Industrial buildings
6. Hotels
7. Unimproved (industrial)
8. Unimproved (residential)
9. Farms

10. Other—Special-purpose (includes churches, theaters, lodge halls, fraternity houses, garages, service and gas stations, golf courses, and bowling alleys)

Some lenders specialize in loans other than home loans. For example, in industrial centers there is a great activity in loans on industrial properties. Some large life insurance companies do a great deal of hotel-loan business. On the other hand some lenders make no loans except on homes. Mutual savings banks and savings and loan associations make virtually no farm loans. It is important therefore that a person engaged in mortgage lending activities know the types of properties on which each lender will consider making loans.

Processing the Application

In the initial interview in which the application for the loan is made an able interviewer will quickly review the facts shown by the application and will be able to judge the soundness of the proposed transaction. If there are any doubts about possible approval of the loan, the applicant will be informed in the initial interview.

If the facts indicate that a loan will be approved, the application will be recorded and numbered and sent to the appraisal department. After appraisal has been completed, the entire transaction will be analyzed by a loan officer or the loan committee. The security, the applicant's credit and ability to repay the loan, the interest rate, and maturity of the loan will be analyzed, and if the decision is to make the loan, the application will be approved and signed. After this the applicant will be notified by telephone, by letter, or by the interested broker.

STANDARD SPECIFICATIONS FOR RESIDENTIAL CONSTRUCTION

Residence for

MR. & MRS. WILLIAM R. BROWN

to be built on

Lot 5, Block 3
Sunset Park Subdivision No. 2
Palo Alto, California

GIBSON CONSTRUCTION COMPANY
Contractors
Palo Alto, California

SPECIFICATIONS

1. GENERAL CONDITIONS:

   A. The plans which shall accompany these specifications, including all figures and references which may be inscribed in same, shall hereby be considered a part of these specifications, and the General Contractor and all Sub-contractors shall be governed by both. If, however, there is

Figure 5

a discrepancy discovered in either the plans or the specifications, or both, the Sub-contractors shall request a
definition or interpretation from the General Contractor
and same shall be final.

B. The General Contractor shall give his personal supervision
to the work or shall at all times have some competent person on the work to act for him. The General Contractor and
all Sub-contractors must comply with public laws and ordinances, and shall protect the Owners against all damage
from violations of same.

C. The Owners shall apply for the installation of a water
meter and pay for same. All water used by the Contractor
and Sub-contractors during the course of construction shall
be paid for by the General Contractor.

2. STRIKES AND LOCKOUTS: The General Contractor or Sub-contractors in his employ will be held strictly responsible for the construction and proper execution of the work herein defined, but
shall not be held responsible for delays which may result through
strikes and lockouts, acts of God, and conditions which may develop from same which are beyond control of the General Contractor or his Sub-contractors, or those in his employ. Should same
occur, the General Contractor or Sub-contractors shall not be released from the responsibility of satisfactory completion of the
work.

3. COMPENSATION INSURANCE: The General Contractor must carry
Compensation Insurance, Public Liability and Property Damage to
amply protect himself from losses due to accident or other cas-
ualty to men employed by him or his Sub-contractors, or others
for which he could be responsible. General Contractor shall be
responsible for any and all damage to his work by reason of the
action of the elements until the entire building is completed and
accepted.

4. FIRE INSURANCE: The building shall be covered by fire insurance in the amount of not less than $18,000.00. In case of fire
the General Contractor and Sub-contractors shall be reimbursed
from said insurance for any losses which they may have incurred.

5. BUILDING PERMITS, LICENSE, ETC.: City building permit shall be
secured and paid for by the General Contractor for the general
construction. Sub-contractors shall secure and pay for all permits, licenses and inspection services as may be required by the
City of Palo Alto in the County of Santa Clara in the State of
California, and when required, must give sufficient evidence of
same.

Figure 5. (Continued)

6. <u>STATE UNEMPLOYMENT ACT AND</u> The General Contractor and all
   <u>FEDERAL OLD AGE PENSION</u>:   Sub-contractors must give suffi-
                                  cient evidence that they have com-
plied with the Federal Old Age Pension and State Unemployment Act
and must promptly pay when due moneys collected for same on this
project.

7. <u>OWNER'S RIGHTS</u>: The Owners to have free access at all times
for inspection of work, but shall not direct building operations.
No changes will be made unless ordered in writing by the Owners
and accepted by the General Contractor. The work shall not be de-
layed because of anticipated changes.

8. <u>MATERIALS AND WORKMANSHIP</u>: Any materials and labor necessary
for the proper construction and thorough execution of the work
must be furnished and performed, whether the same be particularly
specified and illustrated or not. All materials to be the best of
their respective kinds as specified, and the workmanship to be
performed in the most approved and skilled manner.

9. <u>EXCAVATION</u>: General Contractor shall first examine premises
and become familiar with existing conditions. Do all excavations
and back filling for foundations and floor.

10. <u>CONCRETE WORK</u>: Execute all concrete work on plans as follows:
Foundations, walls, piers and floors. All concrete work for footings, walls, columns, curtain walls and fire walls to be composed of 1-94# sack of cement of standard brand, two parts of
fine and four parts of course aggregate; or 1-94# sack cement of
a standard brand to $2\frac{1}{2}$ parts of fine and $3\frac{1}{2}$ parts of coarse
aggregate; with water ratio not to exceed $7\frac{1}{2}$ gallons. Concrete
for floor slab shall be of same mix as above described and shall
be a monolithic finish, left with a smooth surface.

11. <u>REINFORCING STEEL</u>: All reinforcing steel as shown on plan
shall be installed according to the best practice of the trade.
Steel shall be held free from all woodwork and shall be held in a
perpendicular or horizontal position or as formed by being wired
together with No. 14 tie-wire.

12. <u>CARPENTER WORK AND LUMBER</u>: The lumber used in the building
shall be free from imperfections impairing its durability or
strength. All framing lumber shall be Douglas Fir, mill sized and
framed in accordance with local practice and ordinances. All
framing lumber shall be of the following sizes:

   A. <u>Plates</u>: Shall be single 2x4, #2, D.F., SISIE.
   B. <u>Girders</u>: Shall be 4x6, No. 1, D.F.
   C. <u>Joists Floor</u>: Shall be 2x10, No. 1, 16" on center.
   D. <u>Studs</u>: Shall be 2x4 #2, D.F. 16" on center.
   E. <u>Rafters</u>: Shall be 2x4, #1, D.F. SISIE, 24" O.C.

Figure 5. (Continued)

F. <u>Roofing Sheathing</u>: Shall be 1x6 or 1x8, #3 D.F., SISIE.
G. <u>Subfloor</u>: Shall be 1x6, 1x8, No. 3 & Better, D.F.
H. <u>Wall Sheathing</u>: Shall be water repellent gyplap as manu-
   factured by the U. S. Gypsum Company.

13. <u>EXTERIOR PLASTERING</u>: Exterior plastering shall be applied in
four coats as follows:

<u>First</u> shall be composed of one part waterproofed cement and
   three parts clean, sharp, washed sand of a standard grade.

<u>Second</u> coat shall be of same mix as first coat.

<u>Third and Fourth</u> coats shall be of a standard brushcoat mate-
   rial applied as specified by Acme Stucco Company of San
   Francisco.

First and Second coats shall be applied with a trowel and at
least twenty-four hours shall elapse between application of the
first and second coats. The total thickness of these two coats
shall be at least 3/4". The cement shall be placed firmly against
all woodwork and shall be applied to approximately 4" below
grade.
   The Exterior Plastering shall be applied over 18 gauge 1"
mesh wire, which shall be secured to the studs with Gem Furring
nails. The building shall be covered with 15# building felt prior
to the application of the wire.

14. <u>INTERIOR PLASTERING</u>: The entire interior shall be lathed with
5/16" gypsum lath. All interior angles, except closets shall be
reinforced with a strip of metal lath or chicken wire. All
arrises shall have a metal corner bead applied to same, which
shall reach from floor to ceiling.

Plastering shall be done in two coats. The First Coat shall be
composed of one part of gypsum plaster of any standard brand to
2½ parts of clean, sharp sand. After this coat has been applied
to a thickness which should be flush with 3/4 grounds, it shall
be allowed to set before the Second Coat shall be applied.

Second Coat shall be applied of California Stucco throughout
the interior of the building and shall be a light texture, except
Kitchen and Bath, which shall be trowelled smooth for painting.
After the plastering has been completed, the building shall be
thoroughly clean of all lathing and plastering material, both interior and exterior, and all debris shall be hauled away from the
job by the Plastering Contractor.

15. <u>DOORS AND DOOR FRAMES</u>: All outside and inside door frames
shall be wood.

Figure 5. (Continued)

16. INTERIOR FINISH: All interior finish shall be best quality Oregon Pine and interior jambs to be 3/4 Oregon Pine. Trim for doors and windows to be moulded wood trim.

17. SHEET METAL WORK: Flash roof with 26 gauge galvanized iron. All flashing and galvanized iron shall be shop painted. Provide vents for furnace and water heater as shown on plan. Furnace to be 120,000 B.T.U. input of a Standard Brand.

18. ELECTRICAL WORK: All electrical work shall be furnished and installed by the Contractor and shall be in accordance with the latest edition of the National Code and Regulations of the Board of Underwriters and City Ordinances. The distribution of lighting is to be as shown on plans and elevations. All panel and switch boxes shall be installed and of a size as made and required by law.

19. ROOFING: The entire roof shall be covered with No. 1 cedar shingles.

20. FIXTURES: All lighting fixtures shall be furnished and in-stalled by Contractor. (Cost of fixtures not to exceed $60.00.)

21. PAINTING: All exterior metal shall be painted with red lead. All exterior woodwork shall be given three coats of paint of a color selected by the Owners. All exterior metal shall have a second coat of the same color. All interior finish woodwork to receive two coats of flat and one coat of enamel with colors as selected.

22. PLUMBING: Plumbing contractor to furnish and install all water, gas and sewer pipe. Also, furnish and install all plumbing fixtures, dig and fill trenches for pipes, make all connections between meters and sewer and building. All work is to comply with Rules and Regulations of the City of Palo Alto and County of Santa Clara.

Furnish and lay cast iron sewer for building with necessary connections, elbows, traps, clean-outs, fresh air inlets, etc. and connect with sewer in street. All sewer pipes to be standard cast iron, and to have proper pitch joints, caulked with oakum and molten lead. All vents and fixtures properly trapped with sanitary fittings, and all fixtures to have proper air chambers. All shut-off valves and pipes connected to fixtures and exposed shall have a chromium finish. All water pipe to be copper tubing. A shut-off valve shall be provided between meter and building, and in supply line to water heater. Provide four water faucets for exterior of building, install where directed.

FIXTURES: All fixtures shall be Kohler or equal. All white.

Lavatories: 1-Kohler white enamel, 18" x 20 tile in, complete with chromium faucets: 1 — standard lavatory, No. F367, Size 18x20, white

Figure 5. (Continued)

Toilets: Shall be Glenco bowl with white Church seat.
Water Heater: 1 – 30 gal. Day and Night "Crest", or equal,
  automatic gas storage heater.
Sink: Shall be two compartment 18" x 30".
Showers: Shall be installed as shown, including copper pans.
Gas Piping: Gas shall be piped and connected with furnace.
  All piping shall meet the requirements of the Pacific Gas &
  Electric Co.

23. HARDWOOD FLOORS: Floors throughout shall be white clear oak
except kitchen and bath. Same shall be 3/8 x 2" or if their size
is not available, the size and thickness obtainable shall be
used. The oak floors shall be sanded, stained and sealed and
given two coats of shellac and thoroughly waxed.

24. LINOLEUM: The kitchen floor shall be covered with $\frac{1}{4}$" ply-
wood. After this has been done, the entire surface shall be
covered with a standard grade inlaid linoleum of a pattern and
color as selected by Owners. The kitchen shall have a cove base.

25. TILE: The walls of baths shall be tile 4' up from floor,
shower 7' up from floor; both baths #1 and #2 shall have a tile
floor; bath #1 shall have a tile top vanity case and kitchen sink
shall be tiled as shown. The selection of this tile must meet the
approval of Owners and Contractors. Any standard brand of tile
may be used if acceptable to the Contractors. The tile shall be
set in cement and after same has become thoroughly hard and firm,
the tile joints shall be filled with pure white waterproof tile
grout. All work shall be left in a neat and workmanlike manner.

26. HARDWARE: The General Contractor to furnish and install all
rough and finished hardware, complete.

27. CLEANING: After construction has been completed, the premises
shall be left clean and free from material or debris.

28. FINALLY: The time required by the General Contractor shall
not be more than 65 working days. All Sub–contractors shall install and complete their work as required by the Gibson Construction Company, the General Contractors.

Dated 11–8 , 1960   Signed   *William R. Brown*

Dated 11–8 , 1960   Signed   *Fredda S. Brown*

                           GIBSON CONSTRUCTION CO.
                           General Contractors

Dated 11–8 , 1960   Signed by   *W. A. Gibson*
                                          W. A. Gibson

Figure 5. (Continued)

Need for a Written Application for a Mortgage Loan

A written application establishes a clear-cut basis for the deal and also establishes a legal relationship between the parties, which includes terms of loan, costs, insurance, taxes, and many other items. Probably just as important are the customer-relations and public relations aspects of the transaction.

Conventional-loan Applications Covering Construction Loans

Individuals

If an application for a construction loan to an individual is filed, the same form of application as previously described is used. Together with this form there should be submitted two copies of the plans and specification (Figure 3), the contractor's bid, and two copies of description of materials. Two copies of plans and specifications and description of materials are usually required, as the lender submits a copy of each to the VA or FHA if it is to be such a loan.

Operative Builders

The same form is used for applications covering conventional construction loans to builders and must be accompanied by a construction loan control sheet.

No work of any nature should be done, or material delivered, on the property on which a construction loan is to be made prior to recording the mortgage or deed of trust through the title company.

Plans and specifications must be submitted to the lender for examination and approval prior to the granting of the loan and must be left with the lender until the building is completed. Plans and specifications should be signed and dated by the borrowers and the contractor at the time the contract is signed.

The building contract should be carefully analyzed by the lender and should be recorded after the mortgage. A bond should be required of the builder when there is any question as to his ability to perform the contract. During the course of erection of the building, hazard insurance should be taken out with loss, if any, payable to the lender.

Importance of Construction Loans

Making loans to finance new construction has become a very important factor in the mortgage lending industry. A lender who makes such a loan to an individual usually retains the mortgage after the loan is made or obtains a mortgage from the purchaser of the home built with funds loaned to the builder. Such financing also enables the mortgage lender to participate in the development of new-home building programs that result in community improvement and rehabilitation of old areas. Construction loans lead to better-planned homes, hence better mortgage security.

Types of Construction Loans

Construction loans are made to an individual or to an investor on a long-term conventional basis or on a short-term interim-financing basis where the ultimate loan is to be purchased by an insurance company or some other type of investor on a prior-commitment basis. Such loans are also made to operative builders who develop tracts and subdivisions on (1) conventional-loan basis, (2) FHA dual-commitment basis, or (3) blanket-project basis. In the latter case one conventional loan is made to cover the construction of all the homes in the tract. Individual loans, such as FHA, VA, or conventional loans, are then made to the purchaser of the homes.

The Individual Borrower

Construction loans are made available to the individual by banks, savings and loan associations, mutual savings banks, insurance companies, mortgage companies, and individuals. Some lenders will make larger construction loans than others, but a bank loan usually amounts to approximately 60 to legal maximum of 75 per cent of the current cost, a savings and loan association loans about 80 to a legal maximum of 90 per cent, and an insurance company loans approximately 60 to a legal maximum of 75 per cent of the current cost.

Consideration of the Application

The cost of the project, including the cost of the lot, the cost of construction, and the cost of financing, is carefully analyzed by the interviewer. The borrower's investment should be known—whether the lot has been paid for and the amount of cash he has for handling the transaction. The amount to be loaned is based on the appraisal of the plans and the lot and the borrower's ability to service the loan. In addition to this, the cost of the entire project, the ability and financial status of the builder, and the contract between the borrower and the builder must also be carefully analyzed.

Loans to Operative Builders

These financing problems involve:
1. Land purchase and development
2. Construction financing
3. Financing of sales

Many operative builders have funds available for purchase and development of a tract or will borrow commercial funds for this purpose. Most lenders are very conservative in lending on such developments, and private financing is often required. When they do make such loans, they want to be assured that they will also be in position to make loans to ultimate purchasers of the homes.

Builders Control Service

Some lenders handle the inspection and progress reports and the disbursements on construction loans in their own mortgage loan departments, but most lenders use a builders control service to handle these technical operations and procedures.

The basic function of a builders control service is to ensure that a proposed construction project is sound from the point of view of all interested participants: the builder, the owner, the land developer, and the investor.

This service usually includes a systematic analysis of plans, financing, independent cost estimates, establishment of building funds, inspections, and disbursements and accounting.

Through the method of establishing separate control accounts for each project, all accounting pertaining to one project is isolated from other projects. In this manner clients are provided with accurate figures for each building control project and are relieved of a great deal of clerical work.

Construction loan proceeds are assigned to the builder control service by the lender for each project handled. Such moneys are ear marked for specific construction objectives. This is important for the builder because it assures him that funds will be available as needed during all phases of construction.

The general disbursal of funds is accomplished through a budget established with the builder. This budget includes all items covered in the reconciled construction cost breakdown.

All receipts and disbursements for a specific project are channeled through its specific bank account, and the builder pays all his bills by issuing disbursements orders on the particular builder control service.

Amount of Loan and Data Required

As previously stated, a lender will usually loan 60 to 75 per cent of the estimated current market price of the property, and such a loan must have a release-price schedule which will pay off the loan in full when 60 per cent of the lots are released.

A map of the tract, a cost estimate for improvements, proposed sales prices, and information about the homes to be built must be submitted to the lender in complete detail.

Building Contracts

The filing in the office of the county recorder, before the commencement of work, of the original contract (see Figure 6) between the owner and the contractor is the equivalent of giving actual notice of the terms of the contract by the owner to all persons performing work or furnishing material thereunder. The contract though not so filed is valid as to all persons, except that when not filed, liens, other than those of the contractor, are not limited by the contract price.

Evidence of Commencement of Work

It is important that evidence of commencement of work at the site be completely understood. Any one of the following comprises such evidence:

1. Building materials or equipment deposited—whether on the property in question or on an adjoining property if designed for use on the first-mentioned
2. Foundation stakes set by surveyor (not land boundary stakes)
3. Test holes dug
4. Load of dirt deposited
5. Trees and weeds removed
6. Water meter set in parking place
7. Preliminary landscaping started
8. Installation of sprinkling system begun
9. Demolition of old buildings started
10. Any action visible by an inspection of the land

Original Contractor

The original contractor is one who contracts directly with the owner or his agent to do the work or furnish the materials for the whole work of construction or for a particular portion of the work. These arrangements with the owner or agent are usually accompanied by a written contract, which, if satisfactory, is signed by both parties.

C O N T R A C T

between

GIBSON CONSTRUCTION CO.
General Contractors

and

WILLIAM R. & FREDDA S. BROWN
O w n e r s

for a one story dwelling
to be erected on Lot 5, Block 3,
Sunset Park Subdivision, Palo Alto
Santa Clara County, California

CONTRACT FOR CONSTRUCTION OF A ONE STORY, WOOD FRAME DWELLING
To be erected on Lot 5, Block 3, Sunset Park Subdivision #4
Palo Alto, California

- 0 -

Contract between WILLIAM R. BROWN and FREDDA S. BROWN, hereinafter known as owners, and GIBSON CONSTRUCTION CO., a California
Co-partnership, hereinafter known as contractor, is made with respect to the construction of a one story wood frame dwelling to
be erected on property described as follows: Lot 5, Block 3, Sunset Park Subdivision #4, Palo Alto, California.

There is attached to this contract, and by reference made a
part hereof, the following:

1. An instrument entitled Specifications.

2. Architectural Plans.

3. Both the Specifications and the Architectural Plans are
hereby referred to and by such reference incorporated in and made
a part of this contract. The Owners and Contractor shall sign
each and every sheet of the plans and two copies of the Specifications.

4. The Contractor agrees to perform and complete work described
in the Specifications and as shown on drawings, and to furnish
all services, materials and supplies necessary and to complete
the construction, using the materials as shown or specified in
sixty-five (65) working days, with the following exceptions:

(a) If materials specified are not available, contractor reserves the right to use other materials, which are in his opinion
of equal quality and which would pass requirements as set forth
and required by the City of Palo Alto, and as set forth in the
requirements of the Federal Housing Administration.

Figure 6

(b) Contractor shall not provide Fire Insurance. Such insurance is to be carried by the owner and a copy of Loss Payable Clause in favor of the contractor shall be forwarded to the contractor within ten days after construction work has begun.

5. Contractor agrees to leave the building broom clean and free from all excess construction materials, ready for occupancy by the owner, and agrees to protect the owner from any liens for materials, men and all mechanics.

The owner agrees to pay upon demand of the contractor the sum of Eighteen thousand dollars ($18,000.00) as follows:

When foundation has been completed and sub-
    flooring installed $3,600.00

When building has been framed, roof shingled, and
    exterior closed in   3,600.00

When first coat of plaster is completed on interior
    and exterior   3,600.00

Upon completion of building   3,600.00

Thirty-five days after Notice of Completion has been
    filed, or building accepted by owner, or after
    work has been completed by contractor $3,600.00

Owner agrees to pay for Extras when presented with
    statement for same by contractor. Extras will only
    be installed when owner has approved same in
    writing.

Should owners fail to make payments as outlined above, it shall be deemed cause for cessation of performance by the contractor, and the entire amount of contract price shall immediately become due.

Owners agree to refrain from interfering with the construction work and to accept the work and sign a Notice of Completion when advised by the contractor that the work has been completed, but reserves the right to notify the contractor if, in his opinion, the specifications and plans and terms of this contract are not being adhered to, and contractor shall accept such notice and make proper correction to conform to plans and specifications. Owners also reserve the right, should the contractor abandon construction of the building, or fail to complete or carry on the work as specified, and upon ten days' written notice to the contractor, to terminate this contract and to perform and complete any and all portions of the work which may remain uncompleted and to charge costs of same to contractor.

Figure 6. (Continued)

Contractor agrees for the period of one year after the Notice of Completion has been filed to remedy any defect, either in material or workmanship, at his own expense. However, this is not a guarantee against earth movements or that contractor will remedy such defects as cracks and settlements or shrinkage of lumber due to factors beyond his control.

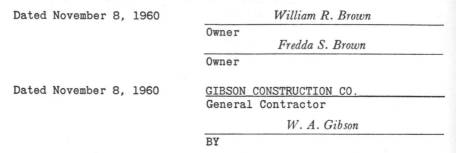

Dated November 8, 1960   *William R. Brown*
                             _____
                             Owner
                                    Fredda S. Brown
                             _____
                             Owner

Dated November 8, 1960   GIBSON CONSTRUCTION CO.
                             General Contractor
                                    W. A. Gibson
                             _____
                             BY

Figure 6. (Continued)

Completion

The occupation or use accompanied by cessation of labor therefrom, or the acceptance of a building or improvement by the owner or his agent, or the cessation of labor thereon or upon any contract for 90 days, or the filing of a notice of completion by the owner in the county recorder's office comprises completion of the project.

Notice of Completion or Notice of Cessation of Labor

Notice of Completion or Notice of Cessation of Labor must be filed in the office of the county recorder of the county in which the property is located within ten days after completion of any contract or work of improvement, or within ten days after cessation from labor for a period of 90 days. This Notice of Completion or Notice of Cessation of Labor must show date of completion or cessation, names and addresses of all owners, description of property (legal and street address), and name of original contractor, if any.

The notices must be signed by at least one of the several owners.

Lien Period

Original contractors have sixty days in which to file any liens for unpaid services, while all others have thirty days after the filing of a valid notice of completion of the project to take such action. If no Notice of Completion or Notice of Cessation of Labor is filed, or if these documents are not properly drawn, or properly signed, or if not filed within proper time, all claimants have ninety days in which to file liens.

Mechanics' Liens

This is probably the most difficult lien for a lender to control. State statutes generally contain provisions which specify that one who furnishes labor or materials that go into buildings constructed upon land or one who brings about other improvements of real estate is given a statutory lien upon the premises which have been improved by his contribution.

On compliance with statutory requirements as to technical notices to be given and as to time limitations on steps to be taken, anyone having an unpaid claim for either labor or materials may maintain a suit to enforce his lien. The lender through the title company by a preliminary report will be informed of any suits of this nature that are pending.

In most states such liens run from ninety days from filing the date of the Notice of a Mechanic's Lien. If during this period the lender started foreclosure proceedings, the lien would remain in full effect. In most jurisdictions foreclosure proceedings must be prosecuted to trial within two years.

Disbursements on Building Loans

Disbursements on a construction loan are quite complicated, and various methods are used. The building cost can be divided into four equal parts and disbursements made as follows: (1) twenty-five per cent when the building is framed, roof decked, and walls enclosed, and provided a written certification is made by a competent member of the mortgage lender's staff that the building is being constructed on the lot securing the loan and the building conforms substantially to the description which appears in the plans and specifications; (2) twenty-five per cent when the interior and exterior have been rough-plastered or covered with a substitute described in the plans and specifications, or written certification by a competent member of the lender's staff that the work has been satisfactorily completed; (3) twenty-five per cent when the building has been completed, Notice of Completion filed, and on written certification by a competent member of the lender's staff that the building has been completed and decorated as per plans and specifications; (4) twenty-five per cent and final payment after the expiration of the lien period if no liens appear on record. From this payment a sufficient sum must be withheld by the lender to pay loan fees or other charges which remain unpaid.

In some construction cases the building costs are divided into five equal payments, which are as follows: (1) twenty per cent when subflooring has been laid in the case of a one-story building, or in the case of two-story buildings when the first story has been framed and the subflooring for the second story laid, when accompanied by a written certification by a competent member of the lender's staff that the building is being constructed on the lot securing the loan and that the building is substantially as described in the plans and specifications; (2) twenty per cent when the building has been enclosed and roofed and the rough plumbing and wiring installed, on written certification by a competent member of the lender's staff; (3) twenty per cent when the interior and exterior have been rough-plastered, or covered with a substitute described in plans and specifications, on written certification by a competent member of the staff that the work has been completed satisfactorily; (4) twenty per cent when the building has been completed, Notice of Completion filed, and on written certification by a competent member of the lender's staff that the building has been completed and decorated as per plans and specifications; (5) twenty per cent and final payment after the expiration of the lien period and if no liens appear on record. From this payment a sufficient sum must be withheld to pay loan fees or other charges which remain unpaid.

The proceeds of a building loan are usually disbursed upon the inspector's report of progress, usually indicated on a Loan Progress and Disbursement Record. Inspections are made only after notification by the borrower and the contractor that the building has progressed to such a state that a disbursement is desired on the loan.

As outlined above, the cost of the proposed building and the amount of the loan are closely related. The difference between the cost of the proposed building (contract price plus extras) and the amount of the loan must be furnished by the borrower, to be applied on first payments due. This places the lender in a position where it has at all times sufficient funds to complete the building. Where a substantial difference exists between the cost of the building and the amount of the loan, the contributions by the owner should be deposited with the lender and applied to the first payments due. This method also tends to keep prospective borrowers from overestimating building costs. A specific example, showing clearly this method, is as follows:

Mr. A is to construct a building to cost........... $9,500.00
Lender has a building loan of.................... 5,000.00
To be provided by borrower.................... $4,500.00

State of Construction	By Borrower	By Lender	Total
Frame erected............	$2,375.00	....	$2,375.00
Brown coat plaster........	2,125.00	$ 250.00	2,375.00
Completion..............	....	2,375.00	2,375.00
After lien period..........	....	2,375.00	2,375.00
Totals................	$4,500.00	$5,000.00	$9,500.00

In some cases second-mortgage loans may supply the money to be furnished by borrowers. In this event the foregoing table is unchanged; the proceeds of the second mortgage are applied on the payments before drawing payments from Loan Commitments.

Where there is no contract the receipted bill for amounts paid by borrowers must be furnished. When any doubt arises on a building loan as to the ability of the contractor, or borrower, to complete the building, all receipted bills must be checked carefully by the lender.

Liens

If any liens are filed before the expiration of the lien period (as indicated below), or if the contractor or owner should become involved in bankruptcy proceedings, or die, the portion of the loan not yet advanced is held by the lender and no further advance made, until authorized by agreement of all parties concerned, or by court order.

The summary regarding mechanics' liens which follows should be borne in mind in connection with mortgage loans. It is not intended to be exhaustive or to cover all questions which may arise. All legal questions regarding mechanics' liens and similar matters should be cleared with the lender's attorneys.

Priority of Mechanics' Liens over the Mortgage or Deed of Trust

Some mechanics' liens take precedence over a deed of trust or mortgage when the work of improvement is started before the deed of trust or mortgage is recorded, unless the lender files in the county recorder's office a bond signed by the owner or contractor of not less than 75 per cent of the face amount of the deed of trust or mortgage. Furnishing such a bond by an owner or contractor may in some instances render a loan ineligible for FHA insurance or VA guaranty, therefore, it is important to record the deed of trust or mortgage before any materials are delivered or any work is started.

Notice to Withhold Funds (Stop Notice)

In most jurisdictions, if a Notice to Withhold (Stop Notice) is filed within the statutory time for recording claims of lien and is accompanied by a bond of $1\frac{1}{4}$ times the amount of the claim, the lender must withhold enough funds from disbursement to answer the claim. Sureties on the bond may be individuals or a surety company. If individuals, the lender may give notice in writing within twenty days that the sureties are insufficient, in which case a corporate surety must be furnished within twenty days. No assignment of these funds by the owner or contractor takes priority over such a claim. The withheld funds must be released if the contractor has filed a bond of at least 50 per cent of the amount of the contract before work was commenced, guaranteeing payment of all such claims, or if after the Stop Notice is filed, the owner, contractor, or subcontractor delivers to the lender a bond in the same amount as that which accompanied the Stop Notice.

Notice of Completion and Notice of Cessation

If there is more than one original contract for a job, the owner may file a Notice of Completion within ten days after completion of each contract instead of waiting for completion of the entire job. An incorrect date of completion does not invalidate the Notice of Completion, if the actual date of completion is within ten days preceding the date of filing. The owner may file a Notice of Cessation of Labor at any time not less than thirty days after such cessation. The general contractor has 60 days and others have thirty days after each Notice of Completion or Notice of Cessation of Labor to file claims. Notice of Completion and Notice of Cessation of Labor must include the street address of the property, but if the address is incorrect or is not given, a sufficient legal description is satisfactory. If no Notice of Completion or Notice of Cessation of Labor is filed, the lien period expires ninety days after the date of actual completion or 150 days after cessation, as the case may be.

Interest on Building Loans

As disbursements are made on building loans, the amount disbursed is entered on the lender's loan journal at the applicable rate, with a corresponding entry on the ledger card. Interest is charged only on the loan as cash is disbursed. Some lenders charge this interest on the entire amount of the loan. Any changes of a loan interest rate should be recorded on the loan journal, crediting the principal amount at the old rate and debiting the amount at the new rate.

Advances to Borrowers

All incidental expenses advanced for the account of borrowers in connection with making mortgage loans, such as notary fees, recording charges, cost of title search and policy, preparation of papers, appraisal fees, and other items necessary to complete the loan transaction are usually charged to an account called Advances to Borrowers. All these items must be cleared from the account at the time of the disbursement of each loan by deduction from the amount disbursed to the borrower. On renewal loans where no funds are available, the lender should be reimbursed by the borrower as soon as possible to clear the item from the account.

Taxes and Insurance Paid by Lender

During the life of a loan where it is necessary for the lender to pay insurance premiums or taxes, the amount of these payments is usually carried under Advances to Borrowers—Loan Charges and is collected from the borrower at the earliest opportunity and cleared from the account. This delinquency constitutes a default in the mortgage or deed of trust. When it is necessary to advance funds to pay taxes or insurance for borrowers, a service charge is usually collected at the time the borrower reimburses the lender for the advance. This charge when paid is usually credited to Operating Income—Loan Charges.

Payment of Fire Insurance Premiums

When paying fire insurance premiums, lenders usually make a cashier's check payable to the insurance company or authorized agent. It is forwarded to the broker or agent with the bill which is to be receipted and later filed in the loan folder. In the event the cashier's check is returned by a broker with instructions to make check payable to him, the check is then forwarded direct to the insurance company, or authorized agent, requesting a receipted bill.

Collection of Loan Charges

Loan Charges Collected in Advance is usually credited with charges collected in advance from borrowers to be paid to appraisers not on the lender's payroll, to title insurance companies, or to others. Operating Income—Loan Charges is usually credited with amounts collected for appraisals and other such services, when the work is done by someone on the payroll of the lender to whom special fees are not paid.

Disbursement of Loan

Loans are not disbursed to borrowers until all necessary papers have been recorded and a title-company policy showing the property free of all encumbrances, except the loan and taxes or special assessment districts, has been received. The form of disbursement is usually by a cashier's check, or by credit to the account of the borrower if it is a bank construction loan. When a new loan is completed for disbursement, a detailed recapitulation of the entire transaction is prepared in duplicate on a form called Loan Settlement Statement. The original copy is for the borrower's record of the transaction, and the duplicate copy is filed in the lender's loan folder. The loan ledger card is always given the same number as the related note and loan papers. All blank spaces are carefully filled in, and particular care must be taken in noting the outlaw date.

Uniform Agreement of Sale and Deposit Receipt

In practically all real estate transactions covering the sale or purchase of a particular property a Deposit Receipt, Sales Agreement, Purchase Agreement, or combination of these forms is involved. In many states this document is called a Deposit Receipt; in others, a Sales Contract or Purchase Contract. There are many combinations and types of such forms.

The exhibit attached is a combination form called Uniform Agreement of Sale and Deposit Receipt (Figure 7). It is a vitally important part of any real estate transaction and must be submitted to the mortgage lender for analysis. The VA requires this document on any veteran loan transaction. The FHA also requires a copy of the Sales Agreement on any firm commitment. In many states the sale of real estate must be in writing if such a sale is ever to be subjected to court action.

The lender who is considering a loan on any type of property always makes a careful analysis of the Agreement of Sale and Deposit Receipt. The transaction must be very clearly described, and there should be no requirements in this form which would be unfair to either the borrower or the seller. There have been many lawsuits over the interpretation of the wording of this document.

The importance of this document also lies in the fact that the Agreement of Sale and Deposit Receipt clearly states for the benefit of future reference the intentions and desires of the parties in the real estate transaction.

On homes that are five or more years in age a clause is usually included in the Agreement of Sale and Deposit Receipt which reads along the following lines: "In case there is evidence of termite infestation the cost of correction is to be borne by the seller while if only preventive work is required the cost of such preventive work is to be borne by the purchaser."

Figure 7 should be carefully analyzed, as it is a very up-to-date type of document and embodies all requirements of such a document. It consists of a receipt covering the down payment, also a description of the property, the terms of the sale, the conditions of the sale, any special conditions, and the signatures of all interested parties.[1]

---

[1] Statements regarding building contracts, commencement of work, completion, disbursements, lien periods, mechanics' liens, and related items are from the *Wells Fargo Bank–American Trust Company Real Estate Loan Manual*. The laws vary widely in various jurisdictions, and the student should ascertain their effects as they govern in their own particular state, city, and county.

Uniform Agreement of Sale and Deposit Receipt

(Adopted by The San Francisco Real Estate Board, October 25, 1955)

San Francisco, California............ January 30 , 19 61

RECEIVED FROM...ELMER K. DOAKES and MARY DOAKES, his wife

....*hereinafter designated as the purchaser,*

the sum of.....ONE THOUSAND and No/100...(*$* 1,000.00 *) DOLLARS,*

evidenced by cash ☐, *personal check* ☒, *Certified check* ☐, *Cashier's check* ☐, ...*being deposited on account of*
TWENTY THOUSAND and No/100...(*$*20,000.00 *) DOLLARS,*

lawful money of the United States of America, the purchase price of the herein described property in the City and County of San Francisco, State of California, upon the following terms and conditions:

> LAND AND IMPROVEMENTS ON THE SOUTHEASTERLY LINE OF SANTA FE
> STREET, COMMENCING AT A POINT 75 FEET FROM RAMONA AVENUE,
> SAN FRANCISCO, CALIFORNIA.
> PROPERTY ADDRESS - 464 SANTA FE STREET - CLOSING EXPENSES
> TO BE PAID BY THE BUYERS.

.......60.....*days from the date of approval hereof are allowed the purchaser to examine the title to the property and to report in writing any valid objections to the marketability thereof, to the agent for the seller. If no such objections to title be reported the balance of purchase price shall be paid by the purchaser on or before the expiration of said time to*
CALIFORNIA PACIFIC TITLE INSURANCE COMPANY, 148 Montgomery Street, San Francisco
for accounts of the seller and the seller shall within the above specified time deliver to said office a properly executed and acknowledged grant deed of the property. If any such objections to title are reported, the seller shall use all due diligence to remove such objections at his own expense within ninety (90) days thereafter, and if so removed, the balance of the purchase price shall be paid within five (5) days after notice to purchaser that such objections have been removed and upon delivery of the deed as herein provided; but if such objections cannot be removed within the time allowed, all rights and obligations hereunder may, at the election of the purchaser, terminate and end, and the deposit shall be returned to the purchaser, unless he elects to buy the property subject to such objections.

In the event that the purchaser fails to pay the balance of the purchase price, or to complete the purchase as herein provided, the amounts paid hereunder may be retained by the seller at his option as consideration for the execution of this agreement by the seller.

Subject to any public utility easements and to zoning and set-back ordinances of the City and County of San Francisco.

Taxes, premiums on insurance acceptable to the purchaser, rents, interest and other expenses of the property shall be prorated as of the date of the recordation of the deed.

Possession of the property shall be delivered to the purchaser upon the date of recordation of the deed. of Trust

Deposit to be increased to $.......None........*upon approval. Time is of the essence of this agreement.*

.......30.......*days from date hereof are hereby irrevocably allowed the agent for obtaining the seller's approval hereof.*

The undersigned purchaser hereby agrees to purchase the herein described property for the price and according to the conditions herein specified, and HEREBY ACKNOWLEDGES RECEIPT OF A COPY HEREOF.

M. T. DOME, Realtors
Agent for The Seller

(Signed)   ELMER K. DOAKES ....*Purchaser*
(Signed)   MARY DOAKES ....*Purchaser*

By...M. T. DOME, President

APPROVAL

San Francisco, California, ...January 30 , 19 61

The seller hereby approves the foregoing contract and agrees to sell the property herein described upon the terms and conditions herein set forth, and agrees to pay, on demand, to......M. T. DOME, REALTORS

the sum of.....TWELVE HUNDRED and No/100...(*$*1,200.00 *) DOLLARS*

for services rendered. In case the seller receives or retains any money as consideration for the execution of this agreement, the agent shall receive or retain one-half thereof but in no event shall be entitled to receive or retain an amount in excess of the commission earned. In case suit is instituted to collect this commission or any portion thereof, the seller promises and agrees to pay such additional sum as the court may adjudge reasonable for attorney fees to be allowed in said suit.

THE SELLER HEREBY ACKNOWLEDGES RECEIPT OF A COPY HEREOF.

(Signed)   HAROLD B. DIXON ....*Seller*
(Signed)   MARY A. DIXON ....*Seller*

CALIFORNIA PACIFIC TITLE INSURANCE COMPANY

SAN FRANCISCO

Figure 7

SUMMARY

The mortgage loan application forms the basis for analysis of the loan transaction. All information regarding the amount of loan desired, description and location of the property, and detailed information regarding the borrower should be contained in the application.

An application for a home loan is usually the largest financial investment in the life of the average family, and great care is necessary in order to be as certain as possible that the borrower is making a sound investment and is not overbuying. Rigid examination of the borrower's credit standing and ability to repay the obligation is now a part of the requirements of all prudent lenders.

A mortgage lender today must take a keen interest in the applicant for a mortgage loan, and his interests as well as the lender's interests should be protected to the greatest possible extent.

There are many different forms of loan applications in use today, but nearly all of them vary in form only as all loan applications must contain certain basic information which is necessary if the loan application is to be properly analyzed. The major difference in any mortgage loan application is that a few companies have the appraisal report incorporated in the actual application itself while all others have an appraisal report which is a completely separate document. There are usually eight major sections to the average form of application for a conventional loan, namely: (1) formal request for loan and statement of the applicant; (2) description and location of the property; (3) description of improvements; (4) encumbrances, mortgages, or other liens against the property; (5) credit information covering the potential borrower; (6) the appraisal report (in nearly all cases a separate document); (7) signature and summary statements; and (8) loan approval or disapproval by the loan committee.

There are several methods of filing an application for a mortgage loan in addition to the written application, namely, by telephone and by mail and verbally, but even in these cases the detailed information must eventually be assembled in written form.

Most loan portfolios are classified according to ten different types of properties, and the type of property on which a loan is being considered has a great bearing upon the manner in which the proposed transaction will be handled.

Construction loans are particularly hazardous, and such applications require a great deal more information than an application covering a loan on an existing structure. In addition to the written application signed by the potential borrower, supporting documents must include the plans and specifications covering the proposed construction, the contract between the builder and the borrower, and a credit statement covering the builder. The contract must contain the method by which the contractor is to be paid as the construction progresses. There are various methods of making disbursements on construction loans, but the most popular seems to be the four-payment or five-payment plan and in most cases through a builders' control service.

The Uniform Agreement of Sale and Deposit Receipt is one of the most important documents required in connection with a proposed mortgage loan. It is highly important that this document be very carefully analyzed in order to make certain that all parties engaged in the transaction under consideration are properly protected.

QUESTIONS

1. On construction loans to speculative builders explain why the lender is interested in making a loan to the ultimate buyer of the property.
2. Give a description of how funds are supplied by the borrower and the lender on a four-payment plan covering a loan for $12,000 on which the cost of construction according to the contract is $16,000. Borrower owns land: $3,000—price paid for lot.
3. Define a mechanic's lien.
4. In the construction of a home for an individual the funds of the borrower are used first for what reasons?
5. List five types of properties on which most lenders will make mortgage loans.
6. Why should the applicant sign the mortgage loan application?
7. Explain why a sales agreement should always contain a clause regarding the buyer's and seller's responsibilities concerning termites.
8. Explain why a few companies have applications with the appraisal report incorporated in the application form.
9. Name four parts of a typical conventional-loan application.
10. Many applicants for a mortgage loan have very little information available about the property. Describe how this can be corrected.
11. Give reasons why plans and specifications are important to the lenders.
12. Name the first concern of the mortgage lender regarding the proposed loan transaction.
13. Give reasons why the information submitted by an applicant on an application must be complete and accurate.
14. Explain why a written application is preferable to any other type of application.
15. Give reasons why it is important that the financial stability of a builder be known.
16. Name three evidences of commencement of construction.
17. List ten items which are always required in a loan application.
18. Outline the five-payment plan on a construction loan and describe the functions of a builder control service.
19. State why a construction loan is particularly hazardous.
20. Explain "completion of structure."

21. Name four methods of filing an application for a mortgage loan.
22. Define a conventional loan.
23. Explain how FHA and VA applications for a home loan are more complex than the application forms used by most institutional lenders.
24. Describe the reasons why the down payment on home loans during the past several years has been relatively small.
25. Give reasons why a careful credit analysis of the borrower is necessary.
26. Why should the lender carefully analyze the Deposit Receipt and Agreement of Sale?
27. State the conditions under which a completion bond should be required.
28. Explain why the description and location of the property is important in a loan application.
29. If you believe in low down payments on a mortgage loan covering a home, give your reasons.
30. Give your reasons why you are of the opinion that the appraisal report should be a part of the loan application or should be a completely separate document.
31. Name some important problems involved in making loans to operative builders.
32. Describe three important parts of a Uniform Agreement of Sale and Deposit Receipt.
33. In case of termite infestation, name the party responsible for the cost of the corrective work.
24. Explain why the occupation of the potential borrower is of particular importance in a loan application.
35. Name three different types of construction loans.

ASSIGNMENTS

1. Make up an application covering a loan on a home in your neighborhood which you might be interested in purchasing.
2. Explain how loan applications in a company of your selection are processed.
3. Describe the development of subdivisions in the community in which you live.
4. Describe some of the methods used by lenders in your community covering applications for mortgage loans.

BIBLIOGRAPHY AND SUGGESTED READING

Home Mortgage Lending, chap. 3, American Institute of Banking, Section American Bankers Association, New York, 1953.

Mortgage Loan Advances during Construction, American Bankers Association, Savings and Mortgage Division, New York, 1952.

Pease, Robert H., and Homer V. Cherrington (eds.), *Mortgage Banking,* chaps. 2, 11, McGraw-Hill Book Company, Inc., New York, 1953.

5

Personal Interview with Borrower

and Credit Analysis of Borrower

PURPOSES

1. To explain the development of the importance of the borrower as a factor in the mortgage risk
2. To discuss the importance of the initial interview and the vital responsibilities of the interviewer
3. To list the basic problems which confront lending institutions in processing the application and closing the loan
4. To explain the risks involved
5. To describe methods of analyzing the loan application
6. To explain the imperative need for proper credit analysis
7. To discuss some of the basic factors, procedures, and policies that determine a sound loan and therefore a successful transaction

Borrower Now Recognized as a Vitally Important Part of Mortgage Lending Operations

After the end of the Great Depression, while endeavoring to return to a peacetime economy, hundreds of thousands of applicants for home loans and other types of mortgage loans entered lending institutions for the first time. Many of these potential borrowers were wholly unacquainted with the ramifications of mortgage financing and unaware of the dangers awaiting the buyer of a home or other type of property.

As a result of these conditions, lenders were required to counsel with many of these applicants to prevent "overbuying" while at the same time keeping themselves informed of pending legislation concerning the industry, values, the mortgage market, and countless other items. It was also necessary to understand and interpret existing laws and regulations and to adjust lending policies in order to meet changing conditions. There have been thousands of such interviews that did not result in the closing of a mortgage loan. There is no doubt that most lenders during this period interviewed every conceivable type of person concerning mortgage financing. Many such applications were extremely strong credit risks while others were extremely weak. The development of techniques to handle these potential borrowers has been an important new phase of mortgage lending operations.

Condition of Mortgage Market in 1948

In February and early March, 1948, mortgage credit had begun to tighten. FHA Title VI was to end on March 31, and it was not known whether it would be extended. President Truman had delivered his housing message to Congress. Many lenders were loaned up. There was no secondary market on VA loans. Some mortgage lenders had indicated that too much money at a 4 per cent interest rate had already been loaned on a long-term basis. More selective home purchasing had developed. Would Title II of the FHA be liberalized? Interest rates, which were at their lowest possible point, were also strengthening a little.[1] Increased cash equity in the home purchase was required. Appraisals were firming down. Credit analysis of the builder and the home purchaser and other mortgage borrowers was becoming more technical and severe. During 1948 and 1949 the combination FHA-VA loan became the main type of loan used to meet the needs of veterans.

Definite indications of trends which would vitally affect mortgage lending were in evidence. Conditions were uncertain and "caution" continued to be the watchword. At this time, FNMA was very active in purchasing Veterans Administration home loans at par. Intensive analysis of mortgage loan portfolios was being made by most lenders. Would the portfolio be strong enough to weather another depression or period of deflation?

Improvements in Mortgage Lending Practices

During the Great Depression of the early thirties, many painful lessons were learned about mortgage financing. As a result of these lessons great improvements in mortgage lending operations had already been made. It was realized that additional safeguards would have to be established to protect mortgage lenders against the risks of loss. Important among these was the need of recognizing the borrower as one of the major safety factors in any loan transaction. As a result of the recognition of this need, improved and efficient interview and credit analysis procedures were developed— procedures which have helped humanize mortgage lending, have aided lenders in reducing the risks of loss, helped improve the quality of loan

---

[1] The interest rate on FHA Title II loans was reduced from 4½ per cent to 4¼ per cent on April 24, 1950, and on May 2, 1953, was increased from 4¼ per cent to 4½ per cent. The interest rate on VA home loans was increased from 4 per cent to 4½ per cent on May 5, 1953.

portfolios, and been responsible for the development of advanced credit techniques in mortgage lending operations.

Development of the Importance of the Borrower

The following pages show how the borrower, chiefly the individual borrower, has developed in importance and how interview and credit analysis procedures are now used to evaluate his strength. Basic factors, operational procedures, and lending policies in connection with this phase of mortgage lending factors, procedures, and policies that determine a sound loan and, therefore, a successful transaction are reviewed.

Interview and Credit Analysis

Interview and credit analysis are two closely related phases of operations in mortgage lending. The interview with the borrower could cover any one of a number of different types of transactions. It could be the discussion or application for a loan covering the purchase or construction of a home, for a possible loan on a farm, apartment house, or any other type of real estate security. Interview also involves the various methods of reception of the potential borrower, since in many cases only an informal discussion concerning mortgage lending is desired. The interview could also be, and usually is, the preliminary or tentative analysis of the proposed transaction.

The Application Form

Since a mortgage transaction is a new experience to the average borrower, the interviewer should begin the discussion by explaining why a detailed application form as described in Chapter 4 is necessary. A prospective borrower will then have no reluctance about furnishing information requested when he realizes (1) that a study of an application which contains all the required information makes possible an analysis of the loan transaction, (2) that the purpose of the loan analysis is to determine that he will be able to make the payments in accordance with the loan contract, (3) that such analysis has prevented many borrowers from assuming obligations which could not be handled satisfactorily, and (4) that the interests of both the lender and the borrower in the transaction are somewhat similar.

Qualifications Required of the Interviewer

The interviewer should be qualified to arrange effectively for proper reception of the potential borrower and should create the impression that the request for a loan will be carefully studied and analyzed. In addition to this he should have the ability to assemble all pertinent details in order to have a clear understanding of the given problem and should know how to analyze character and credit data and financial statements as an aid in judging the soundness of the proposed transaction. To be completely successful in this work the interviewer should also have a background of years of experience in mortgage lending, including a knowledge of operating procedures, loan policies, and mortgage values in the areas served by his firm.

In making the credit analysis all the pertinent details that have been assembled in the personal interview must be analyzed. Additional information which has been assembled from the required credit report, the financial statement, and from other sources must also be analyzed. With this information borrower risk is evaluated, and the strength of the borrower is judged and rated.

On the one hand the interviewer, or loan officer, is dealing with a personality and assembling all possible facts pertaining to the transaction such as location of the property, type of property, amount of loan desired, terms, borrower's personal history, assets, and liabilities, and other necessary details that will have a bearing on this particular case. On the other hand the tentative credit analysis of this borrower, which is usually made by this same interviewer after receipt of the credit report and other data, is concerned with all factors affecting the borrower which will enable the loan committee to rate the borrower as a factor in the mortgage pattern. The interviewer should have keen analytical ability, sound judgment, a flexible mind, and a thorough knowledge of human nature. The interview and credit information assembled must be complete in every respect. Otherwise, the credit analysis cannot be complete, and there will be weaknesses in the over-all analysis.

Objectives of Interview and Credit Analysis

One of the major objectives of interview and credit analysis, therefore, is to develop, analyze, and determine the strength of the borrower. Many analysts, including those employed by the FHA, now use in their operations a method known as *rating of the mortgage pattern*. The rating is based on all risks already determined and is mainly a recapitulation of property, neighborhood, and borrower ratings; in addition it takes into consideration the mortgage terms. It is a method used to ascertain and judge the economic soundness of the proposed transaction. Interview and credit analysis are also used to evaluate the quality and strength of the borrower in connection with the control of loanable funds in the mortgage lending field. In other words, a study of all underlying borrower risk factors must indicate that the borrower has the ability to service the debt.

Processing of an Application in the Late 1920s

Weaknesses of Interview and Credit-analysis Procedures

Thirty years ago the average mortgage loan department of most lenders was not staffed with efficient interviewers nor was credit analysis considered of major importance. In those days an applicant for a mortgage loan would usually be directed to a "taker of the application," who was probably some employee who had been with the institution for many years and was not blessed with any remarkable personality or desire to please anybody. The applicant for a loan would state his case, which would be recorded on a loan-application form. The property would be appraised, and upon receipt of the appraisal report the loan committee or branch manager would figure 60 per cent of the appraisal, or whatever the legal limit might be, write a loan for one year, which would outlaw in four years, and advise the applicant that a loan for a certain amount was available. In those days the record contained little, if any, information concerning the borrower, and no credit analysis was made. Important factors having to do with the likely ability of the borrower to make payment on the loan in accordance with the note terms were seldom taken into consideration. In other words, a loan was made on a piece of property in accordance with existing Federal or state legislation.

Improvements in the 1930s

In the early thirties it became evident that the mortgage lending system needed certain fundamental changes for the sake of making lenders more liquid and for the sake of providing protection for borrowers. Long-term installment loans began to replace one-year loans. Second-mortgage financing, which had been disastrous to so many borrowers, was largely abandoned. Prior to the advent of the National Housing Act of 1934, which created the FHA, many lenders had already swung to ten-year installment loans, and the borrower ratings were developing. It is probably true that each lender follows a somewhat different pattern in establishing borrower rating, but all have the same objective, namely, sound loans and reduction of risks.

Credit Criteria

Both the FHA and VA have always determined the credit criteria upon which the FHA insurance and VA guaranty are predicated and which protect lenders against loss by reason of defaults on the part of mortgagors.[2]

FNMA has always reserved the right to pass upon borrowers' credit, since, under the FNMA Charter Act, mortgages purchased by the Association are required to be related to their salability in the general secondary market. The mortgages which FNMA purchases are intended to be resold to private investors and consequently the Association's purchasing activities are not directed at establishing FNMA as a permanent investor in long-term mortgage obligations.

The mere fact that a mortgage is insured or guaranteed by an agency of the government does not automatically provide assurance that it is also a readily marketable asset; credit can, and does, have a vitally significant effect on mortgage marketability, particularly since many adverse factors may enter the picture during the period between the date of the credit approval by the insuring or guaranteeing agency and the date on which the mortgage is offered for purchase to FNMA.

The experience of the FNMA in the mortgage business and the experience of mortgage originators and sellers show generally that investors recognize these factors and take them into consideration in their mortgage investment programs.

Mortgage Loan Quality Today

Today, most lending institutions have a higher quality of mortgage loans in their portfolios, less delinquencies, and less owned real estate than at any time during the past twenty-five or more years. This has been due to improved economic conditions, good wages, and concentrated efforts during those years to eliminate as many old and unsatisfactory loans as possible. This has also been due to the development of improved techniques and improved operational procedures covering the processing and the administration of mortgage loan portfolios. However, since 1934, there has been a rising market in real estate. A complete real estate cycle has not been experienced. At some future date, which is unpredictable, the number of delinquent loans is bound to increase as will the number of foreclosures. Practically every leader in the field of finance, business, and economics will acknowledge this fact. Under the circumstances, if proper interview and credit analysis procedures are not now in use, it is important that such

[2] On April 20, 1961, the Commissioner of the Federal Housing Administration issued a letter to all approved mortgagees reading in part as follows: "Effective July 1, 1961, lending institutions will be required to order direct from reporting agencies the credit reports submitted in connection with insured loan applications. Further, the standard of such reports must at least equal the minimum quality and amount of information required by FHA in its contract awards to agencies supplying reports to FHA. The credit report forms must contain direct answers to and compliance with the language of our standard factual data report."

operations be established at this time. Efficient loan analysis and interviewing procedures should have been developed and established long ago by all mortgage lenders as a result of lessons learned during the Great Depression of the early thirties.

Types of Applications and Problems Involved Will Determine Interviewer

In addition to applications received from individual borrowers for the purchase or construction of homes, or requests for help and guidance concerning such purchase, there are many other types of mortgage loan applications, and different interviewers are available for each particular case. Operative builders, for example, are usually interviewed by a senior loaning officer, or branch manager, or by an officer handling builders relations in the mortgage loan department. Subdivision financing is usually handled by the senior loaning officer, or by the officer handling subdivision mortgage loans. Farm-loan applicants are interviewed by officers in charge of farm-loan financing. Such officers of firms that maintain branch operations are usually located at both the main office and certain key branch offices in farming areas. Applicants for apartment-house loans or industrial-property loans are usually interviewed by a member of the mortgage loan committee, or an officer or manager of a branch office. Loan applications and interviews covering conventional loans on properties other than home loans are far more technical and detailed than home-loan applications. Income and expense, leases, tenants, location, credit reports, cost, type of improvements, surveys, financial statements, and numerous other items must be analyzed. Real estate brokers usually contact a loan officer or a branch manager. A major point to realize is that every loan officer or branch manager is an interviewer.

In addition, most large lenders maintain a separate FHA division, which processes builders' loan applications, as well as individual applications, strictly on an FHA basis. Such lenders also maintain a separate VA loan division through which all applications for VA loans are processed. In some branch offices of large lenders the manager, or the assistant manager, of the office is required to perform the functions involved in all types of mortgage lending. Most lenders have loaning limits for each loan officer, and any loan in excess of the limit must be approved by both the executive committee and the board of directors. In a highly efficient mortgage lending institution the principal interviewers are men who are fully capable of handling any type of loan application. Interview and credit analysis, therefore, in their broader sense embrace all the many types of mortgage financing that comprise the activities of a large and active mortgage lending firm.

Problems Directly Affecting Interview with Borrower and Credit Analysis

The efficiency of operations in interview and credit-analysis procedures depends greatly upon proper understanding of affirmative answers to the following:

1. Does the interviewer know his subject? Has he the ability to obtain information for evaluation of risk?

2. Does the lender make a thorough analysis of each transaction?

3. Have lenders set up efficient and uniform operating procedures covering the processing of each application?

4. Are all basic factors understood in order to get a clear understanding of the potential borrower?

5. Should a lender get confirmation of applicant's employment in all cases? Should a lender get confirmation of his bank balance?

6. Should any consideration be given to the income of the applicant's wife?

7. Is the value of the security enhanced by a guaranteed note signed by the applicant's father and mother?

8. What is value? Who determines it? By what methods?

9. Do lenders and the potential borrower or speculative builder fully realize the dangers of individual construction?

10. Do lenders sometimes assume the individual builder needs no credit checking?

11. Do builders, or real estate brokers, properly screen applicants for a home loan or other types of loans?

12. Is it true that second-mortgage financing, which proved disastrous in the late twenties, is again creeping into the mortgage lending picture?

The foregoing questions are but a few of the many which are a part of the interviewing and credit analysis of a borrower who is desirous of obtaining a mortgage loan. There are many others.

Proper Relations with the Public Important

Our relations with the public are interesting and important to all of us. We want to be popular, we want to attract loyal friends. Lending institutions, like people, have personality. They wish to attract prospective customers and make friends of such customers. Their customer relations program is a factor that will determine the share of good will they will command. The public- or customer-relations program of many lending institutions has been a rather haphazard and erratic activity. These relations can be defined as the sum of all impressions registered by the business and the people in it. They come from many sources. The nature and efficiency of services rendered, including the reception of any prospective customers by the lending institution, are of major importance. We all desire new business, and we desire to cultivate good will. We should also desire to make it easy and comfortable for a customer to do business with us. It is very gratifying to know that great advances have been made in this field in the past few years.

Basic Qualifications Required of an Interviewer

The interviewer will help maintain good public relations for his firm if he has these four qualifications:

1. He must know his product.
2. He must be satisfied with his product.
3. He must have innate desire to create good will for his own institution.
4. He must take fast and efficient action in handling the application.

Contacts with potential borrowers take the form of personal contact, telephone conversation, and correspondence. The attention the potential borrower received and the impression created in his mind are accepted by him as having come from the institution itself. Mortgage lenders must be well equipped for such contacts. The results obtained by some lenders by proper training of personnel to interview potential borrowers would be surprising to those who have given little attention to this phase of mortgage lending. When a potential customer enters a lending institution, a pleasant smile, a warm welcome, courteous attention, and intelligent and understandable answers to questions may determine his future connection with that institution. This is a vital, important, and significant role in business today. Interviewers handling mortgage loan applications should understand and have an interest in human nature. They should know how to please people. They should be experienced and enthusiastic.

Objectives of the Interview

Every interview is an interesting adventure. Each personality is different. The interviewer should be prepared to develop the conversation into channels that will reveal the kind of information he wishes to get. His analysis of the potential borrower starts the minute he looks at him, and the potential borrower is undoubtedly making a similar analysis of the interviewer at the same time. The objective is to assemble all details covering the transaction while analyzing the applicant and winning the applicant's confidence. This is not always easy. The interviewer must give this visitor his complete and undivided attention. He must be a good listener. He should take notes of the conversation. His desk should not be cluttered with papers. Such papers as he has should be to one side. He should stand up to greet this visitor and should also stand up when the visitor leaves. He should make the most of the initial interview. He should refer requests for certain information to others in his department who might know more about a particular question than he does—for example, a legal question, a question of lending policy, a doubtful case.

Original Interview and Procedures

All the following points must be taken into consideration in the original interview:

All the necessary and required preliminary information covering both the property and applicant must be obtained and filed.

There must be as great speed as possible in the processing of each applicant. Builders, upon selling a house, insist on immediate action in closing the loan. They do not understand and are not interested in the intricate details required in processing a loan application.

The interviewer must be diplomatic, must have understanding, and must be a sympathetic listener. He must have the ability to analyze the transaction as completely as possible during the interview and to give financial counsel and guidance when needed.

In case a sales agreement has been signed, it should be given minute analysis.

A contract covering individual construction of a home should be carefully analyzed. Many such contracts are vague and revocable. Most important, the interviewer must be able to decide whether or not the loan should be made in such cases, particularly where the transaction appears to be unsound. In coming to this decision, he must have a knowledge of the basic requirements and factors that mean a sound loan, and he must always bear in mind that risks of loss must be kept at a minimum at all times. In addition to this, as no two borrowers or no two properties are exactly alike, each case must also be judged on its own individual merits. The interviewer must always be flexible in his analysis of each individual transaction at all times.

The borrower's interest as well as the lender's must at all times be protected.

Discussion of the Loan Transaction: Important Factors to Be Developed

The interviewer should never subject an applicant to the third degree. When a prospective borrower calls at a lending institution to make inquiries about a loan for a home or any other type of property, it is usually the most important financial undertaking of his life, and it might be the beginning of a friendly relationship with the lender which could last for many years. The representative who first meets this borrower must have a sound knowledge of mortgage lending policies and practices, including the dangers awaiting a new buyer of a home or other type of property who is not aware of such possibilities. A borrower should use the services of a sound and prudent lender with years of experience in this field. The responsibility for wise counsel rests with all lending officers, and they should fully realize that one of the major problems facing the housing industry today is progressive improvement in mortgage financing operations and procedures.

The Borrower

The borrower himself has come into the limelight. He is no longer a spectator, but today he is a part of the team. The lender has faith in his abilities to perform, and the borrower has faith in the lender. In other words the lender and the borrower are teammates and want to make a success of their particular transaction.

Analyzing Borrower Risk

In analyzing borrower risk, the fact must be established that the borrower will be able to comply with the terms of the mortgage contract and that the investment in mind is sound. How does a lender go about establishing these facts? Are there certain factors which will quickly give the borrower's position? What factors are subject to measurement? There are certain tangible factors which probably are subject to measurement, namely, income, assets, and liabilities. There are also many intangible factors, which are subject to estimate only, such as character, responsibility, ambition, reliability, reputation, future prospects, earning power, family background, motivation, health, education, and personality, as well as countless other items. How does a lender obtain this information?

1. From the personal interview
2. From the mortgage loan application
3. From the credit report
4. From the appraisal report
5. From many other sources, some of which might require ingenuity or special investigation on the part of the lender

Interview with Borrower Purchasing New Home in a Subdivision

In a large lending institution where there is considerable financing of operative builders, these builders sell the homes either direct or through brokers. In such cases the contracts of sale are signed, and the potential buyers of the homes are sent to the lender for filing of the home-loan application. The lender in nearly all cases is the same firm that financed the operative builder.

In such cases when the applicant calls at the office of the lender, the interviewer already knows the maximum amount of loan that can be made on the property, the type of property, the neighborhood, the builder, and all such circumstances. In the original interview he can quickly analyze the transaction. His first objective is to ascertain if the applicant's monthly income is sufficient to carry the loan desired and whether the cash and credit position of the applicant warrants the purchase of the property at the listed selling price. During the past few years both builders and brokers have screened some home purchasers by checking the prospective buyers' financial positions in order to eliminate those purchasers who were not qualified to buy the homes in question because of lack of sufficient income or some such reason. However, analyzing the ability of the prospective home purchaser to handle properly the payments on a loan should not be the function of a builder or broker.

Interview Covering Transactions Where No Sales Agreement Has Been Signed

Another interviewing procedure which comprises a great deal of the work on the part of the interviewer concerns loan applications submitted by real estate brokers or received directly from applicants who call and are interested in a certain property but as yet have signed no sales agreement. In nearly all such cases the interviewer will make a very tentative analysis of the applicant's financial position but will take no additional action concerning the processing of the application until the appraisal report has been received giving the location of the property, neighborhood, condition of the property, and the appraisal figure. The interviewer in this way ascertains whether the property involved and the selling price asked are satisfactory before obtaining a credit report, a financial statement, and other data. Unnecessary expense including a great deal of extra paper work and time in connection with obviously unsound transactions should be avoided.

Construction Loans

In the case of any potential borrower who files an application for a construction loan for a home or other type of property, together with plans, specifications, and a firm bid from a building contractor, the interviewer is immediately on notice that grave dangers of loss are always present unless every factor involved in the transaction is completely satisfactory. The builder is checked carefully, the borrower must be an especially strong risk with sufficient cash and financial background to warrant the undertaking, and other conditions must also be carefully analyzed.

Rating of the Borrower

Income stability and ability to meet the obligations of the mortgage are probably the most important of the factors involved in the analysis of the transaction from the borrower-rating standpoint covering a home-loan application.

In many lending institutions today a great deal of the analysis of the borrower is done at the time of the first interview followed by a more intensive analysis after receipt of the credit report and the appraisal report.

Establishment of Borrower in a Particular Community

In some areas a large number of purchasers of homes today have been living in a particular community for only short periods of time. This presents a constant challenge to any interviewer to cover as many points as possible in the original interview. To cite an example of this, the following experience of a typical large lender in the handling of VA home loan applications during the first few years of this problem might be of interest: During a two-year period applicants were interviewed for home loans involving $10 million, and approximately half of these applicants were approved for a loan total of $5 million. In other words, half of the applications were withdrawn for one reason or another, many of them before a credit report was ordered. In those cases it was quickly established that the borrower's income would not warrant the making of a loan to purchase the house because of inability to meet the monthly payment required, and the applicant was undoubtedly protected from "overbuying."

FHA and VA Loan Applications

Each loan application should be approved by the lender in all respects for any type of FHA loan or VA loan prior to submitting the application to the FHA or to the VA. It should be remembered that these agencies do not see this potential borrower. Over a period of more than twenty-seven years of handling FHA loans and seventeen years of VA loans, because of preliminary screening by the mortgagee, the number of applications disapproved by FHA and VA after preliminary approval by lenders is almost negligible.

Ability of Borrower to Handle His Financial Affairs

In the general discussion about the applicant and his life and business experience the interviewer is able, in most cases, to judge quite accurately whether the applicant has the ability to handle his financial affairs. The credit report will show whether there has been any disregard of obligations or certain difficulties over finances. The failure of a borrower to establish a savings account, purchase bonds, or develop insurance equities could indicate poor management, unless there are logical reasons which prevented such savings. Past records of payments are nearly always shown in a commercial credit report. Any legal proceedings, bankruptcies, domestic difficulties, suits, judgments, and the like will also be revealed in the credit report.

Domestic Relationship

Unsatisfactory domestic relationships are usually revealed by the applicant. Information concerning the family life of the applicant can be developed, and in case there has ever been a divorce or other family trouble, the credit report should disclose that information. Today marital difficulties are the basic reason for a goodly number of delinquent loans.

Borrower's Income Compared to Required Monthly Payments on the Loan

Probably the most important item to be considered in making a credit analysis of the borrower is the amount of his present income compared with the required monthly payments of the proposed mortgage and the amount of his other obligations. This is subject to fairly accurate analysis. Monthly payments of interest, fire insurance, and taxes, according to most lenders, should not exceed 20 per cent of the net monthly income, provided everything else is satisfactory. Exceptions to this ratio should never be made unless there is positive information covering an expected increase in income.

New Housing Expenses Compared with Previous Housing Expenses

It is very important that new housing expenses and previous housing expenses be carefully compared, as the purchase of a home usually means considerably increased expenses. Added to this should be other obligations required, in case the borrower purchases and moves into the home, such as refrigerator, stove, or furniture, and possibly an automobile or increased transportation expense. Also, estimated loan-closing costs should be considered to include proration of taxes and insurance as well as cost of title search, appraisal fees, and miscellaneous items. These latter items are extremely important and should be carefully explained to the borrower.

Family Obligations

Family obligations and family responsibilities should be analyzed. Only the net income of the family as stated above should be taken into consideration, and the income of a wife under thirty-five years of age should not be considered. Endorsement of the note by father and mother of the applicant does not necessarily eliminate the risk. Most individuals who want to purchase a home should first of all have assets, including sufficient cash available to take care of the difference between the selling price or cost of construction of the home, plus costs and incidentals, and the amount of the loan. In addition there should be funds available for incidentals, which nearly always appear. The borrower should always carry sufficient life insurance and health and accident insurance to take care of the mortgage in case of a castastrophe.

Young Applicants

The future prospects of younger applicants to earn a living cannot be seriously considered as a basis for granting a loan. Young applicants should be fairly well established in business and have some savings before becoming involved in what is usually the major financial investment of a lifetime. Homes are paid for out of present and future income, and with young borrowers, particularly, the dangers of overbuying are always present. These conditions have been especially true since the end of World War II.

Confirmation of Employment

Confirmation of employment and bank balances should be obtained in all cases. In most instances the employer is willing to cooperate by giving an unofficial opinion of the present and future prospects of the borrower. This information is important particularly if it is a borderline case based upon present income.

Borrower's Reasons for Need of a Loan

The reasons why the applicant wishes to purchase the property are always noted, but the importance of this item is very difficult to evaluate. The amount of cash equity, or amount of the initial investment, is one of the most important factors in the transaction and can be evaluated. Most applicants for a home loan willingly give the reasons for wishing to purchase the particular property, and thus the motivation in the transaction is known.

Most Stable Applicants

Junior executives, accountants, attorneys, skilled workers, clerks, skilled mechanics, buyers, and professional men are generally very stable and conservative individuals who are well established and equipped in all respects to repay an obligation. However, in all such cases it is important that the number of years the applicant has been engaged in a certain skilled profession be noted. If his experience has been of short duration, the risk in the transaction is increased.

Application Forms

Although application forms used by lending institutions vary greatly, there has been an endeavor during the past few years to use forms that provide for more detailed and comprehensive information about the borrower than was previously considered necessary, and to have such applica-

	NO. LOANS	AMOUNT
TOTAL MORTGAGE LOAN PORTFOLIO 12/31/45	15,400	$ 67,500,000
TOTAL MORTGAGE LOAN PORTFOLIO 12/31/47	20,000	100,000,000
NUMBER OF OFFICES WITH MORTGAGE LOAN PORTFOLIOS	18	

MORTGAGE LOAN ACTIVITY YEAR 1946

	NO. LOANS	AMOUNT
NEW LOANS PLACED IN PORTFOLIO	4,500	$ 33,250,000
TOTAL INTERVIEWS	7,500	
RUN OFF INCLUDING PRINCIPAL PAYMENTS	2,700	20,750,000
NET GAIN	1,800	12,500,000

LOAN COMMITMENTS TO BUILDERS 12/31/46		$ 8,500,000

MORTGAGE LOAN ACTIVITY YEAR 1947

	NO. LOANS	AMOUNT
NEW LOANS PLACED IN PORTFOLIO	6,000	$ 47,000,000
TOTAL INTERVIEWS	9,500	
RUN OFF INCLUDING PRINCIPAL PAYMENTS	3,200	27,000,000
NET GAIN	?,800	20,000,000

LOAN COMMITMENTS TO BUILDERS 12/31/47		$ 7,900,000

NUMBER OF INTERVIEWS DURING TWO YEAR PERIOD	17,000	
NUMBER OF LOANS GRANTED	10,000	
NUMBER OF LOAN APPLICATIONS WITHDRAWN	6,500	

Figure 8. Actual Figures on a Proportionate Basis Covering the Activity of a Typical Large Lender

```
LOANS PAST DUE 90 DAYS OR MORE 1/1/46                    $    250,000
LOANS PAST DUE 90 DAYS OR MORE 12/31/47                       500,000


AVERAGE AMOUNT OF LOAN IN PORTFOLIO                     $      5,000
LOANS UNDER $10,000                        87%
LOANS ON ONE- TO FOUR-FAMILY DWELL-
   INGS                                    88%
```

F.H.A. ACTIVITY SINCE 1934
```
FHA TITLE II AND TITLE VI LOANS PLACED
   IN PORTFOLIO                                         $100,000,000
BALANCE FHA LOANS IN PORTFOLIO AT END OF
   THIS 15 YEAR PERIOD                                    45,000,000
FORECLOSURES DURING THIS 15 YEAR PERIOD        46            208,000
LOSS BY LENDER                                                  NONE
```

Figure 8. (Continued)

COMMENTS ON FIGURE 8

1. These figures represent the mortgage loan activities during 1946 and 1947 of several of the larger lenders in the country on a proportionate basis. These activities should not vary more than 15 per cent for any one of these lenders.

2. Note large increase in portfolio amount during the years 1946 and 1947.

3. Figures reveal a very active mortgage market and liquid portfolios.

4. Loan activity during 1947 was considerably larger than for year 1946.

5. Note slight drop in loan commitments.

6. Note number of interviews during the two-year period and fact that 6,500 loan applications were withdrawn. What were the basic reasons for these withdrawals? Interviews on which no applications were filed are estimated at an additional 2,500 in number. Most of these were thousands of "borderline" cases that tax the ingenuity and ability of the interviewer or loan officer, or the loan committee. There were also many "pressure" cases by the real estate broker, or builder, or a friend of a friend, or by a branch manager. There were also many outright "policy" cases that particularly required diplomacy, discretion, and flexibility in the credit analysis and loan processing.

7. During the two-year period, the number and amount of delinquencies has doubled. A majority of the new delinquencies are on loans made during the past three years. It is a warning signal and points directly to increase in cost of loan-servicing operations. It also reveals faults in interview and credit-analysis procedures and weak borrowers.

8. Amount of average loan in portfolio, percentage of loans under $10,000, and percentage of loans on one- to four-family dwellings indicate strength and liquidity, provided these are sound loans on good properties to strong borrowers, all on an amortized basis.

9. Figures covering FHA loan activities point to outstanding success of this program.

10. Need for highly efficient interview and credit-analysis procedures is directly indicated by these statistics.

11. *Statistics for the years 1946 and 1947 are purposely cited in order to show the lending activity which developed shortly after the end of World War II. This phenomenal growth steadily continued through the years 1948 to 1961 (see Table 2)*

TOTAL MORTGAGE LOAN PORTFOLIO 12/31/47   4,000 $20,000,000

<u>VETERAN LOAN REPORT AS OF MARCH 31, 1948</u>

ACTUAL LEDGER BALANCES OF MARCH
31, 1948

SECTION 501 −	348	$ 2,817,974
SECTION 502 −	1	7,753
SECTION 503 −	3	70,891
SECTION 505 −	96	1,016,933
TOTAL	448	$ 3,913,551

AN ADDITIONAL 10 LOAN APPLICATIONS
TOTALING $99,960 HAVE BEEN FULLY
PROCESSED AND ARE NOW READY TO BE
PLACED ON THE BOOKS.

LOANS PLACED ON THE BOOKS DURING
MARCH, 1948 AND INCLUDED IN ABOVE
TOTALS

SECTION 501 −	11	$ 102,050
SECTION 505 −	17	177,725
TOTAL	28	$ 279,775

<u>PROOF OF MARCH, 1948 CONTROL SHEET</u>

50 APPLICATIONS TAKEN DURING MARCH, 1948	$	477,170
4 APPLICATIONS PLACED ON THE BOOKS	$	40,090
4 APPLICATIONS PLACED ON FULLY PROCESSED LIST		36,340
18 APPLICATIONS WITHDRAWN		167,800
24 APPLICATIONS PLACED ON PARTIALLY PROCESSED LIST		232,940
50 TOTAL AND PROOF	$	477,170

<u>CUMULATIVE FROM FEBRUARY 1, 1946 to MARCH 31, 1948</u>

502 APPLICATIONS SUSPENDED OR WITHDRAWN	$ 4,755,954
446 LOAN APPLICATIONS APPROVED AND ON BOOKS	3,874,229
20 LOAN APPLICATIONS FULLY PROCESSED AND READY TO BE PLACED ON BOOKS	199,920
92 LOAN APPLICATIONS PARTIALLY PROCESSED	906,305
39 LOANS PAID OFF	284,289
17 LOANS TRANSFERRED TO OTHER BRANCHES	146,800
2 LOANS FORECLOSED	17,500
1118 GRAND TOTAL	$10,184,997

Figure 9. Actual Figures on a Proportionate Basis Covering Veteran
Mortgage Loan Activity of a Typical Large Lender

COMMENTS ON FIGURE 9

1. Figures reveal that approximately one-fifth of this portfolio is now comprised of loans to veterans.

2. Indicates that this lender has actively endeavored to assist veterans in the purchase of homes and to aid them in their economic readjustment. Financial counsel and guidance have been given in all cases.

3. Only one farm loan made. Farm prices have been too high, and typical veteran who desired to purchase a farm had little or no knowledge of the farming industry.

4. Almost 50 per cent of the VA loan applications filed at this office were withdrawn. Are these figures out of proportion compared with most mortgage lenders throughout the country?

5. These statistics reveal the great responsibilities placed on the interviewer in handling this type of loan application, the importance of knowing the fundamentals of mortgage lending, and why the ability to analyze credit data is essential.

6. *Statistics for the years 1946 and 1947 are purposely cited in order to show the VA lending activity which developed shortly after the end of World War II. This phenomenal growth steadily continued through the years 1948 to 1961 (see Table 2).*

I. FINANCIAL

    a. Analysis reveals that monthly payment required on loan is in excess of proper relation to net income. (Financial capacity — Relation of income to transaction.)

    b. Selling price of home not in proper relation to annual salary of applicant. (Financial capacity — Relation of income to transaction.)

    c. Other obligations, such as need for purchase of furniture, stove, refrigerator, plus closing costs, including title search, added to purchase price of house would cause applicant to overextend himself. (Financial capacity — Relation of income to transaction.)

    d. Insufficient cash on hand to cover difference between maximum loan available and selling price. (Motivation.)

    e. Income insufficient to service loan unless wife's total income taken into consideration and possibility of her working steadily is very uncertain. (Financial capacity — Relation of income to transaction.)

II. INDIVIDUAL

    a. Attitude toward obligation indicates that a loan, if made, would quickly become a collection problem. (Personal financial management — Motivation.)

    b. Motivation or desire for home indicates property would only be a temporary home and would quickly be sold. (Motivation.)

Figure 10. Reasons for Withdrawal of Loan Application

    c. Character and reliability unsatisfactóry.
(Family and social relationships – Social and economic characteristics.)

    d. Unsatisfactory domestic relations indicated.
(Social and economic characteristics.)

    e. Divorce proceedings started during loan processing.
(Social and economic characteristics – Family and social relationships.)

    f. Duration of employment few months only. Steady employment doubtful.
(Employability and income stability.)

    g. Not living within income.
(Personal financial management – Social and economic characteristics.)

    h. Student with note to be endorsed by father and mother. Part time work only. (Relation of income to transaction.)

    i. Analysis of transaction indicates subterfuge, fraud, collusion or misrepresentation.

       (Social and economic characteristics – Family and social relationships.)

III. CONTRACTOR

    a. Individual construction case – credit report shows builder weak.

    b. Contract unsatisfactory – not a firm bid.

IV. PROPERTY

    a. Property unsatisfactory because of age, type or location.

    b. Property not in lender's lending area.

    c. Reasonable value of property lower than selling price.

    d. Furniture included in Selling Price.

Figure 10. (Continued)

COMMENTS ON FIGURE 10

1. This typical lender never rejects an application. It is either withdrawn or suspended. Basic reasons for withdrawal or suspension are explained in detail to the applicant.

2. Specific reasons for withdrawal or suspension are always noted on each specific application.

3. Analysis reveals that reasons for withdrawals fall into four major categories, namely:

    Financial, 80 per cent

    Individual, 15 per cent

    Contractor, 3 per cent (financial position weak)

    Property, 2 per cent

4. The lender's own appraised value of the property must be used as the basis for establishing the maximum amount of loan available. Federal and state legislation and regulations of other regulatory bodies specify the percentage of the appraisal value that may be loaned.

5. This information also strongly indicates the importance of interview and credit analysis in the handling and analyzing of any loan application.

DUTIES AND RESPONSIBILITIES OF AN INTERVIEWER TOGETHER WITH THE PERSONAL ATTRIBUTES REQUIRED TO BE SUCCESSFUL IN THIS WORK.

DUTIES AND RESPONSIBILITIES	PERSONAL ATTRIBUTES
PROPER RECEPTION OF POTENTIAL BORROWER	PLEASANT PERSONALITY
PROTECTION OF BORROWER'S INTEREST	GOOD APPEARANCE
FINANCIAL COUNSEL AND GUIDANCE	TACT
WIN CONFIDENCE OF BORROWER	DISPOSITION
	CONVERSATIONALIST
ABILITY TO ASSEMBLE ALL POSSIBLE DETAILS COVERING PROPOSED TRANSACTION	POPULAR WITH CUSTOMERS
	LIKED BY STAFF
ABILITY TO ANALYZE CREDIT DATA	UNDERSTANDING
ABILITY TO ANALYZE FINANCIAL STATEMENT	SYMPATHETIC LISTENER
ABILITY TO JUDGE SOUNDNESS OF TRANSAC-TION	VERSATILITY
	SOUND JUDGMENT
ABILITY TO ANALYZE SALES AGREEMENT	ANALYSIS ABILITY
ABILITY TO ANALYZE CONTRACT FOR CON-STRUCTION	DEPENDABILITY
	ACCURACY
ABILITY TO ANALYZE PLANS AND SPECIFICA-TIONS	THOROUGHNESS
	LOYALTY
ABILITY TO ANALYZE THE BUILDER	COOPERATION
KNOWLEDGE OF OPERATING PROCEDURES	INDUSTRIOUSNESS
KNOWLEDGE OF LENDING POLICIES	FLEXIBLE MIND
KNOWLEDGE OF MORTGAGE VALUES	PERSONAL INTEGRITY
	LEADERSHIP
	INTELLIGENCE
	RESOURCEFULNESS
	INITIATIVE

Figure 11. The Interviewer

COMMENTS ON FIGURE 11

1. Under "Duties and Responsibilities" of the interviewer, the items directly concerned with credit analysis have been listed and also indicate the great responsibilities that rest on the shoulders of the interviewer. He should have knowledge of practically every phase of mortgage lending.

2. Personal attributes listed probably apply to any person in any type of business. These attributes are particularly important in any duties that are concerned with meeting potential customers.

tions more uniform. Forms in use today itemize detailed information about the borrower's employment, income, resources, liabilities, and in many cases also include a financial statement (see Chapter 4). It enables the interviewer to make a more detailed tentative analysis of the transaction.

```
PROCESSING OF  ( 1. PERSONAL INTERVIEW WITH THE      ) WITH THIS
APPLICATION    (     BORROWER.                       )
               (                                     )
               ( 2. THE LOAN APPLICATION.            ) INFORMATION
               (                                     )
ANALYSIS OF    ( 3. APPRAISAL OF THE PROPERTY.       ) THE LOAN IS
TRANSACTION    (                                     )
               ( 4. CREDIT ANALYSIS OF THE BORROWER. ) RATED AND
EVALUATION     (                                     )
OF RISKS       ( 5. RATING OF THE PROPERTY, NEIGH-   ) APPROVED OR
               (     BORHOOD, THE BORROWER AND THE   )
               (     MORTGAGE PATTERN.               )
               (                                     ) WITHDRAWN
               ( 6. APPROVAL OF LOAN, OR WITHDRAWAL. )

               ( 7. NET INCOME.                      )
               (                                     )
               ( 8. CUSTOMER RELATIONS.              )
               (                                     )
               ( 9. PUBLIC RELATIONS.                )
               (                                     )
    MAJOR      (10. COMPETITION.                     )
               (                                     )
  OBJECTIVES   (11. MAINTENANCE OF INTEREST RATE.    )
               (                                     )
 AND POLICIES  (12. LIQUIDITY OF THE PORTFOLIO.      )
               (                                     )
 THAT AFFECT   (13. MAINTENANCE OF QUALITY.          )
               (                                     )
PROCESSING OF  (14. GENERAL LENDING POLICIES.        )
               (                                     )
 APPLICATION   (15. COUNTLESS OTHER REQUIREMENTS     )
               (     WHICH ARE ESSENTIAL IN ORDER TO )
               (     INSURE HIGHLY EFFICIENT OPER-   )
 AND ANALYSIS  (     ATION AND MANAGEMENT.           )
               (                                     )
    OF         (16. CONTINUOUS STUDY AND ANALYSIS OF )
               (     OPERATIONS, STATISTICS AND LOAN )
 TRANSACTION   (     TRENDS IN ORDER THAT IMPROVE-   )
               (     MENTS IN OPERATIONS AND MANAGE- )
               (     MENT CAN BE MADE.               )
               (                                     )
               (17. REDUCTION OF RISKS INVOLVED.     )
               (                                     )
               (18. ECONOMIC STABILITY.             )
               (                                     )
               (19. SOUND LOANS.                     )
```

Figure 12. Technical Operations and Objectives Covering Application
and Processing of Loan

IF THE BORROWER DEFAULTS PERMANENTLY IN PAYMENTS, AND A SALE OF THE PROPERTY BY THE BORROWER, OR OTHER SOLUTIONS FOR A SATISFACTORY WORKOUT, FAIL, THE PROPERTY ITSELF THEN BECOMES THE PROTECTION AGAINST LOSS IN CASE OF FORECLOSURE AND EVENTUAL SALE OR TRANSFER TO FHA OR VA ON SUCH TYPE LOANS

RISKS ARE ALWAYS PRESENT AND INCLUDE THE POSSIBILITY OF

RISKS

(1. INABILITY OF <u>BORROWER</u> TO REPAY THE OBLIGATION.

(2. <u>LOSS OF INTEREST OR SOME OF THE PRINCIPAL.</u>

(3. <u>INCREASED SERVICING AND FORECLOSURE COSTS ON
(DELINQUENT LOANS.</u>

(4. COST OF REHABILITATION AND CARRYING PROPERTY
(UNTIL SOLD OR ASSIGNED TO FHA OR VA.

(5. LOSS ON RESALE.

FACTORS

WHICH

CONTRIBUTE

TO RISKS

(6. RECURRING DEPRESSION PERIODS, WHICH PROBABLY
(WOULD QUICKLY CHANGE THE ECONOMIC OUTLOOK OF
(MORTGAGE LENDING.

(7. UNCONTROLLABLE AND PERIODICAL CHANGES IN GENERAL
(ECONOMIC CONDITIONS.

(8. FLUCTUATION OF VALUE ELEMENTS INVOLVED IN THE
(MAKING OF ANY MORTGAGE LOAN.

(9. ACTS OF GOD.

(10. WAR.

(11. <u>THE HUMAN ELEMENT.</u>

(12. CHANGES IN NEIGHBORHOODS.

(13. STRUCTURAL DURABILITY OF HOMES.

(14. MARKETABILITY OF THE PROPERTY.

(15. <u>EARNING POWER OF BORROWER, ABILITY TO PAY AND
(FUTURE PROSPECTS.</u>

(16. <u>UNSOUND LENDING.</u>

Figure 13. Risks Involved in Analyzing Strength of Borrower in Transaction

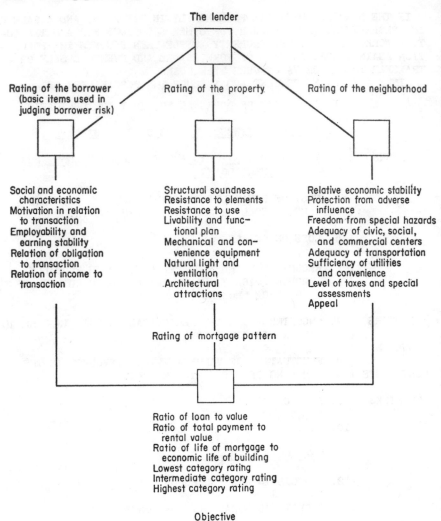

The lender

Rating of the borrower
(basic items used in
judging borrower risk)

Rating of the property

Rating of the neighborhood

Social and economic
characteristics
Motivation in relation
to transaction
Employability and
earning stability
Relation of obligation
to transaction
Relation of income to
transaction

Structural soundness
Resistance to elements
Resistance to use
Livability and func-
tional plan
Mechanical and con-
venience equipment
Natural light and
ventilation
Architectural
attractions

Relative economic stability
Protection from adverse
influence
Freedom from special hazards
Adequacy of civic, social,
and commercial centers
Adequacy of transportation
Sufficiency of utilities
and convenience
Level of taxes and special
assessments
Appeal

Rating of mortgage pattern

Ratio of loan to value
Ratio of total payment to
rental value
Ratio of life of mortgage to
economic life of building
Lowest category rating
Intermediate category rating
Highest category rating

Objective

Evaluation of economic soundness of the transaction

Figure 14. Position of the Borrower in Mortgage Lending

COMMENTS ON FIGURE 14

1. This chart shows in a general way the position of the borrower in a mortgage loan transaction today. He now is recognized as representing so many safety factors that his strength has a great bearing on the evaluation of risks involved.

2. Although there are hundreds of items which are involved in the rating of any borrower, they have been reduced to five basic items in number.

3. The lender has been added to this chart to stress the fact that the lending policies of each lender must be sound and the borrower should do business with sound lenders only.

ATTITUDE		ABILITY TO PAY		
*CHARACTER.	*CASH IN- VESTMENT.	*VERSATILITY.	NATURE OF OBLIGA- TIONS.	*RATIO OF PROPERTY VALUE TO
*FAMILY LIFE AND RELA- TIONSHIPS.	*MOTIVES FOR BORROWING.	*PERSONALITY. *EMPLOYMENT.	*EFFECT OF OBLIGATIONS	ANNUAL IN- COME.
*ASSOCIATES. MATURITY.	*IMPORTANCE OF PROP- ERTY TO BORROWER.	OCCUPATIONAL IMPAIRMENT. RE-EMPLOYMENT	ON CAPAC- ITY.	*RATIO OF TOTAL MONTHLY PAYMENTS TO
*ATTITUDE TOWARD OB- LIGATIONS.		POSSIBIL- ITIES. *RESERVES AND		INCOME. CO-MAKERS.
*ABILITY TO MANAGE AFFAIRS.		CONTRIBU- TIONS. *AGE. *HEALTH.		CO-SIGNERS. ENDORSERS. GUARANTORS.
WEIGHT 15	WEIGHT 25	WEIGHT 20	WEIGHT 15	WEIGHT 25
SOCIAL AND ECONOMIC CHARACTER- ISTICS.	MOTIVATION IN RELA- TION TO TRANSAC- TION.	EMPLOYABILITY AND EARNING STABILITY.	RELATION OF OBLIGATIONS TO TRANS- ACTION.	RELATION OF INCOME TO TRANSAC- TION.

Figure 15. List of Major Factors That Have a Bearing on Borrower Risk and Reduction to the Five Basic Relationships That Represent All Factors. These Are Known as Elements of Risk to Which Weights Have Been Given

COMMENTS ON FIGURE 15

1. FHA major factors that have a bearing on borrower risk are listed, and the reduction to the five basic relationships that represent all factors are also listed. This list is based upon the FHA *Underwriting Manual.*

2. This is a simple explanation of the development of the system of weights which are used to measure borrower risks—weights which are employed in the over-all rating of the loan involved.

Credit Report

Before a lending officer can properly evaluate any loan transaction, it is necessary that he know and understand credit, what a credit report should show, and how the credit department of a typical large lender, mainly commercial banks, mutual savings banks, and savings and loan associations, has developed into the major position which it holds today. He should learn to make full use of the credit department and to take full advantage of the abilities of the credit-department personnel, who are particularly trained to review and analyze a credit report or financial statement.

Importance of the Credit Department

Because of constant efforts in education and training during the past many years, employees of lenders engaged in this type of work are experienced in this field and, almost without exception, are able to develop an accurate judgment of all factors involved in each particular case. Many loan officers today have had actual training in the credit departments or mortgage risk analysis departments of their firms. Information obtained from the commercial credit report is extremely valuable, particularly concerning any pending litigation, suits, judgments, or bankruptcies. It is no doubt true that the average commercial credit report today merely confirms much of the information obtained at the time of the interview, but it is an additional and necessary protection. It gives the past record of the applicant as well as present position, but does not predict potentials. Commercial credit reports give confidential factual data on the borrower.

Not so many years ago loan officers were the credit departments of both commercial and mutual savings banks. The credit department in a bank gradually was developed to handle credit inquiries of these loan officers and of other lenders. In addition to making complete credit checkings on individuals and business firms, credit departments began to establish records on specialized subjects, such as business statistics and business trends. For example, on the item of lumber alone most credit departments of mortgage lenders have price ranges covering the past thirty years or more, plus a record of supply and demand covering lumber for this period. It would perhaps be possible to multiply lumber by thousands of other items on which credit departments keep up-to-date records. Commodity files are maintained, as are industry figures. For example, a complete history of the canning industry is maintained. All such records and statistics are aids to some loan officer.

*FUTURE CONTINUITY OF INCOME. *PAST EMPLOYMENT HISTORY. *VERSATILITY. *PERSONALITY. EDUCATION. *HEALTH. *AGE.	*ABILITY TO HANDLE HIS FINANCIAL AFFAIRS. (CREDIT REPORT) *REGARD FOR OBLIGATIONS. ABILITY TO ACCUMULATE RESOURCES.	*MOTIVE FOR BORROWING. *IMPORTANCE OF PROPERTY TO BORROWER. *RATIO OF INITIAL INVESTMENT TO PROPERTY VALUE. PURPOSE.	*REFLECT CHARACTER AND REPUTATION. (CREDIT REPORT) *ASSOCIATES.	*ADEQUACY OF BORROWER'S INCOME TO MEET THE OBLIGATIONS OF THE PROPOSED MORTGAGE. *RATIO ESTIMATED HOUSING EXPENSES TO BORROWER'S INCOME. RATIO AMOUNT OF MORTGAGE TO BORROWER'S NET WORTH. ESTIMATED HOUSING EXPENSES TO PAST HOUSING EXPENSES. *RATIO OF VALUE OF PROPERTY TO BORROWER'S CURRENT INCOME.
WEIGHT 14	WEIGHT 10	WEIGHT 8	WEIGHT 8	WEIGHT 10
EMPLOYABILITY AND INCOME STABILITY.	PERSONAL FINANCIAL MANAGEMENT.	MOTIVATION IN THIS TRANSACTION.	FAMILY AND SOCIAL RELATIONSHIPS.	FINANCIAL CAPACITY.

Figure 16. List of Elements of Risks to Which Weights Have Been Given

COMMENTS ON FIGURE 16

1. List of elements of risks and weights contained in *Home Mortgage Lending Manual,* American Institute of Banking.

2. Asterisks indicate those items that are also contained in the FHA manual.

3. Are these weights sound and accurate? Experience will probably cause them to be adjusted from time to time.

4. Improvements in analytical techniques and procedures are being made constantly.

Credit Analysis

Credit analysis in many cases can be made informally by one of the loan officers in a small community where the personal contact with the customer is easily maintained. In the case of larger lenders special arrangements for assembling and analyzing credit information are necessary. Credit departments have been developed to meet this need. The operations have increased in importance with the increasing development of business in this country and with the increase in large-scale financing.

Sources of Credit Information

Information maintained is assembled from many sources. Reports furnished by commercial agencies are particularly valuable, as they furnish a history of the business experience of individuals and firms. Credit associations, both local and national, assemble information covering promptness with which obligations are paid. Credit information is exchanged by lenders on customers who have dealings with more than one firm. Bulletins, newspapers, and trade journals furnish a great deal of general information. Many borrowers make a practice of keeping mortgage loan departments, or credit departments, fully informed of their operations. Financial statements, when needed, are furnished periodically.

Elements of Credit

Credit involves two basic elements, namely, postponed payment and confidence. Without confidence credit cannot exist.

There are certain factors which affect credit in mortgage lending over which there is little or no control. They can be classed as political, which include price ceilings, tariffs, laws, income taxes, changes in government policies, public attitudes, antitrust laws, banking laws, insurance laws, and the HHFA policies; and economic, which include economic trends and cycles, market prices, public acceptance, supply and demand, and the money market.

	SOURCES OF INFORMATION				
	INTER- VIEW	APPLI- CATION	CREDIT REPORT	FINAN- CIAL STATE- MENT	OTHER SOURCES
INFORMATION REQUIRED					
CHARACTER (INTANGIBLE)			X		X
REPUTATION (INTANGIBLE)			X		X
HEALTH (INTANGIBLE)	X				
AGE (TANGIBLE)	X	X	X		
FAMILY HEALTH (INTANGIBLE)	X		X		
DEPENDENTS (TANGIBLE)	X	X	X		
INCOME (TANGIBLE)	X	X	X	X	
ASSETS (TANGIBLE)				X	
LIABILITIES (TANGIBLE)		X		X	
OTHER INCOME (TANGIBLE)		X		X	
LIFE INSURANCE (TANGIBLE)	X	X	X	X	
LOANS ON POLICIES (TANGIBLE)	X	X	X	X	
CASH SURRENDER VALUE (TANGIBLE)	X	X	X	X	
OTHER PROPERTIES OWNED (TANGIBLE)	X	X	X	X	
BANK BALANCES (TANGIBLE)	X	X	X	X	
LITIGATION (TANGIBLE)			X		
BANKRUPTCIES (TANGIBLE)			X		
INTELLIGENCE (INTANGIBLE)	X		X		
FUTURE EARNING PROSPECTS (INTANGIBLE)	X		X	X	X
ESTIMATED PRESENT LIVING EXPENSES (TANGIBLE)	X	X		X	
ESTIMATED FUTURE LIVING EXPENSES (TANGIBLE)	X	X		X	
STOVE (TANGIBLE)	X	X			
REFRIGERATOR (TANGIBLE)	X	X			
FURNITURE (TANGIBLE)	X	X	X		
WASHING MACHINE (TANGIBLE)	X	X			
AUTOMOBILE (TANGIBLE)	X	X	X	X	
RATING OF BORROWER					
EMPLOYABILITY AND EARNING STABILITY	X	X	X	X	X
MOTIVATION IN RELATION TO TRANSACTION	X	X	X	X	X
SOCIAL AND ECONOMIC CHARACTERISTICS	X	X	X	X	X
RELATION OF OBLIGATIONS TO TRANSACTION	X	X	X	X	X
RELATION OF INCOME TO TRANSACTION	X	X	X	X	X

Figure 17. Analysis of Borrower

Rating of borrower after study of application, credit report, and information from all other sources, based upon A.I.B. home mortgage lending manual

John Doe—Mary Doe   100 points

	2	1	0	1	2	Weight	Grade
Employability and income stability					X	14	28
Personal financial management					X	10	20
Motivation in this transaction				X		8	8
Family and social relationships					X	8	16
Financial capacity				X		10	10
	Total grade						82

John Doe—Mary Doe   100 points

		Reject	1	2	3	4	5	Rating
Attitudes	Social and economic characteristics					X		12
Attitudes	Motivation in relation to transaction					X		20
Ability to pay	Employability and earning stability					X		16
Ability to pay	Relation of obligations to transaction					X		12
Ability to pay	Relation of income to transaction					X		20
	Total rating of borrower							80

Complete amortization provisions required.
Periodic payments required not in excess of his reasonable ability to pay.
Analysis of all credit factors required.
Complete information on borrower must be assembled.
Requires careful study.

Figure 18. Grids Covering Rating of Borrower

COMMENTS ON FIGURE 18

1. Grids covering the borrower rating of John Doe and Mary Doe are set forth in a manner similar to FHA and AIB grid rating procedures.

2. Analysis has revealed that John Doe and Mary Doe are strong financially and of good character. John Doe has steady employment with a well-established firm. He has a good monthly income, and prospects for advancement in his firm are excellent. The grade given in each grid is above average.

Credit Analysis of the Operative Builder

During the past few years billions of dollars have been loaned to operative builders, large and small, by lenders to aid in solving the housing crisis. In view of building-material shortages and other uncertainties, some risks of loss were involved. Thousands of new builders had entered the field. Their ability to perform was not certain or assured. The record of accomplishment in the construction of homes during this period reveals that this program has been successful.

CONSTRUCTION OF HOME LOT 4, BLOCK 2, SAN MATEO

COST OF CONSTRUCTION	$15,000
LOAN REQUIRED — FHA TITLE II	$12,000
4½% INTEREST	

BUILDER — JOHN SMITH
CONTRACT — SATISFACTORY
PAYMENT PLAN — SATISFACTORY

MONTHLY INCOME		PRESENT EXPENSES		ESTIMATED FUTURE EXPENSES	
SALARY	$450.00	RENT	$ 80.00	LOAN PAYMENT	$ 95.00
ANNUITY	15.00	GAS &		WATER	5.00
MISCELLANEOUS	5.00	ELECTR.	5.00	TELEPHONE	4.00
GROSS TOTAL	$470.00	TELEPHONE	4.00	GAS &	
		COMMUTE	12.00	ELECTR.	5.00
LESS		LIFE INSUR–		PROPERTY UP–	
TAX WITH–		ANCE	15.00	KEEP	10.00
HOLDING	$ 40.00	MILK	10.00	COMMUTE	12.00
GROUP INSUR–		PROPERTY		LIFE INSUR–	
ANCE	9.00	TAXES	6.00	ANCE	15.00
RETIREMENT	12.00	FOOD	100.00	MILK	10.00
S.S. & U.C.		PHARMACY	6.00	PROPERTY	
TAX	4.00	LAUNDRY	10.00	TAXES	6.00
	$ 65.00	CLOTHING	12.00	FOOD	100.00
		DOCTOR	10.00	PHARMACY	6.00
NET INCOME	$405.00	ENTERTAIN–		LAUNDRY	10.00
		MENT	30.00	CLOTHING	12.00
		AUTO. INSUR–		DOCTOR	10.00
		ANCE	4.00	ENTERTAIN–	
				MENT	30.00
		MISCEL–		AUTO. INSUR–	
		LANEOUS	20.00	ANCE	4.00
				MISCEL–	
				LANEOUS	20.00
		TOTAL	$324.00	TOTAL	$354.00

FINANCIAL STATEMENT

ASSETS		LIABILITIES	
BANK ACCOUNTS	$ 4,500.00	CURRENT ACCOUNTS	
WAR BONDS	1,000.00	PAYABLE	0
PROPERTY (LOT ABOVE)	3,000.00	REAL ESTATE MORT–	
PROPERTY SANTA CLARA	4,000.00	GAGES	0
AUTOMOBILE	900.00	OTHER LIABILITIES	0
TOTAL ASSETS	$13,400.00	TOTAL LIABILITIES	0
		NET WORTH	$13,400.00

LIFE INSURANCE	$20,000.00	CASH SURRENDER VALUE	$ 3,000.00
		LOANS ON POLICIES	NONE

Figure 19. Financial Information, John Doe—Mary Doe

COMMENTS ON FIGURE 19

1. Financial information analysis form used by some lenders in order to compare present expenses and estimated future expenses. Net monthly income together with a list of assets and liabilities itemized in the financial statement discloses financial strength or weakness of the borrower.

2. In case the borrower does not present information concerning present expenses and estimated future expenses, he should have such figures available for his self-analysis of the possible increase in his budget. Purchase or construction of a new home entails many additional expenses that must be taken into consideration.

Credit Records of Builders Maintained by Lenders

In the case of builders who are now so active in the building industry, most credit departments have complete and accurate records of all materials that go into the building of a home and other properties, including supplies of materials and price records. In addition to checking the financial responsibilities of the builder, his ability to perform, as well as the ability of subcontractors to perform, is checked. As we all know, there are a certain number of business failures occurring nearly every day. The major reasons for failures in building operations, according to the records, are lack of capital, poor management, inability to perform, and overexpansion. In credit, there is the famous doctrine called "the three C's."

1. Capital
2. Capacity
3. Character

Some credit men add a fourth called "Collateral."

Financial Statement of Builder Required

In analyzing the operative builder, the lender first requires a financial statement and a balance sheet, plus a profit and loss statement which shows operating figures. The mortgage loan officer will analyze this statement to find out if the borrower has first of all made up the statement correctly, ascertaining working capital and fixed assets, and whether they are in proper proportion to each other. The profit and loss, or operating, statement will show whether this builder has made money in his operations. His major items of expense will be checked to find out if they are correct, and also whether the gross-profit margin is correct.

In addition to this it will be necessary to ascertain whether the builder is in good balance or bad balance. What is working capital for a builder? Lots and houses in course of construction, if they can be moved within one year, are considered working capital. A builder is different from a mercantile firm, and analysis of one as compared with the other differs just as an analysis for a utilities firm would differ from either of them.

Through such credit agencies as Dun & Bradstreet, Inc., and the Credit Managers' Association, information including the following is obtained:

1. History of the firm
2. Its method of operation and quarters
3. Financial information
4. Conclusion and rating

Credit procedures are used to see factors with which to evaluate each transaction. There is not a great deal of difference between the basic factors in the analysis of the individual borrower and the builder of a large business operation. It is a question of potentials.

Analyzing the Loan Application and Effect upon Interview and Credit Analysis

Mortgage lending institutions must analyze each loan application and the status of the applicant by intelligent methods in order that the possibility of any loss or additional expense of any kind be kept at a minimum at all times. The best manner in which procedures can be improved is by using the wisdom gained by many years of experience in this field, by continuous study and analysis of operating expenses, gross income, net income, and operation and administration expenses, and by analyzing losses during a given period to see whether they vary from experience of others in the same endeavors. Inadequate credit analysis of the borrower at inception of transaction had a great deal to do with the losses experienced in the Great Depression.

Assuming that on every individual home-loan application received by every lender in the United States each property involved has been properly appraised, the amount of the loan is satisfactory, the amortization program is fundamentally sound, the credit record of the borrower is satisfactory, the type of loan is based upon factors which would indicate that it is the best type of loan possible for the lending institution to make, and that all other underlying factors involved in the making of such a loan have been used, nevertheless, in spite of this care, delinquencies will arise continually, and there will be some losses. To keep delinquencies and losses at a minimum the entire mortgage loan portfolio must be subjected to searching examination as well as constant supervision at all times. Value factors and credit-analysis procedures must be adjusted frequently. In other words, mortgage loan portfolios and lending practices are subject to almost daily change.

CONFIDENTIAL

FHA LOAN

DATE 3-30-61

CREDIT ANALYSIS OF BORROWER

REL NO. 12345

APPLICANT   DOE, JOHN AND MARY

Age 41   Age 38

	WEIGHT	RATING	TOTAL WEIGHT
1. AMOUNT OF LOAN APPLIED FOR: FHA TITLE II	10	$12,000.00	7
2. REQUIRED MONTHLY PAYMENT INCLUDING TAXES $75.96 AND INSURANCE: 4.77 MORT. INS. AND TERM OF LOAN..20 YEARS......... 12.00 EST. TAXES 2.27 FIRE INS.	10	$95.00	8
3. MONTHLY INCOME: $470.00 GROSS (SEE FINANCIAL STATEMENT)	10	$405.00	NET
4. RATIO OF MONTHLY INCOME TO REQUIRED MONTHLY PAYMENT ON LOAN WHICH INCLUDES PAYMENT OF TAXES AND INSURANCE:	20	23%	14
5. RATIO OF LOAN TO SALE PRICE OF PROPERTY: $ 3,000 LAND 15,000 CONSTRUCTION	15	12,000 / 18,000	12
6. CHARACTER CREDIT REPORT: (EXCELLENT) (SATISFACTORY) (UNSATISFACTORY)	15	EXCELLENT	15

7. RATING OF ANTICIPATED INCREASED EARNINGS OF BORROWER:	10	SATISFACTORY	10

8. OTHER OBLIGATIONS REQUIRED IN ORDER TO OCCUPY HOME:	10		8
5 ROOMS (FURNITURE)		CLEAR	
(STOVE)		CLEAR	
(REFRIGERATOR)		CLEAR	
1953 OLDS. (AUTOMOBILE)		CLEAR	

9. CONCLUSION: SIZE OF LOAN COMMENSURATE WITH APPLICANT'S INCOME – PAYMENTS LESS THAN 1/4 OF NET. FINANCIAL STATEMENT SHOWS APPLICANT HAS BEEN LIVING WITHIN INCOME AND THAT THIS IS A SOUND INVESTMENT.	100	SATISFACTORY	82

ANALYSIS OF LOAN MUST SHOW:

1. THAT THE CONTEMPLATED TERMS OF PAYMENT REQUIRED IN ANY MORTGAGE TO BE GIVEN IN PART PAYMENT OF THE PURCHASE PRICE OR THE CONSTRUCTION COST BEAR A PROPER RELATION TO THE BORROWER'S PRESENT AND ANTICIPATED INCOME AND EXPENSES: AND THAT THE NATURE AND CONDITION OF THE PROPERTY IS SUCH AS TO BE SUITABLE FOR DWELLING PURPOSES: AND

2. THAT ALL UNDERLYING FACTORS NECESSARY TO INDICATE A SOUND LOAN HAVE BEEN ANALYZED AND APPROVED.

APPROVAL RECOMMENDED _____ CLYDE BROWN _____ DISAPPROVAL RECOMMENDED _____

    TO BE ATTACHED TO BANK REAL ESTATE LOAN APPLICATION.

Figure 20

COMMENTS ON FIGURE 20

1. Lenders who do not use borrower ratings, such as are used by the FHA, analyze the borrower by means of a credit analysis sheet similar to the example shown in this figure. It should be noted that the basic items analyzed are similar to the items listed by the FHA. The objectives are the same, and a very clear and sound analysis of the transaction is necessary before the ratings can be indicated.

2. The interviewer or loan officer, in studying and rating this case, must make an exhaustive study of every possible factor involved; otherwise the transaction cannot be properly rated and evaluated.

3. Weights shown in this exhibit are not generally used by lenders but if used would vary only slightly from weights and rating arrived at by either the FHA or AIB weight and rating methods. For example:

> AIB total rating of borrowers John and Mary Doe.......82
> FHA total rating of borrowers John and Mary Doe......80
> Lender total rating of borrowers John and Mary Doe....82

Tests Covering Efficiency of Interview and Credit-analysis Procedures

There are numerous methods by which the efficiency and success of interview and analysis procedures can be tested by a lender.

One of the most important is by checking the trend of delinquent loans and analyzing the basic reasons for defaults. In analyzing any specific chronic delinquent the lender will undoubtedly find a definite fault that existed at the time the loan was made. By noting these faults and reasons for the faults, loan-processing methods are improved.

A recent analysis of a typical large lender indicated these basic reasons for delinquencies in home loans which have occurred during the past few years.

1. Frequent changes in occupation
2. Downward trend in monthly income
3. Unsatisfactory domestic relationships
4. Excessive installment purchases, i.e., furniture, weather stripping, automobile, landscaping, washing machine, television set; indications of complete inability to budget income and expenses
5. Sickness, doctor bills, unexpected expenses not covered by a reserve
6. Progressive increase in cost of food, clothing, and other items
7. Temporary unemployment due mainly in strikes or inclement weather
8. Lack of understanding of necessity for meeting obligations promptly
9. Inability to adjust existing working conditions and family problems
10. Carelessness, lack of responsibility, and improper attitude toward obligations

A study of the amount of interest earned but not collected on a comparative basis gives some indication of strength of the original interview and credit analysis.

Analysis of number of loans under foreclosure and reasons for foreclosure action will also reveal weaknesses or strength in interview and credit-analysis procedures.

Attitude of borrowers toward the lender and the regard held for the firm by other lenders will also indicate the efficiency and success of these procedures.

Most important, perhaps, is self-analysis of each individual interviewer's endeavors and accomplishments. It is not very difficult for a person to judge his success or shortcomings in interview and credit-analysis work.

Lastly, another depression would very quickly reveal strength or weakness in lending procedures, including interview with borrower and credit analysis of borrower.

Soundness of Lending Procedures Have Been Tested

New loans placed in portfolios since V-J Day have been completely tested. Over $50 billion in VA real estate loans have been made by lenders since the passage of the Servicemen's Readjustment Act of 1944 and amendments thereto. This has been a highly successful program. The potential loans for apartment houses, industrial expansion, and farms total many billions of dollars, as do home loans to nonveterans and veterans. The United States is progressively developing into a country of homeowners because of improved transportation, shopping centers in outlying areas, spectacular growth of subdivisions, and decentralization. These statements very clearly outline the future of mortgage lending in this country. We are on the threshold of great opportunities in this field which can be and should be handled mainly by private enterprise. It is well to repeat that new borrowers wholly unacquainted with lending operations or policies have contacted lenders by the hundreds of thousands to discuss or apply for mortgage loans. Many more will be contacting lenders during the next few years. Lenders who meet these potential customers every day are charged with the responsibility of seeing that in the mortgage lending field the economic stability of the country is strengthened.

Personal interview with the borrower and credit analysis of the borrower are two of the vital factors in mortgage loan operations which control loanable funds and have a great bearing on the success of this program.[3]

[3] For additional coverage of this subject, refer to Bibliography and Suggested Reading at the end of this chapter.

CREDIT ANALYSIS OF BORROWER   DATE   4-20-48

SERVICEMEN'S READJUSTMENT ACT OF 1944 AS AMENDED

REL NO.   12345

APPLICANT   BROWN, JOHN AND SUSAN
Age 36   Age 33

	WT.	RATING	TOTAL WT.
1. AMOUNT OF LOAN APPLIED FOR: "501" $6,000 / 4,000	10	$10,000.00	5
2. REQUIRED MONTHLY PAYMENT INCLUDING TAXES AND INSURANCE: TERM OF LOAN...25 YEARS.............	10	$64.80	6
3. MONTHLY INCOME:	10	$225.00 NET	6
4. RATIO OF MONTHLY INCOME TO REQUIRED MONTHLY PAYMENT ON LOAN WHICH INCLUDES PAYMENT OF TAXES AND INSURANCE:	20	*28%	0
5. RATIO OF LOAN INCLUDING GUARANTEE TO SALE PRICE OF PROPERTY:	15	10,000 / 12,000	4
6. CHARACTER CREDIT REPORT: (EXCELLENT) (SATISFACTORY) (UNSATISFACTORY)	15	SATISFACTORY	10
7. RATING OF ANTICIPATED INCREASED EARNINGS OF BORROWER:	10	SATISFACTORY	7

8. OTHER OBLIGATIONS REQUIRED IN ORDER TO OCCUPY HOME: (FURNITURE) NONE (STOVE) NONE (REFRIGERATOR) NONE (AUTOMOBILE) NONE	10	0
9. CONCLUSIONS: *APPLICANT'S CREDIT RATING IS SATISFACTORY, BUT IN- COME IS NOT SUFFICIENT TO HANDLE LOAN OF THIS SIZE. SHOULD NOT BORROW MORE THAN $8,000, BUT DOES NOT HAVE THIS MUCH READY CASH.	100	38

ANALYSIS OF LOAN MUST SHOW:

1. THAT THE PROCEEDS OF SUCH LOAN WILL BE USED FOR PAYMENT OF THE PROPERTY PURCHASED, OR CON-
STRUCTED, OR IMPROVED, AND THAT THE PROPERTY WILL BE OCCUPIED BY THE APPLICANT.

2. THAT THE CONTEMPLATED TERMS OF PAYMENT REQUIRED IN ANY MORTGAGE TO BE GIVEN IN PART PAYMENT OF
THE PURCHASE PRICE OF THE CONSTRUCTION COST BEAR A PROPER RELATION TO THE VETERAN'S PRESENT AND
ANTICIPATED INCOME AND EXPENSES: AND THAT THE NATURE AND CONDITION OF THE PROPERTY IS SUCH AS TO
BE SUITABLE FOR DWELLING PURPOSES: AND

3. THAT THE PRICE PAID OR TO BE PAID BY THE VETERAN FOR SUCH PROPERTY OR FOR THE COST OF CONSTRUC-
TION, REPAIRS, OR ALTERATIONS DOES NOT EXCEED THE REASONABLE VALUE THEREOF AS DETERMINED BY PROP-
ERTY APPRAISAL MADE BY AN APPRAISER DESIGNATED BY THE ADMINISTRATOR.

APPROVAL RECOMMENDED _____ DISAPPROVAL RECOMMENDED *Raymond Royal*

TO BE ATTACHED TO BANK REAL ESTATE LOAN APPLICATION.

Figure 21

CREDIT ANALYSIS OF BORROWER   DATE   4/20/48

CONFIDENTIAL

SERVICEMEN'S READJUSTMENT ACT OF 1944 AS AMENDED

REL NO.   54321

APPLICANT   DOAKES, ELMER AND HYACINTH

　　　　　　　Age 38   Age 36

	WT.	RATING	TOTAL WT.
1. AMOUNT OF LOAN APPLIED FOR: "501" $5,900 4,000	10	$9,900.00	6
2. REQUIRED MONTHLY PAYMENT INCLUDING TAXES AND INSURANCE: TERM OF LOAN...25 YEARS............................	10	$64.15	8
3. MONTHLY INCOME:	10	$260.00	7
4. RATIO OF MONTHLY INCOME TO REQUIRED MONTHLY PAYMENT ON LOAN WHICH INCLUDES PAYMENT OF TAXES AND INSURANCE:	20	25%	13
5. RATIO OF LOAN INCLUDING GUARANTEE TO SALE PRICE OF PROPERTY:	15	9,900 / 11,500	5
6. CHARACTER CREDIT REPORT: (EXCELLENT) (SATISFACTORY) (UNSATISFACTORY)	15	*UNSATISFAC- TORY	0
7. RATING OF ANTICIPATED INCREASED EARNINGS OF BORROWER	10	QUESTIONABLE	0

10		0

8. OTHER OBLIGATIONS REQUIRED IN ORDER TO OCCUPY HOME:
    (FURNITURE   ) NONE
    (STOVE   ) NONE
    (REFRIGERATOR) NONE
    (AUTOMOBILE) NONE

100		39

9. CONCLUSION: *CREDIT REPORT SHOWS SEVERAL VERY QUESTIONABLE ITEMS
BOTH AS TO APPLICANT'S CHARACTER AND HIS PAST ABILITY
IN MEETING OBLIGATIONS. HAS HAD TWO SUITS AND JUDG-
MENTS FOR NON-PAYMENT. WAS DISCHARGED FROM LAST POSI-
TION BEFORE WAR FOR BEING ARROGANT, SURLY AND USING
INTOXICANTS TO EXCESS.

ANALYSIS OF LOAN MUST SHOW:

1. THAT THE PROCEEDS OF SUCH LOAN WILL BE USED FOR PAYMENT OF THE PROPERTY PURCHASED OR CONSTRUCTED, OR IMPROVED, AND THAT THE PROPERTY WILL BE OCCUPIED BY THE APPLICANT.

2. THAT THE CONTEMPLATED TERMS OF PAYMENT REQUIRED IN ANY MORTGAGE TO BE GIVEN IN PART PAYMENT OF THE PURCHASE PRICE OR THE CONSTRUCTION COST BEAR A PROPER RELATION TO THE VETERAN'S PRESENT AND ANTICIPATED INCOME AND EXPENSES: AND THAT THE NATURE AND CONDITION OF THE PROPERTY IS SUCH AS TO BE SUITABLE FOR DWELLING PURPOSES: AND

3. THAT THE PRICE PAID OR TO BE PAID BY THE VETERAN FOR SUCH PROPERTY OR FOR THE COST OF CONSTRUC-TION, REPAIRS, OR ALTERATIONS DOES NOT EXCEED THE REASONABLE VALUE THEREOF AS DETERMINED BY PROP-ERTY APPRAISAL MADE BY AN APPRAISER DESIGNATED BY THE ADMINISTRATOR.

APPROVAL RECOMMENDED   DISAPPROVAL RECOMMENDED   A. Flinthead

    TO BE ATTACHED TO BANK REAL ESTATE LOAN APPLICATION.

Figure 22

CONFIDENTIAL

CREDIT ANALYSIS OF BORROWER   DATE   3/30/61

CONVENTIONAL BANK REAL ESTATE LOAN

REL. NO.   23456

APPLICANT   BOTTS, ALEXANDER AND GRACE

Age 46   Age 42

	WT.	RATING	TOTAL WT.
1. AMOUNT OF LOAN APPLIED FOR: STRAIGHT BANK LOAN 5% INTEREST	10	$10,000.00	9
2. REQUIRED MONTHLY PAYMENT INCLUDING TAXES $111.00 INT. & INSTALL. AND INSURANCE: 20.00 TAXES 5.00 INSURANCE TERM OF LOAN...10 YEARS	10	$136.00	9
3. MONTHLY INCOME: $700.00 GROSS (SEE FINANCIAL STATEMENT)	10	$600.00 NET	9
4. RATIO OF MONTHLY INCOME TO REQUIRED MONTHLY PAYMENT ON LOAN, WHICH INCLUDES PAYMENTS OF TAXES AND INSURANCE:	20	22.6%	15
5. RATIO OF LOAN TO SALE PRICE OF PROPERTY:	15	$\frac{10,000}{25,000}$	15
6. CHARACTER CREDIT REPORT: (EXCELLENT) (SATISFACTORY) (UNSATISFACTORY)	15	EXCELLENT	15
7. RATINGS OF ANTICIPATED INCREASED EARNINGS OF BORROWER:	10	EXCELLENT	9

8. OTHER OBLIGATIONS REQUIRED IN ORDER TO OCCUPY HOME:		
(FURNITURE)		CLEAR
(STOVE)		CLEAR
(REFRIGERATOR)		CLEAR
(AUTOMOBILE)	10	CLEAR 9
9. CONCLUSION: SOUND LOAN – STRONG BORROWER	100	EXCELLENT 90

ANALYSIS OF LOAN MUST SHOW:

1. THAT THE CONTEMPLATED TERMS OF PAYMENT REQUIRED IN ANY MORTGAGE TO BE GIVEN IN PART PAYMENT OF THE PURCHASE PRICE, OR THE CONSTRUCTION COST, BEAR A PROPER RELATION TO THE BORROWER'S PRESENT AND ANTICIPATED INCOME AND EXPENSE: AND THAT THE NATURE AND CONDITION OF THE PROPERTY IS SUCH AS TO BE SUITABLE FOR DWELLING PURPOSES: AND

2. THAT ALL UNDERLYING FACTORS NECESSARY TO INDICATE A SOUND LOAN HAVE BEEN ANALYZED AND APPROVED.

APPROVAL RECOMMENDED   *Clyde Brown*   DISAPPROVAL RECOMMENDED

TO BE ATTACHED TO BANK REAL ESTATE LOAN APPLICATION

Figure 23

COMMENTS ON FIGURE 23

1. This figure described what is known as a conventional real estate loan, which is based strictly on 75 per cent, or under, of the bank appraisal of the property, plus an exact credit analysis of the borrower, which reveals that this borrower is a strong credit risk. Amortization provisions are satisfactory, as is the interest rate. The type and location of the property are also satisfactory.

2. The bank appraisal of the property is $20,000.00, cash investment in the property, $15,000.00. Margin of safety is high. The likelihood of loss on this loan is negligible.

SOCIAL AND ECONOMIC CHARACTERISTICS	(COVERS NAME, AGE, RACIAL DESCENT, MARRIAGE, (GENERAL REPUTATION AS TO CHARACTER, HABITS (AND MORALS, STEADINESS AND DEPENDABILITY, (DOMESTIC DIFFICULTIES, CLASS OF BUSINESS (ASSOCIATED, REPUTATION OF SOCIAL ASSOCIATES, (ABILITY TO MANAGE HIS AFFAIRS, LIVING WITHIN (INCOME, GENERAL ATTITUDE TOWARD CONTRACTUAL (OBLIGATIONS, ANY BANKRUPTCIES, FORECLOSURES, (SUITS, AND IF A CHRONIC LITIGANT.
EMPLOYABILITY AND EARNING STABILITY	(WHAT IS NATURE OF HIS BUSINESS AND POSITION (HELD? (HOW LONG IN PRESENT CONNECTION? (DOES HE WORK FULL TIME STEADILY? (WHAT ARE HIS FUTURE PROSPECTS? (IS HE MAKING EFFORTS TO IMPROVE HIMSELF IN HIS (WORK? (HAS HIS HEALTH INTERFERED WITH HIS PROGRESS?
INCOME AND OBLIGATIONS	(ANNUAL EARNED INCOME FROM HIS EMPLOYMENT OR (BUSINESS. (WHAT INCOME, IF ANY, FROM OTHER SOURCES. (ESTIMATE OF NET WORTH. (IF MARRIED, DOES HIS WIFE FOLLOW A GAINFUL (OCCUPATION? (WHAT IS HIS WIFE'S INDEPENDENT INCOME AND ESTI- (MATED NET WORTH? (AMPLIFICATION OF BUSINESS HISTORY. (AMPLIFICATION OF ALL UNUSUAL AND UNFAVORABLE (INFORMATION SUCH AS BANKRUPTCY, DIVORCE, ETC. (IF A WOMAN, COVER HUSBAND'S OR FATHER'S REPU- (TATION, BUSINESS HISTORY, INCOME, AND NET (WORTH. (INTENSIVE ANALYSIS OF CREDIT REPORT SHOULD BE (MADE.

Figure 24. Commercial Credit Report

MERCANTILE AGENCY, INC.   RATING CHANGE

BROWN, John A.   Genl. Contr.   SAN FRANCISCO, CALIF.
                                                 SAN FRANCISCO COUNTY
                                                 300 CAPITAL AVENUE

CD 101 52 December 30, 1960

SYNOPSIS

BACKGROUND: Present business commenced early in 1960 by owner
            with over 20 years experience in this line.
NET WORTH: $62,476 (Incl. real estate)   SALES: $45,300 (1-1-60
            to 12-1-60)
PAYMENTS: Prompt.
CONDITION AND TREND: Cash more than covers current debt. Volume
                     appears adequate for profitable operations.

HISTORY

Brown is 49, married and a native of San Jose, California. He has
lived most of his life there, in Sausalito or Santa Rosa, California, and engaged in the general contracting business in 1924,
operating from Santa Rosa, Calif. He came to San Francisco during
November, 1945, and from that time until very early in 1960 engaged in the buying of homes and speculating on them. He sold all
of his equipment except one crane. He only recently started to
build homes again after many months of inactivity due to labor
and material shortages. He commenced the subject line during
November, 1945.

METHOD OF OPERATION – FIRE HAZARD

Operates as a general contractor, engaged in buying lots and
building homes thereon and then selling the homes. He has five
homes under construction at the present time. Operates from his
residence at the above address. There are three employees.
OWNS this residence which is in good repair. Adjoining to either
side are similar residential structures.
FIRE RECORD: No fires reported.

FINANCIAL INFORMATION

From estimates of Dec. 30, 1960.

ASSETS

Cash-savings	$ 7,200.00	Accts. payable	$ 3,500.00
Cash-commercial	4,801.00		
Mdse.	300.00	Total current	$ 3,500.00
Total current	$12,301.00	Mortgages	$16,200.00

Figure 25. Hypothetical Credit Report

ASSETS

Real Estate	67,000.00		
Machy. & Fixts.	275.00		
'41 Buick auto	1,600.00		
Cash Val. Life Ins.	1,000.00	NET WORTH	62,476.00
Total Assets	$82,176.00	Total	$82,176.00

REAL ESTATE

1 lot Sausalito   Self & Wife $ 1,000 Clear
5 homes under construction Self & Wife $52,500 Mtg. $9,500
                                      (Bldg. Loan)
Home— 300 Capital Ave., Self & Wife $13,500 Mtg. 6,700
   NET SALES: 1-1-47 to 12-1-60 $45,300 Fire Ins.: Covered
          (Signed) Dec. 30, 1960 (by) John A. Brown

Cash was confirmed from passbooks and statement was favorably
accepted in quarter consulted. Valuation given for the five
homes under construction is selling price when finished. Real
estate on Capital would be subject to claim of exemption under
homestead laws, and mortgage is being retired at the rate of
$67.45 monthly.

PAYMENTS

Periodic trade clearances have shown this account to maintain a
prompt payment record in the trade.

Figure 25. (Continued)

COMMENTS ON FIGURE 25

John A. Brown wants to borrow $15,000 to complete his project.

1. Rating 3 to 2 indicates change from previous rating. Rating 3 indicates $2,000 to $20,000 Net Worth. Indicates he did not give the Mercantile Agency a financial statement. Net Worth equals assets minus liabilities.

2. In the process of conducting building operations, John A. Brown should show profit or loss, which should be reflected by increase or decrease in Net Worth.

3. Is Net Worth correctly stated?

a. To ascertain—must be sure that all assets and liabilities are included in the statement.

b. To evaluate assets—are they too high, too low, or satisfactory?

c. Real estate should be appraised, if real estate figures appear doubtful.

d. How much money does he need to carry through with his project?

4. Under financial information note the word *estimates*—

a. Means this is not a true and accurate statement. Is it a round figure or estimate?

b. Indicates not willing to give the Mercantile Agency an accountant's statement.

c. How much faith can we place in this statement?

d. If Brown is honest, the figures can be accepted as being aproximate. The statement is dated and signed.

5. Mortgage loan department enters the picture by making an analysis of the builder's building project now in progress. Is it sound—will he make a profit—does he build a good house? Shows $43,000 equity in the project upon completion, which should be available for investment in new projects.

6. Include in liabilities—cost to complete, which immediately raises a question as to the $43,000 equity stated above. How far along are the houses in the present project? If the houses are finished, it is a different story.

7. Current assets show $300 merchandise—very loose statement. Where are building materials? Has he enough on hand to finish project?

8. *Evaluate the project—most major information needed in order to analyze this applicant is missing. Need:*
   a. Location of project—is it satisfactory?
   b. Type of house—type of construction.
   c. Percentage completed.
   d. Cost to complete.
   e. Availability of materials and labor.
   f. Outstanding bills (which could become liens on the project).
   g. Selling prices of homes—are they correct?
   h. Can properties be sold on completion?

9. Do we want to retain account or get this new business?

10. Why not lend his own money—savings-passbook loan and loan on cash surrender value of life insurance?

11. Cannot do anything with this builder until accurate financial statement is obtained.

12. *Points to importance of interviewer and need to ascertain facts.*

13. Examine history—
   a. Verify his activities and reputation through San Jose, Sausalito, and Santa Rosa offices.
   b. Many builders went through bankruptcy in the 1930s as a result of heavy building operations. No bankruptcy indicated for John Brown.
   c. Perhaps he operated in a very small way and just made living expenses.

14. What is John Brown doing now?
   a. Is he qualified to expand?
   b. What is his ability, organization, program?

15. Examine method of operation—smart to operate from own home as it reduces overhead. If larger operations planned, he would need an office, yard, tools, materials, and assistants.

16. Why is "Fire hazard" noted—it means that property has been reported to insurance companies as a fire hazard.

17. Note "Payments"—
   a. Pays promptly—takes care of bills in the trade.
   b. Suppliers primarily interested in this item.

18. Ascertain principal supplier of John Brown.
   a. Talk with this supplier—lender must be ethical in inquiries.

19. *Sift all facts. Use information obtained with discretion.*

20. A decision concerning this case cannot be made until complete information as set forth above is obtained.

The exhibits and comments in this chapter explain some of the technical aspects of these operations by means of charts, graphs, and examples.

SUMMARY

The borrower has become a major element in each loan transaction. Many applicants for home loans and other types of mortgage loans have entered lending institutions for the first time. The average age of applicants has lowered greatly during the past several years.

Full use should be made of advanced interview and credit-analysis procedures; otherwise lenders could easily revert back to lending procedures which existed prior to the Great Depression of the early 1930s. Many new borrowers require counsel and guidance against the danger of "overbuying."

Ability to interview should be developed, as it is recognized today as a valuable asset in business success.

One of the most important improvements in mortgage lending since the Great Depression is recognition of the borrower as one of the major safety factors in any loan transaction.

Interviews should be thorough, accurate, analytical, and handled by highly capable personnel. Such interviews are concerned with many types of loans, with personalities of borrowers, and with customer and public relations aspects of each transaction.

All factors that are required to assure a sound loan should be known by the interviewer. This takes years of study, application, and attention to duty.

Every person engaged in mortgage lending today should become a student of human relations in order to understand the importance of efficient interviewing procedures. Qualifications required for an able interviewer should be developed.

Lenders should learn how their credit departments operate and make full use of them.

Credit departments have experts who have the equipment with which to get the facts.

Analysis of credit of an operative builder requires special procedures.

Mortgage risk analysis has been developed to the point where it is hoped losses due to the personal elements have been reduced to a minimum.

QUESTIONS

1. State one of the most important improvements made in mortgage lending since the Great Depression of the early 1930s.
2. Explain how borrower risk is evaluated.
3. Describe the present position of mortgage lending in the field of finance and industry.
4. Explain why improvements in mortgage lending procedures and policies were necessary during the Great Depression of the early 1930s.
5. Will the type of loan application determine the interviewer who will discuss the proposed transaction with the applicant?
6. Why do large lenders maintain separate FHA and VA divisions to handle these types of loans?
7. The efficiency of operations in interview and credit-analysis procedures depends upon what particular attributes in the interviewer?

8. Name some of the basic qualifications required of an interviewer.
9. Explain why a potential borrower planning to purchase a home should use the services of a sound and prudent lender.
10. Give reasons why a loan covering the construction of a home is particularly hazardous.
11. Why is it necessary to compare new housing expenses with previous housing expenses?
12. List some sources of credit information.
13. Name the three C's in credit.
14. Name a fourth C used by some credit men.
15. The analysis of an application for a VA home loan should show what three satisfactory facts if it is to be processed?
16. Explain how a study of the trend to delinquencies in the portfolio reflects the efficiency of interview and credit-analysis procedures.
17. Credit records of speculative builders are of special importance for what reasons?
18. Outline the borrower's position in the mortgage pattern.
19. Name the most important factor involved in the analysis of the rating of the borrower in the proposed mortgage loan transaction.
20. Explain the change in the pattern of mortgage lending which has taken place during the past twenty-five years.
21. Name some of the weaknesses of interview and credit-analysis procedures during the 1920s.
22. Name some of the elements of risk used in rating the borrower.
23. Why should the interviewer explain to the potential borrower the need for a detailed loan-application form?
24. Name the most important source of information covering the potential borrower.
25. Name five types of loan transactions which could be covered by an interviewer.
26. List some of the reasons for withdrawal of loan applications.
27. In large firms what officer usually handles transactions covering subdivisions?
28. Name one of the major objectives of interview and credit analysis.
29. Explain why sound and prudent lending policies have a beneficial effect upon the business health of the nation.
30. List the tangible factors covering the analysis of the borrower that can be accurately measured.
31. Describe the development in importance of the borrower in a mortgage loan transaction.
32. Name some of the items of information which ought to be obtained in the initial interview.
33. Describe the functions of the credit department covering proposed mortgage loan transactions.
34. List the information that is usually contained in the credit report covering a builder.
35. Name some of the tests used to analyze the efficiency of interview and credit-analysis procedures.

ASSIGNMENTS

1. Select two or three homes in your neighborhood, and analyze the ability of each home owner to maintain payments on the loan.
2. Obtain a copy of a credit report covering some borrower who has a mortgage loan with a company of your selection, and carefully analyze this report.
3. List all items which you think might be important in analyzing the credit strength of a potential borrower.
4. Describe how the mortgage risk section in a company of your selection operates.

BIBLIOGRAPHY AND SUGGESTED READING

Bryant, Willis R., "Personal Interview with Borrower and Credit Analysis of Borrower," lecture, Mortgage Bankers Association of America Seminar, Northwestern University, Evanston, Ill., June 21, 1948.

"Credit Standards," *Technical Bulletin* TB4A-137, Veterans Administration, Loan Guaranty Division, Washington, 1953.

Home Mortgage Lending, chaps. 6, 9, 10, American Institute of Banking, Section American Bankers Association, New York, 1946.

McMichael, Stanley L., *How to Finance Real Estate,* chaps. 2, 26, Prentice Hall, Inc., Englewood Cliffs, N.J., 1951.

Mortgagees' Handbook, rev. ed., pp. 109–115, Federal Housing Administration, 1950.

Pease, Robert H., and Homer V. Cherrington (eds.), *Mortgage Banking,* chaps. 7–9, McGraw-Hill Book Company, Inc., New York, 1953.

CHAPTER 6

Appraisal of Real Estate Security

PURPOSES

1. To explain the purposes of the appraisal of real estate security
2. To describe the relationship between the security and the position of the borrower in the transaction
3. To discuss the steps involved in the appraisal of real estate security
4. To discuss the importance of the appraisal report in the mortgage loan transaction
5. To explain the need for comprehensive appraisal reports
6. To outline the information which should be contained in the appraisal report

In the preceding chapter the importance of the borrower in a mortgage loan transaction was described in some detail, as were the methods of analyzing the borrower's ability to repay the obligation. It has only been since 1934 that the borrower has been recognized as a highly important safety factor against the risks of loss; and this development, added to better appraisal techniques, has brought about a great improvement in mortgage lending procedures and practices, has reduced loss exposure, and has had a profound effect upon the mortgage market as well as upon customer relations.

Underlying Security for a Mortgage Loan

The underlying security for any mortgage loan is the real estate itself which the borrower has pledged to the lender by means of the mortgage. In case of a serious default in payments on the loan or failure to comply with some other covenant of the mortgage or deed of trust, it might become necessary for the lender to start and complete foreclosure proceedings in order to protect his investment. In view of this possibility the lender will undertake to be as sure as possible that, in selling the property after its acquisition through foreclosure, there would be no loss involved. It is by making a sound appraisal of the property that a major safeguard against loss is established following foreclosure and acquiring title. On VA loans the lender has the privilege of transferring title to the VA and receiving cash; in the case of an FHA loan, of transferring title to the FHA and accepting debentures from the FHA. On such loans practically no loss is sustained by the lender, but the lender is required to handle the portfolio administration and loan collection procedures of both FHA and VA loans efficiently.

Margin of Security Defined

At the time a mortgage loan is made, the difference between the amount of the loan and the appraised value of the property is known as the "margin of security." In analyzing this margin of security and the risks involved today, a prudent lender will also evaluate the quality of the borrower as an important factor in judging the soundness of the loan.

Purpose of Inspection and Appraisal of the Collateral

The purpose of the inspection and appraisal of the property is to determine that the value of the property in support of the contemplated loan is sufficient in every respect to warrant such a loan. National banking laws, state banking laws, and laws and regulations covering the lending operation of insurance companies, savings and loan associations, and other institutional lenders all require such an appraisal. Also the VA and FHA regulations require an appraisal of the real estate. The percentage of the loan to the appraised value of the property is established by law in the case of almost every institutional lender.

Appraisal Forms Are of Various Types

There are two basic types of appraisal forms used by mortgage lenders on conventional loans including the lender's own appraisals of farm properties, FHA loans, and VA loans. Most lenders make a practice of appraising properties for FHA and VA loans, even though the FHA and VA also appraise such properties, such appraisals being set up on the forms furnished by these administrations. Appraisals by the lender are usually made prior to submission of the application for insurance or guaranty to the FHA or VA. One type of appraisal form is combined with the loan application, while the other type is an entirely separate form. In the latter case the appraiser does not see the loan application itself at any time. Opinions vary widely regarding the use of these two types of forms, as some lenders strongly favor the separate appraisal form. The use of either type of form probably depends largely on the nature of the operations of a company and the part the chief appraiser plays in the executive operations of the department. If a lender has its own appraisal staff, it would be more inclined to use the combined form, while if independent appraisers are used, it would seem that a separate appraisal form would be desirable.

Contents of an Appraisal Form Consist of Numerous Sections

There are numerous sections to the appraisal form itself, the most important of which consist of the following:

1. Legal description and location of the property including lot number, block number, and name of tract as well as lot dimensions including street identification.

2. Description and condition of improvements, which includes type of construction, number of stories and rooms.

3. Analysis of the neighborhood.

4. Taxes and special assessments, assessed valuation.

5. Statement of income and expense if income property.

6. Total valuation of property including land and valuations covering land and improvements. Improvements are shown separately.

Other information which is required and is usually included in the appraisal report is the following:

1. Age of improvements

2. Information regarding streets being paved and sewer installations and whether both have been accepted by the municipality

3. Details regarding occupancy

4. Availability of transportation

5. Nearness to schools, churches, recreation, and shopping

6. Growth trend in the area

7. Compatibility of population

8. Proximity to existing or potential nonresident types of development

9. Any special features or conditions

10. Report of termite condition if house is over five years old

11. Conservative capitalization on income properties after deduction for vacancy allowance

12. Recommendations as to chattels or rental assignments on income properties

13. Detailed description covering interior and exterior of building including type of heating and square-foot or cubic-foot measurements of the improvements

Need for Comprehensive Report Form if Adequate Appraisal Is to Be Made

From the above it can readily be observed that a comprehensive appraisal report form is necessary. Otherwise it would be possible for the appraiser to omit important items which have a direct bearing upon the establishment of the appraisal value of the property. In addition to this, the judgment and recognized ability of the appraiser himself have an important bearing upon the quality and accuracy of the appraisal. Nearly all prudent lenders who maintain a staff of appraisers within their own organizations require that the chief appraiser review, approve, and sign each appraisal report before the loan application and appraisal report are submitted to the loan committee, sometimes called the "finance committee."

Establishment of Value of the Collateral

In establishing the value of the collateral for lending purposes the appraiser has a major responsibility. He must not only set a value based on present economic conditions, but he ought to forecast the stabilized value of the collateral for a reasonable period of time. It follows that the value set by the appraiser who is a member of the staff of a conservative mortgage lender will generally be somewhat below the existing current market value of the property during boom periods.

A great many elements must be considered in establishing this stabilized value: changes in the neighborhood, obsolescence, physical deterioration, possible change of ownership, as well as likely changes in the value of the collateral itself. Also, constant changes will occur in the loan itself, as practically all loans are now written on an amortized basis. Under these circumstances the appraisal of the property at the time a loan is made is not sufficient to indicate the measure of risk involved in making a loan. Even though an able appraiser may have the ability to make a careful estimate of the future value of the property, complete elimination of risk is not to be expected.

Great Improvements Have Been Made in Appraisal Techniques

Appraising real estate during the past twenty years has become more standardized and specialized. Many new techniques covering appraisal methods have been developed. These improvements have to a great extent been the result of the efforts of the Society of Residential Appraisers and the American Institute of Real Estate Appraisers. Practically all staff appraisers of mortgage lending institutions are members of one of or both these fine organizations. Education of members in improved appraisal methods and procedures has been one of the major objectives of these associations.

Economic and Physical Characteristics of Real Estate

As stated in Chapter 1, there are certain physical and economic characteristics of real estate itself that are of basic importance in mortgage lending and have a direct bearing upon appraisal procedures, namely:

1. Properties are fixed in their location and unique in character.
2. Properties have relatively long lives, and the existing supply has a direct effect upon the market at all times.
3. All improved properties are complex and in construction loans require a large volume of labor at the site.
4. Property values are subject to extreme fluctuations.
5. Neighborhoods are also subject to great changes in conditions including fluctuations in value and appeal.

Appraisal Techniques and Practices

Appraisal techniques and practices have been greatly improved since the Great Depression of the early thirties, and our discussion of this subject will cover some of the basic phases of these subjects only. Before discussing these appraisal techniques and practices, the types of values involved in appraising properties should be briefly described.

Market Value Defined

"The highest price expressed in terms of money which a property will bring if exposed for sale in the open market, allowing a reasonable time to find a purchaser who buys with full knowledge of all the uses to which it is adapted and capable of being used, both buyer and seller acting intelligently and willingly, without compulsion."[1]

Another definition of "market value" given by the American Institute of Real Estate Appraisers reads:

The quantity of other commodities a property will command in exchange; specifically the highest price estimated in terms of money which a buyer would be warranted in paying and a seller justified in accepting, provided both parties were fully informed, acted intelligently and voluntarily, and further, that the rights and benefits inherent in and attributable to the property were included in the transfer.

[1] These definitions of value and numerous definitions of other terms used in appraising are adequately described in *Appraisal Terminology and Handbook,* American Institute of Real Estate Appraisers, Education Committee, Chicago, 1950.

There are many other definitions of "market value" including those that are to be found in the statutes of almost every state. For a number of reasons market value of real estate differs from the market value of merchandise and probably is best defined as "fair price which a buyer is justified in paying for a property." Each property is different in many respects, and consequently no general and standardized market price can be established such as is used in the sale of clothing, automobiles, food, and other items.

Justified Price

This is usually defined as the price that a buyer would be economically justified in paying for a property. It must take into consideration the utility of the property over a period of years and actually represents the present and future value of the property. It is obvious that such a price would be very difficult to determine.

Cost and Value

Cost and value although closely related are hardly ever identical. Cost does not determine value, although it does have a definite effect upon it.

Value Defined

Value is an amount representing the price which a prudent buyer would be justified in paying if he knew all the pertinent facts and could foresee and measure all future services of the property during its life.

The value of a property can never be exactly determined, and at best it is an estimate which is evolved from a very thorough consideration of facts and circumstances and appraisal of the property.

Normal Value

This is a most difficult value to define, as a study of the mortgage market over the past fifteen years would indicate that at no time has there been a "normal" value. Existing conditions would indicate that today's values are abnormal rather than normal.

Subjective Value

This type of value mainly concerns the purchaser of the property, as the term is used to indicate the special value or worth of a particular property to a particular person.

Objective Value

Objectives value, which could also be identified as market value, is usually determined by competitive bidding in the market. The market value on homes is usually restricted to the local area and never exists on a nationwide or even a state-wide basis. Thus the competitive effect is localized and could vary considerably even in a small community.

The Appraisal Process

An adequate appraisal cannot be made unless certain basic elements are analyzed. This analysis is termed "the appraisal process" and investigated the following:

1. The property
    a. Size of land and buildings, detailed inspections
    b. Liens, leases, estates, rights of way, encroachments
    c. Assessed valuation, taxes, special assessments
2. The neighborhood
    a. Schools, churches, recreation, shopping
    b. Utilities, transportation
    c. Growth trend
    d. Compatibility of population
3. Purpose of the appraisal and effective date
4. An analysis of the best use of the land
5. Determination of the relative importance of the "three approaches," namely, the cost approach, the comparison, or market data, approach, and the income capitalization approach
6. Gathering, processing, and a correlation of the data necessary to the making of a sound value estimate

The Property

In analyzing and appraising the property, the exact size of the land and building must be known, and a detailed inspection of the land and improvements must be made.

The location of the property is usually obtained from the applicant for a mortgage loan or from a broker, agent, or other interested party. In most cases the applicant will not know the lot and block number or the exact boundaries and measurements of the lot but will know the street number. This information, if not given by the applicant, will be added to the report by the appraiser. Some applicants present a legal description of the property which is of considerable assistance to the appraiser. If a complete description and location of the property is given by the applicant, it will aid in speeding the processing of the application.

In describing the site of the property the appraiser will describe the contour of the lot and the condition of the yard including landscaping. No appraisal report can be complete and accurate unless it includes a report covering liens, leases, estates, rights of way, and any encroachments which might affect the value of the property.

In addition to the above the appraisal report should show the assessed valuation of the property, the annual property taxes, and any special assessments. In the case of existing special assessments such as sewer bonds, street bonds, or other items, the amount of the outstanding assessment is always taken into account in arriving at the appraised value of the property by the appraiser.

The Neighborhood

An analysis of the neighborhood involves the following:
1. Schools, churches, recreation, shopping, transportation
2. Pride of ownership, owner occupancy, utilities
3. Growth trend
4. Compatibility of population

If schools, churches, recreation, transportation, and shopping facilities are within a reasonable distance from the neighborhood, it is of distinct advantage to the homeowner and makes the property much more marketable. The appraiser in his report should comment upon the presence or lack of any of these facilities.

A careful inspection of the condition of the yards in the neighborhood as well as the outside condition of the property and whether the houses are well maintained will reveal pride of ownership in the area. Well-kept yards with good landscaping will also indicate that the owners are reliable individuals who are desirous of having the appearance of the entire neighborhood in excellent condition at all times.

The appraiser will also report how completely the land is built up and will determine the percentage of owner occupancy. On the homes which are rented the average rental or rental value of dwellings in the vicinity will be determined. Any features which detract from the desirability of the neighborhood, such as billboards, gasoline stations, or stores, should also be reported. The types of structures found in the area should be listed, and the most typical should be described.

The availability of utilities is a very important part of a property appraisal. It covers gas and electric facilities as well as garbage service and telephone service.

It is important that the growth trend of the neighborhood be described, including the possible future stability of property values. An analysis should be made of the fields of business in which the homeowners in the neighborhood are engaged as well as an estimate of the income level of the group. The economic and cultural activities within the neighborhood should also be described.

The marketability of properties in the area should be described, and the amount of vacant properties, whether held for sale or rent, should be noted. It will usually be found that in most neighborhoods there will be some vacancies and some homes for sale, which should be considered a normal condition.

The range of prices of newly built or partially constructed homes should be listed, as this information has an important bearing upon trend of values. The appraiser will also estimate the future trends of values in the neighborhood, as a mortgage loan is predicated to a great extent upon the future value and marketability of a particular property.

The type and character of population should be observed to ascertain whether a change in neighborhood stability and compatibility should be anticipated.

The Three Approaches to Establishing the Value of the Property

The three approaches generally used in the valuation process are the following:
1. The cost approach
2. The comparison, or market data, approach
3. The income capitalization approach

By examining, weighing, and comparing these evidences of value, the appraiser is able to arrive at an estimate of the value of the property, which value must take into consideration all the pertinent data which may affect that value.

Some appraisers in setting a value on a property use (1) rental value, (2) estimated reproduction cost less depreciation, (3) current sales price of comparable properties, and (4) capitalization method of establishing value on income properties.

The Cost Approach

The sources of data used by an appraiser in establishing this value comprise cost manuals and services, reports on studies on the subject by appraisal groups and local builders, contractors, and building-material dealers.

On new construction builders are usually required to submit cost of labor and materials in detail together with the specifications, and from this source an analysis of costs can be made.

The cost of replacement plus the land value sets the upper limit of value, and from this figure the appraiser deducts depreciation and arrives at his estimate of the proper value of the property.

The methods used in estimating cost of replacement vary widely in different parts of the nation. The five most commonly used are (1) comparative cubic feet of content, (2) comparative square-foot method, (3) quantity survey method, (4) unit in place method, and (5) the index method.

The number of cubic feet in a building is ascertained by multiplying the width by the depth by the mean height.

The number of square feet in a dwelling is ascertained by multiplying the outside width by the depth. In case a garage is a part of the dwelling, this area is not included as a part of the livable area of the dwelling. In order to establish the value of the structure a cost factor is used by the appraiser, which factor is based on current building costs, taking into consideration quality of construction, type of materials used, and other items. To this total figure is added the estimated cost of garages, porches, enclosed patios, and any other buildings on the premises. From the total estimated replacement cost an amount to cover depreciation must be deducted. Depreciation is usually described as a loss in value for any reason. Depreciation can be divided into three main categories: physical, functional, and economic. Physical depreciation results from use—call it wear and tear. Functional depreciation, or obsolescence, is the result of characteristics of the property itself—such as poor design, inadequate heating or plumbing, etc. Economic obsolescence is the result of factors entirely outside the property—such as unfavorable influences caused by commercial or industrial encroachment into a fine residential area.

The land itself is not in most cases subject to depreciation and this value is usually established by comparison with the selling price, offers, and asking prices of similar land in the immediate area, or in comparable neighborhoods.

Quantity survey method is ascertained from construction-loan files of mortgage lending companies, the builder's cost figures, the FHA or VA cost-of-materials records covering specific areas, as well as cost manuals. By adding overhead, profit, and indirect costs the appraiser is able to estimate accurately the total construction cost. This cost can then be converted into square-foot cost or cubic-foot cost.

The use of replacement-cost data in establishing value is particularly useful in making construction loans. However, in addition to this information, the appraiser is required to estimate the future of the property, as value is based largely on future usefulness. Thus we find that cost is not necessarily value, although the two are related. The cost approach establishes the top limit of value and is especially useful in the appraisal of new homes or other types of new properties which have been well planned and executed.

In the index method, a certain percentage of value is added or subtracted from known values of a previous year.

The Comparison, or Market Data, Approach

The actual sales prices, listing prices, and offering prices of other similar properties must be taken into consideration, especially where comparable units are concerned. The entire appraisal process involves comparison. It is not always possible to find identical buildings in the same neighborhood, but even though certain buildings are slightly different in design and size, it is not difficult to establish a comparative value for each dwelling. The more up to date the comparative values are, the more important such values are in appraising a particular property.

Capitalization Method Valuation

This method valuation is used most frequently in appraising income properties and is seldom used in appraising a home. In the latter case ownership and use are of more importance than monetary returns.

There are four steps usually used in the capitalization method of valuation, namely:

1. Estimate of the probable effective gross income, which is the gross income less allowance for vacancy and loss of rents

2. Estimate of the probable expenses of operation, including taxes and an allowance for management

3. Estimate of net earnings before depreciation (the difference between effective gross income and expenses of operation) both as to amount and as to the period of years during which net earnings may be expected to continue

4. Conversion of expected net earnings before depreciation by use of a capitalization rate, which includes a depreciation factor and an investment-return factor, into an estimate of the value of the property

The allowance for vacancy and loss of rents is generally a small percentage of the gross income. Operating expenses include cleaning and maintenance, repair and replacement of equipment, management, cost of heat, electricity, water, etc. Generally taxes and insurance costs are classified as fixed charges.

Determining the capitalization rate is extremely important, and a slight variation in the rate can produce a considerable difference in the final valuation of the property. An adequate capitalization rate can only be determined by a competent appraiser who has had many years of experience in appraising similar properties and who is thoroughly acquainted with market conditions in the area where the property is located. Capitalization rate can also be determined by examination of sales that will reflect returns from typical properties.

Establishing the Final Estimate of Value

After the three estimates of value previously mentioned have been established, the appraiser proceeds to establish the final estimate of value. The "fair market value" is first established, after which the appraiser will apply any corrective factors the mortgage lending firm may require for lending purposes.

It is important that an appraiser use the three approaches in all appraisals or such of them as apply in certain special cases.

Judgment and experience are the most important factors in every appraisal. Appraising is an analytical and evaluation science, not an exact science. A difference of 5 to 10 per cent between the valuation estimates of any two able and qualified appraisers in a dwelling appraisal should not be considered as a serious reflection on ability or qualifications of either appraiser. The real estate market is dynamic and subject to frequent changes. For this reason valuations should be realistic and the data and information on which they are based should be current and up to date. Personal prejudice should never be permitted to influence the analysis of a property or the analysis of an appraisal report.

There are no arbitrary rules to be followed in reaching a final estimate of value. A qualified appraiser will give weight to the figures arrived at by the three approaches as dictated by the type of property under appraisal. Obviously, the figures arrived at by the use of the three approaches should not be averaged. A conservative appraiser often uses the lowest valuation of the three approaches as his basis of certification to the final estimate of the value. In some cases, the final estimate of value might be lower than any of the three items. Lengthy narrative reports covering an appraisal of a property are usually unnecessary. If an appraiser has adequately demonstrated his knowledge and ability to use appraisal techniques properly, a short appraisal report should be sufficient.

During the past fifteen or more years, it has been the requirement of most mortgage lenders to have at least two photographs in the appraisal report. One is a photograph of the property itself, while the other shows a view of the adjoining properties. Such photographs are very important and necessary for the chief appraiser and the loan or finance committee.

Today independent appraisers, appraisers who are members of the staffs of mortgage lending companies, and FHA and VA appraisers are all interested in the exchange of ideas and in the promotion of more widespread knowledge of appraisal techniques. These are accomplished by (1) meetings of appraisal groups, (2) real estate board activities, (3) appraisal conferences and seminars, and by membership in the Society of Residential Appraisers, or the American Institute of Real Estate Appraisers, or both.[2]

SUMMARY

The underlying security for any mortgage loan is the real estate which the borrower pledges to the lender by means of the mortgage or deed of

[2] Refer to Bibliography and Suggested Reading at the end of this chapter for more complete coverage of subjects.

trust. In case of default in payments or in some other covenant of the mortgage or deed of trust, the lender will want to make as certain as possible that no loss would be sustained if foreclosure were to occur. An appraisal of the property prior to the time the loan is made establishes the margin of security, which is the difference between the amount of the loan and the appraisal value of the property. Such appraisals are required by national and state banking laws as well as by the regulations of other regulatory bodies including both the FHA and VA.

The purpose of the inspection and appraisal of the property is to determine that the value of the property in support of the loan is sufficient in every respect to warrant such a loan.

There are various types of appraisal forms in use today, but the two basic types are one which is part of the loan application itself and used by only a few companies, and one which is an entirely separate form.

The use of a form of some type is very necessary, as an appraiser must determine both the present and probable future value of the property. Every item which may affect value must be taken into consideration, and consequently a comprehensive report form is used by most mortgage lenders.

There are generally three approaches used in appraising a property, namely, the cost approach, the comparison, or market data, approach, and the income capitalization approach. By examining, weighing, and comparing these evidences of value the appraiser is able to arrive at a carefully considered estimate of the value of the property, which estimate must take into consideration all the pertinent data affecting value.

The methods used in computing cost of replacement vary, but the five most commonly used are the following:

1. Comparative cubic feet of content
2. Comparative square-foot method
3. Quantity survey method
4. Unit in place method
5. The index method

From the total estimated replacement cost an amount to cover depreciation will be deducted, which is known as loss of value due to (1) physical deterioration, (2) functional obsolescence, and (3) economic obsolescence.

After the five estimates of value have been arrived at, the appraiser will then proceed to establish the final estimate of value. The fair market value is first established, after which the appraiser may apply certain corrective factors which the mortgage lending firm requires for lending purposes.

Judgment is a very important factor in each and every appraisal, and appraising is generally recognized as an analytical and evaluation science rather than an exact science.

APPRAISAL REPORT

ON A

SEVEN—ROOM, SINGLE—FAMILY DWELLING

AT

1942 YALECROSS AVENUE
SALT LAKE CITY, UTAH

AS OF

AUGUST 1, 1961

BY

RALPH B. WRIGHT, M. A. I.

(A photograph of the property and a photograph of the adjacent properties are normally included at this point in the report.)

APPRAISAL REPORT

Subject property located at 1942 Yalecross Avenue, Salt Lake City, Utah.

PURPOSE AND EFFECTIVE DATE

To determine the fair market value of the property as of August 1, 1961, in connection with the owner's application for a mortgage loan.

LEGAL DESCRIPTION

The West 55 feet of Lot 6, Block "B", Yale Gardens, Salt Lake City, Salt Lake County, Utah.

CITY AND NEIGHBORHOOD

SALT LAKE CITY AND ITS SUPPORTING AREA

Salt Lake City was founded in 1847 by the Mormons, under the leadership of Brigham Young, and incorporated as a City in 1851. It is the capital of the State of Utah and County Seat of Salt Lake County. The city of Ogden, with a population of 57,000 lies about thirty—eight miles North, and Provo, the County Seat of Utah County, with a population of 29,000 is forty—five miles to

Figure 26

the South. Salt Lake City has had a continuous growth; the census
of 1880 gave it a population of 20,700; 1910, 92,800; 1920,
118,000; 1940, 150,000; 1950, 181,900; and 1960, 189,500. Salt
Lake County, which essentially constitutes the metropolitan area
of the city, had a population in the 1950 census of 274,200, a
63,000 gain over 1940, and the census shows a population of
380,800 in 1960.

The city is well served by railroads, with lines of the Oregon
Short Line (Union Pacific), Western Pacific, Denver and Rio
Grande Western, and Los Angeles and Salt Lake (Southern Pacific).
Its Municipal Airport is the hub of air travel for the entire
West.

Salt Lake County is the manufacturing center of the State of
Utah. In 1960 there were 1,068 manufacturing plants in the State
of Utah, and establishments employed over 38,900 wage earners on
a payroll of well over $195,000,000. Included in its large list
of manufacturing industries are petroleum refining, railroad
repair shops, printing, and publishing, slaughtering and meat
packing, foundry and machine shops, and copper, tin and sheet
iron work. Smelting and refining of copper is done largely outside the city limits, but within Salt Lake County. Also outside
the city limits are the refineries for silver and lead and the
beet sugar plants. At Provo, in Utah County, are the large plants
of U.S. Steel (Geneva), Columbia Steel (Ironton) and the Pacific
States Cast Iron Pipe Company. Many steel fabricators and related
industries are located in Salt Lake City and County. The tribu-
tary territory to Salt Lake includes a strong agricultural background of sugarbeets, wheat, wool, sheep, cattle and poultry.
There is also a large volume of mining of silver, copper, lead,
zinc, gold, uranium, coal and oil.

Salt Lake City serves as a distributing center for not only the
wholesale and retail trade within its confines, but much of the
outlying territory as well, drawing trade from Western Colorado
and Wyoming, Southern Idaho and Nevada.

As the metropolis of the State of Utah, as well as the location
of the University of Utah, professional and semi-professional
service is of considerable importance, as is the employment in
the City, County and State Government offices, which are centered
in Salt Lake City. The City has a commission form of government,
adopted in 1911.

The people of Salt Lake City and Utah have always been a homemaking type, who have a serious regard for their obligations, and
there is found a degree of stability as to homemaking and homeownership, which if equaled, is not surpassed by any other community in the Country.

Figure 26. (Continued)

NEIGHBORHOOD

Subject property is approximately four miles from the central downtown shopping district, in what is known as the "Southeast Bench" residential area. There is a rather sharp incline extending Eastward from Eleventh East Street to Fifteenth East, all the way from Second South to Twenty-first South Street, and it is on this high ground, East of Nineteenth East Street, which commands a view Westward over the Salt Lake Valley, looking toward Great Salt Lake, where some of the best and most recent residential development has taken place in Salt Lake City.

Within this "Southeast Bench" area is a rather definitely defined neighborhood, bounded on the North by Sunnyside Avenue, on the South by Thirteenth South, on the West by Seventeenth East, and on the East by Twenty-first East, in which subject property is located. This neighborhood is over 95% built up at this time, many new homes are now under construction, and strong demand exists for the relatively few remaining unimproved building sites. After full development, which will be accomplished in the near future, the decline of this neighborhood is expected to be very slow.

No vacant dwellings, with the exception of those held open for sale, were noted. Owner occupancy is at such a high level, that little data is available to establish a range of rentals, although there are a few duplex units scattered through the area which bring from $85.00 to $150.00 per month. The age of the typical house in this neighborhood runs from six to ten years in its West half; from four years to new in the East half. After allowing for a few exceptions, it can be said that the whole area has been built new since 1940. The typical home in this neighborhood is worth between $20,000 and $30,000, with a few in the $15,000 to $20,000 range; many well into the range between $30,000 and $37,500.

The higher salaried executives, business and professional people constitute chiefly the type of residents in this neighborhood. There are no nuisances or other unfavorable factors evident or in prospect to detract from its good residential character; a high degree of pride in ownership is evident throughout.

The property is served with all public improvements, including street lighting, street paving, curb and gutter, sidewalks, gas, water and sewer, all assessments paid. Transportation to downtown is provided by bus one-half block West along Nineteenth East; a new grade school fronts Nineteenth East, just three blocks South of subject property, and the East High School is about one mile distant.

Figure 26. (Continued)

The University of Utah is about one and one-half miles distant, and a new L.D.S. Church stands at Michigan Avenue and Twentieth East, about one block East. A majority of the inhabitants of the neighborhood surrounding subject property are of this faith. Two neighborhood shopping centers have been developed, one at Thirteenth South and Seventeenth East; the other at Thirteenth South and Twenty-first East; both easily accessible to subject property and providing all necessary facilities to meet the ordinary needs of the residents of this and adjacent areas.

SITE

The lot is rectangular, fronting 55 feet on the South side of Yalecross Avenue, 310 feet East of Nineteenth East, and has a depth of 123.10 feet. There is a slight slope from East to West; not sufficient to require retaining walls, but providing good drainage. The lot is for all practical purposes flat and level, having been graded slightly downward from the front of the house to the front sidewalk. The lot has been shrubbed and planted to evergreens, grass and flowers; all in nice condition. The rear yard is enclosed with a woven wire fence on steel posts set in concrete, with gate opening on driveway.

Zoning

Residential "A" - One- and two-family dwellings permitted. (The building restrictions which run with the land in Yale Gardens Subdivision permit only single-family detached dwellings.)

Assessed Valuation, Taxes and Assessments

Assessed valuation for 1961:
    Land $630.00 - Improvements $2,575.00
                    Total $3,205.00
    Salt Lake City levy in 1960 expected to be about $62.00
For 1960:
    Land $630.00 - Improvements $2,680.00
                    Total $3,310.00
                    Tax $ 193.30
    Salt Lake City levy in 1960 was $58.40

Utah statute provides that "all tangible property must be assessed at 40% of its reasonable fair cash value." The last general reassessment of property in Salt Lake County was in 1937. There is no reliable comparison between assessed values and fair market value.

Assessment for installation of street lighting. $123.55 in 1961, paid in full. Annual maintenance charge of $7.75 due November 30th of each year.

Figure 26. (Continued)

DESCRIPTION OF BUILDINGS

Dwelling

The house was built in 1940, and is a well constructed one and one-half story single-family seven-room dwelling with two baths, as per floor sketch shown in this report.

Footings and foundation are of poured concrete, exterior walls are of heavy cedar shakes painted light gray, over Celotex Vapor Seal Sheathing, which serves as insulation; the roof is covered with 5-2 perfect cedar shingles, stained green and laid five inches to the weather. Gutters and downspouts are installed, and painted to match the exterior. All windows are Curtis Silentite, equipped with screens and storm sash, ceilings are insulated with Rock Wool. Ornamental, fixed shutters have been added for decorative effect to the front windows. Sidewalks, front and rear steps and stoops are concrete and there is a concrete patio at the rear, with permanent roof over, and equipped with canvas valance and sunshades.

Basement

The basement is full, straight wall, with poured concrete walls and floor and has been partitioned into a 15' x 16' knotty pine bedroom, furnace room, food and fruit storage room, and laundry. All rooms, except the laundry, are finished with asphalt tile floor covering, furred-out walls and Celotex ceilings. The bedroom has two large closets, overhead light fixtures, ample convenience outlets, a telephone outlet, and is quite acceptable from all angles as a boys' room, or utility bedroom. The basement is dry, of good depth, allowing ample head room, and has several windows providing good light and ventilation. Hot air ducts connected into the furnace system heat all basement rooms. Proper precautions have been taken against damage by termites or dry rot.

Main Floor

The main floor has an area of 1,023 square feet, containing four full sized rooms, a bath, and breakfast bay off the kitchen. There is a front entry closet, broom closet with linen storage cabinet in rear hall off kitchen, and closet in the rear bedroom.

All floors are oak, except kitchen, which is fir covered with inlaid linoleum, and bath, which is polished terrazzo laid in square block design. Sub-flooring is tongue and groove fir, laid diagonally over 2" x 10" joists, 16" on center, properly bridged.

The interior woodwork and trim is fir, walls and ceilings are plastered. Colors and decorating scheme well selected and in good taste.

Figure 26. (Continued)

Electrical wiring meets code requirements, and fixtures are of modern design, in keeping with the balance of the interior. Dining room has Czech crystal cut-glass chandelier; convenience outlets are ample throughout. All closets have lights, with pull-cord switch.

Living room fireplace has colonial type wood mantel, polished terrazzo hearth; all rooms on main floor, including kitchen, and both upstairs bedrooms, have decorative cornice boxes over windows.

Kitchen drain and splash are tile; Curtis custom-built kitchen cabinets above and under sink. Bath has polished terrazzo wainscot four feet high, except stall for shower, which is seven feet; walls above, and ceiling canvassed and painted. Bath has metal medicine cabinet with mirror over lavatory, lights in chrome fixtures on each side of medicine cabinet.

Second Floor

The second floor, reached by front stairway with oak risers and treads, has two good bedrooms, full tile bath, and five closets as shown on floor sketch. Finish and trim throughout are the same as the main floor, except bath, which has tile floor and wainscot, and full-sized recessed tub, with shower over.

Plumbing and Heating

Plumbing and fixtures are of good quality and installation.

Hot and cold water is piped to the laundry in the basement where a floor drain is provided, with two soapstone laundry tubs.

Double kitchen sink is acid-proof, strainer type with swing spout and spray attachment, hot and cold water combination faucet. General Electric disposal and dishwasher units were installed new in February, 1960.

Tub in upstairs bath is recessed, tiled in; lavatories are china, attached to wall, and have side towel bars of chrome, toilets are wash-down, exposed tanks, Church seats.

Hot water is supplied by a fifty gallon oil-fired automatic heater, installed in basement and connected to one hundred fifty gallon fuel tank buried in West sideyard of lot. Hot water piping is equipped with valves to connect a rental cylinder for water softening. Cold water lines run to silcocks at front and rear of house for watering lawn and gardens.

Heating plant is an American Radiator warm air furnace, oil-fired and with built-in blower unit and automatic controls. Oil-O-Matic low pressure oil burner, new in 1960. Blower and burner

Figure 26. (Continued)

motors very quiet running and in good condition. Plant of ample capacity, warm and cold air ducts of sufficient size and properly installed to insure economical and efficient operation. A five-hundred—gallon fuel tank for furnace is buried near front of house on East side.

GARAGE

The garage is 12' x 20' for one car. It is of frame construction with overhead door and cedar shingle roof; painted to match the house. It has a concrete floor, and concrete ribbons extend from the garage to the street.

GRADE AND RATING OF PROPERTY

My rating of this property according to the following table is:

1. Excellent, highest grade   3. Good, average
2. Very good, above average   4. Fair, below average
                          5. Inferior

xxxxxxxxxxxxxxxxxxxxxxxxxxxx

Architectural style...2   Interior finish.........3 to 2
Construction..........2   Plumbing & heating......3 to 2
Floor plan...........3 to 2 Location & surroundings..2 to 1
     Present physical condition....1 (as to interior & exterior)

The following deficiencies, which might be cited by a critical purchaser, are noted:

1. Garage for only one car.
2. Cost of operating oil furnace and water heater is some-what higher than natural gas, which is widely used in Salt Lake City. Natural gas has not been available for space heating for several years past, but owner has just obtained a connection permit for this property.
3. No toilet to accommodate basement bedroom; must use bathroom on first floor.
4. No sprinkling system in yard, which facility is common in this neighborhood.

All of the above are "curable" and would not constitute serious objections to the ready marketability of this property in the current market.

HISTORY

Property was purchased from builder by present owner, in 1940 for $8,500. It has had good care and maintenance throughout, and since purchase many improvements have been added, including basement rooms and finishing, grading lot, planting, fencing, landscaping, and covered patio at rear. In the Spring of 1960 over $750.00 was spent for interior decorating of all rooms; a new

Figure 26. (Continued)

dishwasher and disposal were installed at a cost of $500.00, and a two-coat paint job on the exterior of house and garage, including roof, at a cost of $498.00 was done.

HIGHEST AND BEST USE

In my opinion the present improvements closely approach the highest and best use of this land.

COST APPROACH

I estimate the construction cost of this house, if reproduced today, as follows:

Main dimensions: 34-6 x 32-0		1,104	sq. ft.
Less offset:	5-0 x 19-0	95	" "
	Net area........	1,009	
Average height for this building		26	ft.
	Cubical content.	26,234	cubic ft.
Add breakfast bay, 7-0 x 2-0 x 15'			
average height		210	" "
	Total content...	26,444	" "

Cubic foot factor, based on local costs	$ .755
	$19,965.00
Add for: Extra bath with shower	900.00
Finished basement rooms	1,400.00
Covered patio at rear, 10' x 20'	600.00
Estimated cost new, of dwelling..........	$22,865.00
Garage	600.00
Concrete walks and drive	200.00
Total for improvements.................	$23,665.00

Depreciation and obsolescence:
Physical 7% — Functional 3% —

Economic 1% — Total 11% — approximately	2,615.00
Estimated cost, less depreciation	$21,050.00
Landscaping, shrubs, fencing, etc.	1,000.00
Land: 55-0 x 123-10 @ $75.00 per front foot	4,125.00
TOTAL FOR THE PROPERTY...............	$26,175.00

Through close contact with operative builders and contractors who have similar, as well as other types of homes under construction in Salt Lake City, I am able to maintain current cost figures, on which the above estimate is based.

MARKET DATA

The following sales, listing and offers have been carefully considered in appraising the value of subject property:

Property A — Sold in June, 1960 — $22,500. One block West, on North side of street; built in 1939. Two bedrooms

Figure 26. (Continued)

one and one-half baths, full basement with finished rumpus room, 1½ story brick. Lot 60' front
with sprinkling system, detached two-car frame
garage. Excellent landscaping and planting, top
condition throughout.

Property B – Sold in April, 1960 – $35,000. One and one-half
blocks West, same street, built in 1939. Three
bedrooms 2½ baths, full basement with knotty pine
rumpus room, bedroom and bath, two-story brick.
Lot 65' in width, good landscaping, sprinkling
system, two-car detached frame garage.

Property C – Sold in March, 1960 – $37,500. One block East and
one block South, built in 1942. Three bedrooms,
large den, two baths, partial basement with finished rumpus room, two-story brick. Large corner
lot, sprinkling system, and good landscaping. Two-
car garage with attached patio.

Property D – Sold in November, 1959 – $29,500. Two blocks East
and one block South, built in 1948. Three bedrooms, one bath main floor, full basement with
finished rumpus room, bedroom and bath, one-story
brick rambler. Lot 70' x 125', nicely landscaped,
sprinkler system, two-car detached frame garage.

Property E – Sold in July, 1959 – $24,000. One block East and
one block South, built in 1949. Two bedrooms, one
bath, partial basement, one-story frame. A 65'
width lot with sprinkling system and two-car
attached garage with breezeway. Lot beautifully
planted; excellent condition throughout. This same
property sold in May 1952 for $23,500.

Property F – Sold in June, 1959 – $28,500. Same block, same
side of the street, built in 1940. Three bedrooms, two baths, full basement with finished
rumpus room, 1½ story brick. Price includes full
electric kitchen. Lot 70' front, with full sprinkling system; two-car frame detached garage.

Property G – Sold in June, 1959 – $17,500. Two blocks South,
built in 1941. Two bedrooms, one bath, full basement, one-story frame. Lot 50' front with sprinkling system, one-car detached garage. A small
house in fair to good condition.

Property H – Sold in May, 1958 – $27,500. Same block, same side
of the street, built in 1940. Three bedrooms, two
baths, partial basement, one-story brick. Same
size lot with sprinkling system, two-car garage.
Condition not as good as subject property.

Figure 26. (Continued)

Property I — Sold in July, 1958 — $25,000. Same block, on North side of the street. One and one-half story brick, four bedrooms, two baths, full basement, built in 1941. Same size lot with sprinkling system, two-car garage. Originally listed four months ago at $34,500, sold at above price due to very small kitchen and generally poor condition of house. Owner became anxious to sell.

Property J — Sold in February, 1958 — $18,000. One-half block West and one block North. One-story brick, two-bedroom, five rooms and full basement, built in 1949. Comparable lot, no sprinkling system, one-car garage.

Property K — Sold in April, 1958 — $29,500. One block East and one block South. One-story brick, three bedrooms, part basement, built in 1948. Same size lot, no sprinkling system, two-car garage.

LOTS

Property 1 — One block East, 1½ blocks South, all utilities and improvements; 60' x 135' lot sold for $5,000 in June, 1960.

Property 2 — Two blocks East, one block South, same utilities and improvements; lot irregular shape, 60' front at curb; 75' wide at building line, 110' across rear and about 130' deep, sold for $7,500 in March, 1960. One other lot of similar size in same block is now offered at $7,500.

Property 3 — Two blocks East, two blocks South, same improvements; two adjoining vacant lots about 60' x 125' each, held in same ownership, numerous offers of up to $6,000 each have been declined during past 2 years.

Property 4 — One block North, three blocks East, near golf course, same improvements. Lot 75' x 160'; owner holding for own future use, has declined several $7,000 offers during spring of 1960.

Property 5 — One block East, one and one-half blocks South, same improvements; 80' lot sold for $6,000 in April, 1960.

Property 6 — One block East, one-half block North, same improvements; 105' corner lot sold for $8,000 in February, 1960.

Figure 26. (Continued)

Property 7 — One block East, three blocks South, same improvements; 72' front lot with 110' width at rear, sold
for $7,500 in April, 1960.

Property 8 — One block East, one block South, same improvements; 80' lot sold for $5,700 in 1958.

It is my considered opinion in the light of the above market
data and other sales information on many properties, some in the
neighborhood, others in various locations of the city, but comparable in size, quality, etc., and not detailed herein, that a
value of $75.00 per front foot is justified for the land under
appraisal, and that this property would sell, under prevailing
market conditions, if given a reasonable time to find a buyer,
for from $26,000 to $28,500.

INCOME

Since this property is occupied by the owner, and has never
been rented, no actual rental figure can be given for it. In my
opinion however, it would bring, if offered in the current rental
market, from $150.00 to $175.00 per month. This figure could be
expected while the house retained its present good condition,
and contemplates its being kept in first—class condition and repair by the owner. I would be inclined to establish a figure
under $175.00 per month as a stabilized rental for the property
in setting up an income and expense statement, if the use of such
a statement and the capitalization of the net income arrived at
by that process could be used as an approach to value, but it
cannot, where a single—family dwelling is being appraised.

Ordinarily, the use of a gross income multiplier cannot be considered as a reliable approach, although it may be used under
certain conditions as a guide to check roughly the value of a
single—family dwelling. As noted elsewhere in this report, there
is insufficient data available on rentals for this class of property to set up a table of gross multipliers which could be used
with any degree of confidence or safety, in appraising the value
of subject property.

UNDERLYING ASSUMPTIONS

It is assumed that the title to the property is good and marketable. No survey has been made of the property and the value
estimate is given without regard to any question of title, boundary, encumbrance or encroachments.

VALUATION CERTIFICATE

In view of the facts set out in this report and in the light of
the data considered in the making of this appraisal, it is my

Figure 26. (Continued)

opinion that the fair market value of the property described, as of August 1, 1961, that is the present worth of the future bene- fits which would accrue to typical users or persons through long- term use and ownership of the property, as per the assumptions and limiting conditions stated, is

TWENTY–SIX THOUSAND DOLLARS – ($26,000.00)

which for convenience may be divided as follows:

Land	$ 4,000.00
Improvements	22,000.00
Total	$26,000.00

CERTIFICATION

I hereby certify that I have personally inspected both interior and exterior of the foregoing described property; that my employ- ment is not contingent in any way upon the value reported; that the statements made, and information contained in this report are true to the best of my knowledge and belief, and that this ap- praisal has been made in accordance with the standards of prac- tice approved by the American Institute of Real Estate Appraisers.

Ralph B. Wright
_____
Appraiser
Member of American Institute of
Dated at Salt Lake City, Utah   Real Estate Appraisers
August 3, 1961

Figure 26. (Continued)

COMMENTS ON FIGURE 26

1. This exhibit covers a portion of an appraisal report on a seven-room, single-family dwelling at 1942 Yalecross Avenue, Salt Lake City, Utah, as of August 1, 1961.

2. This appraisal report was made by Ralph B. Wright, chairman of the board, First Security State Bank, Salt Lake City, Utah, and member of the American Institute of Real Estate Appraisers.

3. It will be noted that this exhibit includes the many items and techniques men-tioned in this chapter and should prove an ideal reference for students of appraisal practices as well as those already engaged in this profession. The names of streets and avenues of the city are fictitious; otherwise the entire appraisal report is factual.

4. This appraisal report has been written in great detail mainly for educational purposes. Most large mortgage lenders who maintain an appraisal staff within their own organizations do not make reports containing such detailed information covering home loans, as the large volume of business would not warrant it. Experienced lending officers are always well acquainted with the city, the particular neighborhoods where loans on properties are made, and all other pertinent details of this nature which affect a transaction.

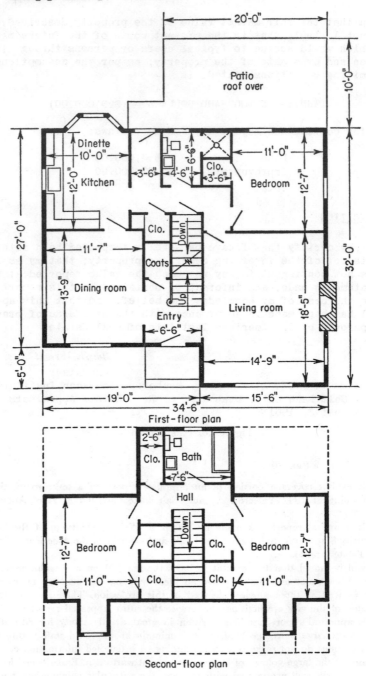

First-floor plan

Second-floor plan

Figure 26. (Continued)

ANGUS HOLDEN
Real Estate Appraiser
1182 Market Street
San Francisco 2, California

October 15, 1961

Mr. and Mrs. R. W. Brown
1234 Main Street
Your Town, California

Dear Mr. and Mrs. Brown:

I have made a thorough analysis of your flats, located at 1234
Main Street, Your Town, and am of the opinion that the fair
market value of the property on this date is $27,500.

You also have requested my opinion of the sound value which
should be applied, in this case, to establish a fee ownership in
one owner.

Your having a half interest, only, in my opinion the fair value
of the half interest is $12,500.

Pertinent data covering this property and the explanation of my
opinion is attached.

                    Very truly yours

                    /s/
                    Angus Holden
AH:rt

LEGAL DESCRIPTION

Commencing at a point on the Easterly Line of Main Street, 100
feet South of Beacon Way, thence at a right angle Easterly 125
feet, thence at a right angle Southerly 25 feet, thence at a
right angle Westerly 125 feet, thence at a right angle Northerly
and along said Easterly line of Main Street 25 feet to the point
of beginning.
Assessors Lot #12, Block #20.

SIZE OF LOT

25 x 125

DESCRIPTION OF IMPROVEMENTS

Two-story, full basement; woodframe, concrete foundation; stucco
front; redwood rustic sides and rear; tar and gravel roof. Built
in 1926.

Figure 27. Appraisal Report Covering Flats

UPPER FLAT

Entry hall and stairs (oak)
Living room across front; fireplace.
Dining room – separate
Breakfast room – separate
Kitchen – ample cabinets, tile drain and splash,
linoleum floor. Service porch.
Two bedrooms, good size. Large closets.
Bath – tub, lavatory, separate toilet, tile floor,
plaster walls.

LOWER FLAT

Entry hall
Living room across front; fireplace.
Dining room – separate
Breakfast room – separate
Kitchen – ample cabinets, tile drain and splash,
linoleum floor. Service porch.
Two bedrooms, good size. Large closets.
Bath – tile stall shower, lavatory, separate toilet,
tile floor, plaster walls.

BASEMENT

Two–car garage, storage and utility area. Two servants' rooms.
Bath; lavatory and toilet only.

INTERIOR FINISH

Oak floors, gum trim, plaster walls and ceilings, good quality
hardware and electric fixtures.

The over–all plan is good and the construction appears excellent.
There is a minimum of physical deterioration. The exterior has
just been painted. The roof, plumbing, and electrical work are in
good condition.

TAXES AND ASSESSMENTS

Land	$2,070
Improvements	3,950
Total Assessment	$6,020
Tax rate 1960–1961	$ 6.27
Total taxes	$377.45

Figure 27. (Continued)

LOCATION AND NEIGHBORHOOD

This is one of the best rental residential neighborhoods in Your Town. Close to schools, shopping, transportation. Typical incomes: $5,000 to $8,000 per year. The area particularly appeals to clerical and executive types without children, who desire a maximum of convenience regarding closeness in time to employment and shopping facilities. Frequent electric bus system services this area to the main shopping and commercial center of the city within 15 minutes. Convenience to parks, playgrounds, and Your Town Yacht Harbor. All contribute to good recreation and to the over-all desirability of the neighborhood.

REPRODUCTION LESS DEPRECIATION ESTIMATE OF VALUE

Living area	—	3,050 sq. ft.	$26,000.
Basement	—	1,250 sq. ft.	2,500.
Servants' rooms, ½ bath		325 sq. ft.	1,500.
			$30,000.

Observed physical depreciation (loss in value) due to wear and tear and functional obsolescence   10,000.

Built 1926 —Age 35 years

Net value of improvements	$20,000.
Land	7,500.
	$27,500.

ECONOMIC (INCOME) APPROACH TO VALUE

INCOME

Upper Flat	$110.		
Lower Flat	100.		
Income per month	$210.		
Income per year	$210.	x 12	$2,520.

EXPENSES

Taxes	$380.	
Insurance ($20,000)	35.	
Water	60.	
Maintenance & Repairs	210.	
Management & Vacancy	210.	
Depreciation	400.	
Total expenses		$1,295.
Net income		1,225.

$1,225. capitalized at 6% indicates a value of $20,417.

Round figure $20,500.

Figure 27. (Continued)

SUGGESTED IMPROVEMENTS FOR ADDITIONAL INCOME

The rents, shown in the economic schedule, are fair by comparison
with similar flats in the area. Rent controls have recently been
removed and there have been many rentals in excess of this figure
in this area but, actually, these higher rents are brought about
by a tight housing shortage at this time. I have endeavored to
establish a fair rental for these units, as is.

Bear in mind that this building is in excess of 35 years old and
to establish a fair, higher income, many improvements should be
made at this time. The exterior is in excellent condition, having
been entirely repainted. The interior is in good condition and in
order to justify a higher income the following improvements are
warranted at this time:

> Tile wainscoting in the baths.
> Stall shower in upper flat.
> Modernize the kitchens.
> Installation of fans, garbage disposal, and dishwashers.

The total cost of these improvements, together with the rehabilitation of the entire interior would cost approximately $3,000 and
would enhance the income by at least $600 per year. Therefore,
this expense is warranted at this time.

COMPARABLE SALES

I have checked many sales in the neighborhood and actually have
found but one which I consider comparable. Namely, 3519-21 Main
Street, which sold for $25,000 in November of 1960. Other, more
recent sales, have been in excess of this figure but those were
second mortgages and other favorable financing which boosted the
price and did not indicate a fair market value. There have been
other sales of much higher-priced flats in the newer neighborhood
East of Channel Street, which I do not consider comparable. There
are many listings of flats from $30,000 to $35,000, similar to
the subject property. Many have been on the market for several
months with no takers, which is proof that by comparison $27,500
is the fair market value at this time.

CONCLUSION

Upon analyzing this and similar properties in the area I am of
the opinion that the market value of the subject property on
October 15, 1961, is $27,500.

I wish to review the analysis of the several approaches to value
on this property. The cost and comparable sale approach indicates

Figure 27. (Continued)

$27,500. The economic approach indicates $20,500 only. Experience shows that flats or small apartment buildings with less than 8 units, actually do not earn an income in relation to cost. The reason being that these properties are usually owner-occupied and the owner obtains other benefits, together with nominal income. In the case of flats, the owner, usually, has a good place to live in the area in which he desires to reside and the income from the other flat pays his miscellaneous expenses and, in a sense, he lives free, except for any income on his investment, plus the inconvenience of an additional family in his residence. Therefore, the reason for flats selling far in excess of their earning capacity.

PURPOSE OF APPRAISAL

You have informed me that the purpose of this appraisal is to establish a value on the premises for the reason that the property is jointly owned by the occupants of the upper and lower flat. One occupant wishes to sell, the other desires fee ownership of the entire premises. I wish to call your attention to the fact that, in this case, I think it is only fair that the cost of selling should be discounted from the fair market value. Not only would there be the 5% commission to the real estate broker, and other minor expenses, but there would be the inconvenience of remaining on the premises and showing the property, perhaps for three or four months.

I think that it is only fair that in this case the total value not exceed $25,000. Therefore, one-half interest be $12,500, one selling to the other.

Figure 27. (Continued)

COMMENTS ON FIGURE 27

1. This exhibit covers an appraisal report on a two-story structure with full basement and concrete foundation, containing two flats, at 1234 Main Street, Your Town, California.

2. This appraisal report was made by Angus Holden, real estate appraiser, and member of the Society of Residential Appraisers.

3. This appraisal report includes many items and techniques mentioned in this chapter and should be of particular interest, as it covers a small income property. The names of the streets, avenues of the city, town, and county are fictitious; otherwise the entire appraisal report is factual.

4. It should also be noted that this appraisal was made for the specific purpose of establishing the sound value of the property in order to establish a fee ownership in one owner. Numerous appraisals are made for other purposes than the lending of mortgage funds.

_____ *Head* _____ OFFICE

STATEMENT OF INCOME AND EXPENSE ON REAL ESTATE   LOAN OR APPLICATION NO. *1234*

HOUSE NO. *corner of West and South Streets* STREET _____ CITY *Metropolis*

MONTHLY INCOME			ANNUAL EXPENSE		
APT. # ROOMS FURNISHED UNFURN. OWNER		BANK		OWNER	BANK
Retail shopping center $		$	TAXES	$	$ *5,000*
consisting of 12 stores			INSURANCE		*1,000*
having a total building			WATER		
area of 35,000 sq. ft.			LIGHT		*300*
Leases are on percentage			POWER		
basis with minimum			GAS		
of $3,000 per month.			OIL		
Rentals are considered			REFRIGERATION – POWER		
equitable.			REFRIGERATION – SERVICE		
			SCAVENGER		
			LICENSE		
			MANAGEMENT		*1,800*
			GARDENER		*600*
			ELEVATOR INSPECTION		
			INCIDENTALS		
			UPKEEP – BLDG.		*1,800*
			DEPRECIATION – BLDG.		
			DEPRECIATION – FURN.		
			10 % VACANCY		*3,600*
GARAGES @ $			% VACANCY		
TOTAL $ *3,000*		$ *3,000*	TOTAL $		$ *14,100*

REMARKS: _____

OWNER		BANK	
GROSS ANNUAL RENTAL	$	ESTIMATED ANNUAL RENTAL	$ *36,000*
ANNUAL EXPENSE	$	ESTIMATED ANNUAL EXPENSE	$ *14,100*
NET ANNUAL RENTAL	$	ESTIMATED ANNUAL NET RENTAL	$ *21,900*
CAPITALIZED AT % NET	$	CAPITALIZED AT *8* % NET	$ *273,750*

DATE *6-30-61*   *J. Doe*   *R. Roe*
                    OWNER OR AGENT   APPRAISER

Figure 28. Example of Capitalization Method of Appraising

Head _____ Office   City_Metropolis_

Mortgage Loan ____ Dept.   County · Metropolis

A P P R A I S A L OF R E A L E S T A T E

NAME_____John Doe_____ADDRESS_Corner of West and South Streets_

DESCRIPTION:____Corner_____Line of_____West_____Street

_____   _____   _____and South_____Street;

Thence____400____Feet by____300____. House No._____

Lot____20____Block____12____Tract____SUNSET____

ENCUMBRANCES: Trust Deed) with balance due $__175,000__Interest paid to_12-1-60_

Note dated____12-11____1960 Term____10____years, Interest rate____5 %

Second Lien$__none____Owed to_____none____

Annual Taxes $_5000_____Insurance $__1000____

Occupied by_____Tenants_____Monthly Rental $_3000_

Street Assessment $__none____Date Acquired_12-11-60__Purchase Price $_325,000_

APPRAISER'S REPORT

I have made a personal examination of the above property and report as follows:

Property is situated in the suburbs of Metropolis in an area largely developed with Tract Homes in the low to medium priced bracket. The land consists of a parcel 400 x 300 and is improved with a retail shopping center containing a food market, drug store, hardware store, and nine various similar service shops. The stores are contained in one building of frame and stucco construction, and the store fronts are of the modern type. Building is about 5 years old, of fair construction and is well maintained. Building area is 35,000 s/f, and the remainder of the land of 85,000 s/f is paved and used as parking area. Most of the stores are leased on a percentage basis, and although current rents are in excess of the established minimums, a proposed development of similar type in an adjacent district indicates that a loan appraisal should be based on the value established by the minimum rents only. However, despite the impending competition, the stores should remain rented at a reasonable level. Value on a replacement basis is estimated to be - Land, $35,000; Improvement, $288,000; or a total of $323,000; however, as indicated on the attached capitalization analysis, the property shows a return of 8% net on a value of $273,750 which is considered to be a sound value for the purpose of basing a mortgage loan.

	V A L U E S	
Real Estate $ _____	$	35,000
Improvements $ _____	$	240,000
Proposed Improvements $ _____	$	
Totals $ _____	$	275,000

West Street

South Street

R. Doe
_____
Appraiser

Richard Rowe
_____
Reviewed by Chief Appraiser

Date _6-30-61_

Figure 28. (Continued)

COMMENTS ON FIGURE 28

This exhibit gives a general outline of the capitalization method of appraising, which is usually used in appraising income properties of all types. The steps taken in using this appraisal method are the following:

1. The actual physical value of the land and improvements is established by the lender's appraiser.

2. The owner furnishes operating income and expense statements usually on an annual basis.

3. The appraiser checks the rentals and expense very carefully, as the income is generally high and the expense is generally low. The appraiser adjusts the income and expense to realistic or stabilized amounts.

4. Expense schedules supplied by principals are usually stripped down with certain important items omitted, for example, expense of management or maintenance, as well as vacancy allowance, the latter of which should run from 5 to 10 per cent.

5. The appraiser makes a careful analysis in order to ascertain if the building is well or poorly managed.

6. If the submitted income and expense figures are on a monthly basis, the appraiser will adjust them to an annual basis and then determine the net return.

7. There are two types of capitalization methods, one of which takes into consideration the depreciation factor while the other excludes this factor. In the latter procedure, depreciation is treated as an expense item and deducted from income prior to application of the capitalization factor.

8. Age of improvements and desirability of the investment have an important bearing on the capitalization factor. Seven per cent is considered a prime rate, and the conversion figure is dependent to a great extent upon the judgment and skill of the appraiser.

9. The capitalization method usually results in a lower appraisal figure than does the physical appraisal value.

QUESTIONS

1. If an estimate of value is a basis on which a home mortgage loan is granted, name another important basis used.
2. Name the two uses in the valuation process of rental value.
3. Describe the four steps in the capitalization method of valuation.
4. Define depreciation.
5. State why the present value of a mortgaged property is of great importance to the lender.
6. Name six parts of an appraisal form.
7. Give the reasons why it is necessary to have a comprehensive appraisal report.
8. Explain why sound valuation is dependent to a great extent upon the skill, experience, training, and judgment of the appraiser.
9. Give reasons why the capitalization method of valuation is used more frequently in appraising income-producing properties than in appraising homes.
10. Name the five most commonly used methods of estimating replacement cost.
11. Explain why an estimate of the probable future value of the property is also of great importance to the lender.

12. Define justified price.
13. Explain why the exact location of the property is of major importance in an appraisal.
14. Define objective value.
15. Define normal value.
16. Explain why the real estate market is highly restricted.
17. Name three evidences of value used in making an appraisal.
18. Land itself differs in many respects from other commodities. Name three such differences.
19. Name the three approaches in the appraisal process.
20. Define market value.
21. Explain why the neighborhood is of particular importance to an appraiser.
22. Explain why cost may differ from value.
23. Do you believe in conservative or liberal appraisals? Give reasons.
24. State what the purposes are of making observations regarding the condition of lawns, fences, and landscaping of the neighborhood.
25. Explain why it is important for the appraiser to ascertain or estimate the amount of the annual taxes on a property.
26. Give reasons why the appraiser should know about any special assessments on the property, such as sewer or street bonds, and take these into consideration when making an appraisal.
27. Name one of the major tests in measuring the quality of a mortgage loan.
28. Define deterioration as it applies to a property.
29. Define fair market value.
30. Give reasons why there is no general uniformity of opinion as to the meaning of "value" or "appraised value" for mortgage loan purposes.
31. Name some classifications of properties that are used for development of a concept of value.
32. Name one of the most important factors which have a direct bearing on the value of an apartment property.
33. Explain the importance of the market area in comparison with the property itself in appraising a store property.
34. Give the generally accepted definition of use value covering an industrial property.
35. Describe a new type of commercial development which has expanded rapidly during the past several years.

ASSIGNMENTS

1. Describe a recent or newly planned shopping center in the community in which you live.
2. Analyze and explain the trend of property values in the area in which you live.
3. Ascertain the cost per square foot of the construction of a home in the community in which you live, and compare this with the selling price of the home.
4. Describe the appraisal methods of a company of your selection.

BIBLIOGRAPHY AND SUGGESTED READING

Appraisal Terminology and Handbook, American Institute of Real Estate Appraisers, Education Committee, Chicago, 1950.

Handbook for Appraisers, American Institute of Real Estate Appraisers, Chicago, 1948.

Home Mortgage Lending, chaps. 4, 5, American Institute of Banking, Section American Bankers Association, New York, 1953.

McMichael, Stanley L., *How to Finance Real Estate,* chaps. 5, 6, Prentice-Hall, Inc., Englewood Cliffs, N.J., 1951.

Pease, Robert H., and Homer V. Cherrington (eds.), *Mortgage Banking,* chaps. 4-6, McGraw-Hill Book Company, Inc., New York, 1953.

Schmutz, George L., *The Appraisal Process,* Prentice-Hall, Inc., Englewood Cliffs, N.J., 1949.

Thorson, Ivan A., *Essentials of California Real Estate: Law and Practice,* Realty Research Bureau, Inc., Los Angeles, 1951.

Thorson, Ivan A., *Simplified Appraisal System: Land Economics,* Realty Research Bureau, Inc., Los Angeles, 1951.

Wright, Ralph B., "Analyzing Appraisals for Mortgage Purposes," lecture, Western Mortgage Banking Seminar, Stanford University, Stanford, Calif., 1953.

CHAPTER **7** Legal Aspects of the Mortgage

PURPOSES

1. To explain the technical phases of this subject
2. To define the term "mortgage" and explain what it implies
3. To explain the necessity for establishing the mortgagor's interest in the property
4. To describe the various forms of mortgage instruments that may be used in a mortgage loan transaction
5. To explain the rights of the borrower and the lender
6. To explain the purpose of the Title Insurance Policy and describe the work involved in a title search
7. To explain briefly foreclosure action
8. To describe the expenses and hazards of FHA and VA foreclosures

The use of mortgages in real estate transactions dates back to ancient times. Throughout world history, property has been sold and purchased; and the instrument involved to pledge the property is known as a mortgage or deed of trust—a conveyance of the property as security for the payment of the debt incurred. In the case of the deed of trust, the property is conveyed to a trustee. These instruments contain provisions which must be strictly adhered to by both the borrower and the lender.

Laws Governing Mortgage Transactions

Many technical and legal principles and practices are involved in mortgage lending, and these have been slowly developed throughout history. In ancient times and even as late as the eighteenth century the borrower had little if any protection in case he found it impossible to repay the obligation. In such a case the property was forfeited to the lender regardless of the amount of the equity which the borrower might have in the property. Thereafter courts of equity came into being, and such courts allowed the use of procedures which would protect the borrower to some extent even though his payments were in default. His right to redeem the property is known today as "right of redemption," or "equity of redemption." This right of redemption would naturally have to be restrictive as to the time permitted for clearing up the existing delinquency.

Throughout our nation, the allowable time for redemption varies considerably between the states, and some are for short periods only, while others give the borrower a year or more to reclaim his property by payment of the past-due payments and other charges. The laws of the various states also differ greatly but nonetheless are based on the same general background. This right, or equity, of redemption may be extinguished only by completion of foreclosure in a manner prescribed by the law of the particular state concerned. The equity of the borrower in the property itself is the difference between the amount of the mortgage and the market value of the property. In the event of foreclosure this market value would be the price of the property obtainable at the time.

During the twentieth century there has been a definite trend by the states of the nation toward uniformity of the legal procedures involved in any mortgage transaction, and the pledging of real estate as security for a mortgage loan is governed by the laws of the state in which the property is located. Also each state has its own statutes which must be fully complied with wherever a mortgage is placed upon a property in that particular state. Nevertheless the major principles of mortgage law are now fairly uniform throughout the nation.

The Lien Theory

The lien theory regarding the mortgage is now generally accepted by most states. According to this theory the courts interpret the mortgage or deed of trust as a lien on the property only and not a conveyance of title. In such a case title to the property can be obtained by the lender only provided there has been a default by the borrower and the lender has taken the necessary steps prescribed by the laws of the particular state to acquire title.

Basic Steps in the Loan Transaction

In order to comply properly with existing laws which govern mortgage transactions there are certain basic steps which must be taken when a mortgage loan is made, namely:

1. A note which covers the amount of the loan, the interest rate, the term, the installment payment, and other conditions must be signed by all the borrowers who have an interest in the property involved.

2. The interested borrowers must sign a mortgage or deed of trust, which instrument is legally sufficient to pledge the real estate.

3. The lender must make certain that there is a merchantable title and that the property pledged as security for the loan is as free and clear as possible of all encumbrances and that the borrowers have clear title to the property and merchantable title. These encumbrances which might exist could be taxes, convenants, conditions and restrictions of record, easements, rights of way, etc. Such encumbrances would not adversely affect the transaction.

4. The mortgage instrument must be properly recorded in the proper public office in order to give the required notice to all parties.

There are many forms of notes, mortgages, and deeds of trust. Both the FHA and the VA have excellent note, deed of trust, and mortgage forms for such loans, which should be studied and carefully analyzed by students of mortgage lending.

Pledge of the Property

The property is pledged by the borrower as security for the mortgage loan by the mortgage or deed of trust, which is signed by the borrowers and properly recorded. In other words the mortgage is the instrument by which the pledge of the security for the loan is accomplished. There is no need for a mortgage or deed of trust if there is no debt involved. This instrument when recorded constitutes a lien on the property, and the lender has the right to institute foreclosure proceedings in case the borrower fails to make payments on the loan in accordance with the note terms or fails to comply with the other covenants of the mortgage.

A loan on real estate in which a mortgage is involved is far more complicated than a commercial loan made with stocks or bonds as security. In the latter case if the borrower fails to repay his obligation in accordance with the terms of the note or if there is a severe drop in the prevailing market price of the security, the lender has the right to sell such security in the market without the necessity of complying with certain legal procedures such as are prescribed for mortgage lending. The basic legal difference between the two types of loans is the right of redemption by the borrower before foreclosure is completed as an inherent right in every mortgage, and although the wording of the law might differ from state to state, every state law contains this protection for the borrower in one form or another.

Construction Loan Advances under the Mortgage

When a property is mortgaged, the mortgage attaches to the land as well as to the improvements on the land. This is true whether such improvements are placed on the land before or after the execution of the mortgage. This interpretation permits the type of financing known as construction loans, which were described in Chapter 4. It permits the borrower to borrow on the land itself as well as the improvements which are to be constructed. The percentage of loan to appraisal would be higher in such cases on both FHA and VA loans than on conventional loans. These funds, as previously mentioned, are paid out as construction of the building progresses. In all construction cases, however, a prudent lender requires that the borrower's funds are to be paid out first, and these funds represent the difference between the amount of the cost of construction and the amount of the loan. On a construction loan the lender will include a percentage of the appraisal of the land itself in the over-all appraisal of the property which in turn affects the total amount of the loan that can be made. Most large building projects are financed by construction loans, as are most subdivision developments.

A large amount of home building is done by individuals who first acquire the land and have their homes constructed in accordance with their own desires and needs. Mortgage lenders in many instances will lend a portion of the appraised value of the land to assist the borrower in purchasing the land, usually with the understanding that when construction is to begin, that lender will handle the construction financing. The lender furnishes the funds to the borrower as the construction progresses. Such loans are especially hazardous because of possible mechanics' liens which could be filed for services performed by subcontractors and material dealers who have not been paid by the builder for services rendered or materials furnished. The lender should therefore through some medium carefully check the payments for labor and materials, the progress of construction, and make certain that the building is being constructed in exact accordance with the plans and specifications and for this purpose the lender employs inspectors and appraisers to perform the above services. A mortgage is therefore so worded as to cover advances to be made in the future by the lender and is a guard against the possible interests of third parties such as creditors where the lender has definitely obligated himself to make such advances to the borrower. There are various methods of advancing such construction funds. Many lenders use a draft form for a certain dollar amount signed by the borrower, which is drawn on the title company involved, ordering the title company to pay the builder the amount specified. Other lenders use building control companies which handle all disbursements and assume full responsibility covering progress payments, compliance inspections, and safeguards against possible liens. Construction-loan mortgages are drawn in such a manner as to obligate the lender to lend a certain amount when certain conditions are performed and therefore automatically become prior to claims of third persons filed after the first mortgage has been recorded, regardless of whether or not the full amount of the loan has been paid out at the time of the claim of the third party is filed. It is therefore imperative that the progress payments be strictly adhered to in accordance with the loan-commitment schedule.

Recording of the Mortgage

All mortgages must be recorded in order to guard against claims of third parties. Also, unless recorded, the owner of the property could make numerous loans on the same property. Also, the property owner could sell the property and obtain all the net proceeds of the transaction even though he might have a sizable loan on the property. The first concern of a lender, therefore, is to make sure that the evidence of the security covering the loan is properly recorded, and other recorded matters which might have an effect upon the title are analyzed.

The Obligation

It should be obvious that there can be no mortgage unless there is a debt or an obligation to secure one. It follows that if a borrower executes a note and mortgage as evidence of a loan but the funds are never disbursed and therefore a debt has not been incurred, there is no enforceable mortgage. Occasionally a mortgage is given on a piece of property by the owner of that particular property to secure the loan or debt of another party.

The mortgage and the note are held by the lender during the life of the loan. In the case of a deed of trust they are held by the beneficiary during the life of the loan. The Title Policy and Fire Insurance Policy or policies are also held by the lender until the loan is paid in full. Some borrowers obtain copies of these documents and keep them for reference. This is a very sensible plan, and such documents should be read very carefully from time to time by the borrower. In this manner he is better informed regarding his rights and his obligations under the contract.

If a borrower holds a Title Policy, or Title Certificate, an Abstract is not necessary except in a few states. An Abstract is the legal description of the property and a history and record of the previous ownership.

The actual deed to the property is partial evidence that the borrower is the owner of the property. In some states the deed with revenue stamps on it is recorded and given back to the borrower. In other states the deed is held in trust by a third party usually known as a trustee and is not returned to the borrower until the loan is repaid in full.

The Borrower's Title

It is not necessary that a borrower own an entire piece of property in order to obtain a loan, but he may mortgage his interest in that property, whether it be a one-half interest or a one-third interest, provided he can find a lender willing to make such a loan. Many a transaction involves a borrower who owns a half interest in a property and wishes to purchase the other half interest. The above conditions are cited in order to stress the necessity and importance of establishing the interest of the prospective borrower in the realty and to ascertain if there are any possible encumbrances which might have a direct effect upon that interest. A title search will disclose any unpaid property taxes or street or sewer-bond assessments as well as other types of liens and encumbrances. It frequently happens on loans which are in default and which are in the process of foreclosure that a search of the title will reveal liens covering unpaid income taxes as well as the other items mentioned above.

The general practice covering search of title is to have this work performed by a competent and responsible title company, which will issue a Title Insurance Policy which protects the lender against loss in case a defect in title develops at a later date. Also, the borrower's claim to ownership is protected as long as he owns the property if he obtains an owner's policy or has a joint protection policy with the lender. If the property is registered under the Torrens system, the checking of the Torrens Certificate will be done by the title company.[1] In most communities lenders have an attorney handle these phases of mortgage lending with the title company.

At the outset, title to all real estate came from the power of government or from a sovereign power. Following this many methods covering conveyance of title developed, such as by deed, by will, by descent, by foreclosure, by sale, by award in court decree, and in many other ways. The complete title to a property is dependent upon the record of previous changes of title; if any defect appears, the value of the security would be seriously affected.

Estate in Fee Simple

The closest approach to complete title to real property is termed "fee simple" or "estate in fee simple," as a person's interest in a property is known as an estate. The fee simple title is subject always to the rights of the state. Some of these rights include condemnation of property for public use, by

[1] According to *Essentials of California Real Estate* by Ivan A. Thorson, Realty Research Bureau, Inc., Los Angeles, p. 139, a Torrens title is a system of land registration originated by Sir Robert Torrens of Australia and intended to shorten and simplify transfer of land title. Authority was granted by statutory provision under the so-called Torrens Act of December 19, 1914. Obtaining Torrens title is done by examination, as in an abstract, and by court action, similar to that of quieting title. The decree of registration is issued by a court following action to register under Torrens title. Evidence of title is given by a registrar's Certificate of Title. This system is used very little in the nation. Buyers and lenders generally prefer the regular Title Insurance Policy.

payment of a fair price for the property, right to enforce the collection of taxes, as well as the right to continue the use made of the property, except in cases where it is unlawful to continue to use it, such as police power regulations.

Loans on Estates Less than Fee Simple

A principle of common law recognizes that where buildings are erected on a piece of unimproved land and there is no agreement to the contrary, the structures become a part of the land itself. The owner of such land and improvements may lease the property to another for a term of many years. The party who leases such property continues to own it subject to the lease he has made, and any mortgage made thereafter will be subject to the lease unless the lessee subordinates his lease to the mortgage. Such an estate is termed "leasehold estate." Throughout the nation land is improved by the erection of expensive and permanent buildings in which the ownership is not in fee simple and will revert back to the owner in fee simple at the time of expiration of the lease unless the lease provides otherwise. Also in many subdivision developments the contractor or speculative builder who has developed the project and sold the houses will retain ownership of the lot in each case and lease them to the buyers of the houses for periods of fifty to ninety-nine years at whatever rentals have been agreed upon. Many such leases contain provisions which give the individual an option to buy the lot at the end of any five-year interval for the price previously established when the lease was made. Prudent lenders who make loans on such improvements usually require that the lease on the land be subordinated to the mortgage. A prudent lender will also arrange to collect the lease payment from the borrowers along with the interest, installment, and trust funds on the first mortgage. Trust funds cover payments made by the borrower to the lender and held by the lender to pay for property taxes, hazard insurance, and lease payments and other items as they become due and payable.

Other Types of Estates

There is also an estate known as "homestead," in which the law of the state applies. States in such estates have provided by statute that the owner of the property is exempted from the payment of some debts in the case of a forced sale if the owner has a family. In some states it also applies to other designated persons.

There are estates which are acquired by a marriage relationship, and in most states the rights of the wife to real estate are called "dower," while the husband's rights are called "curtesy." There are also so-called "community property rights" acquired by the spouses in community property states.

There are numerous other estates, not all of which are generally subject to a mortgage.

Prior Liens

There are numerous liens which might seriously affect the borrower's title to the property. These include taxes, special assessments for local improvements such as sewer bonds, street assessments, judgments, mechanics' liens, partition suits, ad valorem taxes, and other litigation. Obligations of the government always take precedence over the first mortgage, and in case there is such a lien on a property on which foreclosure has been started, a prudent lender will promptly pay such taxes in order to avoid the payment of interest and penalties and will add these charges to the outstanding loan balance, or to the loan trust funds, depending upon the type of loan involved.

Types of Mortgages

There are several different types of mortgages, but the ones most commonly used are termed a mortgage, a trust deed, or a deed of trust. Other types are regular mortgages, equitable mortgages, and absolute deeds which are given as security for debts.

Equitable mortgages cover any document which shows an intention that real estate be used as security for the payment of a debt and which, for some reason, cannot operate as a regular mortgage or deed of trust and permits foreclosure in a court of equity.

An absolute deed is not generally used in real estate transactions. Parties have attempted to avoid the legal consequences flowing from the right of redemption by the borrower giving the lender an outright deed of conveyance, with the understanding that if the debt was not paid, the lender would own the mortgaged premises clear of all rights of the borrower and could thereafter deal with the real estate so conveyed with freedom. While the mortgage and trust deed, or deed of trust, differ greatly in form, they are both well adapted for use in pledging the security for the debt.

The form of mortgage which is used in most states is known as the "regular" mortgage, and it represents the conveyance or deed of the property by the borrower to the lender. It contains a description of the security, the amount of the debt, and a provision to the effect that the mortgage shall be null and void upon complete payment of the debt. The terms of the transaction are set forth in this instrument. Such a mortgage states whether a note is involved, and if so, the mortgage will adequately describe the note, including the date, amount, maturity, interest rate, place of payment, amortization, and all other important details. In the trust deed, or deed of trust, form of mortgage the borrower conveys the property to a third party as trustee in trust for the benefit of the holder of the note, namely, the lender. The trust deed is used extensively in several states in the nation.

Regardless of the type of mortgage instrument used there are other agreements set forth in the mortgage instrument which must also be recited in exact detail. These agreements are termed Express Covenants, and include the rights of the borrower and the lender in the transaction. Of particular importance to the lender is that the covenants contain provisions which will protect the lender in case there are defaults in the mortgage contract. The most important of these covers the procedures to be followed by the lender in case foreclosure of the mortgage becomes necessary.

Other Express Covenants include the following:

1. Provisions regarding the payment of the debt and the interest and any other required payments

2. Provisions that the borrower maintain adequate insurance on the improvements at all times

3. Provisions that the borrower pay the property taxes when due as well as all other types of taxes

4. Provisions regarding maintenance of the premises

5. Action which can be taken by the lender in case of default

6. Right of lender or trustee to take possession of the premises

7. Methods used for obtaining the income of the property in order to satisfy the debt, such as right to assign the rentals

8. Detailed provisions regarding foreclosure and the right to apply the foreclosure proceeds to the satisfaction of the debt

Description of the Mortgaged Property

In all mortgage instruments it is necessary that the mortgaged premises be accurately described, for unless the property involved can be accurately identified, the mortgage could be voided. In most parts of the nation the actual legal description of the premises is embodied in the mortgage instrument. This description shows lot and block numbers, subdivision, range, section, township, and exact boundaries and measurements of the property.

Fixtures

The term fixtures has been a controversial subject among mortgage lenders for many years. Originally the term meant any piece of property or chattel which upon becoming affixed to the property became a part of that property. Many of these items are removable, and this condition has caused some misunderstanding between buyers and sellers of properties.

During the past several years, many homes in new subdivisions have been sold with the washing machine, stove, garbage disposal, and other such items included in the price of the home being sold. There is no doubt that these items are gradually becoming classified as permanent fixtures, and when such is the case, the mortgage instrument is identified as, or termed, a "package mortgage."

Mechanics' Liens

In construction-loan operations there is always the danger of mechanics' liens being filed which in some states take precedence over the first mortgage or deed of trust. Statutes of each state contain provisions which protect the work done on the premises by either laborers or subcontractors or others, and if the contractor or builder fails to make payment for services rendered or for materials furnished, these persons are permitted to file mechanics' liens in order to protect their interests. They cover such items as plumbing service and supplies, brickwork and supplies, lumber furnished, other types of building materials, and services. Any person who has an unpaid claim for either labor or materials may sue to enforce the lien.

The mortgage lender must therefore watch this phase of operations very closely. Some lenders arrange to pay all the bills rendered and charge the borrower, while others merely check the paid bills. In some cities there are independent companies which perform all such services for the lender. These are usually termed "builders control companies."

Mechanics' liens not only apply to new construction but also to improvements to existing structures.

In cases where a builder is not too strong a credit risk, the lender might require that the builder obtain from a surety company a lien and completion bond which will guarantee the completion of the structure free and clear of all mechanics' liens.

Restrictions

There are many restrictions which pertain to the use of real estate. These are generally known as "private restrictions" and "public restrictions" and are made up of the following:

1. Restrictions imposed by the owner of the premises
2. Restrictions imposed by some government or regulatory body

These restrictions have to do with the types of buildings which can be erected on a property and the use to be made of the land. They have usually been imposed by deed, by a map, or by provisions of a zoning or building ordinance. When a mortgage loan is made, it is necessary for the lender to make sure that the type of building and use of the property conform to these restrictions. Sometimes deed restrictions contain a reversionary clause which states that if the restrictions are violated, the title to the property will revert to the grantor in the deed.

Illustrative of privately imposed restrictions are the following:
1. The use to which the premises may be put, such as residential or commercial
2. Types of buildings which may be erected
3. Location relative to building lines
4. Cost of buildings
5. Liquor restrictions and numerous others
Illustrative of public restrictions are the following:
1. Zoning laws issued by municipalities
2. Building codes issued by municipalities
3. Fire and health regulations issued by municipalities

Recording of the Mortgage

Every mortgage or deed of trust must be properly recorded if it is to become effective. Every state has provided statutes which have established a system of public records relating to real property. These records are designed to give notice to anyone who may purchase or in some other manner deal in real estate, and they are also a means of protecting innocent persons against fraud.

Not only mortgages but deeds of conveyance and other instruments which affect title to a property may be filed for record in the office provided by the law, and thereafter they constitute notice of the rights of the property owner. In case a mortgage is not properly recorded, a lender would run the risk of losing his security in the property in case of a sale to a third party who promptly records his deed. The party who did not record his mortgage would not be known as holder of the lien on the property.

Borrowers' Rights and Liabilities

Unless there is a default in one of the covenants of the mortgage or deed of trust, the borrower, as owner of the property, may deal with the property in any way he desires except that he may not abuse the property in violation of the deed of trust or mortgage. These privileges are known as Express Covenants and give the borrower complete right to possession of the property, and, just as important, the borrower may sell or convey the property subject only to the rights of the lender, which in nearly all cases consist of the lien of the mortgage or deed of trust.

There Are Numerous Types of Foreclosure

In case there is a default in one or more of the convenants of the mortgage or deed of trust, the lender has several permissible methods of taking action to protect the investment, such as:

1. Action to foreclose in accordance with local statutes

2. Court action by means of a suit to collect the debt from the borrower and other interested parties

3. Possession of the mortgaged premises for the purpose of taking over control and management of the property

4. Serving an Assignment of Rents on the tenant if property is rented and applying proceeds to the debt

Each state has statutes which prescribe the procedure to be followed in foreclosing a mortgage or deed of trust. Some statutes permit a sale of the mortgaged premises under the terms of a deed of trust or mortgage without the borrower's and other interested parties' having recourse to court action. Other statutes require the lender to foreclose through court action only. The former is termed "foreclosure under power of sale," while the latter is termed "foreclosure by court action," or "judicial foreclosure."

Foreclosure under Power of Sale

Numerous state laws permit the lender, in the event of a default in a covenant of the deed of trust or mortgage, to sell the mortgaged premises after giving the required notices in accordance with statutory provisions, provided the mortgage instrument permits such action. Legal requirements include:

1. Recording notice of default and registered-letter notice to the borrower and certain others who may record a request for notice

2. Publication of a notice in a newspaper of general circulation giving time and place of sale. Periods required for such posting are prescribed in the statutes

3. Posting of notices in prescribed public places

If, before termination of the foreclosure period, the borrower and other interested parties have taken no action to reinstate the loan, an officer of the lender will conduct a fair sale of the property at an appointed place, which is usually the steps of the county courthouse.

Foreclosure by Court Action

Numerous state laws require that all foreclosure procedures must result from court action, even though the mortgage or deed of trust might contain provisions authorizing foreclosure without court action.

Where court action is required a suit is brought by the lender against the borrower and all other interested parties. Other interested parties include holders of second and third mortgages, if any, and government officials interested in the collection of unpaid property taxes or other claims. Unpaid property taxes claims are usually prior to the liens of first mortgages, and most mortgage lenders advance these unpaid property taxes before starting foreclosure in all such cases.

The court usually renders a decree which determines the existence of the debt as well as the lien which secures it and directs that if the debt is not paid within the time fixed by the decree, the mortgaged premises shall be sold by a designated court officer after prescribed notices.

Strict Foreclosure

There is another type of foreclosure which is permitted in a few states and is termed "strict foreclosure." Foreclosure is accomplished by an action brought by the lender for the purpose of having a court of equity fix a time within which the mortgage must be paid if the borrower is not to lose his rights in the property. The decree of the court in such an action does not order a sale of the property but confirms the absolute title to it in the mortgage in case the borrower does not redeem the property within the time fixed by the court. Strict foreclosures are permitted only where the mortgaged premises do not exceed in value the amount of the mortgage debt.

Redemption after Sale

In addition to the right of redemption, which exists as an element of every mortgage until foreclosed or until it is otherwise legally barred, many states provide a right of redemption known as a statutory right to redeem after a judicial sale. This right is distinct from the equity of redemption and does not come into existence until the foreclosure has been completed. The redemption period ranges from a few months in some states to up to two years in other states.[2]

Expenses and Hazards of FHA and VA Foreclosures[3]

What are the present principal hazards and expenses of foreclosure to the lender in the various states on FHA and VA loans?

In answering this question, the discussion must of necessity be limited to loans on single-family residences, either guaranteed by VA or insured by FHA. A thorough discussion of the hazards and expenses of foreclosure on conventional loans would be more involved and require an analysis of the laws and practices of each of the fifty states.

Foreclosure proceedings on FHA and VA loans must be carried out pursuant to, and in compliance with, the laws of the state in which the property is situated. This is normal legal procedure. The hazards and costs which a lender may suffer, however, are determined not by state laws but by the contract of insurance or

[2] Refer to Bibliography and Suggested Reading at end of this chapter for further study of this subject.

[3] Adapted from Samuel E. Neel, "Expenses and Hazards of FHA and VA Foreclosures," *Banking, Journal of the American Bankers Association,* vol. 46, no. 10, April, 1954.

guaranty into which the lender has entered with either the FHA or VA. Since these contracts are standard regardless of the location of the real estate, a lender's rights may be safely determined in general from the rules and regulations of FHA and VA. In the case of FHA, however, while the contract of insurance is standard, certain rights of the lender thereunder are dependent upon state laws. These need special comment.

Foreclosure costs and expenses vary from state to state. As typical examples of average expenses, it is estimated that the cost of foreclosing a $10,000 mortgage on a single-family residence in the District of Columbia, assuming no unusual complications occur, would approximate $225 to $250. The estimated cost of foreclosing the same mortgage in the state of Florida would be approximately $350. Whichever cost might be incurred would make little difference if the mortgage is a VA mortgage. It will make a difference if the mortgage is an FHA mortgage.

With VA loans, where the VA fixes an upset price and the lender elects to convey the property to the VA, the lender receives cash in exchange for title to the foreclosed property. Sections 36:4313 and 36:4320 of the VA regulations lists those foreclosure expenses which may be included in the claim submitted by the lender to the VA for payment. In brief, the lender is allowed to include all reasonably necessary and proper advances for maintenance or repair of the security and payment of accrued taxes, insurance, special assessments, ground or water rents, court costs, advertising expenses, trustee's commissions, sheriff's fees, and other foreclosure expenses reasonably necessary. Also "a reasonable amount for legal services actually performed not to exceed 10 per cent of the unpaid indebtedness as of the date of the first uncured default, or $250, whichever is less." The portion of the regulation dealing with attorneys' fees has been the source of some controversy, principally because the VA decides whether the fee included is "reasonable" even though it may be $250 or less.

The upper limits set out in the VA regulations are not fixed by statute and therefore may be exceeded at the discretion of the VA. In an unusual case, for example, where there is considerable extra legal work involved, the loan guaranty officer may approve a higher attorney's fee or any other fee in excess of any of the above regulatory limits. It is important to bear in mind that this approval must be obtained in advance of the fee or charge being incurred. In case of any doubt as to the allowability of a particular item or the amount of a fee or charge being incurred it would be advisable to check with the local loan guaranty officer in advance in order to resolve the question.

If the property is conveyed to VA, the holder is also reimbursed for United States revenue stamps, state and documentary stamp taxes as required, the customary cost of title evidence in favor of the administrator, and recording and notary fees [Section 36:4320 (f)]. The Internal Revenue Service has ruled that deeds of conveyance from Federal savings and loan associations are exempt from affixing documentary stamps. Interest at the contract rate may also be included up to the date of the foreclosure sale or other acquisition.

Thus, except for some very unusual circumstances, a lender may safely expect to be reimbursed for 100 per cent of the out-of-pocket expenses incurred in foreclosing a VA loan, no matter where the property is situated or whatever the local costs may be.

With FHA loans, the situation is less favorable to lenders in several respects than that of the VA. For example:

1. The mortgagee receives debentures, not cash, from FHA in exchange for title to the real estate.

2. The FHA's regulations as to the foreclosure costs that may be included are not as liberal as those of the VA and vary considerably, depending upon which section of the act the mortgage is insured under.

3. The FHA limits on includable expenses are fixed by statute and may not be exceeded even in troublesome cases.

Mortgages on single-family homes are insured by FHA under several sections (Title I, Section 8; Section 203; Section 603; Section 611; and Sections 213, 220, 221, and 223). A great majority of loans come under Section 203. Since there are various subsections within Section 203, however, the regulations as to foreclosure costs, even under this one section are not uniform. With specific regard to subsections 203 (b), (2) (A), and Section 203 (b) (2) (C), the regulations provide that, except for advances the mortgagee has made for the protection of the security (such as taxes, ground and water rents, insurance, etc.), no other foreclosure costs will be included in determining the amount of FHA debentures which will be issued in exchange for the property in case of foreclosure.

As to all mortgages accepted for insurance under Section 203 on or after the effective date of the Housing Act of 1954 there shall be included in debentures, foreclosure costs or costs of acquiring the property otherwise (including cost of acquiring the property by the mortgagee and of conveying and evidencing title to the property of the Commissioner) actually paid by the mortgagee and approved by the Commissioner in an amount not in excess of two-thirds of such costs or $75, whichever is the greater.

The FHA regulations provide that a "certificate of claim" will be issued to the mortgagee in an amount sufficient to equal everything due if not covered by debentures, including a reasonable amount for necessary foreclosure expenses and attorney's fees. However, since the mortgagee can expect to receive payment under the "certificate of claim" only upon final liquidation of the security (which may take some years to effect) and not even then unless the net amount received by FHA after expenses exceeds the face amount of the debentures plus interest paid thereon, this provision understandably elicits something less than tumultuous applause from lenders.

In this field the item which probably occasions the most worry among lenders is the question of "rights of redemption." Here again the provisions of the various state laws vary widely. For example, in the District of Columbia there is no statutory period of redemption. Following an uncured default and proper notice of intent to sell, the trustees named in the deed of trust may effect a sale of the property. When this sale is ratified by the court, the foreclosure is complete. The entire process usually takes less than thirty days. The opposite extreme occurs under the laws of the state of Michigan, for example: here the statute requires publication of a notice of foreclosure for a period of twelve weeks and then provides that for a period of one year from the date of the sheriff's deed the original owner may regain title to the property by payment of the full amount of the debt and foreclosure costs. Thus, a period of at least fifteen months must elapse before all rights of the original mortgagor are eliminated, during which time the mortgagor is entitled to possession.

So far as VA loans are concerned, it does not make the slightest difference whether the laws of the jurisdiction where the property is located do or do not provide for any period during which a right of redemption is in existence. Nor does the question of adverse occupancy of the premises by the mortgagor give any trouble. The VA regulations provide that occupancy of the property by the mortgagor, his grantee, or tenants, or others will not be an objection to the acceptance of title by the VA, provided the occupants do not claim rights of ownership other than redemption rights [Section 36:4320 (h) (3)]. Therefore, immediately following the foreclosure sale, a lender is in position to file a final accounting with the VA and to receive payment under the guaranty.

With FHA loans, the mortgagee is again not in as favorable a position as when a VA loan is involved. First, as to possession, it has consistently been the FHA position that the commissioner has the right under the regulations to require the mortgagee to tender actual phyical possession of the property free from tenants. It is the policy of FHA to require delivery of the property vacant except where, at the FHA election, the existing tenancies are entirely consistent with their program of property management and disposal. Therefore, until a mortgagee can tender actual physical possession of the property, he is not in a position to deliver good title or to apply for debentures. This might mean the necessity of waiting until an eviction suit can be completed.

This same rule applies where a right of redemption exists under the laws of the jurisdiction where the property is located. "In those cases where the right of redemption exists, the mortgagee is not in a position to tender the property until the redemption period expires . . . " (FHA *Mortgagee's Handbook,* at page 43). Here again the mortgagee's position ultimately is favorable. When the debentures are issued, following expiration of the redemption period, they are dated and bear interest from the date as of which foreclosure proceedings were instituted. It is true, however, that under present provisions the lender cannot deliver title to the FHA in foreclosure proceedings until the expiration of the redemption period. Therefore, the property remains on his books during that period. Some lenders justifiably consider that to this extent the FHA tag does not remove their objections to making residential loans in those states where rights of redemption exist.

The conclusion seems justified that in the case of VA loans the lender is almost entirely protected against local expenses and hazards of foreclosure, and in the case of FHA loans such expenses and hazards are at least minimized.

Abstract of Title

An Abstract of Title is a complete history of the record of title of a designated parcel of land.[4] It consists of a summary of the material parts of every recorded instrument of conveyance or other transaction appearing of record which affects the title to the land or any estate or interest therein, together with a brief statement of all liens and encumbrances which have

[4] Land Title Guarantee and Trust Company, Cleveland, Ohio.

ever appeared of record against same. The facts, together with reference maps, are arranged in chronological order and show the origin and the incidents of the title without the necessity of referring to the original instruments or to the records wherein they are recorded.

The purpose of an Abstract is to afford a prospective purchaser, mortgagee, or lessee of real estate a convenient means of ascertaining the condition of the title. The party in interest, through his attorney, may readily pass upon the validity of the record title in question without resorting to a laborious search of the records. The attorney's function is to interpret properly the effect of each instrument in the chain of title and determine the ultimate condition of the record title.

Limited Abstract of Title

A Limited Abstract of Title is a compiled history of the record title, similar to an Abstract of Title, but covering only a given period of time.[5] Limited Abstracts are sometimes called "continuations," or "extensions."

The purpose of a Limited Abstract is to afford a purchaser, mortgagee, or lessee of real estate information as to what has transpired of record regarding a designated parcel of land during a short period of time, usually from the date of a previous title examination.

A Title Guarantee

A Title Guarantee is an indemnity contract whereby the title company, as insurer, guarantees that, so far as appears of record, the title to a designated parcel of land is good in a certain party subject only to such defects, liens, and encumbrances as are set forth in the Title Guarantee as shown by the indices of the records.[6]

The purpose of a Title Guarantee is to afford a purchaser, mortgagee, or lessee of real estate a short and convenient way of ascertaining the condition of the record title as of a certain date, and also it guarantees that the record title is as shown therein.

Title Insurance

Title Insurance is a contract of indemnity whereby the title company, as insurer, guarantees that the title of an owner, mortgagee, or lessee is good and is free from defects, liens, or encumbrances existing at the date of the policy, excepting such as are specifically mentioned therein. By it, the title company obligates itself to pay any loss, up to the full amount of the policy,

[5] *Ibid.*
[6] *Ibid.*

suffered by the insured by reason of any defects, liens, or encumbrances found to exist at the date of the policy and not excepted therein, and to defend the title at its own cost against any such defects or encumbrances alleged to be in existence at the date of the policy.[7]

Purpose of a Title Insurance Policy

The purpose of a Title Insurance Policy is to protect the owner, mortgagee, or lessee of real estate against a great many defects which would not be disclosed by the most thorough examination of the record title.[8] Here are some of them:

1. Forged deeds
2. Forged mortgages
3. Forged waivers, assignments, and cancellations of mortgages
4. False impersonation
5. Mortgages canceled by mistake
6. Undisclosed heirs
7. Undisclosed dower
8. Missing heirs presumed to be dead
9. Deeds and mortgages made by insane parties, the insanity proceedings not being of record in the county
10. Deeds and mortgages made by minors, there being nothing of record in the county to disclose the fact of minority
11. The undisclosed existence of children born or adopted after the execution of a will
12. Release of dower by a minor husband or wife, there being no record evidence of minority
13. Deeds made under power of attorney that has been revoked by the death of the person executing the power
14. Divorce proceedings in a foreign county or state
15. Foreign bankruptcy proceedings
16. Probating of will after deed executed and delivered by heirs
17. A recorded deed that was never delivered, delivery essential to the passing of title by deed

In addition to the issuance of Abstracts, Limited Abstracts, Title Guarantees, and Title Insurance Policies, title companies furnish judicial sale reports, special tax searches, Federal court searches, and location services for mortgage loan purposes. They also close real estate loans for clients and render a general escrow and trust service in connection with the transfer or holding of title to real estate.[9]

[7] *Ibid.*
[8] *Ibid.*
[9] *Ibid.*

Recorder's Office

1. Deed Index
2. Mortgage Index
3. Lease Index
4. Mechanics Lien Index
5. Miscellaneous Index
6. Release Index
7. Powers of Attorney
8. Subdivision Plats
9. Bond Records
10. Attested Accounts
11. Federal Tax Liens
12. Personal Property Tax Liens
13. Authority to Pay Taxes
14. Corporation Records
    Change of Names
    Delinquent Franchise Tax
    Cancelled Charters
15. Industrial Commission Liens
16. Chattel Mortgages

Auditor's Office

1. Plat Books
2. Tax Sale Books
3. Transfer Records
4. Tax Addition Book
5. Tax Abatement Book
6. Affidavits for Transfer
7. Special Tax and Assessment
   Records

Treasurer's Office

1. General Tax Duplicate
2. Liquor Taxes and Licenses
3. Public Utility Corporation
   Taxes
4. Church Property Exemptions
5. Tax Addition Book

Surveyor's Office

1. Road Records

Sheriff's Office

1. Foreign Execution Dockets
2. Order of Sales
3. Decrees in Partition, etc.

Clerk's Office

1. General Index to Suits
2. Files
3. Levy Records
4. Judgment Liens Docket
5. Divorces
6. Transcripts
7. Partnership Records
8. Record of Notaries
9. Court of Appeals Index and
   Files
10. Old Insolvency Court
    Records Both as to Di-
    vorces, Appropriation
    Proceedings and Assign-
    ments for Benefits of
    Creditors
11. Sales Tax Liens

Court of Appeals

1. Appeals from All Courts in
   County

Probate Court

1. Estates — Index and Files
2. Guardianship — Index and
   Files
3. Insanity Proceedings
4. Civil Cases
5. Marriage Records
6. Inheritance Tax
7. Adoptions
8. Birth Records
9. Death Records
10. Will Contests
11. Land Sales
12. Appropriations
13. Change of Name
14. Inquests
15. Assignments

Figure 29. Work Involved in a Title Search[10]

[10] *Ibid.*

<u>Municipal Court</u>

1. Index to Suits (General)
2. Index to Suits (Conciliation)
3. Stay Bonds
4. Levy Bonds

<u>Municipal Health Department</u>

1. Birth Records
2. Death Records

<u>Municipal Engineer's Office</u>

1. Street Records
2. House Numbers

<u>Municipal Clerk's Records</u>

1. Ordinances — Vacating, Widening, Narrowing or Changing Names
   of Streets
2. Special Tax and Assessment Records

<u>Office of Collector of Internal Revenue</u>

1. Federal Estate Tax

<u>United States Court</u>

1. Index to Suits
2. Bankruptcy
3. Revenue Law Liens (including income tax, liquor tax, social
   security, unemployment tax and amusement tax)

<u>Department of Taxation</u>

1. Information as to Corporation Franchise Tax

<u>Secretary of State's Office</u>

1. Information as to Cancellations, Dissolutions, Reinstatements
   of Corporations

Figure 29. (Continued)

SUMMARY

The use of mortgages in some form in a real estate transaction dates back to ancient times, and throughout world history property has been sold and purchased. The instrument used to pledge the property in modern times has been known as a mortgage or deed of trust.

Many technical and legal principles and practices are involved in mortgage lending, and these have been slowly developed throughout history. Even as late as the eighteenth century the borrower had little, if any, protection in case it developed that he was unable to repay the obligation properly.

The right of the borrower to redeem the property is known today as "right of redemption," or "equity of redemption." Throughout our nation, the time for redemption varies considerably among states. Some are for short periods only, while others give the borrower a year or more to reclaim his property by payment of the past-due payments or other charges. In some states there is no "right of redemption" after sale.

In order to comply with existing laws which govern mortgage transactions, there are certain basic steps which must be taken when a mortgage loan is made, namely:

1. A note covering the amount of the loan, the interest rate, and the installment, and other conditions must be signed by all borrowers who have an interest in the property involved.

2. The interested borrowers must also sign a mortgage or deed of trust, which instrument is legally sufficient to pledge the real estate.

3. The lender must make certain that the property pledged as security for the loan is free and clear of all encumbrances and that the borrowers have clear title to the property except such encumbrance as approved by the lender.

4. The mortgage instrument must be properly recorded in the proper public office in order to give the required notice to all parties.

The property is pledged by the borrower as security for the mortgage loan by the mortgage or deed of trust, which is signed by the borrower and properly recorded. In other words the mortgage is the instrument by which the pledge of the property is accomplished.

When a property is mortgaged, the mortgage attaches to the land as well as the improvements on the land. This is true whether such improvements are placed on the land before or after the execution of the mortgage. This interpretation permits the type of financing known as a construction loan.

All mortgages must be recorded in order to guard against claims of third parties. Also, unless recorded, the borrower could make numerous loans on the same property.

The closest approach to complete title to real property is termed fee simple, or estate in fee simple, as a person's interest in a property is known as an estate. The fee simple title is subject always to the right of the state.

The form of mortgage used in many states, known as the regular mortgage, represents the conveyance, or deed, of the property to the lender. It contains a description of the security, the amount of the debt, and a provision that the mortgage shall become null and void upon complete payment of the debt. The terms of the transaction are also set forth in the instrument.

In the trust deed, or deed of trust, form of mortgage the borrower conveys the property to a third party as trustee in trust for the holder of the note, namely, the lender.

Regardless of the type of mortgage instrument used, there are other agreements which must be recited in exact detail. These agreements are termed Express Covenants and include the rights of both the borrower and the lender in the transaction. It is of particular importance to the lender that the covenants contain provisions which will protect the lender in case there are defaults by the borrower on the mortgage contract.

There are many restrictions which pertain to the use of real estate that are generally known as private restrictions and public restrictions. Private restrictions are imposed by the owner of the premises while public restrictions are imposed by some government, state, city, or regulatory body.

Unless there is a default in one of the covenants of the mortgage or deed of trust, the borrower, as owner of the property, may deal with the property in any way he desires, except that he may not abuse the property in violation of the deed of trust or mortgage. These Express Covenants also give the borrower complete right to possession of the property, and, just as important, the borrower may sell or convey the property subject only to the rights of the lender, which in nearly all cases consist of the lien of the mortgage or deed of trust.

In case there is a default on one or more of the covenants of the mortgage or deed of trust, the lender has several permissible methods of taking action to protect the investment, such as:

1. Action to foreclose in accordance with local statutes

2. Action by means of a suit to collect the debt from the borrower and other interested parties

3. Possession of the mortgaged premises for the purpose of taking over control and management of the property

4. Serving Assignment of Rents on the tenant if the property is rented and applying the proceeds to the debt

There are numerous types of foreclosures, and each state has statutes which prescribe the procedures to be followed in foreclosing a mortgage or deed of trust. Some statutes permit a foreclosure sale of the mortgaged premises without the borrower's or other interested parties' having recourse to court action, while other state statutes require the lender to foreclose through court action only. The former is termed foreclosure under power of sale while the latter is termed foreclosure by court action.

All prudent lenders will cooperate fully with a borrower who through no fault of his own has defaulted on one or more of the covenants of the mortgage or deed of trust. A majority of such default cases are cleared prior to completion of foreclosure action by complete cooperation between the borrower and lender.

QUESTIONS

1. Explain how a grantee becomes bound by the terms of the mortgage.
2. What is the basic source covering title to property records?
3. Is real estate and the pledging of it as security governed by the law of state in which the security is located?
4. Does each state have its own statutes? Explain.
5. When a piece of personal property permanent in character is annexed to the mortgaged premises, does it become subject to the mortgage?
6. Why is the original mortgagor (borrower) in case of sale of the property still liable to the mortgagee (lender) if sold subject to the mortgage?
7. Why should every mortgage or deed of trust be promptly and properly recorded?
8. May a minor make conveyance of a property the title to which is in his own name?
9. Explain why a deed of trust usually provides for more simple foreclosure operations than does a mortgage.
10. Describe "milking" of an income property.
11. Name five Express Covenants usually contained in a deed of trust.
12. Explain an absolute deed.
13. Give reasons why the instrument (deed of trust or mortgage) should recite whether the debt is evidenced by a note, and also should recite with exactness all the other agreements between the parties to the transaction.
14. What are the above agreements termed?
15. Do all title companies endeavor to maintain their own records on ownership of properties, lien records, tax records, in other words, the status of the properties in all respects?
16. Describe plant records.
17. Name the two types of instruments which are most commonly used in mortgage transactions.
18. Restrictions relating to the use of real estate fall into what two groups?
19. The term mortgage has what two distinct meanings? Explain.
20. Would you be willing to hold a mortgage on property if the house is only partially located on a lot owned by the mortgagor? Explain.
21. Name the two basic elements required in order to create a mortgage.
22. Explain why obligations of the government take precedence over all individual rights in property.
23. Explain why a search of title is required.
24. Distinguish between public and private restrictions.
25. Explain foreclosure under power of sale.
26. Explain foreclosure by court action.
27. Explain strict foreclosure.
28. Describe what is meant by title-theory states.

29. Describe what is meant by lien-theory states.
30. Explain why leases which have been made subsequent to a mortgage on a property are terminated by completion of foreclosure action.
31. Explain the basic legal difference between a mortgage loan and collateral loan.
32. Name five methods by which title to property may be conveyed.
33. Explain an open-end mortgage.
34. Define a purchase money mortgage.
35. Explain why an extension of time in which to pay the debt sometimes releases the original mortgagor.

ASSIGNMENTS

1. Explain two deed restrictions and their importance in mortgage lending.
2. Obtain a mortgage agreement and carefully study the express covenants contained therein.
3. Describe the system of public recording required by the statutes in your state.
4. Obtain an assignment of a mortgage form and explain a transaction in which this document is used.
5. Explain the type of foreclosure proceedings which are used in your state.

BIBLIOGRAPHY AND SUGGESTED READING

Berhaus, George H., *Know Your Real Estate,* Mercury Press, San Francisco, 1946.

Home Mortgage Lending, chaps. 2–4, American Institute of Banking, Section American Bankers Association, New York, 1946.

Kratovil, Robert, *Real Estate Law,* Prentice-Hall, Inc., Englewood Cliffs, N.J., 1952.

MacChesney, Nathan W., *The Law of Real Estate Brokerage,* The Foundation Press, Chicago, 1938.

McMichael, Stanley L., *How to Finance Real Estate,* chaps. 4, 18, 36, 37, Prentice-Hall, Inc., Englewood Cliffs, N.J., 1951.

Pease, Robert H., and Homer V. Cherrington (eds.), *Mortgage Banking,* chap. 2, McGraw-Hill Book Company, Inc., New York, 1951.

Thorson, Ivan A., *Essentials of California Real Estate: Law and Practice,* Realty Research Bureau, Los Angeles, 1951.

Title Insurance and Trust Company, *Handbook for Title Men,* The Ward Ritchie Press, Los Angeles, 1948.

8 Development of New Business

PURPOSES

1. To explain the need for effective methods to develop new mortgage business
2. To describe methods and mediums used to promote new business
3. To explain the competitive considerations that influence methods of developing new mortgage business
4. To explain the responsibilities of prudent mortgage lenders in the new-business phase of mortgage lending

Marketing Objectives of Mortgage Lending Institutions

No two lenders have exactly the same new-business-development problems or objectives. Variations occur largely as a consequence of differences in the nature and extent of the area served and differences in the amounts and character of loans that make up the portfolio. There is relatively little uniformity in lending policy among lenders. Nor is there uniformity in permissible ratios of mortgage loans to assets or time deposits. Generally speaking, these ratios are restricted by Federal regulations in the case of federally chartered lending institutions and by state laws and company policies in the case of life insurance companies, state-chartered banks, mutual savings banks, and state-supervised savings and loan associations. A few states impose no limitations. See Appendix C, "Loan Limitations by States," covering life insurance companies. New-business-development activities vary widely even among companies with similar operations. Notwithstanding these varying or dissimilar considerations, the major objective of every prudent lender is to obtain as much sound business as desired in the different types of loans which it is willing to make.

Basic Conditions Which Control New-business-development Objectives

Among the conditions that affect a mortgage development program, the following are most important:

1. The funds earmarked for mortgage investments
2. The optimum of total loans for a particular lender
3. The runoff of the portfolio
4. Methods by which a lender makes sure that a fair share of the business is being obtained
5. The soundness of the lending policies of the particular lender
6. Earnings
7. The quality of the portfolio
8. The flow of funds and the availability of funds for investment in mortgage loans
9. The government-bond market and the Federal Reserve bank rediscount rate and reserve requirements for member banks

Several times each year the board of directors and executive officers of a lender meet and decide upon the amount of funds which they estimate will be available and should be invested in mortgage loans and in other securities. Practically all mortgage lenders establish each year the optimum of loans they will want to carry in the portfolio during that year. In establishing such a figure many factors must be taken into consideration, among them the economic conditions of a particular locality, the position of the investment portfolio with respect to interest accrual, types of loans, delinquencies, geographical distribution, and operating income and expense.

It is particularly important in arriving at a decision regarding the amount of funds to be invested during a given period to determine the runoff of the portfolio. Most lenders keep a runoff record on a weekly basis. It includes a report of all new loans made during the week, loans on which payments have been made, loans paid off, and the corresponding increase or decrease in the loan ledger balance by types of loans. Most large lenders that are active in the construction-loan business also keep a record of the dollar amount of loan commitments to builders. These future commitments must be watched carefully because of their direct bearing on plans for the acquisition of new business.

An aggressive lender does not leave to chance the maintenance of its competitive status. It keeps informed daily of the activities of its competitors and knows as much as possible about their lending policies, the types of loans they are seeking aggressively, and their requirements for various types of loans. Specifically, it is desirable to acquire information on loan maturities, loan fees, interest rates being charged, the amount of down payments required on FHA or VA loans, specific areas in which loans are made on subdivisions and individual properties, and the names of the builders who are obtaining construction financing through competitors.

Importance of Mortgage Recordings

Mortgage recordings in the various counties are analyzed to ascertain how much business is being done by each type of lender. By assembling all available information an astute lender will be kept informed of the possibility of business being obtained in each county by type of loans. He will also be able to determine if his company is obtaining a fair share of the business. Title companies in most states issue reports monthly covering the number and dollar amount of loans made in each county by type of lender, and also give the name of the lender in each case.

The soundness of lending policies has a marked effect on business development objectives. Some lenders who are conservative in their lending policies are often satisfied with the normal run of business and do not press for new business. A conservative appraisal basis and strict credit requirements are characteristic of this type of lender. In most communities, however, there are many lenders whose policies are liberal as to down payment and credit requirements. This is sometimes found to be the case when loans are made for eventual sale to other investors. The builder-lender program, previously described, wherein VA 501 loans are sold at a considerable discount to purchasing mortgagees, is an example of this type of operation.

It is generally true that all mortgage lenders regardless of type must continuously stay in the mortgage market. If a lender leaves the market for a time, it is difficult to reenter and acquire, without a considerable time lag, a fair share of the business. An aggressive lending organization will endeavor to meet competition at all times, provided it does not become necessary to change or sacrifice any of its basic lending policies. It is important that such lenders handle the potential business of old customers and regular depositors at all times.

Basic conditions controlling the acquisition of new mortgage lending business are affected by the relationship of the mortgage loan department to other operations of large institutions. In many banks commercial loans are the major investment. In others bonds are the major investment, and in still other institutions the mortgage loan department is the major operation. The very nature of savings and loan associations suggests that the major activity is mortgage lending. Nearly all large insurance companies are active in mortgage lending but from time to time will withdraw from the market on certain types of loans such as FHA and VA loans and stress their own conventional loans. They also purchase government obligations either for the purpose of diversifying their investments or, whenever it can be done, for the purpose of maximizing income. Such practices basically affect their business-development operations.

The quality of the mortgage loan portfolio is carefully analyzed at all times by prudent lenders. The maintenance of quality at a high point has a direct effect upon the activities in seeking new business. If quality is the paramount consideration, the lender will rarely make or seek new loans which call for little or no down payment or repayment over an excessively long term. In this case safety and liquidity of the portfolio are regarded as more important than the acquisition of new business.

Services Offered by Mortgage Lenders

The services offered by different mortgage lenders will have a direct bearing upon the mortgage development activities. These services are based to some extent on the following:

1. Adoption of policies which underlie sound lending practices
2. Promptness in meeting competition
3. Necessity for constant mortgage lending activity
4. Organization of the lender
5. Mortgage bankers (loan correspondents) and agents who handle other business in addition to mortgage loans

Numerous mortgage bankers as such not only engage in mortgage lending business but also handle fire insurance, real estate sales, rentals, leases, property management, and business locations, as well as the servicing of loans for purchasing mortgagees. Their business-development activities are dependent to some extent upon the objectives of the investors they represent, as well as their operations covering local activities.

Determination of Business-development Policies and Practices

The types of properties on which loans are made by a lender will determine to some extent its business-development policies and practices. In Chapter 4 the types of properties on which loans are made by most mortgage lenders are listed. They consist of the following:

1. Dwellings (one- to four-family)
2. Flats (with stores below)
3. Apartments
4. Stores and office buildings
5. Industrial buildings
6. Hotels
7. Unimproved (industrial)
8. Unimproved (residential)
9. Farms

10. Special-purpose (includes churches, theaters, lodge halls, fraternity houses, garages, service and gas stations, and golf courses)

Many lenders specialize in home loans. Others specialize in the other types of properties listed above and do no home loan business. Some lenders invest in all these types of properties. A lender who specializes in loans on homes would use a different market promotion pattern for new business from that of a lender who specializes in apartment buildings or industrial buildings or all types of properties other than homes. Mutual savings banks and savings and loan associations make no farm loans, while some large life insurance companies do a considerable amount of business in hotel loans. Some life insurance companies do not want a loan under $50,000 in their portfolio. All mutual savings banks and savings and loan associations and some commercial banks doing a savings business specialize in home loans. The type of activity governs to a great extent the promotional planning and marketing activities of the lender.

The Role of the Mortgage Banker in the Development of New Business

In the development of new business, the mortgage banker (loan correspondent) actually sells money. Money, like any other commodity, has a value based on the laws of supply and demand. The mortgage banker attempts to buy and sell his commodity to the greatest advantage to his customer and his investor.

Much like the stock market where each broker must buy and sell for his clients at the same price as every other broker, the successful mortgage banker must give service as well, since his volume of business largely depends on the excellence and the amount of service he renders his clients.

An advertisement in a recent issue of the *Mortgage Banker,* the national magazine of the Mortgage Bankers Association of Amercia, read in part: "One call to our mortgage department is the equivalent of calling on the mortgage officers of fifteen large institutional investors."

In other words, the mortgage banker claims that in representing more than one source of mortgage money he can by experience, and through a knowledge of policies of his various lenders, perhaps fit a mortgage into a portfolio with the most advantageous terms to his clients and this can be a great time saver. If a client seeking a mortgage loan calls on a mortgage banker, he has a choice of five, ten, fifteen, or even twenty lenders. Thus he makes a single interview and a single application in one stop.

Some mortgage bankers also operate as real estate brokers and try to bring buyers and sellers together after the process of matching the buyer's wants with the right property. Some mortgage bankers, also, act as bankers, using their own funds, coupled with a commercial bank line of credit. Thus they make loans, package the loans, and then sell from their own portfolios of mortgages to various investors. A considerable volume of this business is done in FHA and VA loans, with mutual savings banks and FNMA.

Some mortgage bankers do a combination business; other activities include the processing and making of construction loans and the appraisal of real estate.

In recent years, the mortgage banker, with a view to getting new business, has been the creator of real estate investment opportunities by financing the purchase of land for a builder-developer, in order to get the future mortgage business of both the construction loan for the builder and the eventual mortgages from purchasers of the homes, or owners of apartment houses, or developers of shopping centers, and other commercial and industrial types of properties.

The heart of any real estate transaction or any building operation is the financing. The knowledge of this financing and the research and sources of financing are the tools with which the mortgage banker works. Also there are the tools with which the mortgage banker can best serve his community.

In many large cities in the nation, city officials place some reliance on the mortgage banker in pushing slum-clearance projects, downtown redevelopment projects, and urban renewal.

Methods and Techniques Used in Developing New Business

Modern marketing methods are required in the mortgage lending business because of the tremendous growth of this industry and the progressive increase in competition for loans. These methods of developing the market can be classified broadly as personal contact, advertising, and services rendered.

Personal Contact

1. Individuals
2. Builders
3. New construction (individuals planning to build a home)
4. Architects
5. Lumber firms and other material dealers
6. Homeowners
7. Real estate brokers
8. Individuals desiring to refinance
9. Owners of land
10. Holders of insurance policies (contact by life insurance companies)
11. Members of trade associations and similar organizations

Advertising

1. Radio
2. Television
3. Newspapers
4. Booklets
5. Magazines
6. Billboards
7. Direct mail
8. Home models and other displays
9. Trade journals
10. Memo pads
11. Appointment books
12. Wall calendars

Services Rendered

1. Efficient and speedy handling of applications
2. Reputation of lender for efficiency of services in the mortgage lending industry
3. Ability to maintain a satisfied clientele
4. Relationship with competitors
5. Actual adoption of the most improved and modern merchandising methods designed to stimulate and create interest
6. Adequate and efficient personnel

Personal Contact

Excellent sources of new business are individuals who are looking for a home or some other type of property. They require the services of a reputable mortgage lender to suggest the best method of finding suitable properties, the soundest method of investment, and the maximum amount that should be invested or could be loaned on particular properties.

The largest volume of new home-loan business is obtained by lenders who provide construction funds for developers *of subdivisions.* The lender who provides the construction financing in nearly all cases has an agreement with the builder to provide loans to the individual home purchasers. So important is this phase of business development that large lenders have contact men on their staffs to develop builder relations. Nor is the small but growing builder overlooked.

Still another prospect for new business is the person who has his own ideas about the home he wishes to build. Generally he prefers to make all arrangements regarding the construction and the type of architecture with his builder and architect and calls upon the mortgage lender for financial assistance and guidance in the transaction. Although it is generally the individual about to build a home who provides this kind of opportunity, mortgages are also in demand by builders of commercial and industrial properties. It is good practice for the mortgage lender to advise individuals regarding plans and specifications and types of building to be constructed and to offer opinions regarding the financial needs of the principals.

Contacts should be developed with architects. Most potential borrowers who are planning some type of construction use the services of an architect before discussing the transaction with a mortgage lender. Architects as a general rule know the lending policies of the various lenders in the area and are able to direct business to individual lenders.

Contacts with lumber firms and national dealers are of extreme value. It is through such firms that new building programs are often obtained. Builders and individuals planning to have a home constructed customarily price building materials at the inception of a transaction.

Persons who own or are buying their homes are also potential sources of new business. A homeowner planning the sale of a property may refer the potential buyer to the lender who holds the existing loan. This is also an excellent field for conventional loans to cover modernization and improvements on existing dwellings.

Major Source of New Home-loan Business

Perhaps the major source of new home-loan business is real estate brokers whose business is to bring buyers and sellers of properties together. Real estate brokers have a keen knowledge of the mortgage market. They also know the lending policies of the various types of mortgage lenders. A friendly real estate broker is able to bring a great deal of good new business to a lender.

Refinancing of Loans

There is a large amount of refinancing of loans for a variety of purposes. This includes borrowers who desire to obtain loans for larger amounts than can be obtained from present lenders. In many cases lenders may be looking for more attractive interest rates and will transfer their loans to other lenders if lower interest rates are offered and appear to be advantageous to borrowers. Some borrowers refinance in order to obtain longer maturities on existing loans. All lenders desire to hold as many mortgage loans as possible in their loan portfolios. One method of accomplishing this objective is to impose a penalty on a pay-off of a loan before maturity. The FHA, for example, imposes a penalty of 1 per cent of the original amount of the loan if the loan is paid off before maturity. Many institutional lenders follow this same practice on conventional loans. Many refinancing transactions cover the purchase of properties by other individuals who desire to carry the loans with different lending firms.

Contacts should be developed among individuals who own unimproved land and desire to improve their properties.

Many large insurance companies use the method of contacting insurance-policy holders within their own company for mortgage business.

The purchase and sale of existing properties of all types is continuous and one of the major activities in the real estate market. A careful follow-up of all such transactions will be maintained by an alert lender.

Importance of Trade Associations

It is good business to join associations. Among them are the Mortgage Bankers Association of America, the Savings and Mortgage Division of the American Bankers Association, the Associated Home Builders, the National Association of Real Estate Boards, and local trade associations. Most of these associations issue magazines or bulletins which contain valuable information regarding the mortgage market and related activities.

Mortgage Development Program by Banks

The form of a bank's mortgage development program will depend upon whether it is an independent bank with only one office or a branch bank with numerous offices. From the loan applicant's viewpoint there is little difference between the independent bank with one office and a branch of a large bank having many offices. Convenience is the important thing to him. For that reason, a bank with only one office finds it necessary to be unusually aggressive in its solicitation programs and to use every possible means of developing desirable applications.

A method used by many lenders with considerable success is a team effort on the part of the employees. In some instances, extra compensation is offered, and in others promotions and salary increases are the motivating forces. In cases where extra compensation is not offered, it is important that effort on the part of the employees be confined to regular banking hours. If work is done outside regular hours, time and a half must be paid under the Wage and Hour Act regulations.

Employees are usually directed by a special committee consisting of the head of the mortgage loan department as chairman, with other members representing the public relations, advertising, and credit departments. Progress bulletins may be issued from time to time announcing the development of the campaign.

There is nothing new about employee campaigns; they have been used for years. They serve not only as a stimulus to the organization as a whole but also as an effective means of acquainting all employees with the services of the real estate loan department, also called the mortgage loan department.

So far as multibranch banks are concerned, each manager usually has been trained to alert his entire branch staff to the importance of mortgage loans, with the result that there is a continuous new-business effort in progress accompanied by a steady flow of loan applications.

Advertising

Most aggressive mortgage lenders keep their company names constantly before the public by means of advertising. Large lenders generally employ the services of independent advertising agencies to perform this service and to handle all the details of advertising.

Radio programs are used extensively by a number of lenders to reach the public and create interest in the mortgage lending facilities of the sponsor. Some lenders sponsor plays on the radio, others musical programs; others have short commercials which are repeated throughout the day.

Newspapers have always been used extensively by mortgage lenders, and any issue of most of the large newspapers in the nation usually will contain advertisements of various sizes and forms covering the facilities of various lenders. This has been an important method of developing new mortgage business for many years.

Many lenders issue booklets containing home designs and information on the manner of constructing or purchasing a home or other types of properties. Such booklets have proved popular during the past few years. Their appeal depends to a great extend on the contents of the booklets themselves, some of which are made up in an excellent manner.

During the past few years the use of television as a means of advertising has been expanding rapidly. There are some excellent programs on television both national and local which have great appeal and have resulted in considerable new business. One example of such a television program is that sponsored by the Wells Fargo Bank called "Science in Action," which started as a local program in the San Francisco area a few years ago. It has proved to be successful and has had such general appeal that it is now presented in several other large cities under different sponsorship.

Advertisements in magazines, including trade journals, follow somewhat the same pattern as newspaper advertising, and advertisements of mortgage lenders appear in practically every nationally known magazine.

Other advertising methods used are billboards, direct mail, home models and displays, memorandum pads, appointment books, wall calendars, and many other items. These things have varying appeal to prospective customers.

The use of these media will be determined by the objectives of the lender and the type of customer and mortgage business the lender desires to attract.

Quality of Services Rendered

Unless excellent service is rendered by a mortgage lender, it cannot expect to retain business or to develop new business satisfactorily. Applications for mortgage loans must be handled efficiently and quickly, and the lender must have a staff of employees who are friendly and enthusiastic. Proper service will promote good will and develop satisfied clients. A satisfied client is the best form of advertising and the best source of new business.

A mortgage lender can develop a reputation for efficient service throughout the area in which it operates. Such a reputation cannot help but generate new business. Efficient and speedy handling of applications is highly important, and satisfied clients invariably tell their friends about the excellent services of such a lender. Efficient services rendered will also place a lender in an advantageous competitive position with other lenders in the area.

To maintain good service a lender must carefully analyze its operating procedures almost daily in order to adjust lending policies and business-development methods. Unless this is done, the lender may lag in his market-development operations.

It is necessary that a constant search be made for new ideas that will develop new business. Many lenders refer to competitors certain loans which they cannot handle themselves. The competitors will usually return the favor, and this not only is a means of promoting a healthy competitive market but is an excellent builder of good will.

The Use of Each Technique

It should be observed that a sound mortgage lending institution would use advertising, personal contact, and services rendered in promoting new business and that no institution should use any of these methods exclusively. However, some institutions may favor the use of advertising over personal contact and services rendered, while others would favor personal contact and quality of services rendered over advertising. A great deal would depend on the objectives of the lender as well as the methods of operation. For example, a small unit bank would not use the same business-development procedures as a large branch banking system. This is also true of life insurance companies that invest only in the local area in contrast with those that invest throughout the nation.

Savings and loan associations and mutual savings banks would undoubtedly stress different media from those of institutions afore-mentioned, inasmuch as both invest mainly in home loans. There are also certain phases of each medium which might be stressed by a particular lender. Some lenders might not favor radio advertising or newspaper advertising. Others will favor direct mail, while some are of the opinion that direct mail is too expensive and is not warranted. There are also many theories regarding personal contact with prospective customers. Some lenders pay finder's fees to brokers or mortgage loan correspondents for obtaining loans, and most of their loans are obtained by personal contact with prospective borrowers. Almost all large lenders who finance operative builders maintain staffs of efficient contact men who spend practically their entire working hours visiting builders and in this way develop new business. This is undoubtedly the most effective method of obtaining this type of new business.

Large Eastern investors obtain a great deal of new mortgage business from mortgage loan correspondents located in key cities throughout the nation. These correspondents use various methods and techniques of developing the market, and their activities in this field are dependent to some extent on the desires of their principals, that is, types of loans to be sought and whether they are to be sought aggressively. In general such correspondents use the three approaches mentioned in developing new business.

Many large Eastern investors seek FHA loans only, while others prefer the VA loans in certain areas. Others, particularly some of the large life insurance companies, stress conventional loans, and this in turn will have a direct effect upon the market-development methods by which the correspondents will seek new business.

In the fast-growing areas of the nation such as Washington, Oregon, California, Arizona, Florida, and Texas, where there has been a tremendous expansion of home building and other types of construction during the past several years, it has been necessary to interest capital from outside these states to invest in mortgage loans. The means of attracting outside capital take many forms. Although a considerable amount of advertising is used for this purpose, most of the business is developed through correspondence and personal contact with potential purchasing mortgagees. The best sources of new business in this type of mortgage activity are frequent personal contacts plus the efficiency of the organization acting within a particular state, and the types and quality of the loans which they have to offer. Many important personal contacts of this nature are made at trade-association conventions and other meetings of such associations. This is an excellent means of promoting new business and also developing good will.

In fast-growing areas many banks that sell loans to purchasing mortgagees not only service such loans for a fee but in many instances are able to obtain other types of business in return, such as increased deposit lines from the purchasing mortgagee. This business is developed by advertising, personal contact, correspondence, quality of services rendered, as well as the financial stability of the bank.

Importance of Training Programs

An important phase of the internal operation of progressive mortgage lenders today is the training of young men and women in the various aspects of mortgage lending procedures. A portion of this training concerns the methods used in the development of new business. Without new business lenders could not survive very long. Institutions which have adopted such training programs are being farsighted and should find this activity well worth the time, effort, and expense involved.

To maintain a sound and healthy mortgage lending business a mortgage lender constantly needs new mortgage loans. Methods best suited for a particular lender must be devised which will ensure the continuous acquisition of new mortgage business.

Loan payments are made on mortgage loans every day, and these principal payments during any one year amount to a large percentage of the loan-portfolio total. For example, even though the average VA loan is written for a period of twenty to twenty-five years, the average life of each loan is approximately ten years. The average life of an FHA loan on a home is approximately the same, while the average life of a conventional loan would be approximately eight years.

The great growth of the mortgage lending industry, together with the tremendous increase in the home-construction industry and the formation of thousands of new mortgage loan companies, has brought with it a keen competition for mortgage loans. This has required efficient business-development operations for each type of lender.

The organization chart in Chapter 3 (Figure 1) sets forth in detail the relationship of the market-development operations within a large mortgage loan department. This exhibit should be carefully studied. There are many variations of these mortgage development activities, which to a great extent are dependent on the size of the mortgage loan department, the types of loans made, and the objectives of the lender regarding the acquisition of new business.

The basic requirements which a lender must have to be placed in a competitive position for a continuous flow of new business would be prudent lending practices, established reputation, excellent service, and a good product, which is sometimes called "good merchandise." Good loans, or good merchandise, are sound loans properly appraised, properly analyzed, and properly related to market values, economic conditions, and all other factors which are essential in making a satisfactory investment. The quality of the loan submission and percentage of delinquencies, as well as the quality of loan servicing, are other very important factors.

The success of any market-development program will be judged by the interest which has been stimulated or created and the amount of new business which has been acquired.

Interest rates on conventional loans are usually dictated by competition and other factors, but on both FHA and VA loans the interest rates are established by Congress. From around 1930 to 1948 the trend of interest rates on conventional loans was downward. Both FHA and VA interest rates were at a very low point. Interest rates on conventional loans began to rise in 1948, and early in the year 1960 reached the highest point in the entire period. On both FHA and VA loans interest rates were increased to 4½ per cent in early May, 1953. Interest rates naturally have a direct effect upon the business-development activities of a lender. During the period of the low interest rates on VA loans, a great number of the large mortgage lenders throughout the nation withdrew from the veteran home-loan market. During this time, no mortgage development activities were conducted by any lenders on this type of loan.

The term of any type of loan will vary with the financial strength of the borrower, the appraised value of the property, and the age of the property. The longest terms are granted on new construction where the life of the improvements is expected to continue for a maximum number of years. In recent years there has been a marked uniformity among mortgage lenders covering term of loan, the interest rate, and the various fees which are charged in granting and processing the loan. All these items also have a direct bearing upon the business-development operations of a lender.

Savings and Loan Associations

Savings and loan associations in general charge higher interest rates on home loans than do other institutional lenders, but this is offset to some extent by the fact that such associations are permitted to make a considerably higher loan based on loan percentage to the appraisal of the property than permitted to other types of institutional lenders. Such associations generally appraise properties at a higher figure than do other institutional lenders. Consequently, their methods of developing new business would differ to some extent from those of life insurance companies, commercial banks, and mutual savings banks.

The success of business-development programs for acquiring new loans cannot be achieved by newspaper advertising alone, even though such advertising does stimulate interest in the products offered by the lender and is used extensively to stimulate this business. Undoubtedly the most effective method of promoting new business is the personal contact by a member of the staff of the lender with the potential borrower after the advertising has resulted in causing the potential customer to contact the office of the lender.

Loans on income properties of various types are usually made as a result of contact with owners or other principals. Income properties would include hotels, apartments, shopping centers, garages, gasoline service stations, and both medical and dental buildings. A considerable amount of this business is new construction, and there is a great deal of competition among lenders for this type of business. Most of it is developed by personal contact with the principals or the builder. Loans on industrial properties are usually based on the appraised value of the property plus the financial strength and earning power of the borrower and the principals in case the property is to be leased. Competition for this type of business is also very keen and is usually developed by personal contact.

In meeting competition for mortgage loans a prudent lender will never resort to making a more liberal appraisal of the property, ease up on rigid credit analysis of the borrower, or reduce interest rates. On conventional loans a reduction of such interest rates would be made only if economic conditions, earnings, and the Federal Reserve bank rediscount rate warranted this action. Thus competition would not be the major reason for any reduction in the interest rate.

Excellence of service will in many instances offset a lower interest rate. Banks in many parts of the country were for many years at a disadvantage in competing for new conventional mortgage loans because of the restrictive loan-value ratios and the fact that bank appraisers have generally been known to appraise properties at lower values than appraisers connected with large insurance companies, savings and loan associations, mutual savings banks, mortgage bankers, and independent appraisers working for individual investors. Thus many banks in the country increased their investments in both FHA and VA mortgages, where the interest rate is set and the final appraisals are made by the FHA and the VA. Banks are permitted to make these loans for a higher percentage of loan to appraisal and consequently are in a competitive position in both the FHA and VA loan market. In developing this business all the methods of promoting previously described are used.

A large mortgage lending company usually has an advertising manager on the staff and also uses an advertising agency to handle practically all the newspaper, magazine, radio, television, and other outlets. The advertising manager usually operates under a senior officer who is directly responsible for the advertising policies of the lender.

It is desirable that all employees in a mortgage loan department be new-business-minded and use their best efforts to develop good will for the company and obtain sound new business whenever and wherever possible. It is important, therefore, that personal contacts be maintained in social, civic, fraternal, and other types of organizations within a community. For example, the officer in charge of the VA loan program for a lender should become affiliated with some veteran organization such as the American Legion. Not only are more personal contacts made in this manner, but the magazines and other publications of such organizations offer valuable information which may lead to development of new business.

In the promotion and development of new business a major share of funds allocated to this activity by a lender is in most cases used in various types of advertising such as newspapers, radio programs, direct mail, and television. As stated previously, some large mortgage lenders in the nation have advertisements in the newspapers in the key cities in the nation every day of the year, and such advertising keeps the names of these lenders constantly before the public.

The officer in charge of the mortgage loan department is required to make final decisions regarding the methods to be used to develop new business, the amount of funds to be loaned, the types of properties on which loans will be made, the maturities of loans, and the areas in which it is desired to develop new business. This executive officer is usually the key personal-contact man within the organization.

SUMMARY

It is natural to expect that each type of lender would have somewhat different new-business-development objectives, and the methods of acquiring new business would be affected to a great extent by the areas in which a particular lender operates as well as the types of loans made by that lender.

Mortgage lending policies differ to some extent between lenders. Each lender may have a different policy regarding the percentage of mortgage loans to be carried in the portfolio in relation to the time deposits or assets. These percentages vary widely even among institutional lenders of any given class.

There are numerous basic conditions which affect the business-development program of every company, such as:

1. The funds earmarked for mortgage investment
2. The optimum of total loans
3. The runoff of the portfolio
4. Methods by which the lender is assured that a fair share of business is being obtained
5. The soundness of lending policies
6. Earnings
7. The quality of the portfolio
8. The flow of funds and the availability of funds for investment in mortgage loans
9. The government-bond market and the Federal Reserve bank rediscount rate and reserve requirements for member banks

In competing for mortgage loans, lenders must keep informed daily of the activities of competitors and know as much as possible about their lending policies and the types of loans being sought aggressively, as well as the requirements covering various types of loans.

The soundness of lending policies has a great effect upon mortgage development objectives. Some lenders are conservative in their lending policies and at times are satisfied with the normal run of business and do not press for new business. The quality of the mortgage loan portfolio is carefully analyzed by prudent lenders, and the desire to maintain this quality at a high point at all times has a direct effect upon their activities in seeking new business.

The services rendered by different mortgage lenders will also have a direct bearing upon the mortgage development activities. It is generally true that regardless of type a lender must stay continuously in the mortgage market to some extent. If a lender withdraws from the market entirely it would be very difficult to reenter the market and to obtain a share of the business without many months of mortgage development activity.

Modern new business development methods are required in the mortgage lending business because of the tremendous growth of this industry and the progressive increase in competition for loans. Thousands of new mortgage lending companies have been organized during these years.

The basic methods of developing new business can be classified as:

1. Personal contact
2. Advertising
3. Services rendered

New business can be developed by personal contact among individuals who are looking for homes, builders who require funds for the construction of subdivisions, and persons planning new construction. Lumber firms, building-material firms, and architects are also sources of new business which can be developed by personal contact. Real estate brokers provide a great deal of mortgage business of all types for lenders.

The purchase and sale of existing properties of all types is continuous and one of the major activities in the real estate market. A careful personal follow-up of all such possible transactions will always be maintained by an alert lender.

In developing new mortgage loan business, advertising is used to arouse or create interest in a particular lending institution and the products offered by that particular lender. There are numerous modern methods of advertising, and aggressive mortgage lenders will at all times keep the names of their companies before the public by one form or another of advertising.

Unless excellent service is rendered by a lender, it cannot be expected to retain business or satisfactorily develop new mortgage business. Applications for mortgage loans which are received must be handled quickly and efficiently, and the lender must maintain a staff of employees who are friendly, efficient, and enthusiastic.

It should be observed that a sound mortgage lending institution would use personal contact, advertising, and services rendered in promoting and developing new business and that no institution will use any one of these methods exclusively. Some institutions might favor the use of advertising over personal contact and quality of services over advertising. This would depend a great deal upon the objectives of the lender as well as the methods of operations and lending policies.

In the fast-growing areas of the nation, where there has been a tremendous expansion of home building and other types of construction during the past twenty years, it has been necessary to interest outside capital in mortgage loans. The means of attracting this capital take many forms, but most of this business is developed by correspondence and personal contact.

In order to maintain a sound and healthy mortgage lending business a mortgage lender needs new mortgage loans constantly. Methods best suited to a particular lender must be devised which will ensure the continuous acquisition of new mortgage loans. The success of any mortgage development program will be judged by the interest which has been created and stimulated and the amount of new business which has been acquired.

QUESTIONS

1. Explain how legal restrictions put some lenders at a disadvantage in competing for mortgage loans.
2. State why mortgage lenders should maintain a "prospect" list.
3. Describe how the VA loan program has had a great effect upon the mortgage lending industry.
4. In your opinion could the new-business-development methods of most mortgage lenders be improved? Give reasons.
5. What is the basic requirement of a successful business-development program?
6. State the primary function of advertising in the mortgage lending industry.
7. Explain why widely different programs of developing new business are used.
8. Name ten methods used by mortgage lenders in advertising mortgage services.
9. Should lenders maintain lists of new building sites and builders who could be recommended for construction of homes and other types of properties? Explain.
10. Effective business development is a builder of good will. Explain.
11. Name the best source of new business for mortgage lenders.
12. List another source which brings in a tremendous amount of new business.
13. Name the type of institutional lender which has been affected most until recently by legal restrictions in making mortgage loans.
14. Explain why the interest rate on conventional loans is controlled greatly by competition.

15. Name four sources from which mortgage business is derived.
16. List the types of loans that are made in order to take care of the above lending requirements.
17. Describe how the success of a mortgage development program can be judged.
18. Explain why modern business-development methods are required in the mortgage lending business today.
19. Give reasons why competition for mortgage loans is keen in most parts of the country.
20. Is the trend of interest rates on mortgage loans going up or down? Explain.
21. Name three types of prospects for a home loan.
22. Why is it important that the mortgage loan department be readily accessible to customers?
23. Why should the name of a mortgage lender be kept constantly before the public?
24. Why is it that the availability of funds and the willingness to use these funds constructively constitute a major source of good public relations?
25. Do good public relations come largely from good customer relations?
26. Explain why a mortgage loan gives a lender an opportunity for developing good customer relations.
27. Describe how most large life insurance companies develop mortgage business throughout the nation.
28. Why do subdivision loans to builders provide a great number of home loans to the lender?
29. Explain why methods employed to obtain mortgage business in one region might not succeed in another region of the country.
30. Give reasons why methods of seeking to acquire new business at one time may not work at another time.
31. Is experience a good teacher in the field of acquiring new mortgage business as in all other fields of business activity? Explain.
32. Name four sources of new business on existing construction.
33. Name five sources of new business on new construction.
34. Describe the important position of the real estate broker in the acquisition of new mortgage loans.
35. Explain the importance of personal contact with respect to obtaining new mortgage loan business.

ASSIGNMENTS

1. Describe in detail the specific geographical area in which a company of your selection makes mortgage loans.
2. Explain five procedures used by this company for developing new mortgage business.
3. Obtain a booklet from one of the mortgage companies in your community which explains their lending operations.
4. Select a newspaper advertisement by a mortgage lender which you think has excellent appeal.
5. Prepare a plan for developing a mortgage market.

BIBLIOGRAPHY AND SUGGESTED READING

Fisher, Ernest M., *Urban Real Estate Markets,* chaps. 3, 5, National Bureau of Economic Research, New York, 1951.

Hammerman, I. H., II, *The Role of the Mortgage Banker,* S. L. Hammerman Organization, Inc., Baltimore, Md.

Home Mortgage Lending, chap. 5, American Institute of Banking, Section American Bankers Association, New York, 1953.

McMichael, Stanley L., *How to Finance Real Estate,* chap. 41, Prentice-Hall, Inc., Englewood Cliffs, N.J., 1951.

Pease, Robert H., and Homer V. Cherrington (eds.), *Mortgage Banking,* chaps. 14, 17, McGraw-Hill Book Company, Inc., New York, 1953.

Savings Banking, chap. 16, American Institute of Banking, Section American Bankers Association, New York, 1946.

Things to Know about Buying or Building a Home, Wells Fargo Bank, San Francisco, 1953.

Urban Housing Survey, Curtis Publishing Company, Philadelphia, 1945.

9

Insured Mortgages—The Federal

Housing Administration Program

PURPOSES

1. To describe the conditions in the mortgage lending industry which led to the passage of the National Housing Act
2. To explain the role of the FHA as an insurer of loans
3. To list and consider the types of loans insured by the FHA
4. To explain the required procedures of the FHA
5. To consider the improvements in the entire mortgage lending industry which have resulted from the FHA program

The National Housing Act of 1934 (Public Law 479, 73d Congress) was passed by Congress in June of that year and was signed by the President on June 27, 1934. The conditions which led to its passage were discussed in some detail in Chapter 1. It created the FHA and the FHA Mutual Mortgage Insurance plan. The preamble reads as follows: "To encourage improvement in housing standards and conditions, to provide a system of mutual mortgage insurance, and for other purposes." This Mutual Mortgage Insurance plan was designed to reduce as much as possible the hazards involved in mortgage lending by the development of methods of analyzing each transaction in such a scientific manner that all risks in mortgage lending could be rated to the fullest possible extent. In addition to this, each FHA loan was to be insured by the FHA, and all the risks involved, with minor exceptions, were to be assumed by the Mutual Mortgage Insurance Fund and the United States government.

Some of the faults that existed in the mortgage lending industry prior to the advent of the FHA program were described in detail in Chapter 1:

1. Loans were typically made for short periods.

2. It was uncommon for borrowers to reduce their loans by periodic repayments.

3. Many borrowers failed to pay property taxes when due.

4. Amount of loan-to-appraisal-value ratios were restrictive.

5. High interest rates prevailed on all types of home loans.

6. Proper credit analysis of borrower was not made by most lenders.

7. There was widespread use of second mortgages and even third mortgages with high interest rates.

8. There was complete lack of adequate loan-servicing procedures, including inadequate accounting and bookkeeping operations and unsatisfactory portfolio analysis.

9. No effort was made to maintain efficient collection methods covering loan delinquencies. Other defaults in the covenants of the mortgage or deed of trust, such as unsatisfactory upkeep of property, were not checked.

Short-term Loans

Prior to the inception of the FHA program, most loans, which were conventional loans, were written on a one-year basis; notes were outlawed in four years, and this meant that renewals or refinancing of loans were frequently necessary. In some parts of the country, loans of three- to five-year maturities were quite commonplace. After the Great Depression got under way and real estate values fell, mortgage lenders were cramped for funds, and borrowers were unable to meet their mortgage obligations. This resulted in an alarming rise in the rate and number of foreclosures by the holders of first, second, and third mortgages.

Lack of Amortization

Before 1934 very few loans were written on an amortized basis calling for monthly payment of the interest and principal. In fact the follow-up covering the collection of the interest alone was almost negligible. Because of lack of reduction of loan balances and declines in equity due to the drop in real estate values, borrowers were handicapped in refinancing when their mortgage notes matured.

Tax Delinquencies

On a short-term conventional loan the borrower was required to pay the taxes and insurance on the property, and there was generally no control set up by lenders to make checks in order to be sure that such obligations had been paid. On many loans on which foreclosure had been completed it was discovered that three or more years of taxes were unpaid. This added materially to the amount of losses sustained by the lender.

Restrictive Loan-value Ratio

No national commercial bank was allowed to make a mortgage loan in excess of 60 per cent of the appraisal value of the property used as security, and most state-chartered banks were restricted to this same ratio. Other types of lenders were also restricted to some extent in the ratio of loan to appraisal. Consequently most purchasers of homes found it necessary to obtain a second mortgage in addition to the first mortgage. Occasionally even a third mortgage was obtained. Second and third mortgages usually called for extremely high rates of interest as well as a commission for making the second- or third-mortgage loan.

Lack of Proper Credit Analysis

The mortgage lender characteristically made no analysis of the ability of the borrower to repay the loan and meet all other terms of the mortgage contract. Most loans were based on the security margin that existed between the amount of the loan and the appraised value of the property. In making such loans the lender was ordinarily unaware of the amounts of the second and third mortgages. This resulted in many defaults and foreclosures which might otherwise have been averted.

Lack of Adequate Loan Administration

Loan administration operations are covered in considerable detail in Chapters 11 and 12, and most of the operating details of servicing and loan administration which are noted were not in use by mortgage lenders prior to the Great Depression of the thirties.

Benefits of the National Housing Act

This act was the most revolutionary change in methods of making home mortgage loans in the nation's history. There is no question that this act accomplished its early purposes, although many lenders were slow to approve the plan, as they questioned the soundness of having the government enter the field of private enterprise; government control of interest rates on such loans they considered to be especially objectionable.

From the standpoint of the borrower the principal changes and benefits which took place when the FHA plan went into effect were the following:

1. Borrowers were enabled to obtain long-term mortgage loans with high ratios of amount of loan to value of the property.

2. Financing costs were reduced by elimination of second and third mortgages.

3. The plan of fixed monthly payments to include interest, principal, taxes, insurance, and other such costs enabled the borrower to take better care of his housing obligations.

4. The borrower's ability to service the debt was carefully analyzed.

5. Minimum housing standards were developed.

6. Techniques covering appraisal of the property and the neighborhood were improved and served as an added protection to the borrower's investment.

From the standpoint of the lender these changes and benefits took place:

1. Mortgage portfolios became more liquid as holdings of FHA loans increased, for such loans were readily marketable.

2. Institutional lenders were enabled to grant FHA loans at a higher percentage of loan to appraised value of the property.

3. Such lenders were in position to liberalize their lending policies and employ somewhat larger percentages of deposits and assets in mortgage loans because FHA loans could in a sense be termed "nonrisk" assets.

The early Title II loans carried an interest rate of 5½ per cent plus ½ of 1 per cent for the mortgage insurance premium plus a ½ of 1 per cent servicing fee, making a total carrying cost to the borrower of 6½ per cent. This was far less than the conventional loan of the days before the Great Depression when the interest on the first loan ran from 6 to 7 per cent and on second and third loans to as high as 10 per cent in some cases.

Amendments to the National Housing Act

Since the National Housing Act came into being, it has been amended by Congress many times.[1] Title II has been amended and amplified in a number of respects and now contains nine separate categories dealing with insured loans on one- to four-family residences, loans on multifamily buildings for private investment, to nonprofit cooperatives, to proposed or rehabilitated rental housing, to aid in elimination of slums and blighted conditions, and to finance proposed or rehabilitated rental housing designed for use and occupancy by elderly persons (see Figure 30).

Title I, which was originally conceived to provide unsecured credit to individuals for repairs, modernization, and improvement, was amended to contain Section 8, an insured mortgage plan, which was designed to provide financing for extremely low-cost homes in suburban and outlying areas. In June, 1955, Section 8 eliminated and replaced Section (h) and Section (i). Section (h) covers loans in disaster areas and Section (i) covers owner-occupancy low-cost housing and permits secondary financing under certain

[1] See housing acts in Appendix B.

conditions. A service charge of ½ of 1 per cent is permitted on this type of loan.

During World War II, in order to provide quickly homes for defense workers in various critical areas, Title VI was added as an emergency measure to the National Housing Act. This amendment was instrumental in housing hundreds of thousands of in-migrant defense and war workers during the period of rearming prior to the war as well as during the period of hostilities. After the end of the war Title VI was revived to provide housing for returned veterans. Under Section 608, thousands of multifamily apartment houses were also financed. When this housing emergency ended and other sections of the National Housing Act were adequate for meeting the mortgage needs of families, Title VI was allowed to lapse, with the exception of certain sections dealing with the financing of prefabricated houses and the construction by operative builders of small homes on a large scale.

In addition to the above, Titles VII, VIII, and IX have been added to the act, which provide for a system of yield insurance on rental housing, loans to finance rental housing for military personnel at, or adjacent to, military establishments, and loans to provide housing for in-migrant workers in critical defense housing areas (refer to Figure 30).

Home Loans Insured under Title II, Section 203

Section 203 loans represent the most important phase of the National Housing Act so far as most mortgage lenders are concerned, and this section will therefore be briefly described.

Under Title II, the FHA insures lenders, to the extent provided in the act, against loss caused by default on the part of the borrower. Congress initially allocated $10 million for the establishment of a Mutual Mortgage Insurance Fund to protect lenders against these losses in connection with loans insured under this title. In addition to this fund, which has been substantially augmented, the credit of the government is pledged, as the debentures issued by the FHA in exchange for titles to real property, obtained through foreclosure or other authorized means of an insured mortgage, are guaranteed as to principal and interest by the United States government.

Mortgages Eligible for FHA Insurance

FHA Title II loans must be made or held by an approved mortgagee.[2] Any member bank of the Federal Reserve System or institution whose

[2] *Mortgagees' Handbook,* Federal Housing Administration.

deposits are insured by the Federal Deposit Insurance Corporation is automatically approved as a mortgagee. Mutual savings banks, Federal savings and loan associations, and life insurance companies are also approved as mortgagees. All approved mortgagees are required to service insured loans in accordance with the mortgage practices of prudent lending institutions. Other requirements for a mortgage to be eligible for insurance are as follows:

1. The mortgage must be executed on FHA forms prescribed by the FHA for use in the jurisdiction in which the property covered by the mortgage is situated.

2. The credit standing of the borrower must be satisfactory to the FHA. Both the lender and the FHA analyze each application in order to make as certain as possible that the proposed monthly payments bear a proper relationship to the borrower's anticipated income and expenses. Also it must be established that after the mortgage is recorded the mortgaged property is free and clear of all liens other than the insured mortgage, and in the case of a home purchase, that there will be no outstanding unpaid obligation involving the acquisition of the property except obligations which are secured by property or collateral owned by the mortgagor independently of the mortgaged property.

The mortgagor need not be the occupant of the property covered by the mortgage, except where the principal obligation of the mortgage is the maximum percentage loan permitted, in which event owner occupancy is a condition of eligibility, unless the mortgagor can show that he is prevented from occupying the property by reason of being called into military service or the mortgagor is a builder, in which event he may qualify for an 85 per cent loan.

3. The mortgage must be a first lien on property that conforms with the property standards prescribed by the FHA and must cover property designed principally for residential use for not more than four families.

4. The mortgage must involve a principal obligation not in excess of $22,500 on a single-family dwelling, $25,000 on a two-family dwelling, and $27,500 on a three-family dwelling, up to the maximum insurable amount.

Within the above limitations, on a property approved by FHA for mortgage insurance before construction starts, or on an existing property completed more than one year, an owner occupant may obtain a mortgage loan representing 97 per cent of $13,500 of the property value as appraised by the FHA, plus 90 per cent of the next $4,500 of appraised value, and 70 per cent of the remaining value. On the existing property completed less than one year and built without prior approval for mortgage insurance, or VA guaranty, an owner-occupant may obtain up to 90 per cent of $18,000 of value plus 70 per cent of the remainder up to the maximum insurable amount.

When the borrower is not the occupant of the property, the mortgage cannot exceed 85 per cent of the amount that would be available to an owner-occupant, and is subject to a debt service limitation of net income not to exceed 85 per cent of the estimated debt service requirements. The down payment made by the borrower must be at least the difference between the purchase price, plus nonrecurring closing costs, and the amount of the FHA loan approval. The term of repayment cannot exceed thirty years, and cannot exceed three-fourths of the FHA estimate of the remaining economic life of the building.

5. As of October 12, 1951, the administrative rules were amended to place FHA financing of one- and two-family dwellings on a par with conventional loans controlled under Regulation X of the Federal Reserve Board, and on January 12, 1951, three- and four-family dwellings were brought under the same regulation. Under these amendments, the mortgagor was obligated to establish to the satisfaction of the FHA that he had invested in cash, or its equivalent, not less than the amount of the down payment prescribed by the FHA as set forth in the commitment for insurance. As long as these amendments were in force, the loan limits set forth above constituted a ceiling for the FHA. The provisions of the credit-control program at that time were the other limiting factors affecting the principal amount of the loan to be insured. Regulation X was suspended September 16, 1952, as housing starts, seasonally adjusted, fell below the rate of 1,200,000 per year for three consecutive months.

6. In addition to the interest charge, each mortgage provides for payment by the borrower of a sum equal to $\frac{1}{2}$ of 1 per cent of the average outstanding principal obligation to provide for payment to the FHA of the annual mortgage insurance premium.

7. The mortgage must also provide for such equal monthly payments in advance which will amortize ground rents, taxes, special assessments, if any, and fire and other hazard insurance premiums, within a period ending one month prior to the dates on which such payments become due.

8. The mortgage must contain provisions for complete amortization of the loan by its maturity. The sum of the principal and interest payments in each month shall be substantially the same. The mortgage must also become due on the first day of a month.

9. The mortgage must be executed with respect to a project which, in the opinion of the FHA, is economically sound.

Application for Mortgage Insurance

It is necessary that an application for mortgage insurance be made on standard forms furnished by the FHA. Most lenders have the application typed in duplicate, in order that an extra copy will remain in the lender's file. It is extremely important that all information called for be completed

In the mortgage business mortgage lenders are concerned mostly with Title II of the National Housing Act. The principal chapters and sections of the entire Act are set forth below:

TITLE I: Class 1(a): Finance repair, alteration or improvement upon or in connection with existing structures.

     Class 1(b): Finance alteration, repair, improvement, or conversion of existing structures.

     Class 2(a): Finance new construction for other than residential or agricultural use.

     Class 2(b): Finance new non–residential farm construction.

TITLE II: Mortgage Insurance.

     Sec. 201: Mortgage definition (means first mortgage on real estate in fee simple, or on lease–hold 99 years renewable, or over 50 years firm).

     Sec. 203: One to four family dwellings.

     Sec. 203(h): To finance homes damaged or destroyed by disaster.

     Sec. 203(i): To finance low–cost residential buildings.

     Sec. 207: Multi–family rental units up to $5,000,000.

     Sec. 210: Multi–family rental units up to $200,000a (repealed).

     Sec. 213: Co–opertive Housing (Housing Act of 1950).

     Sec. 220: To finance slum and urban renewal projects.

     Sec. 221: To finance persons displaced by slum clearance or urban renewal projects.

     Sec. 222: To finance home purchases by those now in the Armed Services.

     Sec. 223: To finance the sale of government acquired property and to refinance war and defense housing.

     Sec. 225: Use of the "open–end" mortgage.

     Sec. 231: Finance proposed or rehabilitated rental housing designed for use and occupancy by elderly persons.

     Sec. 232: Provide facilities for the care and treatment of convalescents and other persons who are not acutely ill and do not need hospital care but do require

Figure 30. Principal Chapters and Sections of the National Housing Act[3]

[3] *Digest of Insurable Loans, Authorized under the National Housing Act as Amended,* Federal Housing Administration; *Administrative Rules and Regulations,* Federal Housing Administration, as of January, 1960.

```
                                skilled nursing and related medical
                                services.
TITLE III:      Federal National Mortgage Association.
TITLE IV:       Insurance on savings and loan accounts.
TITLE V:        Miscellaneous.
TITLE VI:       Insurance of War Housing.
TITLE VII:      Sec. 701:       Insured yield and investment in rental
                                housing for families of moderate
                                income. No mortgage loan is involved.
TITLE VIII:     Sec. 803:       Finance production of housing for
                                military upon certification of need
                                by Secretary of Defense.
                Sec. 809:       Finance production of civilian owner-
                                occupied housing for civilian em-
                                ployees at a research or development
                                installation of one of the military
                                departments of the United States or a
                                contractor thereof upon certification
                                by the Secretary of Defense. Economic
                                soundness of acceptable risk not
                                required.
                Sec. 810:       Finance production of single and
                                multi-family rental housing for mili-
                                tary personnel and essential civilian
                                personnel serving or employed in con-
                                nection with an installation of one of
                                the armed services upon certification
                                by the Secretary of Defense. Economic
                                soundness or acceptable risk not
                                required.
TITLE IX:       Programmed housing in defense areas.
                Sec. 903:       One to two family units.
                Sec. 908:       Twelve or more family units.
```

Figure 30. (Continued)

fully and accurately. It should be borne in mind that the appraisal of the property and analysis of the borrower made by the FHA is predicated to a great degree on the information submitted by the lender in the application for insurance, for FHA representatives usually do not see or interview the applicant for an FHA home loan. The contract of insurance subsequently entered into by the FHA is also based upon, and related to, the information submitted, including the representations made by the lender in the application. It is essential that all special assessments, improvement liens, easements, and other outstanding interests be brought to the attention of the FHA prior to the issuance of insurance, in order that such items may be taken into account in fixing the appraised value. If such information is not available when the application is sent in to the FHA, it should be covered in a supplementary letter before the loan is actually closed.

Each application must be accompanied by a credit report of the borrower, confirmation of employment statement, or in the case of self-employment a financial statement or evidence to substantiate income, and a check to cover the cost of processing the application. In the case of existing construction, the cost is $20, in most jurisdictions; if new construction, the fee is $45, in most jurisdictions, with the provision that, if the note is finally insured, a refund of $25 will be made for account of the applicant. If an application is rejected by the lender as a result of a preliminary examination, the entire fee will be returned by the lender without charge. If the case is submitted to the FHA, it may be rejected after preliminary examination and the fee will be refunded, but if any inspection, appraisal, or other processing is done, there will be no refund. A copy of the preliminary sales contract must be included. If the application concerns new construction, two sets of plans, specifications, and building contract, plot plan, and legal description of the location must be included.

Commitment for Insurance

After the processing of an application has been completed, the FHA will either issue a Commitment of Insurance or forward a letter rejecting the application. Each commitment outlines the terms and conditions under which the FHA will insure the loan. These requirements must be fully complied with in order to obtain the insurance endorsement. In the case of new construction it is essential that compliance inspections be ordered from the FHA at the three intervals designated and that corrections, if any, called for by such reports be taken care of promptly in order to secure the benefits of insurance. If repairs to existing construction are called for, a compliance report must be ordered from the FHA and final approval obtained before the loan is disbursed. Commitments on existing construction are valid for four months and on new construction for eight months.

Loan Closing

Upon receipt of the commitment from the FHA, and provided the conditions listed thereon have been complied with, the note and mortgage forms are completed and the loan closed. The note and mortgage forms must be the FHA forms as prescribed for the state or area in which the mortgaged property is located. The mortgage should then be recorded in the usual manner. It is imperative that care be taken to make certain that the mortgagor has a clear and merchantable title to the property. A mortgage to be eligible for insurance must be on real estate held in fee simple or on a leasehold under a lease for not less than ninety-nine years which is renewable or under a lease for a period of not less than fifty years to run from the date the mortgage is executed.

It is important, therefore, to bear in mind that the insurance contract which will be obtained from the FHA will be no better than the underlying title covered by the insured mortgage.

If default occurs and completion of foreclosure becomes necessary, the premises must be conveyed to the FHA by means of a merchantable title free and clear of outstanding prior liens, including any past due and unpaid ground rents, taxes, or special assessments.

In closing an FHA loan, it is necessary to collect, in addition to the first year's mortgage insurance premium, accrued taxes and hazard insurance premiums, in order that subsequent monthly payments collected will provide sufficient funds to pay the obligations referred to as they become due. These escrow, or trust funds, are maintained in a separate account for each mortgagor.

At the time of closing an FHA mortgage, the mortgagee is permitted to collect, in addition to the usual recording and title fees, an initial service charge not to exceed 1 per cent of the original principal amount of the mortgage, or a charge of $20, whichever is the greater—except that in cases of properties under construction, or to be constructed, where the lender makes partial disbursements and inspections of the property during the process of construction, such initial service charge may be in an amount not in excess of $2\frac{1}{2}$ per cent of the original principal amount of the mortgage, or $50, whichever is the greater.

The Insurance Contract

Each mortgage is insured by the FHA under an individual contract between the FHA and the lender. When the funds covering the loan have been fully disbursed by the lender, the mortgage note together with the lender's check covering the amount of the first year's mortgage insurance premium are sent to the FHA office which issued the original loan commitment for endorsement of the insurance contract.

Operation of the Mutual Mortgage Insurance Plan

The FHA mortgage insurance plan operates on a mutual basis and is controlled in the headquarters office of the FHA in Washington, D.C.

Until August, 1954, all insured mortgages were classified in groups, and the mortgages in any one group had similar risks and maturity dates.

Each group account was credited with any fees, mortgage insurance premiums, and prepayment penalties collected for each mortgage assigned to the group. Each group account was also credited with properties acquired through foreclosure and with any income from such properties.

Each group was charged with a prorata share of the overhead cost of operating the Mutual Mortgage Insurance system. Any debentures issued to mortgagees in exchange for foreclosed properties and with the expenses and any losses incurred in the operation and disposition of such properties were also charged to each group. A General Reinsurance Account was also provided, as a secondary reserve, to cover any deficit in a group account and to cover general expenses not charged against group accounts.

A group account would be closed out when all the mortgages in it were paid off or when, prior to that time, there were sufficient funds in the account (1) to take care of estimated future losses incurred in handling or disposing of the properties held in the account, (2) to enable the administrator to transfer to the General Reinsurance Account 10 per cent of the premium income received in the group account, and (3) to transmit to the mortgagees their prorata share of the funds in the group account, these refunds to be used to liquidate the outstanding balances on mortgages in the group.

The insurance provided by the FHA is thus on a mutual basis.

The Housing Act of 1954, Public Law 560, Section 114, amended Section 205 of the National Housing Act and revised the operations of the Mutual Mortgage Insurance plan.

It required that the FHA commissioner establish as of July 1, 1954, in the Mutual Mortgage Insurance Fund a General Surplus Account and a Participating Reserve Account. All the assets of the General Insurance Account were to be transferred to the General Surplus Account, and the General Insurance Account was to be abolished. It required further that there be transferred from the various group accounts to the participating Reserve Account as of July 1, 1954, an amount equal to the aggregate amount which would have been distributed if all outstanding mortgages in such group accounts had been paid in full on June 30, 1954. All the remaining balances of the said group accounts were to be transferred to the General Surplus Account, whereupon all the group accounts would be abolished.

The aggregate net income thereafter received by the Mutual Mortgage Insurance Fund in any semiannual period is to be credited to the General Surplus Account and for the Participating Reserve Account in such a manner and amounts as the FHA Commissioner may determine.

Upon termination of the insurance obligation of the Mutual Mortgage Insurance Fund by payment of any mortgage insured thereunder, the FHA Commissioner was authorized to distribute to the mortgagor a share of the Participating Reserve Account in such a manner and amount as the

Commissioner may determine to be equitable and to be in accord with sound actuarial and accounting practices.[4]

Monthly Payments

Payments on FHA loans are on a monthly basis and are required to be applied in the following order:

1. Mortgage insurance premium
2. Ground rents, taxes, special assessments, and fire and other hazard insurance premiums
3. Interest on the mortgage
4. Amortization of the principal

These payments are due on the first of each month, and if a payment is not made by the fifteenth of the month, the lender is authorized to collect a penalty of 2 per cent of the total monthly charge in order to pay the expense of collecting the delinquent payment.

If the mortgage is paid in full before maturity, a prepayment penalty of 1 per cent of the principal amount of the loan is assessed. However, the borrower is allowed to pay 15 per cent of the original amount of the loan in any one calendar year without a penalty. No penalty is due and payable if at the time of prepaid pay-off of the loan there is placed on the mortgaged property a new FHA insured mortgage in any amount.

In setting up the monthly amortization payments on an FHA loan the lender is required by FHA regulations to arrange for the first payment to start not more than thirty days after the expiration date that appears on the FHA commitment. It is desirable under these limitations to allow the borrower a few weeks after the loan has been closed and disbursements have been made before he has to make the first installment payment.

The loan must be submitted to the FHA for endorsement as an insured loan prior to the date the first monthly installment is due. This submission must be made thirty days prior to the first installment date if the loan is written at the maximum term allowed by the National Housing Act, which is currently thirty years.

Reporting of Defaults

Notice of Default Status reports covering delinquent loans must be submitted to the FHA. FHA Form 2068 is used for this purpose, and the regulations covering reporting procedures which are reproduced on this form read as follows:

[4] Amount of the Mutual Mortgage Insurance Account as of
12-31-60 .... $603,164,201
Amount of General Insurance Account....................... 441,343,521
Amount of Participation Reserve Account.................... 161,820,950

1. Submit report in duplicate to Insuring Office of the Federal Housing Administration for area in which subject mortgage security is located in accordance with the following illustrative case: Payment due September 1 but not paid by October 1. The mortgage is in default on October 1, and, provided the payment is not made in the meantime, a report is due on December 1.

2. Thereafter, so long as the mortgage remains in default, submit a followup report in duplicate every 60 days giving current information, months in arrears, and efforts toward reinstatement. No report is required between the reporting of the start of foreclosure and the reporting of completion of such action unless in the meantime the default is cured or the foreclosure action is suspended.

Debentures are issued to cover unpaid principal of the loan plus taxes advanced, and including interest at the debenture rate from start of foreclosure. This rate ranges from 2½% to 3%, depending upon the rate specified in the regulation under which the insurance was granted. The maturities vary, depending whether issued under Mutual Mortgage and Housing Insurance Funds of Title II, under the War Housing Fund of Title VI, or under the War Housing Insurance Fund, the latter having to do with war and emergency housing projects.
The maturities are as follows:
Under Section 203: 3 years after July 1 following maturity.
Under Section 207: 20 years after date of default.
Under Section 213: 20 years after date of default.
Under Sections 603 and 608: 10 years from date of debenture.
Under Title VIII: 10 years from date of debenture.
Under Title IX; Section 903: 10 years from date of debenture.
Under Title IX; Section 908: 10 years from date of default.
The debentures are negotiable, and are an obligation of the Mortgage Fund, earning interest payable January 1 and July 1 of each year.
The Certificate of Claim, executed as of the date of conveyance of title to the property to the FHA, is a contingent liability of the particular mortgage insurance fund. There accrues to the holder an increment of 3% per annum. This certificate covers interest from default to the start of foreclosure, interest due over the debenture rate to the face of the note, and reasonable amounts to cover the costs of foreclosure and repair or maintenance of the property prior to the conveyance of the property to the FHA Commissioner.
This certificate specifies the amount to which the holder is entitled, contingent and dependent upon the net amount realized from the property and payable only upon the full liquidation of that property. The Commissioner deducts from the net realized for the property all expenses incurred by him in handling, dealing with, and disposing of the property. If there be an excess then realized over the debentures and cash advanced for interest on them, such excess is paid over to the certificate holder.

Figure 31. FHA Debentures[5]

[5] *Mortgagees' Handbook,* Federal Housing Administration.

3. Report promptly on this form when mortgage is reinstated.

4. Report promptly on this form when foreclosure is started.

5. When foreclosure action is completed, a report should be submitted promptly on this form at which time, unless a redemption period is involved, the mortgagee shall advise whether or not property will be tendered to the Commissioner.

6. Where a redemption period ensues, no further report is required until the expiration of the redemption period, at which time the mortgagee shall advise whether or not the property will be tendered to the Commissioner.

SERVICING—All approved mortgagees are required to service insured loans in accordance with acceptable mortgage practices of prudent lending institutions. In the event of default, the mortgagee should be able to contact the mortgagor and otherwise exercise diligence in collecting the amounts due. The holder of the mortgage is responsible to the Commissioner for proper servicing, even though the actual servicing may be performed by an agent of such holder.

This "Notice of Default Status" may be submitted by either the mortgagee or its servicing agent, but should not be submitted by both.

IT IS IMPORTANT THAT THE NOTICE BE COMPLETELY EXECUTED.

At any time within one year of the default the lender must acquire title to the property by means other than foreclosure or must institute foreclosure proceedings to foreclose the mortgage.

The lender is required to give notice to the FHA on FHA Form 2068 when foreclosure proceedings have been instituted and must carefully proceed with completion of foreclosure action.

After obtaining title to the property the lender may if it likes convey the property to the FHA within a period of thirty days and apply for debentures of the Mutual Mortgage Insurance Fund (see Figure 31). The FHA must receive a good merchantable title to the property, undamaged by fire or other hazards, and undamaged by waste. In addition to the debentures the lender will receive a Certificate of Claim which becomes payable, if at all, after the sale of the property by the FHA.

If the lender decides to hold the property as Other Real Estate after foreclosure has been completed, and not apply for debentures, the FHA insurance contract is terminated. If there is a strong market and if the property is readily salable at a price which will exceed the amount of the loan including all charges, the lender would undoubtedly sell the property and not apply for debentures. Debentures received are guaranteed as to both principal and interest by the United States government and are therefore readily marketable. It is obvious that in a falling market where a loss is definitely involved a lender would transfer title to the property to the FHA and apply for debentures.

"Out-of-pocket" expenses incurred in the foreclosure of an FHA loan are usually not recovered when the lender applies for debentures and files the Certificate of Claim. This small loss, which might reach $150 to $300 in some cases, would naturally cause the lender to sell such properties on a rising market, thus experiencing no loss whatsoever on such loans.

Sale and Purchase of Insured Mortgages

One of the chief factors which has caused the progressive development and growth of FHA lending has been the liquidity of FHA insured mortgages. Almost since the passage of the National Housing Act, there has been a continuous market for insured mortgages. An insured mortgage may be sold and assigned to any approved mortgagee, and the assignee then assumes all the benefits and obligations of the mortgage insurance contract. Both the assignor and the assignee, on forms especially provided for that purpose, are obligated to notify the FHA within thirty days after the sale has been consummated and the mortgage documents delivered.

In arranging the sale of insured mortgages, it is quite customary for the originating lender to enter into a contract agreement with the purchasing institution to service the mortgage in its behalf. Under market conditions which have existed for the past several years, a servicing fee of $\frac{1}{2}$ of 1 per cent per annum on outstanding balances is customary. In many cases, FHA insured mortgages have been sold at a premium, and generally speaking a small premium indicates a healthy and sound condition in the mortgage market.

As a result of the nationwide marketability of insured mortgages, the rapid and progressive growth of the mortgage loan correspondent system developed. These mortgage banking firms act as agents for buyers and sellers (see Chapter 11, the section on Servicing Loans Sold to Others). These firms perform a desirable function; they make it their business to know the financial institutions which have excess funds for mortgage investment and at the same time to maintain an acquaintance with lenders, builders, and others who develop mortgages for sale or are seeking long-term loans on commercial or industrial properties. This has the effect of moving cash from localities in which there are excess mortgage funds to areas which have not been able to generate savings in sufficient amounts to finance their own growth and development.

Because of the excellent reputation the FHA has developed through its scientific approach to mortgage risk analysis, a few financial institutions buy FHA loans with little knowledge of the property or community, and with little to go on other than a photograph of the property and an examination of the borrower's financial statement. Other institutions make a very detailed inspection of the security, and evaluation of the economic background of the community before buying. A very important consideration from the standpoint of the purchasing institution is the reputation of the originator and its experience in the field of mortgage lending and servicing.

The Housing Act of 1954 and Its Effect upon FHA Operations[6]

The Housing Act of 1954 was signed by the President on August 2, 1954.[7] It is Public Law 560, 83d Congress. The new law lifted the maximum mortgage amount for new construction of FHA loans under Section 203. The loan-to-value ratio and maturity terms were liberalized considerably by the act. These ratios applied to all cases where improvements were built under FHA inspection and covered owner occupants. On July 30, 1955, FHA revised down-payment requirement as mentioned earlier in this chapter. Compared with the no-down-payment thirty-year loans then being purchased by certain insurance companies and mutual savings banks, these new FHA loans had ready acceptance by institutional buyers in the secondary market as well as by primary lenders.

Of great interest to many states was the authorization of the open-end clause in mortgages or deeds of trust securing loans insured by FHA.[8,9] Thus, additional advances could be made under the original loan instrument for the purpose of financing repairs and improvements.

The main effect of this act to broaden the area of homeownership, for, to everybody who could meet the required down payments, mortgage maturity, and monthly repayment, it extended terms that had been available previously only to veterans.

Since the end of World War II, there has been a surplus of savings funds, which are primarily and customarily invested in residential mortgage loans. With this surplus of savings money to invest, and with the great demand for new homes under the prevailing liberal terms, it naturally followed that lenders invested heavily in FHA loans.

During this period there has been a growing short supply of conventional residential loans, which loans are not insured or guaranteed by a government agency. These conventional loans have always carried a higher rate of interest and require larger down payments. Many institutional lenders would probably prefer a larger portfolio of conventional residential loans because of the higher earnings and for further diversification, but because of the somewhat short supply of such loans, which are eligible for investment, coupled with the need to put surplus funds to work, most mortgage lenders have engaged actively in both the FHA and VA home-loan market.

[6] See housing acts in Appendix B.

[7] Refer to "Mutual Mortgage Insurance Administration Rules and Regulations," National Housing Act Title XXIV, chap. 11, subchap. C, sec. 203, in *Code of Federal Regulations, 1949,* revised Aug. 9, 1954, Federal Housing Administration.

[8] Refer to *Federal Housing Administration Letter,* all titles and sections, Aug. 31, 1954, to all approved mortgagees, on the subject of insurance of open-end advances made under insured home mortgages.

[9] Refer to "Servicemen's Mortgage Insurance Administration Rules and Regulations," National Housing Act Title XXIV, chap. 11, subchap. C, parts 225 and 226, sec. 222, in *Code of Federal Regulations, 1949,* effective Nov. 5, 1954, Federal Housing Administration.

Another factor which has caused lenders to invest heavily in the FHA and VA market has been the approval by the United States government of the discount system whereby originating lenders who sell their loans at a discount are allowed to pass along such discounts to the builder or other seller of residential property. The originating lenders, by being able to protect themselves in this manner, made it possible for the ultimate mortgage holders, namely, life insurance companies or mutual savings banks, to acquire FHA loans at a sufficient discount to give them a yield, after servicing sufficiently high to keep them in this mortgage market.

Another important factor which increased investments in FHA-insured loans was the increase in the FHA interest rate which was effective in early May, 1953. This action served to restore the more traditional relationship between the yields on FHA loans and those on government bonds and other alternative investments. This increase together with the decline in the yield on long-term government bonds which began in the latter part of 1953 made the FHA loans immediately more attractive. This trend has continued.

An Evaluation of the Merits of the Federal Housing Administration Program

In order to evaluate properly the merits of the FHA program, a brief analysis of its objectives and progressive development in operations and procedures should be made.

It is generally recognized that the most important step in the development of residential mortgage lending since the Great Depression came with the creation of the National Housing Act of 1934.

The principal objectives of the act were the following:

1. To stimulate activities in the fields of repair and modernization

2. To bring about the revival of new construction and thus relieve unemployment in the building trades and associated industries

3. To reestablish the stability and security of mortgage investments and the real estate market

4. To speed recovery following the Great Depression by setting up the regulation for FHA-insured mortgage loans.

5. Urban renewal and other housing development programs

In setting up these regulations the authorities adopted the best features contained in the HOLC procedures. The FHA does not make mortgage loans as did the HOLC. The FHA insures loans made by approved mortgagees. The initial features covered loans for a term of fifteen years, monthly payments on the loan including taxes and insurance, an increase in the ratio of the amount of the loan to the appraised value of the property, and insurance of loans made on FHA specifications and by FHA-approved lenders.

This was the first time that an insured loan had approved in mortgage lending in the nation. The insurance feature was new, and loans were insured 100 per cent by FHA. In the event of default, long-term interest-bearing debentures guaranteed by the Federal government were issued in exchange for a good merchantable title to the property on which the FHA-insured loan had been made.

Gradually the FHA program gained favor, as it became better understood and as recovery from the Great Depression developed. Lenders, builders, and home buyers began to see the possibilities and advantages of FHA-insured loans. The monthly-payment-loan provisions rapidly gained in popularity. During the ensuing years monthly-payment mortgage loans became a rather standard method of handling residential mortgages, and the longer-term, higher-loan-to-appraised-value FHA loan was readily acceptable.

During those years institutional investors made home mortgage loans a major part of their investment program. The total residential debt in the nation at the end of 1960 amounted to $142 billion, which represented 68 per cent of the total real estate mortgage debt.

Each of the four institutional investors held the following amounts of FHA Title II, Section 203, loans in their portfolios as of December 31, 1960.[10]

Commercial banks.................... $6,300,700,000; 23.3% of portfolio
Mutual savings banks................ $8,552,110,000; 22.0% of portfolio
Savings and loan associations.......... $3,567,560,000; 5.9% of portfolio
Life insurance companies............. $5,198,824,000; 19.4% of portfolio

These figures reveal conclusively the important place FHA-insured loans occupy in the portfolios of three of the above types of institutional lenders.

The comparatively small percentage of FHA loans held by savings and loan associations is due mainly to their methods of operations. Savings and loan associations are not actually institutions of deposit but are essentially investment institutions. These associations sell shares on which a high dividend is paid. They obviously cannot pay such dividends and invest heavily in FHA loans, which pay a lower interest rate than conventional loans. These associations are permitted to make conventional loans on a liberal ratio of amount of loan to the appraisal value and also charge higher interest rates than other types of institutional lenders.

Some of the major reasons why the three types of institutional lenders mentioned above invest heavily in FHA-insured mortgage loans are:

1. The insurance is underwritten by the United States government. The FHA insurance comes in the form of debentures, the interest on which was 3⅞ per cent after January 1, 1961. The large Eastern life insurance companies and mutual savings banks that invest funds in nearly every state in the nation are faced with innumerable types of foreclosure laws and various

[10] Federal Housing Administration, Division of Research and Statistic-operating, Statistics Section.

periods of redemption. By use of FHA-insured loans the property-management problem on foreclosed loans is avoided.

2. Marketability, and especially for smaller institutional lenders. If such an investor needs funds at any time it can sell FHA loans at a price, and in all probability close to par, or during some years at a premium. It is difficult to do this on conventional loans except on a case-to-case basis.

3. The rate of interest, which is currently 5¼ per cent, is not competitive with current conventional-loan interest rates even though these loans are insured by the United States government.

4. With FHA-insured home loans the borrowers are not bothered by junior liens, which payments could interfere with the ability to keep up the monthly payments on the mortgage.

5. In case of real trouble on individual loans, a borrower in serious default generally can sell his home to a buyer with cash paid down to the amount of the defaulted mortgage.

6. The FHA has developed and standardized their appraisal and underwriting departments. FHA has sound methods of determining residential values, has practical minimum construction standards, and has sound formulas to determine the credit and financial responsibility of the borrower and the appropriate relation of his income to the home-loan payments.

7. When a loan is made under the FHA insurance plan, even though the time of possible loss remains uncertain, the extent of the loss is entirely covered with the exception of the incidental costs of foreclosure, which in many cases are recovered through payment of the Certificate of Claim.

8. One of the principal weaknesses of mortgage loans prior to and during the Great Depression was lack of liquidity. Lenders can safely invest a larger percentage of their assets in mortgages under the FHA insurance program, as they not only have marketability but are also eligible as security from the Federal Home Loan Bank System and the Federal Reserve banks.

On August 21, 1955, the Federal Reserve Board in Washington, D.C., reported that a recent survey indicated that homeownership had increased one-third in the postwar home-buying boom since 1948. The number of home-owning families increased from about 18 million to nearly 25 million. The United States Census Bureau reported that according to the results of the 1960 Census, some 32.8 million American families live in houses they own (not counting the mortgage). This is the greatest number of home-owners on record. It is also the highest ratio of home-owning families—61.9 per cent—recorded. FHA-insured mortgage loans played an important part in this growth.

Since the Housing Act of 1956, equally favorable insurance terms are available on both new and existing homes. In 1957 FHA instituted its certified agency program (CAP) primarily to serve communities remote from FHA offices. The 1958 Housing Bill eliminated discount controls and permitted an easier flow of FHA and VA loans in the secondary market. In 1959 the money markets entered their tightest phase in many years, with conventional-loan interest rates at a high level. In 1960 the sale of FHA Section 203 (b) loans to individuals was authorized. In early 1961 the President reduced the FHA interest rate from 5¾ per cent to 5½ and shortly thereafter again reduced the rate to 5¼ per cent.

The FHA-insured loan program has greatly broadened the lending activities of most mortgage lenders. It has also placed commercial banks in a better competitive position because of the higher loan-to-value ratio. FHA loans have proved to be a profitable business for many lenders. The record of the holdings of FHA-insured mortgage loans by mortgage lenders clearly establishes the fact that these loans have a very prominent place in mortgage lending and related industries. There is no doubt that the FHA-insured mortgage program has been eminently successful since the beginning of the program and has contributed greatly to the progressive development of all phases of mortgage lending.[11]

SUMMARY

The National Housing Act was passed by Congress in June, 1934, and signed by the President on June 27, 1934. This act created the FHA and the FHA Mutual Mortgage Insurance plan. This plan was designed to reduce as much as possible the risks of loss involved in mortgage lending as well as the factors which contribute to these risks by the development of improved methods of analyzing each mortgage loan transaction in such a scientific manner that all such factors could be rated to the fullest extent. In addition to this each FHA loan was to be insured by the FHA, and the risks and the possible loss were to be assumed by the FHA and the United States government.

Some of the faults which existed in the mortgage lending industry prior to the advent of the FHA program included short-term loans, lack of amortization, tax delinquencies, restrictive loan-value ratios, high interest rates, lack of proper credit analysis, and widespread use of second mortgages with high interest rates.

In addition to these faults there was an almost complete lack of adequate loan administration and loan collection procedures, which included accounting and bookkeeping operations and portfolio analysis. Failure to maintain efficient collection methods covering loan delinquencies and correction of other defaults in the covenants of the mortgage or deed of trust were prevalent.

The FHA program was undoubtedly the most revolutionary change in the methods of making home mortgage loans in the history of the nation.

[11] Refer to *The FHA Story in Summary*, Federal Housing Administration, Washington, 1959.

From the standpoint of the borrower the principal changes and benefits which took place when the FHA plan became effective were:

1. Borrowers were enabled to obtain long-term mortgage loans with higher ratios of loan to the value of the property.

2. Financing costs were reduced by elimination of second and third mortgages.

3. The fixed monthly-payment plan was arranged to include, in addition to interest, the installment and the trust or escrow payment, which included taxes and insurance and other items which enabled the borrower to take better care of his housing obligations.

4. The borrower's ability to service the debt was carefully analyzed.

5. Minimum housing standards were developed.

6. Improved techniques were developed covering appraisal of the property and the neighborhood, which served as an added protection to the borrower's investment.

From the standpoint of the lender the following changes and benefits took place:

1. Mortgage portfolios became more liquid as holdings of FHA loans increased, for such loans were readily marketable.

2. Institutional lenders were enabled to grant FHA loans at a higher percentage of the loan in relation to the appraised value of the property.

3. Such lenders were in position to liberalize their lending policies and employ larger percentages of deposits and assets in mortgage loans, because FHA loans could in a sense be termed "nonrisk" assets.

Since the original National Housing Act was passed, it has been amended many times.

Title II, Section 203, represents the most important phase of the act to most mortgage lenders, as it covers insurance against loss by FHA to lenders on one- to four-family dwellings. In case an FHA loan is acquired by a lender by means of foreclosure action, the lender upon transferring title to the property to FHA will receive debentures issued by the FHA which cover the entire loan and nearly all costs incurred.

FHA Title II loans must be made or held by an approved mortgagee. Any member banks of the Federal Reserve System, or institution where deposits are insured by the Federal Deposit Insurance Corporation, are automatically approved as mortgagees. Mutual savings banks, Federal savings and loan associations, and life insurance companies are also approved as mortgagees.

All approved mortgagees are required to service FHA loans in accordance with the mortgage servicing practices of prudent lending institutions.

The mortgage and note covering each loan must be executed on FHA forms prescribed by the FHA Commissioner for use in the jurisdiction in which the property covered by the mortgage is situated.

The credit standing of the borrower must also be satisfactory to the FHA, and the mortgaged property must be clear of all liens other than the insured mortgage when the mortgage is recorded. In case of a home purchase there must be no outstanding obligations involving the acquisition of the property unless secured by property or collateral owned by the borrower independently of the mortgaged property.

After each loan transaction is closed, the documents, namely, the note and the mortgage involved, are sent to the FHA for endorsement of the insurance contract. In addition to the interest charge, each FHA mortgage provides for payment by the borrower of a sum equal to $\frac{1}{2}$ of 1 per cent of the average outstanding principal balance to provide for payment to FHA of the annual mortgage insurance premium.

If default occurs and completion of foreclosure becomes necessary, the premises must be conveyed to the FHA Commissioner by means of a merchantable title, free and clear of outstanding prior liens including any past due and unpaid ground rents, taxes, or special assessments, unless the lender chooses to retain ownership of the property or his part of it for whatever it will bring.

The FHA program has greatly broadened the lending activities of most mortgage lenders and has aided in placing banks, particularly, in a better competitive position because of the high loan-to-value ratio which is allowed. FHA loans have also proved to be a profitable business for many lenders, and there is no doubt that the entire FHA program since its inception has been highly successful in every respect.

The Housing Act of 1954 was signed by the President on August 2, 1954. It is Public Law 560, 83d Congress. The new law lifted the maximum mortgage amount for new construction of FHA loans under Section 203 for owner occupancy. Other changes and additions includes an increase in loan-to-value ratio, authorization of the open-end clause in mortgages or deeds of trust securing loans insured by FHA, revised regulations regarding fees and charges, provisions for a system of loans and grants for approved projects designed for urban renewal and slum clearance, and provisions for a system of mortgage insurance to assist the financing required for the construction or purchase of dwellings by servicemen.

Lenders in general were of the opinion that these changes and additions to existing FHA regulations would have a beneficial effect upon both the FHA and the mortgage lending industry.

On July 30, 1955, FHA raised the down-payment requirement on FHA Section 203 and reduced maturities to twenty-five years. The new requirements were exclusive of closing costs, which had to be paid in cash by the borrower.

Shortly thereafter, the Housing Act of 1955 was passed, and the basic provisions tended to liberalize the Housing Act of 1954. The basic provisions of housing acts through 1961 are listed in Appendix B, and should be studied by each reader.

QUESTIONS

1. Explain how the FHA program has broadened the scope of lending activities for most lenders.
2. In analyzing a home-loan application name the four ratings which are set up by the FHA.
3. Name the director of your local FHA office.
4. State when and how the HHFA was created.
5. Do you believe the FHA should be made a separate agency in the government rather than a part of the HHFA? Give reasons for your opinion.
6. State the preamble to the National Housing Act.
7. What interest rate did early FHA Title II loans bear?
8. Why was the creation of the FHA in 1934 a revolutionary change in the pattern of home mortgage lending?
9. What is the maximum loan on a Title II, Section 203, loan?
10. What may a lender charge as an initial service fee in processing an FHA Title II home loan application?
11. Describe how mortgage lenders report delinquent FHA loans to the FHA.
12. Name the most important feature in the rating of the borrower category.
13. Was the FHA program readily accepted by mortgage lenders? Explain.
14. How much is an FHA Title II application and inspection fee?
15. Explain how the FHA obtains additional funds for the FHA insurance program.
16. Name six benefits of the FHA program.
17. Give the present interest rate on FHA Title II loans.
18. Explain why FHA mortgage loans of lenders are sometimes called "nonrisk" assets.
19. Does the FHA require that mortgage loans be carefully followed for payments?
20. If the mortgage is paid in full before maturity, a premium of what per cent of the original amount of the loan is collected from the mortgagor?
21. Name the other government agencies that the HHFA embraces.
22. The National Housing Act of 1934 identifies each loan program by title numbers. How many such titles are there at the present time?
23. State the loan-value ratio on FHA Title II, Section 203, loans.
24. Does Title II, Section 203, cover insurance on loans to finance proposed or existing dwellings.
25. What is the maximum maturity of such loans?
26. What does Title II, Section 207, cover?
27. Name the Commissioner of the FHA.
28. An FHA mortgage must be the first lien against the property and conform to property standards set by the FHA. Explain why.

29. In what two titles are mortgage lenders primarily interested?
30. What does FHA Title IX cover?
31. Is Title I of the National Housing Act of 1934 primarily concerned with alteration, repair, or improvement of existing structures of all types?
32. Name the Administrator of the HHFA.
33. Describe how each monthly payment on an FHA loan is applied.
34. Describe FHA regulations covering foreclosure action on an FHA loan.
35. Explain in detail what is covered by the Certificate of Claim which is used by the FHA after transfer of a property on which foreclosure has been completed.

ASSIGNMENTS

1. Rate the neighborhood in which you live in accordance with methods used by the FHA.
2. If you live in a single-family home, rate that property in accordance with methods used by the FHA.
3. Obtain an FHA application form covering an FHA loan on a single-family dwelling. Complete this form covering such an application to be made by yourself on your own home.
4. Explain how the FHA rates the borrower in a real estate loan transaction.

BIBLIOGRAPHY AND SUGGESTED READING

Collins, Rowland, and Julius L. Bogen, *The Investment Status of FHA and VA Mortgages,* New York University, New York.
Digest of Insurable Loans, Federal Housing Administration, Washington, 1960.
The FHA Story in Summary, Federal Housing Administration, Washington, 1959.
Home Mortgage Lending, chaps. 9, 10, 13, American Institute of Banking, Section American Bankers Association, New York, 1946.
Housing and Home Finance Agency, Fourteenth and Fifteenth Annual Reports for 1960 and 1961.
Housing Statistics, Housing and Home Finance Agency, Washington, compiled monthly.
McMichael, Stanley L., *How to Finance Real Estate,* chap. 16, Prentice-Hall, Inc., Englewood Cliffs, N.J., 1951.
Pease, Robert H., and Homer V. Cherrington (eds.), *Mortgage Banking,* chap. 7, McGraw-Hill Book Company, Inc., New York, 1953.
Publications on FHA practice, Federal Housing Administration.
Sherman, Malcolm C., *Mortgage and Investment Guide,* 1961 ed., Spaulding-Moss Company, Boston, Mass.
Taylor, Roy F., *Government Insured and Guaranteed Loans: Their Place in the Institutional Investor's Portfolio,* lecture, Mortgage Bankers Association of America School of Mortgage Banking, Stanford University, Stanford, Calif., Aug. 5, 1955.

CHAPTER **10**

The Veterans Administration
Loan Program

PURPOSES

1. To describe the background and purposes of the Servicemen's Readjustment Act of 1944
2. To discuss the conditions under which mortgage loans to veterans are partially guaranteed by the VA
3. To review the development of this type of lending
4. To describe briefly the provisions of the Servicemen's Readjustment Act of 1944, as amended, and the provisions in Title 38, United States Code, which covers this activity
5. To explain VA loan application procedures
6. To discuss the effect the VA loan program has had upon mortgage lending practices
7. To make an evaluation of the merits of the program

In 1944 Congress passed the Servicemen's Readjustment Act (Public Law 346), which was signed by the President on June 22, 1944. This act was designed to assist veterans of World War II in making the necessary readjustment from conditions of war to life as civilians and for other purposes.

On September 2, 1958, Public Law 85-857 was approved. This law enacted Title 38, United States Code, "Veterans' Benefits." This Title is a codification of all the laws of general applicability in force on January 1, 1959, which are administered by the Veterans Administration.

Section 12 (e) of Public Law 85-857 provides Chapter 37 of Title 38, United States Code, which is a continuation and restatement of the provisions of Title 111 of the Servicemen's Readjustment Act of 1944, and may be considered an amendment to such Title 111.[1]

---

[1] "Veterans' Benefits," Title 38, United States Code, effective January 1, 1959, Washington, House Committee Print 240.

The actual provisions covering benefits established in the act were the following:

1. Title I—hospitalization, claims and procedures
2. Title II—education of veterans
3. Title III—Section 501, purchase or construction of homes; Section 502, purchase of farms and farm equipment; Section 503, purchase of business property; Section 505, secondary financing
4. Title IV—employment of veterans
5. Title V—readjustment allowances for former members of the Armed Forces who are unemployed

A discussion of the subject in this chapter will cover Title III of the act and its amendment by Chapter 37 of Title 38, United States Code, which refers to the guaranty or insurance by the VA of a certain percentage of a VA loan to an eligible veteran on a home, farm, business property, or certain secondary financing.

Shortly after the passage of the act, the VA issued a pamphlet which contained:

1. A reprint of Title III of the act
2. An outline of general administrative procedures and policies
3. Regulations

In December, 1948, this pamphlet was revised and brought up to date. *A Technical Bulletin* and a *Loan Guaranty Information Bulletin* have been issued from time to time by the VA in order to comply with the many changes which have taken place since the act first became law. In addition to this there have been numerous decisions, rulings, interpretations, and opinions rendered by the Administrator of Veteran Affairs and the Veterans Administration Counsel regarding procedures, policies, and practices of the VA as well as of the lenders.

Number and Dollar Amount of VA Loans Made Since Start of Program

As of December 31, 1960, the following number and dollar amount of VA loans on homes, farms, and business properties had been made:

Types of loans	Number	Dollar amount
Home loans...................	5,574,492	$49,214,496,738
Farm loans...................	71,498	283,681,791
Business-property loans.........	235,838	659,806,184
Total....................	5,881,828	$50,157,984,713

SOURCE: Veterans Administration Loan Guaranty Highlights, December, 1960, Department of Veteran Benefits, Office of the Controller, Washington.

When it is realized that the total mortgage debt of the nation as of December 31, 1960, was in excess of $206 billion, it can readily be seen that the VA loan program has been a vital part of mortgage lending operations.

In order to have a fuller understanding of the effect of this program upon the real estate market and upon mortgage lending practices, a brief chronological review of the progressive development and growth of the VA lending operations should be made.

Guaranty Benefits in the Original Act

At the start of the Servicemen's Readjustment Act of 1944 a VA loan could be made by a lender with a guaranty up to 50 per cent of the amount of the loan not to exceed $2,000. These benefits proved unsatisfactory because of the rising prices of homes and for other reasons. On December 28, 1945, Congress passed an amendment to the act (Public Law 268, 79th Congress) which increased the benefits on a home, farm, or business property to 50 per cent of the total loan, but the guaranty could not exceed $4,000. At that time this was a workable program, as the price range of the average home to meet immediate needs of a veteran was approximately $8,500. The original act limited the price which the veteran could pay to the "reasonable normal value," as determined by the VA. This requirement served to prevent returning veterans from competing on the open market for homes at postwar prices. Congress therefore relaxed this requirement to read "reasonable value," which permitted the appraisal to be based on current costs and market conditions.

VA home loans then being made were identified as Section 501 (a) loans. This type of loan was similar to a conventional loan, except that it contained the VA guaranty and consequently could be made for a higher dollar amount than permitted on a regular conventional loan. Most of these loans were made by supervised lenders under automatic procedure in order to speed the processing of such loan applications. Prior approval procedures caused considerable delay in processing because of the great volume of VA loans being processed and also because of the heavy work loads in VA loan guaranty offices.

Establishment of Reasonable Value

The reasonable value was established by a fee appraiser that had been approved by the VA. All lenders were furnished a list of these appraisers by the VA in the area in which they were located. The lender would select the appraiser from this list for appraisal of the individual property. This procedure did not prove satisfactory, and the VA changed these regulations wherein the VA designated each such appraiser upon the request of the lender.

The Combination VA-FHA Loan

In early 1945 some lenders started making 505 (a) FHA-VA combination loans. This type of lending became very active in late 1946 as well as during the years 1947, 1948, 1949, and 1950 until the Housing Act of 1950 rescinded this subsection. This method of VA home-loan financing was authorized in the original Servicemen's Readjustment Act of 1944. This was a combination FHA and VA loan, the FHA loan being the primary loan and the VA loan being the secondary loan. The first and second loan comprised the maximum loan which could be made to the veteran purchaser. The VA-guaranteed portion of such a loan could not exceed 20 per cent of the total cost of the property including the land and cost of construction on construction loans. This 20 per cent guaranty by the VA could not exceed $4,000.

For the first six months of this combination loan activity it was not necessary to use a fee appraiser approved by the VA, as the FHA at that time, in issuing a commitment in the buyer's name, would show two valuations on each commitment, namely, one which was the FHA valuation on which the commitment was based and the other a replacement cost. This replacement cost was acceptable to the VA in establishing the price a veteran could pay for a property, in other words, the reasonable value. In January, 1948, the VA informed all lenders that in the future it would be necessary in making 505 (a) loans that an appraisal be obtained from a fee appraiser approved by the VA. The VA appraisal form used at that time was VA 4-1808. Such loans were fully insured and guaranteed. The VA loan as the second loan behind the FHA first loan constitutes the only time that FHA has ever permitted secondary financing.

Up to December, 1948, a veteran could purchase a home under the provisions of 505 (a) of the act with little or no down payment.

In the Housing Act of 1950, passed on April 20, 1950, the 505 (a) FHA-VA program was terminated.

During the time that the 505 (a) program was in operation, the merits of this program were a topic of major conversation among hundreds of leading mortgage lenders in the nation. It was the opinion of most of those lenders that the program was unnecessary for the following reasons:

1. The veteran paid a higher interest rate for the loan on his home. The average rate paid was 4.4 per cent.

2. Cost of processing such application for the veteran was excessive.

3. A lender had to deal with two governmental agencies rather than one, which caused considerable delay in the processing of such loans.

4. An enormous amount of paperwork was involved in processing each 505 (a) loan application. This added to the cost of processing each loan.

5. During this entire time the VA had authority to increase the rate of interest on VA home loans from 4 per cent to 4½ per cent.

6. Processing of VA home loans is a comparatively simple procedure, and had the VA approved the increase in interest rates when authorized to do so by the National Housing Act of 1948, passed August 10, 1948, nearly all lenders would have again started making Section 501 (a) VA loans. Under such conditions there would have been no need whatsoever for the very complicated 505 (a) combination loan.

The interest rate on VA loans was increased from 4 per cent to 4½ per cent on May 5, 1953.

Liberalization of VA Loan-guaranty Benefits

More liberal guaranty benefits were granted eligible veterans on April 20, 1950, by Public Law 475, 81st Congress, which created the 501 (b) loan. Under these new provisions a veteran could obtain a home loan which could be guaranteed by the VA for 60 per cent of the amount of the loan or $7,500, whichever was less. Although the 501 (a) financing called for a guaranty of 50 per cent or $4,000, whichever was less, most lenders who were processing VA home loans at the time processed VA loans under the new Section 501 (b) procedure.

Discount Practices

The discount practices which developed after the termination in October, 1950, of the 505 (a) combination FHA and VA loan while the interest rate on VA loans remained at 4 per cent and continued on after the rate on VA loans was increased to 4½ per cent have in the opinion of most leading mortgage lenders throughout the nation been very unsound lending and never should have been permitted under a builder-lender program. In addition to this nearly all prudent lenders have opposed the FNMA "one-for-one" program, previously described, which prolonged this practice.

Basic Provisions of Title III, Now Chapter 37, Title 38, United States Code

The important basic provisions of Title III of the act and as amended, covering VA loan guaranty operations, are set forth below. However, students interested in this important program should carefully study all the provisions of Title III of the act, including regulations and the Solicitors' opinions.

Eligibility Requirements Covering a VA Loan

Sections 500, 1507, and 1506 of the act read as follows:
Section 500:

Any person who has served in the active military or naval service of the United States at any time on or after September 16, 1940, and prior to the termination of the present war (Established July 25, 1947, By an Act of Congress) and who shall have been discharged or released therefrom under conditions other than dishonorable after active service of ninety days or more or by reason of injury or disability incurred in the service in line of duty shall be eligible for the benefits of Title III of the Act or at any time on and after June 27, 1950, and prior to such date as shall be determined by Presidential Proclamation or concurrent resolution of the Congress.

Under existing law, the eligibility of World War II veterans expires July 25, 1962. The eligibility of Korean veterans expires January 31, 1965.
Section 1507 of the act covers the following: A person who meets the above conditions may also be eligible while on terminal leave or while hospitalized pending final discharge.
Section 1506:

Certain other individuals who served in the Armed Forces of Governments allied with the United States in World War II and who at the time of entrance into such service were citizens of the United States and are at the time of application residents of the United States are also eligible under the same conditions as shown above. That he has not applied for or received the same or similar benefit from the government in whose forces he served.

VA Benefits to Korean Veterans

The Veterans Readjustment Assistance Act of 1952, approved July 16, 1952, extended these benefits to veterans of the Korean conflict with service after June 27, 1950, and prior to January 31, 1955.

Discharge Certificates

There are many forms and types of discharge certificates and separation papers in all branches of the Armed Forces. It has been necessary for lenders to analyze carefully and learn the contents of each such certificate. In some instances certain discharge certificates or separation papers are not sufficient to warrant VA loan guaranty benefits. During the past few years, most lenders have made a practice of obtaining for the veteran a Certificate of Eligibility (formerly VA Form 1870, now VA Form 26-1870). This is done by submitting the particular veteran's original discharge certificate to the loan guaranty division of the VA in the respective regional office and requesting that a Certificate of Eligibility be issued for the particular veteran, prior to processing the loan application.

In 1945 and 1946, when a very large volume of VA home-loan applications were being processed and it was necessary that the loans be closed as quickly as possible, a great number of supervised lenders processed all VA home-loan applications on an automatic-guaranty basis. By so doing these lenders took full responsibility regarding the eligibility of the veteran and the guaranty entitlement of the discharge certificate. Only in a few rare instances did lenders lose the guaranty by processing loan applications in this manner. Personnel processing such applications quickly learned to identify the many types of discharge certificates and separation papers that were involved.

There were many logical reasons why the automatic-guaranty privileges were used at that time. Builders of large subdivisions throughout the nation were anxious to receive payment on homes sold to veterans and in turn use such funds for additional home-building activities. Lenders processing loans on this basis were anxious to provide the funds for veterans to purchase homes without any delay. The main problem confronting veterans at that time was to obtain shelter for themselves and their families. Processing home-loan applications under prior-approval procedures took much longer, and such delays were not warranted or necessary during those years.

Purpose of Loans

A VA loan may be made for the purchase of a farm or for the purpose of construction of a home, or business property, or for making improvements or repairs thereto. In the case of a business or farm property such property must be the major source of income of the veteran. Loans may also be made to finance business or farm operations.

The loans are subject to guaranty or insurance if made for a lawful purpose within the limitations of the act [see Sections 501, 502, 503, 505 (a) of the act].

A supplemental loan for the alteration, repair, or improvement of real property owned by a veteran when a lien is already outstanding, to secure a guaranteed or insured loan, may be eligible for guaranty or insurance upon the prior approval of the VA.

The act also authorizes the guaranty or insurance of loans to refinance certain delinquent indebtedness (see Section 507 of the act).

A loan for the purchase of residential property for investment purposes is not eligible for guaranty or insurance as a home loan. A loan, however, may be made to an eligible veteran for the purchase of residential property or the construction of a home consisting of not more than four family units, one of which must be occupied by the veteran as his home.

Estate of Veteran in Real Property (Title Requirements)

Section 35.4350 of the VA regulations (as amended July 12, 1950) reads in part as follows:

(a) The estate in the realty acquired by the veteran, wholly or partly with the proceeds of a guaranteed or insured loan, or owned by him and on which construction or repairs, or alterations or improvements, are to be made, shall be not less than:

1. A fee simple estate therein, legal or equitable or

2. A leasehold estate running or renewable at the option of the lessee for a period of not less than 14 years from the maturity of the loan, or to any earlier date at which the fee simple title will vest in the lessee, which is assignable or transferable, if the same be subjected to the lien, or

3. A life estate, provided that the remainder and reversionary interests are subjected to the lien.

The Title to such estate shall be such as is acceptable to informed buyers, title companies, and attorneys, generally, in the community in which the property is situated, except as modified by paragraph (b) of this section by reason of the following:

(b) Any such property or estate will not fail to comply with the requirements in paragraph (a) of this section by reason of the following:

1. Encroachments;

2. Easements;

3. Servitudes;

4. Reservations for water, timber, or subsurface rights;

5. Right in any grantor or co-tenant in the chain of title, or a successor of either, to purchase for cash, which right by the terms thereof is exercisable only if:

a. An owner elects to sell,

b. The option price is not less than the price at which the then owner is willing to sell to another, and

c. Exercised within 30 days after notice is mailed by registered mail to the address of optionee last known to the then owner, on the then owner's election to sell, stating his price and the identity of the proposed vendee;

6. Building and use restrictions whether or not enforceable by a reverter clause if there has been no breach of the conditions affording a right to an exercise of the reverter;

7. Any other covenant, condition, restriction, or limitation approved by the Administrator in the particular case. Such approval shall be a condition precedent to the guaranty or insurance of the loan;

PROVIDED—That the limitations on the quantum or quality of the estate or property that are indicated in this paragraph, insofar as they may materially affect the value of the property for the purpose for which it is used, are taken into account in the appraisal of reasonable value required by the Act:

AND PROVIDED FURTHER—That, as to home loans, guaranteed or insured subsequent to February 15, 1950, the title to any such property or estate shall not be acceptable under section 36.4320(b) if it is subject to restrictions against sale or occupancy on the ground of race, color, or creed, which have been created and filed of record subsequent to that date.

Amortization of Loans

All loans the maturity date of which is beyond five years from the date of the loan or date of assumption by the veteran must be amortized. The payments on amortized loans must be approximately equal and must include a principal reduction not less often than annually during the life of the loan, except that on farm mortgage loans the principal payments may be postponed for not more than two years from the date of the loan.

The final installment on any amortized loan shall not be in excess of 2 times the average of the preceding installments, except that on a construction loan the final installment may be for an amount not in excess of 5 per cent of the original principal amount of the loan. If the maturity date is five years or less from the date of assumption by the veteran, it need not be amortized. This type of loan is a term loan.

The terms of repayment of any loan may be extended to cure a default or to avoid an imminent default, or in any case upon the prior approval of the VA. However, the rate of amortization applicable to an extended loan must be such as to amortize at least 80 per cent of the extended loan balance within the maximum maturity for loans of the same class.

Amount of Loan, Down-payment Requirements, and Maturities

There is no VA restriction regarding the highest amount which may be loaned on a VA-guaranteed mortgage, provided it conforms with all VA requirements. All business and farm loans of $25,000 or more must have the prior approval of the VA Central Office. This is a part of Section 4343.

There are no down-payment requirements by the VA covering VA loans on homes, farms, or business properties. However, lenders in general have established their own requirements covering down payments, the amount of which varies widely among lending institutions. Effective April 28, 1955, veterans had been required to pay loan-closing costs in cash (amendment to Regulation 36:4312). Effective November 11, 1960, Regulation 36:4312 was amended to permit builders and other sellers to pay closing costs for veterans if they so desire. However the prohibition against including in the loan an amount to pay closing costs was still retained in the regulation.

The maturity of a VA home loan may be up to thirty years, of a VA farm loan up to forty years, and of a VA loan on a business property up to ten years.

Until April 20, 1950, the maximum maturity on a VA home loan was twenty-five years, but on that date the maturity on such loans was extended to thirty years by Public Law 475, 81st Congress.

In late 1950 when credit restrictions were imposed by the Federal government and Regulation X was in effect, the VA complied fully with these restrictions and during that time required minimum down payments on loans based on the transaction price of each property. The maturity of a VA loan at that time for purchase, construction, repair, or improvement was restricted to twenty years, except that if the purchase price or cost of construction was not in excess of $7,000, the maximum maturity permitted was twenty-five years.

Prepayments

Regardless of the terms of the note, the debtor has the right to prepay at any time the entire indebtedness or any part thereof without premium or fee. If desired, the lender is permitted to withhold application of the credit for the prepayment until the next following installment date or thirty days after the prepayment, whichever is the earlier.

These privileges can be considered liberal, as not only does the FHA impose a penalty for prepayment but also most life insurance companies, savings and loan associations, and mutual savings banks impose a prepayment penalty. Commercial banks doing a savings business are the only type of institutional lenders that in general do not charge any penalty for prepayment of a conventional loan.

Eligible Properties

The property in support of a VA home loan must not consist of more than four family units, one of which must be occupied by the veteran as his home. If the dwelling is to be owned by two or more eligible veterans, it may consist of four units plus one additional unit for each veteran participating in the loan.

A home loan may be made for purchasing residential property to be occupied by the veteran as a home, for constructing a dwelling to be occupied by the veteran as a home, or for making alterations, improvements, or repairs on property owned by the veteran and occupied by him as a home.

A farm loan may be made for purchasing lands, buildings, livestock, equipment, or construction of buildings to be used in farming operations; for working capital necessary for farming operations; and for purchasing stock in a cooperative association where purchase of such stock is required by Federal statute incident to obtaining the loan.

A business loan may be made for engaging in business, or pursuing a gainful occupation; for purchasing lands, buildings, supplies, equipment, machinery, tools, inventory, and stock in trade for the purposes of engaging in business or pursuing a gainful occupation; for repairing, altering, constructing, or improving any realty or personalty used for the purpose of pursuing a gainful occupation; and for working capital necessary for engaging in business or pursuing a gainful occupation (see Section 3050, *Veterans Administration Handbook*).

Our discussion in this chapter will primarily cover the processing of VA home loans under Section 501 (a) and (b) of the act as amended, as this is the major VA mortgage lending activity under the provisions of Title III of the Servicemen's Readjustment Act of 1944 as amended.

The Lender and the Holder

The lender is the payee, assignee, or transferee of an obligation at the time the loan is guaranteed or insured by the VA. Any person, firm, association, corporation, or governmental agency, either state or Federal, could be an eligible lender. The veteran has the right to make his own choice of an eligible lender. Anyone holding the loan after it has been guaranteed by the VA is the holder (see Section 1030, *Veterans Administration Handbook*).

Supervised Lenders

Supervised lenders consist of Federal land banks, national banks, state banks, private banks, mutual savings banks, savings and loan associations, insurance companies, credit unions, and mortgage and loan companies which are subject to examination and supervision by an agency of the United States or any state or territory including the District of Columbia.

These companies are authorized to do business in VA loans without regard to limitations and restrictions of any other statute with respect to:

1. Ratio of amount of loan to value of the property
2. Maturity of loan
3. Requirement for mortgage or other security
4. Dignity of liens
5. Percentage of assets which may be invested in real estate loans

Supervised lenders may make loans that are automatically guaranteed, which means that they do not need the specific prior approval of the VA [Section 500 (d) of act].

Nonsupervised Lenders

Nonsupervised lenders may make loans for guaranty upon obtaining prior approval of the Administrator. Generally speaking such a lender is required to file an application with the VA requesting approval by the Administrator to act as a nonsupervised lender. Such an application is supported by financial statements, brief history of the company or individual's operations, together with letters of recommendation from three lenders who have previously processed and are still processing VA loans. This, however, is not a standard requirement among regional VA offices.

The builder-lender program described previously operates under the authority covering nonsupervised lenders. Such lenders may process VA loans on a prior-approval basis only and are not permitted to process such loans on the automatic-guaranty basis. The term "holder" includes the original lender, or any subsequent assignee or transferee of a guaranteed or insured obligation.

The VA does not require any notice of assignment of a guaranteed loan, and the assignment does not affect the guaranty.

Reasonable-value Requirements

No loan is guaranteeable or insurable if the proceeds have been expended or will be expended for property, or for construction, alterations, repairs, or improvements, the purchase price or cost of which is in excess of the reasonable value of the same as determined by the Administrator.

This Request for Determination of Reasonable Value is submitted in duplicate to the VA loan guaranty division on VA Form 26-1805. Upon completion of the appraisal the VA will forward to the lender a Certificate of Reasonable Value VA Form 26-1843.

Hazard Insurance

The holder shall require insurance policies to be procured and maintained in an amount sufficient to protect the security against the risks or hazards to which it may be subjected to the extent customary in the locality. All monies received under such policies covering payments of insured losses shall be applied to restoration of the security or to the loan balance.[2]

The VA has cooperated fully with lenders in the handling of this phase of VA lending activities (see Section 36:4326, *Veterans Administration Regulations*).

Credit Requirements—Ratio of Loan to Income

Section 303 of Public Law 550, 82d Congress, amended Sections 501 (a) (2) of the Servicemen's Readjustment Act of 1944 by adding the phrasing "and the veteran is a satisfactory credit risk." As thus amended the law reads that "the contemplated terms of payment required in any mortgage to be given in part payment of the purchase price or construction cost bear a proper relation to the veteran's present and anticipated income and expenses and the veteran is a satisfactory credit risk."

In case of direct loans the requirement that the veteran be a satisfactory credit risk has always been an express legislative requirement since the direct-

[2] See complete discussion of this subject in Chap. 11.

loan program was authorized. Direct loans to veterans by the VA were authorized by Public Law 475, 81st Congress, approved April 20, 1950, and effective July 1, 1950 (see *Veterans Administration Technical Bulletin* TB4A-137, May 6, 1953, "Credit Standards").[3]

Most mortgage lenders have required that a veteran should not obligate himself to pay more than 20 to 25 per cent of his net take-home pay for the monthly payment, which payment covers interest, installments, and trust funds for insurance premiums and property taxes. The composition of the veteran's family and living habits will have some bearing on this ratio. The income of a wife under thirty-five years of age is generally not included by most lenders in the income analysis. If the wife is over thirty-five years of age and steadily employed, one-half of this income is usually taken into consideration.

Prudent lenders also counsel and advise veterans concerning the property, the location, the neighborhood, the cost of the property as related to the financial position of the veteran; they are also particularly careful to analyze the contract of sale or deposit receipt, in order to be assured that the veteran is being adequately protected, and not overbuying.

Processing of VA Section 1810 Loans (Formerly VA 501 Loans)

In processing this type of loan application each mortgage lender will first determine in interviewing the borrower whether the full loan guaranty benefits are available, whether the applicant has sufficient income to service a loan for the amount requested, and whether all other requirements are satisfactory.

If these preliminary requirements prove satisfactory to the lender, the individual interviewing the applicant is cautioned not to have the veteran sign in blank the VA Form 26-1802 (Application for Home Loan Guaranty) on the line designated "signature of veteran" (in triplicate), since this should be done only after the application form has been completed. However, the veteran applicant should complete and sign VA Form 26-1880 (Request for Determination of Eligibility and Available Entitlement) and a combination work sheet and check sheet which is in use by most lenders.

The fee covering the Credit Report and the VA appraisal in cases involving purchase of existing homes should also be obtained from the applicant at the time of taking the VA application. The VA appraisal fee on existing properties is $25, and on proposed construction it is $30 plus $22.50, covering three inspections during construction. These charges vary in different parts of the country. In tract cases the builder must absorb the appraisal fees but may pass the inspection fees on to the veteran.

Upon completion of the mortgage lender's own appraisal of the property

---

[3] *Technical Bulletin* TB4A–137 relates to both guaranteed and direct loans.

and provided the exposed portion of the total loan is not in excess of the required percentage of the lender's appraisal, a request is then submitted in duplicate to the VA for a Certificate of Reasonable Value. This request in all cases must show the sales price of the house on the duplicate copy.

In the case of proposed construction of individual homes the VA Form 26-1805 in duplicate, formerly VA Form 4-1805 (Request for Determination of Reasonable Value), is submitted to the VA together with the plans and specifications, in triplicate, all copies duly signed by the veteran applicant.

Upon receipt from the VA of the Certificate of Reasonable Value, the Application for Home Loan Guaranty is then completed and forwarded to the VA (see Section 36:4303, "Reporting Requirements," *Veterans Administration Regulations*).

The following exhibits are required to be attached to the VA Form 4-1802 (Application for Home Loan Guaranty or Insurance):

1. Copy of the Sales Agreement bearing the autographed signatures of the buyer and seller or a clear legible photostatic copy thereof (or in the case of proposed construction, a copy of the contract)

2. Copy of the Credit Factual Data Report

3. Signed Certificate of Reasonable Value (Form VA 26-1843)

4. Original Discharge Papers (VA Form 26-1880, Request for Determination of Eligibility and Available Entitlement, attached thereto), or

5. Certificate of Eligibility (Form VA 26-1870)

6. Confirmation of Employment

7. Confirmation of other income and assets as applicable

Practically all prudent lenders now process VA home-loan applicants on a prior-approval basis because of the many possibilities of errors in processing such loans, especially the eligibility of the veteran applicant. Since the guaranty on a VA loan has been increased to 60 per cent of the loan or $7,500, whichever is less, the amount of guaranty available for veterans who have already used a part of their guaranty entitlement is quite difficult to determine. Lenders in general ask the VA for determination of this guaranty entitlement.

Other reasons for obtaining prior approval on home-loan applications were:

1. The FNMA ruling that a government agency must pass on the veteran's credit if loan was to be eligible for sale to FNMA

2. Provisions of Public Law 550 as to possible reduction factor when a veteran had used a portion of his guaranty privileges as a veteran of World War II and was now applying as a veteran of the Korean conflict

Upon completion of the processing of the application and provided it is approved, the VA will issue a Certificate of Commitment good for six months, VA Form 26-1866, covering the application. Extensions are usually granted by the VA upon request. This commitment entitles the holder to issuance of the evidence of the guaranty upon the ultimate actual payment of the full proceeds of the loan, for the purposes described in the original application and upon submission within thirty days thereafter of a report showing that the loan meets the requirements set forth in Section 36:4303 of the VA regulations.

Loan-closing Procedures

To comply with the requirements outlined in the preceding paragraph the lender, upon receipt of the Certificate of Commitment from the VA, proceeds with the closing of the loan in the following manner:

1. Title report is obtained from the title company.

2. The lender ascertains that the veteran has or will obtain a fee simple title.

3. The lender obtains a certificate from the veteran's contractor which certifies that the improvements have been constructed totally within the lot lines and building-restriction lines of the mortgaged property and that there have been no violations of zoning or other municipal building ordinances.

4. The loan documents are then completed by the lender. In this connection it is important that a lender obtain and use the note and mortgage forms approved by the VA for use in the jurisdiction involved. This is especially important in the event the loans should later be sold in the secondary market.

5. The lender will then have the borrowers sign the loan documents. The lender will then disburse the loan and place the mortgage of record as is customary on other types of mortgage loans. Closing papers should not be drawn until after the Certificate of Commitment (VA 26-1866) has been received from the VA. It is the lender's responsibility to make sure that no deed of trust or mortgage is recorded prior to the date appearing on the Certificate of Commitment, as otherwise VA regulations prohibit issuance of a loan guaranty. The VA Deed of Trust or Mortgage and VA Deed of Trust or Mortgage Note should be prepared in duplicate. If the loan is later sold, the original set is forwarded to the new mortgagee, and the duplicate set is retained in the original lender's file. It is the lender's responsibility to make sure that the borrower's name appears on both the Deed of Trust or Mortgage and the Deed of Trust or Mortgage Note exactly as it appears on the Certificate of Commitment and that the veteran borrower signs other documents and takes title to the property in the same manner. When preparing a Certificate of Loan Disbursement (VA Form 26-1876, revised August, 1952) the Certificate of Reasonable Value (VA 26-1843) should be carefully checked to make sure that all items have been properly covered. The Certificate of Loan Disbursement must be accompanied by a copy or photostat of each FHA Compliance Inspection Report

(FIIA Form 2051) and acceptable FIIA change orders, if not already submitted, if the structure is constructed under FHA financing and FHA supervision, or by VA final Compliance Inspection Report (VA Form 26-1839) as required by Section II of the Certificate of Reasonable Value.

6. In lieu of issuing Loan Guaranty Certificate (VA Form 26-1899), the VA, upon request of the lender, will indicate the guaranty by endorsement on the note or other evidence of the indebtedness. If the latter is desired, the lender should send the original note or other evidence of indebtedness to the VA with Certificate of Loan Disbursement (VA Form 26-1876).

Guaranty Provisions

Although each eligible veteran is entitled to a guaranty of $4,000 on farm realty loans and business realty loans under amendments to the Servicemen's Readjustment Act, an eligible veteran is now entitled to a guaranty of $7,500 for the purpose of acquiring residential property or constructing a dwelling to be occupied as his home. Under Section 501 (b), his home loan may be guaranteed up to 60 per cent or $7,500, whichever is smaller, less the amount of his guaranty entitlement previously used.

Gratuity Payments

Until August 31, 1953, each veteran was entitled to receive through the lender a gratuity payment, subsequent to the closing of his loan, equal to 4 per cent of the amount guaranteed with a maximum of $160. This sum was applied by the lender on the veteran's loan, and was an outright gift from the government.

On August 31, 1953, the VA reported that the Second Independent Office Appropriation Act 1953, approved July 27, 1953, which made funds available to the VA for payment of benefits under the loan guaranty program, imposed restrictions on the use of funds for payment of 4 per cent gratuities during the period from September 1, 1953, to June 30, 1954. A law passed by Congress in early 1955 permanently eliminated the gratuity payment.

Closing Charges

Any costs or expenses incurred in closing a loan, if normally required under local lending customs, may be collected from the veteran. Now the builder and other sellers may pay closing costs for veterans if they so desire; however, the prohibition against including in the loan an amount to pay closing costs is still retained in Regulation 36:4312.

Interest Rates

The maximum interest rate on any mortgage loan guaranteed under the Servicemen's Readjustment Act as amended shall not exceed 5¼ per cent per annum on the unpaid principal balance. This increase became effective July 2, 1959, the date of publication in the *Federal Register*.

In the National Housing Act of 1948 authority was given for an increase in the interest rates on VA loans to 4½ per cent with the consent of the Administrator of Veterans Affairs and the Secretary of the Treasury. Up until that time the maximum permissible interest rate on such loans was 4 per cent, and although this was not too desirable a rate, it was accepted by most mortgage lenders. However, because of the progressive rise in interest rates on all other types of mortgage financing which began in early 1948, this 4 per cent rate became quite unattractive. Most lenders expressed a desire that the rate on VA loans be increased ½ to 1 per cent in order to be in a competitive position in the mortgage market, as VA home-loan financing became more difficult to obtain. Even though an increase to 4½ per cent was authorized August 10, 1948, the VA did not look favorably on permitting such an increase to occur. As a result of this impasse, more and more lenders gradually withdrew from the VA lending market and concentrated on FHA and conventional home loans. (The part played by VA loans in the mortgage market during the past seventeen years is discussed in detail in Chapter 1.)

The Builder-Lender Program

As a result of the above conditions, the builder-lender program was devised. If the builder met the requirements of the VA, he would be permitted to operate as a nonsupervised lender. Upon completion of the home, the builder as a lender would process the loan to the veteran and would put the deed of trust on record and hold the paper for a future sale. This action, instead of forcing supervised lenders to make VA loans, caused them to withdraw almost entirely from the VA lending market, except that some banks did "warehouse" such loans for builder-lenders. A discount market developed, and bargaining for discounts between the builder-lender and available purchasers of the VA paper dominated the market. These discount rates offset the low 4 per cent interest rate and in some cases brought the yield on such loans to over 5 per cent. This practice continued even after the 4½ per cent interest rate on VA home loans was authorized. In March, 1954, the market on both FHA 4½ and VA 4½ per cent interest rate loans on home started strengthening, and even though the discount practices were still being used by builder-lenders in May, 1954, there was a par market in most areas on both FHA and VA 4½ per cent interest rate home loans which were being processed by supervised lenders.

The discount market on both FHA and VA loans with little or no down payment continued through the remainder of 1954 and for the entire year of 1955. The amount of the actual discount fluctuated considerably during this period. This discount rate was governed by the availability of mortgage funds for these loans. Most large lenders would not purchase these loans at any price. Public Law 85-364, signed by the President of the United States on April 1, 1958, repealed Section 605 of the Housing Act of 1957, which directed VA to regulate the charges, fees, and discounts imposed against builders or sellers.

On the other hand both FHA and VA loans with reasonable owner equity to strong borrowers remained steadily at par during this entire period.

The VA issued regulations (Section 36:4312) effective April 28, 1955, barring the VA guaranties on loans that included the total price of the house plus closing costs. Loans where the buyer made no down payment but paid closing costs were still permitted.

At this same time there was evidence of some tightening of mortgage money for VA loans. It was expected, however, that enough funds would be available through 1957 to meet these needs.

Transfer of Loans

It is not necessary that the VA be notified at the time of assignment or transfer; however, it should be borne in mind that, in the event it becomes necessary to file a claim under guaranty, the holder (claimant) must support the claim with evidence that it is the owner of the guaranteed loan. Inasmuch as it may also be necessary in certain cases that the VA have a transcript of the ledger accounts in connection with the audit of claims, assignees should require such records from the lenders covering all transactions beginning with the inception of the loan.

Partial or Total Loss of Guaranty

No liability arises against the VA if the evidence of guaranty is forged, or with respect to any transaction in which a signature to the note, mortgage, application for guaranty, or any other loan papers is a forgery or in which the discharge papers, or Certificate of Eligibility, are counterfeited, falsified, or not issued by the government.

A holder in due course who acquires a loan before maturity without notice or knowledge of any material misrepresentation or fraud in procuring a guaranty is not chargeable with the consequences of any fraud or misrepresentation. Otherwise, any fraud, or any material misrepresentation willfully made by the lender, or the holder, or by an agent of either, will relieve the VA of liability. On the other hand, the incontestability provisions of Section 511 of the act do accord every reasonable protection to lenders who conduct their operations prudently and in good faith. The holder must obtain a lien on the property, the title to which is such as to be acceptable to prudent lending institutions, informed buyers, title companies, and attorneys, generally, in the community. If the holder fails in this respect, or fails to comply with the act and the regulations with respect to the eleven requirements listed below, no claim on the guaranty shall be paid on account of the loan with respect to which the failure occurred, or in respect to which an unwillful misrepresentation occurred, until the amount by which the ultimate liability of the VA would thereby be increased has been ascertained.

Eleven Basic Requirements in Order to Maintain the VA Guaranty

1. The lender must obtain and retain a lien of the dignity prescribed on all property upon which a lien is required by the act or the regulation.

2. The documents must include power to substitute trustees.

3. Procurement and maintenance of insurance coverage must be arranged.

4. The lender is required to advise the VA regarding defaults.

5. Formal notice must be given to the VA in any suit or action or notice of sale.

6. Formal Notice of Intention to Foreclose must be sent to the VA.

7. Notice to the VA is required regarding the release, conveyance, substitution, or exchange of security.

8. There must be no lack of legal capacity of a party to the transaction incident to which the guaranty or insurance is granted.

9. Lender must see to it that any escrowed or earmarked account is expended in accordance with the agreement.

10. Lenders are required to take into consideration the limitations upon the quantum or quality of the estate or property.

11. Lenders must comply with any other requirement of the act or the regulations which does not by the terms of the act or the regulations result in relieving the VA of all liability with respect to the loan.

The burden of proof shall be upon the holder to establish that no increase of ultimate liability is attributable to such failure or misrepresentation.

Construction Loans

From a loan administration standpoint, particularly in handling construction loans on which a VA guaranty is contemplated, all prudent lenders will have learned the regulations and procedures before attempting to handle such loans. There is always a danger that the structure may not be completed or that the costs will exceed the contract price. (See Chapter 4 for details covering construction loans. See also VA *Technical Bulletin* TB4A-56, December 15, 1948.)

Any VA loan for the purchase or construction of residential property must be made on property which conforms to the minimum construction requirements prescribed by the Administrator covering homes on which construction started after December 8, 1952. In general the FHA minimum construction requirements have been adopted by the VA.

Compliance Inspections

It is essential, in obtaining a valid guaranty, for a lender to see to it that compliance inspections are obtained from a designated VA compliance inspector. These inspections are required at certain stages in the course of construction and are made at the same intervals required by FHA. In all cases involving new construction of one or more proposed dwelling units on which prior determination of reasonable values are sought, compliance inspections are mandatory.

If construction of the improvement deviates from the plans and specifications on which the VA appraisal is based, which deviation would tend to increase the cost to the veteran in excess of the reasonable value as determined, a request for revision of the reasonable value becomes imperative. The obligation to determine whether such deviations have occurred, together with the increased value resulting therefrom, rests upon the lender who is responsible on construction loans. Prior approval from the VA should be secured on any deviation.

VA may accept FHA Form 2051 as evidence of satisfactory completion and compliance.

Loan-servicing Requirements Covering VA Loans

The guaranty of a VA loan by the VA is in part based on the requirement that adequate servicing will be performed. Whenever a Loan Guaranty Officer finds that a lender has failed to maintain adequate loan accounting records or fails to demonstrate proper ability to service loans adequately, or fails to exercise proper credit judgment, he may temporarily suspend the right of such lender to secure the guaranty on loans under this Title III. In the accomplishment of proper servicing prudent lenders advise with and counsel veteran borrowers in an effort to impress upon them the importance of making prompt payments on the loan and to guide them safely to the ultimate maturity of their loans. Every ethical and fair method of curing defaults should be employed, and personal contacts with the veteran should be made whenever such contacts appear necessary. In the event it is determined that there is no possibility of a loan's being reinstated, every effort must be made to minimize the ultimate loss of all parties concerned. Loan administration and servicing of loans are dealt with in Chapters 11 and 12.

Filing of Default Notices

The regulations require the lender to file with the Loan Guaranty Officer written Notice of Default reports on VA Form 4-6850 within 45 days following a default which has continued (1) 60 days from the non-payment of an installment, (2) 90 days after demand is made to cure a default regarding some other convenant or obligation, (3) 180 days by reason of nonpayment of taxes. These reports should include reason for delinquency and report of reinstatement program which has been arranged with the borrower.

Filing Notice of Intention to Foreclose

Except upon the express waiver of the VA, a lender shall not begin proceedings in court or otherwise take steps to terminate the debtor's rights in the security until the expiration of thirty days after delivery by registered mail to the VA of a notice of intention to take such action, but immediate action may be taken if the property has been abandoned by the debtor, or if the property is subject to extraordinary waste or hazard, or if conditions justify the appointment of a receiver. Any right of a holder to repossess personal property may be exercised without prior notice to the Administrator, provided notice of such action is given by registered mail within ten days thereafter. The request form is VA 4-6851, Notice of Intention to Foreclose.

Foreclosure Action

When a lender institutes a suit or otherwise becomes a party to a suit or other proceedings brought on, or in connection with, a guaranteed loan, he must deliver to the VA Loan Guaranty Officer a copy of every procedural paper filed on behalf of the holder or filed by any other party thereto.

If, after default, a lender does not begin appropriate action within two months after written request by the VA to do so, or does not prosecute such action with reasonable diligence, the VA may intervene and prosecute the action to completion and may collect from the holder the costs of such action, including court costs and attorney's fees.

It is important to notify the VA in advance of a judicial or statutory sale, for it has a right to specify the amount to be bid at the sale. Failure to notify the VA and secure its instructions may jeopardize the guaranty of the lender. It is important that the lender and the attorney of the lender work closely with the Loan Guaranty Officer and the VA legal division in all activities pertaining to foreclosure of a veteran's loan.

Filing Claim under the Guaranty

A claim under the guaranty will not be entertained until a default has continued for at least three months, unless the rights of the holder or the VA may be prejudiced by such delay.

A claim under a guaranty is computed as of the date of the claim, but not later than (1) the date of judgment, or of the decree of foreclosure, or (2) in nonjudicial foreclosure, the date of publication of the first notice of sale. Claims are prepared and submitted to the VA on its Form 4-1874 and include the following items:

1. Unpaid principal balance of the loan.

2. Accrued interest at contract rate.

3. Reasonable foreclosure costs and attorney's fees that are approved by the VA. The latter in no case may exceed 10 per cent of the debt or $250 (whichever is less).

4. Reasonable trustee's fees not in excess of 5 per cent of the unpaid indebtedness.

5. Expenditures for payment of delinquent taxes, assessments, water rents, and hazard insurance premiums.

6. Any amount advanced which is reasonably necessary for the maintenance or repair of the security.

7. Any other expense or fee approved in advance by the Administrator.

An Evaluation of the Merits of the VA Loan Program

It is the opinion of those lenders who have been actively and directly engaged in the VA loan program since the start of this program that it has been eminently successful and has accomplished to date most of the objectives set forth in the original Servicemen's Readjustment Act of 1944, and as amended.

These accomplishments have offset to a great extent the numerous difficulties which beset prudent lenders in the processing of such loans. There is no doubt that many of the interpretations of the act, as well as VA regulations, have been too inflexible.

In evaluating the merits of the entire program it should also be stated that the VA loan program has had a profound and beneficial effect on the building industry, the mortgage lending industry, and the economy of the nation as a whole. Aside from the benefits that veterans and their families have secured through the provisions of the VA lending program by being able to obtain needed housing, farms, and business properties on liberal credit terms, the lending institutions throughout the nation have been able to invest substantial sums of money in mortgage loans with the guaranty of the United States supporting each such loan. In part because of the comparatively small monthly payments, the lower rate of interest, and the intensive screening of applicants by prudent lenders, the percentage of veteran loans in default up to the present time has been exceptionally low. This has had a tendency to reduce the costs of servicing VA loans. As an offset to the benefits that have accrued from the VA lending program, the flow of easy credit into the mortgage lending field has tended to have an inflationary effect on construction costs and real estate values. But this tendency was kept under some measure of control as a result of the unwillingness of the VA to allow an increase in the 4 per cent rate (rate is now $5\frac{1}{4}$ per cent) at a time when institutional investors were able to find more remunerative outlets for their funds.

The future of the VA loan program is subject to numerous conditions, the most important of which are the following:

Availability of Funds for Investment in VA Loans

Because of the steady growth of funds available for investments by banks, insurance companies, savings and loan associations, mutual savings banks, and other investors, these $4\frac{1}{2}$ per cent loans have again become attractive. A decline in the availability of funds would adversely affect the VA program. The interest rate is now $5\frac{1}{4}$ per cent.

Builder-Lender Program

The operations of the nonsupervised builder-lender program and the resultant sale of 501 loans at a discount have had a somewhat adverse effect upon the entire VA loan program. It has tended to impair the stature of the VA loan and may well cause prudent lenders to reduce their investments in VA loans.

The FNMA Program and the VA Direct-loan Program

The future activity of FNMA and the VA direct-loan program could retard the loan activity of prudent institutional lenders in VA loans. All such lenders are of the opinion that private enterprise is fully capable of handling the demands for this type of loan provided a satisfactory private secondary market can be maintained.

The Government-bond Market and the Federal Reserve Rediscount Rate

Bond yields in many instances cause larger investors to curtail mortgage investments in favor of government-bond investments. The Federal Reserve rediscount rate has a direct effect upon the credit to be made available by member banks.

The National Economy

It is estimated that there are over 15,190,000 veterans of World War II and 4,500,000 veterans of the Korean conflict in civil life today. Over 5,900,000 have availed themselves of the loan guaranty benefits of the VA program. Millions more will be applying for VA loans in the future. These veterans in the years ahead not only will comprise a large part of the working force of the nation but also by reason of age and earning power should be the most vital part of that force. It is therefore of great importance that this program be administered efficiently if it is to be continued. An important requirement would appear to be broader authority for the Administrator of Veterans Affairs to modify interest rates as conditions in the market change in one direction or the other and in this way eliminate unnatural support of the market by FNMA, by the builder-lender program, and by operations in the discount market. In other words a flexible interest rate is required if the flow of mortgage funds is not to be interrupted as a consequence of upward movements in interest rates. A flexible rate would undoubtedly go a long way toward eliminating the necessity for FNMA except on a standby emergency basis only.

SUMMARY

The Servicemen's Readjustment Act of 1944 was passed by Congress and signed by the President, June 22, 1944. It was designed to assist veterans of World War II in making the necessary adjustments from conditions of war to life as civilians and for other purposes. In 1952 the act was amended to extend benefits to Korean conflict veterans with service after June 27, 1950.

In the study of this subject we are particularly interested in Title III of the act and Chapter 37 of Title 38, United States Code which cover benefits for veterans in the purchase or construction of homes, farms, and business properties under the following sections: 501, purchase or construction of homes; 502, purchase of farms and farm equipment; 503, purchase of business property; 505, secondary financing.

Under these sections the VA does not make loans to veterans but guarantees or insures a percentage of the amount of each loan. The maximum guaranty on a VA home loan is for 60 per cent of the amount of the loan or $7,500, whichever is less. In order that a veteran may obtain a guaranty, all provisions of the VA regulations must be fully complied with, and the forms prescribed to cover such loans must be used.

The VA loan program has been in existence for approximately seventeen years, and the lending institutions in the nation have in general cooperated to the fullest extent in helping make this program a success. The responsibilities in connection with making loans to veterans have been many because of the fact that veterans will progressively represent a predominant influence on American life with the passage of time. As of December 31, 1960, approximately 5,881,828 (all loans) VA loans in number and $50,157,984,713 in amount had been made, and as the total mortgage debt of the nation as of that date was slightly in excess of $206 billion, it can readily be seen why the VA loan program has been a vital part of the mortgage lending operations during the more than seventeen-year period since the beginning of the act.

There are many forms and types of discharge certificates and separation papers in all branches of the Armed Forces, and it has been necessary for lenders to analyze carefully and learn the contents of each certificate, as in some instances certain discharge certificates or separation papers do not warrant VA loan guaranty benefits.

A loan the maturity of which is five years from the date of the loan, or the date as of which it was assumed by a veteran, must be amortized. The payments on an amortized loan must be approximately equal and must include a principal reduction not less often than annually during the life of the loan, except that on a farm mortgage loan the principal payments may be postponed for not more than two years from the date of the loan.

There is no VA restriction regarding the highest amount that can be loaned on a VA loan, provided it conforms with all VA requirements. There are also no down-payment requirements by the VA covering VA loans on homes, farms, or business properties. However, lenders in general have established their own requirements covering down payments, the amount of which varies widely as among lending institutions.

Until April 20, 1950, the maximum maturity on VA home loans was twenty-five years, but the maximum was extended to thirty years by Public Law 475, 81st Congress.

Regardless of the terms of the note, the debtor has the right to prepay at any time the entire indebtedness or any part thereof without penalty or fee. These privileges can be considered liberal, for the FHA imposes a penalty for prepayment and practically all institutional lenders other than commercial banks do likewise.

Supervised lenders consist of Federal Land Banks, national banks, state banks, private banks, mutual savings banks, savings and loan associations, insurance companies, credit unions, and mortgage and loan companies which are subject to examination and supervision by any agent of the United States government or of any state or territory including the District of Columbia.

Nonsupervised lenders consist of lenders who are not supervised lenders and may make VA loans for guaranty upon obtaining prior approval of the Administrator. The builder-lender program previously described operates under the authority covering nonsupervised lenders.

The VA does not require any notice of assignment of a guaranteed loan, and the assignment does not affect the guaranty.

No loan is guaranteeable of which the proceeds have been expended or will be expended for purchase or construction the purchase price or construction cost of which is in excess of the reasonable value as determined by the Administrator.

The holder must insist on insurance in an amount sufficient to protect the security against the risks or hazards to which it may be subjected and to do so to the extent customary in the place in which the property is located.

The VA now requires that the contemplated terms of payment required in any mortgage to be given in part payment of the purchase price or the construction cost bear a proper relation to the veteran's present and anticipated income and expenses and that the veteran be a satisfactory credit risk. Most mortgage lenders feel that a veteran should not obligate himself to pay more than 20 to 25 per cent of his net take-home pay for the monthly loan payment covering interest, installments, and trust funds for insurance premiums and property taxes. Prudent lenders also counsel and advise the veteran concerning the property location, the neighborhood, the cost of the property as related to the financial position of the veteran; they are also particularly careful to analyze the Contract of Sale or Deposit Receipt in order to be assured that the veteran is being adequately protected and is not overbuying. In processing a VA home-loan application each mortgage lender will first determine in interviewing the veteran applicant whether the full guaranty benefits are available, whether the applicant has sufficient income to service the loan for the amount requested, and whether all other requirements are satisfactory.

Upon completion of the processing of the application the VA (if the application is approved) will issue a Certificate of Commitment, VA Form 26-1866. Upon receipt of the Certificate of Commitment from the VA, the lender proceeds with the closing of the loan in accordance with prescribed procedures. This commitment entitles the holder to assurance of the evidence of the guaranty upon actual payment of the full proceeds of the loan for the purpose described in the original report. Within thirty days of the final disbursement the lender certifies on the Certification of Loan Disbursement Form 26-1876 that the loan meets the requirements set forth in Section 36:4303 of the VA regulations. If the loan described on the Certificate of Commitment, VA Form 26-1866, is made by the lending institution to whom it was issued, the Certificate of Commitment need not be returned to the VA. Otherwise the Certificate of Commitment or a copy of the agreement assigning the certificate to another lender must accompany the Certificate of Loan Disbursement, VA Form 26-1876. Upon submission of the final disbursement, VA Form 26-1876, the holder will then be issued a Certificate of Guaranty, VA Form 26, or endorsed evidence of guaranty on note if requested by lender.

QUESTIONS

1. Explain the position of the Loan Guaranty Division with respect to other divisions of the VA.
2. Name the reasonable foreclosure expenses a lender is permitted to deduct from the proceeds of the foreclosure sale.
3. Name the section of Title III of the Servicemen's Readjustment Act of 1944 which covers purchase of business property.
4. List the benefits for veterans of World War II which the Servicemen's Readjustment Act of 1944 (Public Law 346, 78th Congress) established.
5. Name the section of Title III of the above act which covers purchase of farms and farm equipment.
6. Explain the reasonable-value requirements.
7. Explain the hazard insurance requirements.
8. Once VA issues a guaranty certificate to a lender, can the eligibility of the loan be contested except for fraud or misrepresentation? Explain.
9. Explain the term "default" in a VA loan.
10. Describe the term "guaranty" as used in connection with the VA loan program.
11. Describe briefly the builder-lender program with relation to VA home loans.
12. Explain how the gratuity payment was computed.
13. A lender may reflect on the disbursement schedule a flat charge not exceeding 1 per cent of the amount of the loan or $50, whichever is greater, provided that such flat charge shall be in lieu of all charges relating to the costs of origination. Name ten of these charges.
14. Give the date when the Servicemen's Readjustment Act of 1944 which covers loans for the purchase or construction of homes, farms, and business property was enacted.
15. Explain VA compliance inspection requirements.
16. Is there any limit to the amount of loan which may be made?
17. Explain how the VA home-loan program is a loan guaranty program for which neither the lender nor the veteran pays a premium or service fee.
18. Describe how the VA appraisal value differs from the FHA appraisal value.
19. Describe supervised lenders.
20. Does the VA require that it be notified of the assignment or transfer of the security for a guaranteed loan or of the assignment of a guaranteed loan?
21. VA loan privileges are now extended to veterans of the Korean conflict. By what authority was this done?
22. Desribe the gratuity payment on a VA home loan.
23. Name the conditions under which the VA may make direct home loans to veterans.

24. Does the VA prescribe the minimum down payments on VA home loans?
25. Explain how the VA home-loan program since its inception has been a major factor and influence in the field of home mortgage lending.
26. Name the sections of Title III of the Servicemen's Readjustment Act of 1944 (now codified as Chapter 37, Title 38, United States Code) which covers purchase or construction of homes.
27. Explain who was eligible for a VA loan in the original act.
28. State the maximum maturity allowable on a VA home loan.
29. A VA loan may be made on a leasehold estate running or renewable at the option of the lessee for a period of not less than how many years beyond the maturity of the loan?
30. List seven types of mortgage lenders who are eligible to make VA loans.
31. Regardless of the terms of the note, give the authority for the debtor to prepay at any time the entire indebtedness or any part thereof without premium or fee.
32. Explain why supervised lenders may make loans which are automatically guaranteed.
33. Explain the term "prior approval."
34. List the items lenders may charge as reasonable and customary disbursements actually paid out and properly chargeable to the borrower.
35. In prior-approval cases describe how the VA is now required to check the credit report of the veteran applicant and to approve such applicant as a satisfactory credit risk.

ASSIGNMENTS

1. Obtain a VA home-loan application form, and fill it in completely covering an application to be filed by you for a loan on your own home.
2. Describe how a VA appraiser in your area operates.
3. Investigate and describe the VA home-loan market in the community in which you live.
4. Explain the methods used by the company with which you are associated in following up delinquent payments on VA loans.
5. In addition to the home-loan application form itself, obtain all other forms required by the VA covering a home-loan application.

BIBLIOGRAPHY AND SUGGESTED READING

GI Loans: The First Ten Years, Veterans Administration, Department of Veterans Benefits, Washington.
Home Mortgage Lending, chap. 13, pp. 268–275, American Institute of Banking, Section American Bankers Association, New York, 1946.
Lenders' Handbook, Veterans Administration, Washington, 1948.
McMichael, Stanley L., *How to Finance Real Estate,* chap. 15, Prentice-Hall, Inc., Englewood Cliffs, N.J.

CHAPTER 11

The Loan Administration Program

PURPOSES

1. To explain the objectives of the loan administration program
2. To enumerate and explain the principal operations of such a program
3. To discuss the increasing importance of this phase of mortgage lending operations
4. To explain the importance of portfolio analysis and statistics
5. To describe loan-servicing operations for others
6. To explain an investor–loan correspondent contract

Objectives of the Mortgage Loan Administration Program

The purpose of investment in mortgage loans is to earn net income. The purpose is achieved with maximum success if mortgage contracts are paid according to their terms, if losses are avoided, and if the expenses of managing the mortgage portfolio are properly controlled. To see that these conditions are fulfilled is the objective of the administrative and servicing program. Lenders now commonly recognize the fact that if a mortgage loan portfolio is to be maintained in sound condition, it must be constantly supervised. The cost of such supervision is justified if it results in a reduction of defaults and in an avoidance of losses.

It is essential that the officers charged with the administration of the mortgage loan portfolio have direct contact with the policy-making authority of the lender, in order that those responsible for formulating general policies may be informed of current developments and may be assured that established policies are being effectively administered.

The administration, operation, and supervision of a mortgage loan portfolio consists of a group of functions most frequently described as the "loan administration program," "administration of the loan portfolio," or the "general mortgage loan servicing program." Many mortgage banking firms throughout the nation, during the past few years, have changed the title "general mortgage loan servicing" to "loan administration," or "loan portfolio administration."

Most of the routine contacts of borrowers are made through the respective loan collection departments, and favorable customer relations depend to a large extent on the quality of the service provided.

A close working relationship should always be maintained between the executive officers and the personnel of the loan administration department. Such a relationship promotes more pleasant employee relations and improves the efficiency of the mortgage loan department operations.

Loan administration covers the normal administration of the loan portfolio. It is concerned with maintaining loans in a current condition in all respects and the handling of all functions pertaining to delinquent loans. It requires close attention by executive management, and by personnel well trained in each departmental activity. All phases of these operations are highly specialized and technical. It embraces all the following operations and procedures:

1. Collection of all payments in accordance with the note terms
2. Verification of the fulfillment by the borrower of all other covenants of the deed of trust or mortgage
3. Operations of the cashier, accounting, and bookkeeping divisions
4. Operation of the hazard insurance division
5. Operation of the tax division
6. Operation of the delinquent-loan collection and servicing division
7. Maintenance of statistics, portfolio analysis, and other research activities
8. Maintenance of adequate index and filing systems

When a loan becomes delinquent or a breach in one of the covenants of the deed of trust or mortgage develops, the matter is promptly brought to the attention of the delinquent-loan collection and servicing division, which takes control from that point on. It is difficult to distinguish between some phases of general loan servicing and delinquent-loan collection and servicing. In discussing these operations, we must recognize the existence of some duplication of methods and duplicate functions. General loan-servicing operations and delinquent-loan servicing operations must be thoroughly synchronized if effective loan administration is to be maintained. When a loan is added to the portfolio, it becomes the responsibility of the various divisions of this department. It is through them that contacts between the lender and the customer are maintained.

The loan was made with the approval of the loan committee, which had before it the appraisal report, the report of the type and condition of the property, the financial statement of the borrower, a credit analysis report covering the borrower, and other necessary supplemental information. The loan, when made, was considered a good and safe investment. It is the duty of the various divisions of the loan administration department to keep it so. The officer in charge of loan administration, as a member of the loan committee, assists in eliminating all unreliable and doubtful loan applications. In the broadest sense loan administration is concerned with all the functions involved in the handling of a loan from the time the funds are disbursed until the obligation is satisfied in some way.

After the loan is granted and the note and deed of trust or mortgage have been signed by the borrower, the necessary papers are assembled in the individual loan portfolio. The loan is numbered, the index file is set up, and the payment record is given to the borrower. Both the tax division and the hazard insurance division establish the necessary card-record procedures for the handling of their respective duties in connection with the loan. At the time the note and deed of trust or mortgage are signed, the lending officer explains to the new borrower the methods of making payments on the loan; he also explains other items about which the borrower ought to know and which may arise. This procedure enables both the lender and the borrower to gain a complete understanding of the transaction and promotes a feeling of mutual confidence and friendliness.

Despite the care exercised in the selection of borrowers, a certain amount of collection difficulty is inevitably encountered in every mortgage loan portfolio. Also, there are many questions by borrowers which arise daily concerning insurance protection, tax records, loan payments, titles to properties, and countless other items which must be given careful attention. It is important that loan administration activities be so organized that each borrower who requests information or who has a problem confronting him can be assured of individual and courteous treatment from an officer or employee. It is equally important for servicing officers to handle collections and corrections of any breach in the covenants of the deed of trust or mortgage on a personalized basis.

One of the major objectives of the loan administration program is to anticipate and eliminate, to the greatest possible extent, the risks of loss and the factors which contribute to the risks of loss. The safety of the investment must at all times be protected. Another important objective is the maintenance of such pleasant and friendly relations with each borrower as to merit the borrower's confidence and good will.

The officer in charge of these operations seeks to accomplish these objectives by giving close attention to each loan. He endeavors to have all officers, and the personnel of each division, discuss with the borrower any phase of loan operations in a friendly, diplomatic, and courteous manner. The most frequent contact with the borrower is made by a member of the collection division, who receives the payments. These duties, therefore, are very important in the maintenance of pleasant customer relations.

Influence of Origination on Loan Administration

In mortgage lending there is an old saying to the effect that "a well-made loan is half collected." If all the necessary information is assembled at the time the application for a loan is made, including complete details regarding the property, a very accurate credit report and analysis, and a listing of all other conditions which support a sound loan, it will be of great assistance in the handling and supervision of the loan. Conversely, failure to provide this information will prove a handicap in case the loan becomes delinquent or there are other defaults.

Many lenders are of the opinion that a man cannot be a good originator of mortgage loans, that is, take applications and make an acceptable preliminary analysis of the transaction, unless he has been well trained in loan administration operations. If he has had this intensive training, he has learned what constitutes a successful loan, and he has learned, too, the importance of obtaining full particulars at the outset not only for the benefit of persons who examine the applicant but also for the benefit of those who must supervise the loan after it has become a part of the portfolio.

In the mortgage loan department of many lenders meetings are held weekly, or oftener, at which time new loans, loan policies, delinquencies, and other mortgage loan subjects are discussed. These meetings are essential in order that the operating heads of the various divisions may acquire knowledge of the entire operation of the department and learn about one another's duties.

One of the most important phases of loan origination is the need for gaining the confidence and good will of the potential borrower at the first meeting. First impressions are very often lasting impressions, and many loans have not worked out satisfactorily because of the poor initial reception given the borrower. The personality of the interviewer has an important influence in creating cordial relations. The interest and help he shows in understanding the applicant and assisting him with financing problems make a profound impression.

Organization

The size of the department organization depends upon the size of the loan portfolio, the types of loans in the portfolio, and the type of operations of the lending institution. Regardless of the size, certain basic operations are necessary (see Figure 32). This chart applies primarily to an institutional-type investor that has both its own portfolio and a portfolio of loans being handled for other investors.

Proper delegation of authority is essential to the success of mortgage lending operations. The responsibility for all the acts within the department rests with the head of the department. To ensure smoothness in operations, he must allocate authority to his associates in the department according to the necessities of the work they pursue. To accomplish this, he must know the abilities of all members of his department.

Part of the loan administration operation relates to keeping records

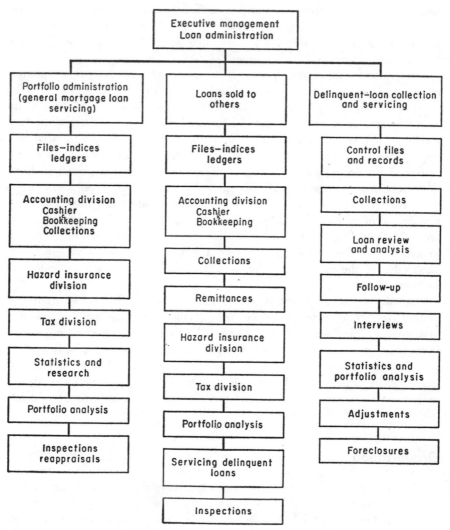

Figure 32. Organization of a Loan Administration Department

of all items of importance up to date. Well-designed forms for good accounting practices and modern methods of posting processes are needed. Keeping inspection reports and tax and insurance records current at all times is part of this work.

Availability of files, which include the loan portfolios, ledger cards, or other types of loan records and index of loans, is an important factor in successful loan administration. In most companies this department is responsible for keeping statistical records, portfolio classifications, and research information up to date. This division maintains the inventory of the loan portfolio and sets up the answers to the examinations of supervisory authorities and the answers to the company's own audit reports. The heads of these various divisions must be constantly on the alert in order to detect any weaknesses in servicing operations.

In handling loans sold to others, it is necessary that the same effective servicing operations be maintained. Such loans must be handled in the same manner as other loans in the portfolio. These operations are no less important when being performed for another party than they are when the investor does its own servicing; they may even be more important.

Personnel: Loan Administration Officers' Qualifications

All major servicing personnel must understand the working requirements and duties of the entire mortgage loan department, including a knowledge of acquiring new loans, of safeguarding present investments, and of operating the mortgage loan department in such an economical and thorough manner as to gain the respect of the lender's officers and employees, and its competitors, its borrowers, and the public.

Each officer should be qualified to arrange for the proper reception of the borrower and should give assurance that the borrower's problem will be carefully studied and analyzed. In addition, the officer should be able to assemble all pertinent details in order to have a clear understanding of the problem and to handle the transaction capably. An officer should have a background of years of experience in mortgage lending, including a knowledge of mortgage loan operating procedures, and an understanding of the regulations of both FHA and the VA in so far as they pertain to loan administration.

In mortgage loan administration operations, lenders must take into consideration the fact that the size and scope of mortgage lending exert an influence on the economy of the country. Lenders must be particularly concerned with their earnings, with the health and liquidity of the loan portfolio, and with the effect of their loan administration operations upon their borrowers. Because of the public relations aspect of mortgage loan administration, lenders are also concerned with the welfare of the communities in which they make loans and the welfare of the persons whom they serve within those communities.

Personnel in these respective divisions should be assigned duties best suited to their abilities. An excellent statistical employee might not have the personality or other qualifications to work as a field representative, or an able tax or insurance officer might not be suited to work in the accounting division. In large operations the highly technical phases of loan administration must be handled by specialists in each field. Highly trained and skilled officers are placed in charge of such divisions as accounting, hazard insurance, tax, delinquent-loan collections and servicing, statistics, research, and portfolio analysis.

There are few occupations as interesting as mortgage loan administration operations, and employees should be encouraged to realize it. They come in contact with many people, each of whom has his individual mortgage problems and is significant from the point of view of human interest. If the loan administrator finds his work interesting and senses its importance, he will grow by continuously applying the things he has learned. The ability of a good loan administrator will be enhanced if he has a good personality and learns to use it. He also needs a good memory, an active and analytical mind, a sense of fair play, and a capacity for hard work.

In addition to learning loan administration methods and operations from senior officers and by experience, the younger employees engaged in various phases of these operations should read and study the many good books which are available on mortgage lending.

Collections

Interest earned and collected represents the major income earned by a mortgage lender from a mortgage loan. It is obvious, therefore, why the item of interest is recognized as foremost in importance in loan collection, why these operations must be set up to cover the collection of this interest when due, and why loan classifications and records should be based primarily on loans on which the interest is current and on loans by degrees of interest delinquency. Other delinquencies should follow in the order of their importance. Collecting interest and amortization payments in accordance with the terms of the loan is one of the major activities of the accounting and bookkeeping divisions of the loan portfolio administration and general servicing. In general, the effectiveness of the lender's general collection program depends almost entirely upon the judgment and skill of its officers and personnel.

One of the most intangible assets of a lender, and one which it must preserve if it is to remain in the mortgage lending business, is a reputation for fair and helpful treatment of mortgagors. A specified date for each payment is set forth at the time the loan is made, and promptness in these payments is essential. If it is necessary to send out notices for delinquent payments, or notices for any special requirement, they must be sent promptly. It is not advisable for the lender to show any tendency toward delay when promptness is expected on the part of the borrower. Proper follow-up of payments according to schedule and a constant review of all loans are mandatory in successful mortgage lending operations.

Information to Be Given the Borrower after Loan Has Been Closed

If the loan application is approved, the officer discussing the closing of the loan with the borrower must be very thorough in talking over the things the lender expects of the borrower. He should discuss prompt payment, proper insurance, maintenance of the property, rate of interest, amount of payment, immediate notice of any change of conditions, and all other items that may affect the handling and supervision of the loan or the relationship between the lender and the borrower. He should also explain all other covenants of the deed of trust or mortgage. Proper explanation of these points will usually mean pleasant relations between the lender and the borrower and will have a profound effect upon loan administration operations.

Accounting Procedures

Cashier operations, also known as "accounting-division operations," have been greatly developed during the past few years. Manual accounting is undoubtedly the best method for small lenders, but it is difficult to know precisely when machine accounting will prove more economical and satisfactory. In large companies the use of a punch-card accounting system has many advantages, since it reduces manpower and facilitates portfolio analysis and statistical records. When considering the installation of mechanical equipment, it is generally advisable for a lender to investigate the systems of other lenders. During the past several years this practice has been followed by a number of large lenders who have considered the installation of the punch-card accounting system. Factors which influence the choice of a system are the volume of business, types of loans made, type of billing required, and types of receipts issued. Another important factor is not only the present volume of business but the expected volume over a period of several years. Many companies recognize that at the point of conversion it may not be economical but the rapid growth in their business will necessitate preparation for the growth by securing the necessary equipment well in advance.

There seems to be a somewhat general agreement that there is a limited need for billing, especially on loans which call for the payment of interest, principal, loan trust funds, and FHA insurance premium for a specific amount each month. Many lenders believe some type of receipt covering each payment on the loan is essential. Customer preference is decidedly in favor of having their payments itemized, with balances of principal and escrow funds shown. In order to systematize these procedures and, if possible, reduce operating expenses, lenders now use some form of receipt other than the passbook. Other forms of receipts include coupon books, mortgage payment notices, payment receipts, copies of installment notices, and amortization schedules. A check is ordinarily considered to be the best receipt in the world, and other type receipt forms are not generally required on a monthly basis.

Accounting work should be so organized that it may avoid as far as possible interruptions of activity and removal of essential records from the department for extended periods. Every accounting system should spread the routine work as evenly as possible over the year and over each month. Some concentration of activity is unavoidable in companies that have a considerable volume of loans on which the payments are due on the thirtieth or on the first of the month. In many companies, counter lines during this period have been reduced by successful efforts to have borrowers mail remittances. In order to reduce such lines, some lenders have arranged for monthly payments on a staggered-due-date basis. This practice has not proved to be satisfactory since it makes delinquency control much more difficult.

In making payments on their mortgage loans, practically all borrowers make contact with the accounting division in person or by mail. These contacts are made far more often than with any other division of the mortgage loan department. The importance of the customer-relations angle of the receiving of these payments, therefore, cannot be too strongly emphasized. To many borrowers the person in the office of the lender receiving the payments is their sole contact with the lender. Some small lenders generally prefer over-the-counter payments, while in general both large and small lenders, in the interest of efficient operations, prefer the mailing of payments. Some lenders have developed this procedure to such an extent that practically all payments are made by mail. It is claimed that payment by mail is the fastest and most efficient method of handling each transaction. However, it is important that payment receipts, if any, be dispatched to borrowers without any delay.

Loan Records

No method of maintaining mortgage loan records can be described as ideal, because the requirements of individual lenders vary greatly. Monthly-payment loans, in which taxes, insurance, and other escrow payments are included, has increased the number of operations involved and in turn the expense in handling mortgage loans. Moreover, supervisory authorities and those charged with the management of operations have a tendency to request portfolio analysis and operating statistics with greater frequency and on an increasingly comprehensive scale. All these changes point to the need for very careful planning of records in order that essential information may always be available, duplication of records avoided, economy of operation achieved, and accounting and bookkeeping operations facilitated. Maintenance of such records is the duty of the accounting division.

Index Cards

In setting up new loans, index cards are necessary. These index cards are generally set up by borrower's name, property location, and loan number. The make-up of index cards varies from the minimum information necessary for identification to rather comprehensive listing of loan data, depending in large measure on the purposes for which the cards are used. A similar file is also maintained for all loans paid off, which provides a valuable source of information for future reference.

Ledger Cards

Ledger cards most frequently used are of two broad types: One type consists of those ledger cards that contain only the basic information necessary for calculating and recording interest, principal, and escrow-account payments. The ledger cards in the other type contain this basic information and, in addition, a wide variety of pertinent data about all aspects of the loans, such as assessments, appraisals, and property descriptions; thus, all the essential information about the loan is available on the ledger card. When this latter type of card is not used, the necessary supplemental information is generally maintained in the loan folder. In any type of operation a ledger card should be provided which can be utilized as a master record for each mortgage loan. Most lenders favor a ledger card with a minimum of pertinent data and find it more desirable to obtain these data directly from the mortgagor's loan file.

Taxes, Tax Follow-up

Prior to closing a loan and before funds are disbursed to borrowers, all general and special assessments and taxes which may be due must be paid to date. In good times or bad times, whether the property is occupied or vacant, taxes continue to accrue against a property in the same manner as that of interest on the loan.

FHA-insured mortgage loans call for one-twelfth of the annual property taxes to be included in the monthly payments. Many lenders follow this same procedure in the collection of VA and conventional loans. Regardless of the type of loan or the method of tax payment, a reliable system is needed for keeping complete tax information about all mortgaged properties.

A separate tax card should be kept for each loan. The tax card should be prepared in such a manner that it offers accuracy for comparison with the tax-collection records. An exact legal description of the property is essential along with other information that may be desired for identification of the mortgage and posting tax-payment records. This includes a record of any special assessments and any other tax data pertaining to the property. It is desirable to have tax records kept as simple as possible within the framework of accuracy. Where only one set of tax records is kept, many lenders file the cards numerically according to the assigned mortgage numbers. Some system for sorting is required when searches of tax records are to be made, and also for separation into loans on which taxes are collected as part of installments and those on which taxes are not collected or paid by the lender. Most large lenders with branches maintain tax records by counties and by branch offices.

The lender has the responsibility of paying taxes when due to the tax collector in all cases where the borrower pays the monthly installment portion of the taxes as part of the payment requirement. When the lender assumes this obligation, he becomes liable for his own errors. He may also be liable for any penalty interest that might accrue if there is a failure to pay taxes when due.

Many lenders prefer to collect tax installments, regardless of type of loan, payable in advance on a monthly-payment basis. On conventional loans, a small fee is charged by many lenders for this service.

The borrower should always be fully informed of the tax requirements and the methods by which payments are to be made to the tax collector and the disposition of the receipted bills. If the loan is to be paid off in full and the lender has assumed the responsibility in the past of paying the taxes when due, it is well to remind the customer of the date when the next tax payment must be made, and what steps he should take to ensure his receiving the proper tax notices. If the lender pays the taxes, it is important that the borrower be informed of the tax payments, the record of payment should be set forth as a separate part of the ledger account, and the receipted tax bills should be mailed to the borrower. Rather than have the borrowers who take care of their own taxes send in their tax receipts to the lender, a more satisfactory manner is for the lender to verify the tax records at the tax collector's office, or have these services performed by a tax service company. This latter procedure is now recognized as part of the responsibility of the mortgage lender.

If a tax search reveals that a delinquency exists, it is important to remedy the default as soon as possible in order to avoid future difficulties. All such delinquencies should be listed in detail and the borrower contacted by letter with the request that the delinquent taxes be paid at once and the receipted tax bills be sent to the lender for notation on the tax card. After this record has been made, the receipts are returned to the borrower. It is important to remember that delinquent taxes may indicate possible trouble with the loan, such as delinquent interest, or some breach in the covenants of the mortgage. In some exceptional cases, the lender will advance the taxes in order to save the borrower interest penalties. Such action is taken where the value of the property is sufficient to warrant such an advance. It is also taken in most cases where the loan is in process of foreclosure. In the former case, arrangements are usually made with the borrower to repay the advanced taxes on a regular monthly basis.

If the lender is responsible for the payment of taxes, and the funds held in the escrow account are not sufficient to cover the tax requirement because loan payments are delinquent or because the taxes have increased, the borrower is contacted immediately in an effort to secure the necessary funds before due date. If the funds cannot be obtained, the lender must decide whether to let the taxes remain unpaid until the owner has accumulated funds with which to pay them or advance the taxes to be repaid at a later date, either in a lump sum or by increasing the regular monthly payments. In practically all cases, however, the lender will advance these funds even though it means an overdraft in the escrow account, as unpaid taxes become a prior lien on the property ahead of the mortgage loan.

Reports covering unpaid taxes should be turned over to the officer in charge of delinquent loans. Each tax delinquency is usually handled on the same basis as other phases of loan collection operations; the method of approach is dependent almost entirely on the circumstances covering the particular case. Nonpayment of taxes constitutes a breach of the mortgage covenants.

A large portion of the losses which mortgage lenders sustained, as a result of foreclosure of mortgage during the Great Depression of the early 1930s, was caused by accumulated tax delinquencies. One of the objectives of loan administration operations is to reduce loss exposure. A well-organized program for the elimination of tax delinquencies is a vital phase of these operations.

Hazard Insurance

Proper insurance must be maintained by a borrower on his mortgaged home or any other type of mortgaged property to provide indemnity against possible loss of the security. The mortgage holder should see that adequate and sound insurance protection is in effect on the mortgaged premises at all times. The kind of insurance protection to be required by a lender must be decided by the administrative officers of the lender. They must also arrange a procedure for selecting acceptable insurance companies and for determining the amount of coverage to be maintained on each mortgage. Control of the insurance contracts requires adequate records, policy amendments, handling of losses and collateral details. There are many insurable hazards to which buildings are subject, and if the laws of the particular state which control do not amply specify the type of insurance to be maintained, a policy may be formulated by each mortgagee to provide complete protection. Fire insurance protection is a primary requisite of all lenders.

The simple form of fire insurance policy may be endorsed to include extended coverage at nominal cost. This endorsement includes insurance against the risks of windstorm, explosion, hail, riot and civil commotion, aircraft, smoke, and also damage caused by motor vehicles not owned by the owner or occupant of the insured premises. Recently the additional extended coverage endorsement also became available on dwelling policies only, in some states, by payment of an additional premium. This endorsement, which is subject to a $50 deductible for each loss, includes protection against water damage caused by faulty plumbing and heating system, vandalism, ice, snow, freezing, falling trees, glass breakage, and damage by a vehicle owned or operated by the insured or an occupant of the dwelling. This kind of protection is becoming more and more popular to the property owner and meets in many instances the requirement for separate fire, windstorm, or explosion insurance specified by financial institution regulations. Some lenders, particularly life insurance companies, have arranged for life insurance on the lives of the borrowers payable to, or assigned to, the mortgagee. This additional protection is becoming widespread. Some mortgage lenders consider it advisable to carry an errors and omission policy, which offers protection where, through error or omission, valid, correct, or sufficient fire insurance protection is not maintained on the mortgage premises. Mortgages or deeds of trust are usually drawn up with sufficiently broad insurance provisions to permit the lender to require almost any form of property damage insurance deemed necessary to provide adequate security.

Insurance companies differ not only by financial standing, size, and experience but also by classification. Financial stability, history, management, and operations should be governing factors in rating companies.

Policies written by some or all companies licensed to transact business in a particular state will be presented to lenders in compliance with mortgage insurance requirements. It is therefore essential for lenders requiring insurance to study their needs in such a manner that they may readily determine what insurance companies' policies will be acceptable as security.

Rules for rating the financial responsibility of insurance companies include certain ratios, such as policy holder's surplus to unearned premium reserves, and loss-and-expense ratio to premiums earned, and policy holder's surplus to assets. A reasonable period of underwriting experience is also necessary.

In addition to the rating of insurance companies, it is not unusual for lenders to place a limit upon the maximum amount of insurance acceptable from a particular company on any one risk. This limitation varies with the estimated financial responsibility of the particular insurance company.

A mortgage lender usually insists upon insurance protection in an amount equal to the mortgage indebtedness. If insurance policies contain a co-insurance clause, the amount of insurance required should always be sufficient to comply with the coinsurance provision. Additional loan advances with new appraisals may call for an adjustment of insurance requirements.

Some lenders require windstorm protection if the loan exceeds a certain figure. Other lenders require windstorm insurance equal to a certain percentage of the loan. If extended coverage is included in the fire insurance policies, the windstorm requirement becomes unimportant, as windstorm protection is one of the hazards covered and will equal in amount the fire insurance maintained.

Before insurance policies are filed, they should be carefully examined by the officer or authorized employee in the mortgage loan department who is responsible for insurance coverage to make certain that the amount of the insurance coverage is sufficient; that the mortgagor is correctly named; that the property and its location are accurately described; that the interest of the lender as mortgagee is properly covered; and that each policy is properly signed. In most states the standard fire insurance policy is a complicated document, and a great deal of study is required for a thorough understanding of the policy and the many endorsements and clauses frequently added to it.

The amount of insurance necessary when a loan is made may be subject to revision during the term of the loan, but as a rule no reduction in coverage should be permitted without the approval of the proper officer or the investor as the case may be.

When a fire occurs in any property on which the lender holds a mortgage, it is essential that the agent or company be immediately notified by the insured. The handling of fire losses is a function of the officer in charge of hazard insurance. Reinstatement of policies to their original amount following payment of loss is a responsibility of the lender's insurance department. The utmost vigilance is called for in all phases of insurance operations.

To prevent any possibility of a lapse in hazard insurance coverage, an index card is usually made up for each policy. This card shows the borrower's name, location of the property, the account number of the loan, and the expiration date of the policy. Space is also provided for the name of the company, the policy number, and the agency. The card could also record the amount of each premium and the date paid.

Insurance index cards should be filed according to the expiration dates of the policies chronologically, by years and by months. Cards for the current month should be filed by day. This constitutes a daily tickler system for expiring policies and may be used as a daily check of renewals or for reference.

When a lender has definite knowledge of a change in the title to a mortgaged property, it is very important that the insurance company be notified and the policy corrected as to the insured as soon as possible. There are many other changes in insurance policies held in connection with mortgage loans made by endorsement or substitution of policies, some of which require changes in expiration dates and index card and the proper filing of the endorsements with the policies.

A renewal notice should be sent out three or four weeks ahead of expiration date, notifying the insured of expiration and also giving him the opportunity of reviewing present coverage to see if it is adequate. Perhaps values have changed considerably; the property may have recently been sold and the new owner may wish to purchase insurance from a new company or broker. It is a common practice to have an authorization signed by the insured on all FHA and VA loans where the lender is obligated to pay the premium from escrow funds. This will avoid possible confusion regarding the responsibility for making the payment. Renewal of policies at other than anniversary dates is very inconvenient and is an additional cost. A reasonable charge is often made for this work.

Insurance increases should be watched carefully, and adjustments in monthly payments should be increased accordingly.

On FHA and conventional loans in a new tract, provisional policies are acceptable, provided the matter is discussed and arranged before disbursements are made. A spread of liability in different companies is recommended on all tract patterns submitted for $250,000 or more. Such a program prevents any one company from assuming all the risk in the event of a catastrophe.

The Servicemen's Readjustment Act of 1944, as amended, authorizes the Administrator of Veterans Affairs to promulgate rules and regulations necessary and appropriate to carry out the provisions of the act. These regulations provide that the holder of the loan shall require insurance policies in an amount sufficient to protect the security against the risks of hazards to which it may be subjected to the extent customary in the locality. All monies received under such policies covering payment of insured losses shall be applied to restoration of the security, or to the loan balance. It is also provided that the regulations issued under the act and in effect on the date of any loan which is submitted and accepted, or approved, for guaranty, or for insurance thereunder, shall cover all rights, duties, and liabilities of the parties to such loan, and provisions of the loan instruments inconsistent with such regulations are thereby amended and supplemented to conform thereto.

Portfolio Analysis and Statistics

Important Part of Mortgage Lending Operations

Constant portfolio analysis is recognized today by all lenders as an important part of mortgage loan operations. It is vitally necessary to provide a basis for adjustments in lending policies and control of loanable funds. Portfolio analysis is also necessary to make certain at all times that loans on the books fully comply with the existing Federal and state laws and housing regulations, such as the FHA and VA regulations. There are no means available that will enable a lender to ascertain the condition of the portfolio except by analysis. It is the responsibility of the officer in charge of loan administration operations to see that these statistical records are maintained to permit proper analysis of the loan portfolio.

Information That Must Be Studied and Analyzed

Some of the information that must be studied in order to obtain a clear picture of the portfolio is set forth below:

1. Classification of loans by types of properties
2. Classification of loans by dollar amounts
3. Report of loans by geographical areas
4. Weekly or monthly runoff, including new loans, loan commitments, and change in ledger balance
5. Average daily accrual rate
6. Net operating income
7. Delinquency records in detail
8. Foreclosure records
9. Loss records on foreclosed loans
10. Maturities
11. Breakdown of amount of loans by interest rates
12. Loans by type, i.e., FHA, conventional, farm, VA, industrial, and commercial
13. Interest earned but not collected
14. Inventory of the portfolio by payment status and appraisal figures

Analysis Will Reveal Strength or Weakness of Loan Administration Operations

Information derived from a detailed analysis of the above will reveal weaknesses or strains in the portfolio and the efficiency of loan administration operations.

A regular increase in the number and dollar amount of delinquent loans could indicate several things, such as increased unemployment, a downward trend in economic conditions, too liberal credit analysis of new borrowers, or a need for more active loan servicing.

Portfolio analysis also serves as a guide to reserve policy. Anticipated losses must be under constant control as the real estate market is subject to drastic and sudden changes.

It is also necessary that the head of the mortgage loan department and his assistants keep informed of economic activities of a community, bank clearings, department-store sales, bank credit, commodity prices, interest rates, bond yields, payrolls, industrial activity, population changes, mortgage recordings, foreclosures, vacancies, new construction, changes in construction costs, building activities, and all other activities that might have an effect upon mortgage lending.

Classification of Portfolio by Size (Dollar Amount)

Classification of real estate loans by size should be made at least once each year and maintained for comparative purposes. Generally accepted breakdown is usually as shown in Table 6. Analysis of this table will quickly re-

TABLE 6   CLASSIFICATION OF PORTFOLIO BY SIZE

	Year 1959		Year 1960	
	No.	Amount	No.	Amount
Under $5,000...........	5,203	$15,780,625	4,707	$13,746,358
5,000–9,999.............	2,852	20,547,694	3,588	26,278,219
10,000–29,999...........	326	4,518,625	446	6,089,369
30,000–99,999...........	28	1,272,637	36	1,627,495
100,000 and over........	3	711,140	6	988,968
Total................	8,412	$42,830,721	8,783	$48,730,409

veal trend of loans in different classifications. Loans for amounts over $10,000 should be closely watched at all times.

Strength of the portfolio, which consists mainly of home loans, is indicated to some extent by the number and amount of loans under $10,000, provided these are sound loans on good properties to strong borrowers, all on an amortized basis. There is a vital need for the mortgage loan portfolio to be classified at least once yearly by types of properties in order that the vice-president in charge, and the president and board of directors, may be informed of each particular type of property on which money is loaned, and this classification should be maintained on a yearly basis for comparative purposes.

Classification of Portfolio by Types of Properties

Classification of properties is usually set up in a manner similar to Table 7. An identification number for each property should be placed on each

TABLE 7   CLASSIFICATION OF PORTFOLIO BY TYPES OF PROPERTIES

	Year 1959		Year 1960	
	No.	Amount	No.	Amount
1. Dwellings....................	7,662	$36,534,287	7,988	$41,379,428
2. Flats........................	190	856,130	198	1,135,565
3. Apartments..................	151	1,342,458	173	1,700,444
4. Stores and office buildings.......	76	908,938	78	984,349
5. Industrial buildings...........	49	591,233	62	603,724
6. Hotels.......................	5	59,933	5	64,555
7. Farms.......................	109	934,113	113	1,018,780
8. Unimproved (industrial)........	6	55,513	7	46,428
9. Unimproved (residential).......	124	1,119,877	110	987,381
10. Special purpose*..............	40	428,239	49	808,755
Total........................	8,412	$42,830,721	8,783	$48,730,409

* Includes churches, theaters, lodge halls, fraternity houses, garages, service and gas stations, and bowling alleys.

ledger card when the loan is made, in order that this report can be easily made up.

Daily Analysis of Loan Delinquencies Must Be Maintained

A daily analysis of loan delinquencies must be maintained. Loan collection in connection with delinquent loans is one of the major operations of a mortgage loan department. An increase in delinquencies indicates trouble and possible losses.

Efficient Delinquent-loan Collection and Servicing Requires Monthly Proof of Loan-delinquency Records

Personal follow-up for loan payments on delinquent loans after analysis is mandatory. This is especially true now, since many new borrowers have purchased homes during the past few years. These loans require constant review in order to discover any tendencies that indicate chronic delinquencies. Many of these borrowers are not acquainted with the necessity for keeping loan payments current.

Reports of loans by geographical areas, particularly for lenders with large portfolios, reveal information covering increase or decrease in amount of loans in each area, and diversification of loans in different communities indicates portfolio strength or weakness. For instance, too large an amount of loans in a community engaged in one major activity only would indicate a weak investment.

Breakdown of Loans by Interest Rates Is Necessary

Breakdown of loans by interest rates is also necessary, for amount of loans in each interest category reveals gross income and trends of interest rates. This should be maintained on at least a semiannual basis for comparative purposes. A breakdown on the basis of dollar amount by types—FHA, conventional, farm, VA, industrial, and commercial—must be maintained on a daily basis. Governmental regulations covering FHA and VA loans must be strictly complied with. Certain Federal and state banking laws and regulations covering other types of lenders also specify that total mortgage loans must not exceed a certain percentage of assets, reserves, or savings and time deposits. This ratio must be under careful supervision.

Another important phase of portfolio-analysis procedures concerns the recording of loan applications received each week, and the number of applications withdrawn together with reasons for withdrawal. Analysis of these figures quickly reveals loan activity as well as information covering reasons why certain loans are not made. There are many other phases of portfolio analysis procedures used that are dependent upon the lender's scope and type of mortgage lending operations.

It has frequently been said that the mortgage lending industry as a whole has less informative statistical information than any other large industry. This is undoubtedly true. In the past few years considerable progress has been made in correcting this condition. The HHFA is now engaged in enlarging statistical records and studies. The Loan Guaranty Division of the VA has excellent statistical records. The Federal Reserve System is expanding its very outstanding and informative mortgage finance statistical records and studies. However, lenders themselves must also improve their own individual statistical records and research activity. Without this adequate statistical information, proper portfolio analysis cannot be maintained.

Loans Sold to Others

Scope of Activity

Surprisingly large amounts of mortgage loans are made for investors by correspondents and agents located in various cities throughout the nation (see Chapter 2). Some large life insurance companies maintain their own mortgage loan offices in key cities, and, in addition to this, such companies also have correspondents and agents who develop mortgage business for them.

Most life insurance companies, however, which do not maintain branch offices but do invest in mortgage loans throughout the country appoint correspondents who acquire mortgage business for them. Some individuals and mortgage companies acting as correspondents or agents represent several large investors, and most of these investors are located in Eastern or Middle Western states. Insurance companies in the Western states which invest in mortgages also appoint correspondents or agents in the areas where they invest in mortgage loans. During the past several years a great many commercial banks in the West and Southwest which have sold loans from their own portfolios to other investors do not act in the capacity of correspondents but only as agents.

Mutual savings banks in New York and New England obtain mortgage loans in many parts of the country through correspondents, agents, mortgage companies, and commercial banks. A tremendous amount of mortgage loan business is developed by mortgage companies for Eastern investors throughout most of the United States and particularly in the South and West.

Fees for Services Rendered

It is the general practice of a correspondent or loan agent to handle collections and to perform all other required services. The usual fee on home loans is ½ of 1 per cent of the principal balance of the loan and continues during the life of the loan. On other types of loans this fee is for a lesser amount, and on large commercial and industrial projects is based on the dollar amount of each loan. Some investors pay a "finder's fee" for loans, but in such cases the servicing is nearly always done by the purchaser of the loan.

The Contract between the Investor and Loan Correspondent

In case the collection of loan payments and the servicing of the loans is to be done by the seller, a contract is always required. There are many forms of contracts some of which are very complex while others are quite simple. However, all such contracts should contain provisions which adequately protect both the investor and the correspondent.

A good contract between the investor and the correspondent establishes the basic rules which will govern this relationship. It also lays the groundwork for settlement of misunderstandings and gives continuity to actions in case of personnel changes. Some well-established mortgage companies operate without contracts, but this method of operation does not seem reasonable, as disagreements might develop at the time of personnel changes or if market conditions cause changes in investment policies. The typical contract does not have a termination date but is a continuing agreement, and a change of contract should not be expected because of a change in business conditions.

Basic Items Contained in Contracts between Investors and Loan Correspondents

An examination of most contracts will generally reveal that, although they may differ in some respects, they all agree on certain basic items as follows:

1. The preamble outlines the parties to the contract and defines the terms used, offering, types of loans, and geographical areas. General terms cover the entire operation and need not be altered for specific cases or changed to fit varying market conditions.

2. The correspondent covenants that it will submit no loans except those which are insured as first liens with satisfactory title insurance; that properties securing the loans are not suffering from waste or abuse; that all loan funds are advanced to the borrower; that no usurious charges have been made; that the FHA insurance or the VA guaranty is valid; that all fees and charges have been paid.

3. After closing the loan, the correspondent must make a diligent effort to collect payments, follow up delinquencies and remit as prescribed, check tax delinquencies, check adequacy of insurance, supervise repair of fire loss, assist in time of foreclosure, maintain a fidelity bond, make reports and inspections as required.

Other items that are likely to be included are as follows:

Investors usually require periodic reinspection of properties, together with a report of the condition of each property, or they may call for specific inspections usually no oftener than once a year. Correspondents are usually required to have separate bank accounts for principals' collections, for escrow accounts, and for different types of loans. An annual financial statement of the servicer and an audit by the investor at his expense are customary and to be expected.

Differences in Contracts

The three items in the contract which usually differ among companies are:

1. Exclusiveness for either party as to other correspondents and other investors
2. Reinspection of guaranty
3. Termination

As to exclusiveness, the correspondent may or may not be permitted other outlets for his loans, and the investor may or may not be permitted other correspondents in a given area. One thing that should be very clear is the area the correspondent will serve. A complete description even to a specific street may be necessary. An area changeable at will by one party only is a poor agreement.

Correspondent Outlets

Usually a correspondent has one major outlet, but additional outlets are often encouraged, provided they do not conflict or at least some agreement is reached about sharing business acceptable to two or more investors. It would seem fair that if an investor grants an exclusive area, it should be given some consideration about the amount of business to be developed in the area. It should have first refusal on the kind of loans it desires. Also the correspondent should be given an area that has enough of the type of loan sought to offer a profitable business to the correspondent.

Guaranty to Repurchase

Some contracts provide for a guaranty to repurchase without cause by correspondent, generally within a specified time, usually three months to one year. Guaranties covering amount of business to be developed are not common, and it is questionable how good the guaranty would be in times of stress if any considerable volume of business were in process. Likewise, repurchase without cause is no longer common. A contract must be based on mutual trust between the parties.

Termination of a Contract

Termination of a contract presents a hurdle of some magnitude in negotiations. Termination for such causes as fraud or bankruptcy is to be expected. An investor ought not to terminate a contract without cause except for some very compelling reason. The investor will want to keep liquid and may reserve the right to sell investments if necessary. At the same time it must know who its servicers will be, and a servicing contract usually cannot be assigned without the approval of the investor. However, a correspondent has a considerable investment in the loans he is handling and managing. Figures available show that present finder's fees do not cover acquisition cost. In general the correspondent must be assured of some reasonable and fair income to justify the expense of operating his business.

In negotiations covering a possible contract the value of the account is affected by the cancellation clause as well as many other items. If two companies are represented by one correspondent, the human reaction would be to favor the investor with the firmest contract and promising the best over-all compensation. An investor or correspondent should not enter into a contract without some cancellation protection. Any agreement that does not offer benefits and profit to both parties will lead to lack of interest and eventual termination or correction.

A contract should be fair to both parties and provide a sound working arrangement through good times and bad. Changing business conditions will emphasize the faults of an unfair agreement.

Fees for Services

There is a great lack of uniformity in fees paid for loan administration and servicing. They often vary with the size of the loan and the rate of interest. Fees on extensions or renewals usually differ from those paid for originations. In all cases, these fees must be earned, and the fee gives no right, title, or interest in the loan. In some instances management fees for foreclosed properties are part of the fee schedule of the contract.

A plain contract is often better than a long contract with many words. A short contract with items described in general is open to different interpretations. The contract should be so worded as to protect all interested parties. If properly written and observed, it gains in value each year, and is important and profitable to both the investor and correspondent.

Duties and Responsibilities of the Mortgage Banker Loan Correspondent

The duties and responsibilities of the loan correspondent or agent will naturally vary depending upon the size of the organization and the extent to which it is required to perform the various functions incidental to servicing mortgage loans. These operations are an exacting and accurate business where mistakes and errors must be kept to an absolute minimum. If the work is to be done quickly and efficiently, it is necessary to have conscientious and accurate employees, a system with proper controls and practices, and good equipment and supplies.

Personnel

The personnel of the department should of course be permanent and efficient. The work must be done thoroughly, accurately, and on schedule; at the same time it should be done at the least possible cost. Unless efficient operations are maintained, the loan correspondent might discover that such an operation is unprofitable when the volume of new-loan originations decreases and collection problems begin to arise. At such a time the investor would expect the loan correspondent to perform additional collection duties which the agent has agreed to perform.

These obligations are usually contractual and are part of the formal contract. They are expensive duties to perform, but the investor requires their strict performance. The cost of performing these duties will undoubtedly increase both because of a normal rise in cost and because of the extra duties required in the handling of collection and default problems.

Handling Defaults

The additional work of handling defaults must usually be done at a time when the mortgage company's income is reduced as a result of the decrease in new business. Therefore, the contract should always be carefully considered, the duties and obligations fully understood and clearly outlined. It should protect and bind both parties to their rights and duties. Both the investor and the loan correspondent or agent should insist upon an equitable and a practical contract.

Basic Obligations of the Mortgage Banker Loan Correspondent

The department of a correspondent which performs these services has the following basic servicing obligations to maintain after the loan has been closed:

1. To the investor:
   a. Prompt and efficient collections and remittances
   b. Safe handling of all funds received
   c. Accurate accounting and records
   d. Prompt attention to insurance, taxes, and miscellaneous items
   e. Efficient handling of defaults
2. To the borrower:
   a. Maintain adequate facilities for payments
   b. Furnish necessary information concerning the loan
   c. Be prepared to counsel and assist with the many problems confronting the borrower

Functions of the Loan Administration Department

These various functions may be separated or combined, depending on the size of the business and local mortgage lending customs. A small department may combine the various functions under one manager, or a larger organization may divide the duties into several departments, making collections, insurance, closing, or taxes as separate departments, leaving the collection department with only the duties of accounting, remitting, and dealing with the mortgagor. In any case the officer in charge of loan administration must know about each detail of his department.

Some companies may assign only detail duties to the department personnel, leaving all contact work with both the investor and the mortgagor to principal officers. Some give the servicing manager responsibility for all phases of servicing.

The Officer in Charge of the Loan Administration Program

The qualifications of this officer will naturally depend upon the company organization and the extent to which the manager is required to perform the obligations and duties to which attention has already been directed. However, any such officer, if he is to operate an efficient department, must understand all the functions and duties involved in the entire department. It is not absolutely necessary for him to be an accountant, but he should know and understand the general principles of accounting.

By necessity the manager must deal with investors, officer personnel, and mortgagors. Therefore, it is most important that he understand human nature and be diplomatic in dealing with the many kinds of persons with whom he must have contact.

The manager must be meticulously accurate in all details, and either he or his accountants should understand the basic principles of insurance, taxes, titles, settlements, government housing regulations, and the basic legal rights of both the borrower and the investor.

An ideal manager is one who knows his department thoroughly, who can train his personnel and mold them into a smooth running team, who has the executive ability to delegate the work of the department, and who can obtain cooperation among his employees and maintain harmonious relationship with his clients.

The manager should strive to improve his department and work out the best system available. However, he should make every endeavor to standardize the operations of his department in accordance with the generally accepted methods and procedures. This will result in better servicing.

The executive officers of a mortgage banking firm will learn much by spending enough time in the loan administration department to understand its problems. It is undoubtedly true that these operations are now being recognized throughout the entire mortgage lending industry as one of the most important phases of mortgage lending.

SUMMARY

The objective of the loan administration program is to anticipate and to eliminate the risks of loss and the factors which contribute to the risks of loss. The safety of the investment must be protected at all times.

Regardless of the care with which mortgage loans are made, defaults in the covenants of the deed of trust or mortgage will be encountered, and it is necessary, therefore, to arrange for efficient supervision and handling of all loans in the portfolio.

It is the duty of these officers to maintain close contact with all loans in the portfolio and to see that adequate accounting and bookkeeping procedures and operations are maintained, that the hazard insurance and tax divisions operate efficiently, and that all borrower relations are handled on a personalized basis.

Continuous portfolio analysis is necessary in order to study the condition of the portfolio and detect any weaknesses which might be developing in the safety of the investment. Statistical records which clearly indicate any changes in the portfolio structure must also be maintained. Statistical records show loans in the portfolio by types, by dollar amounts, by geographical areas, and by delinquencies, as well as by interest rates.

An old saying in the mortgage lending industry is that "a well-made loan is half collected." If all the necessary information is assembled at the time the loan application is processed, it will be of great assistance in the future servicing of the loan.

It is important that this officer understand FHA and VA regulations which pertain to servicing of loans; otherwise the insurance on FHA loans and the guaranty of VA loans could be placed in jeopardy. Government legislation must also be closely studied and analyzed, since legislation which directly affects loan-servicing operations is frequently passed.

The loan administration program consists of "all the functions involved in the administration of a loan from the time the funds are disbursed until the obligation is satisfied in some way."

The setup of the organization which administers the mortgage portfolio varies according to the size and type of the portfolio, but the functions performed are the same. These functions pertain to disbursement of funds, the maintenance of records, collection of payments, and contacts with borrowers.

Working records used in those operations should be located where they are readily accessible. These records include the ledger cards, the loan folders, the insurance tickler file, the tax-payment cards, index cards, follow-up cards on delinquent loans, and other records which may be required.

The handling of loans sold to others is a phase of mortgage lending which has developed very rapidly during the past twenty years. A large volume of mortgage loans is developed by correspondents and agents located in various cities throughout the nation.

Investors who handle a portion of their mortgage lending through correspondents or agents arrange for an agreement between the interested parties which is termed a servicing contract. Such contracts cover the development of new business for the investor and in most cases cover the methods of servicing the loan by the correspondent after the loan is closed. A contract should protect and bind both parties to their rights and duties, and both the investor and the loan correspondent should make certain that the contract is equitable and practical.

In the actual servicing of loans the correspondent is obligated (1) to make prompt and efficient collections, (2) to arrange for the safe handling of all funds received, (3) to maintain accurate accounting and records, (4) to give prompt attention to insurance, taxes, and miscellaneous items, (5) to be efficient in handling defaults.

The correspondent also has the following obligations to the borrower: (1) to maintain adequate facilities for payments, (2) to furnish necessary information concerning the loan, (3) to be prepared to counsel and assist with the many problems confronting the borrower.

The manager of this division must be meticulously accurate in all details, and the accountants should understand the basic principles of the operations in which they are engaged. Loan administration operations should be adequately supervised by the executive management of the company.

QUESTIONS

1. Explain the major objective of loan portfolio administration.
2. Explain why the officer charged with the administration of the mortgage loan portfolio should have direct contact with the policy-making authorities of the lender.
3. The administration of a mortgage loan portfolio is usually divided into two main groups of operation. Name these two groups.
4. Name the two phases of mortgage loan servicing.
5. Name the primary objective of the loan administration program.
6. Explain why loan administration personnel should understand the working requirements and duties of the entire mortgage loan department.
7. Define loan administration.
8. List ten items of information needed by this department to enable it to obtain a clear picture of the condition of the mortgage loan portfolio.
9. Give reasons why lenders usually place a limit on the maximum amount of insurance they will accept from a particular company on any one risk.
10. Explain why favorable customer relations depend to a large extent on the quality of service rendered by loan-servicing personnel.
11. Describe two of the major responsibilities of the escrow division.
12. Name five of the operations and procedures which delinquent loan collection and servicing embraces.
13. Explain why it is important at the time the note and mortgage are signed by the borrower that the lending officer explain the methods of making loan payments.
14. Describe one of the major activities of the accounting and book-keeping divisions.
15. List the ratios studied in rating the financial responsibility of an insurance company which handles hazard insurance.

16. Explain how a regular increase in the number and dollar amount of delinquent loans could indicate a downward trend in economic conditions.

17. Explain why proper delegation of authority is essential to the success of the mortgage loan department.

18. State the reasons why buildings are subject to many insurable hazards.

19. Explain in what way nonpayment of taxes constitutes a breach of the mortgage covenants.

20. Explain how the trend toward monthly payments which include taxes, insurance, and other escrow payments increased the number of operations involved in the handling of mortgage loans.

21. Name four divisions of the loan administration department in which specialists are required.

22. Describe the advantage of a ledger card which provides a master record for each mortgage loan.

23. Explain the reasons why insurance index cards are generally filed chronologically according to the expiration date of the policies.

24. Explain why the amount of insurance necessary when a loan is made is subject to revision during the term of the loan.

25. Give the reasons why a mortgage lender usually requires hazard insurance protection in an amount at least equal to the mortgage indebtedness.

26. In your opinion is payment by mail the fastest and most efficient method of handling mortgage payments? Explain.

27. Explain how the size of the mortgage operations of a lender usually determines the need for departmentalizing mortgage payment procedures.

28. Briefly describe the activity of a correspondent in mortgage lending.

29. Name the basic items which are included in most contracts between an investor and loan correspondent or agent.

30. Describe the importance of accounting in these operations.

31. Outline what the preamble to a contract usually contains.

32. Name three basic items in a contract with respect to which lenders make use of varying policies.

33. Explain the correspondent's obligations to the investor.

34. Explain the correspondent's obligations to the borrower.

35. Give reasons why the investor requires periodic inspections of properties.

ASSIGNMENTS

1. Study and describe the organization of the loan administration operations in a company of your selection, including all forms used.

2. Describe a procedure for analyzing the mortgage loan portfolio of that company.

3. Obtain a simple form of an investor–loan correspondent contract from a mortgage lender, and explain the major provisions in such a contract.

BIBLIOGRAPHY AND SUGGESTED READING

Bryant, Willis R., "A Pattern for Planning Good Loan Servicing Today and Tomorrow," *The Mortgage Banker,* Mortgage Bankers Association of America, Chicago, January, 1955.

De Huszar, William I., *Mortgage Servicing,* McGraw-Hill Book Company, Inc., New York, 1954.

Home Mortgage Lending, chap. 11, American Institute of Banking, Section American Bankers Association, New York, 1953.

Pease, Robert H., and Homer V. Cherrington (eds.), *Mortgage Banking,* chaps. 15, 16, McGraw-Hill Book Company, Inc., New York, 1953.

12

The Delinquent-Loan Collection and Servicing Program

PURPOSES

1. To define a delinquent loan and explain the various ways in which default may occur
2. To outline reasons for delinquencies
3. To explain the objectives of the delinquent-loan collection and servicing program
4. To explain the functions of delinquent-loan collection and servicing
5. To discuss the methods of handling delinquencies
6. To describe briefly the functions of real estate management

Definition of a Delinquent Loan

As a preliminary to discussion of delinquent-loan collection and servicing operations, it is necessary to define a delinquent loan and place the various types of delinquencies in proper sequence. The mortgage note or deed of trust note contains a statement of the terms for payment of the loan, including the principal amount, due date, rate of interest, and installment-payment due date. It specifies whether the interest and installment payments are to be made monthly, quarterly, semiannually, or at other intervals. Practically all types of loans, except farm loans, are now written on a monthly basis.

The deed of trust or mortgage outlines certain requirements of the borrower during the life of the loan and also gives certain rights to the lender in case of default by the borrower. Deeds of trust and mortgages have been explained in Chapter 7.

A delinquent loan is one on which any payment specified in the note or deed of trust or mortgage is not made when due. A loan also becomes delinquent through failure by the borrower to comply with any other covenant of the deed of trust or mortgage.

A delinquency comprises any one or all of the following:

1. Nonpayment of interest.
2. Nonpayment of the installment.
3. Nonpayment on nonaccrual loans. (Covers loans on which interest is not being accrued because of failure of the borrower to make interest payments for one or more of innumerable causes and reasons.)
4. Loans under foreclosure on which reinstatement programs are being enforced, or loans on which foreclosure action will be completed.
5. Unpaid taxes (after final due date). This is a default that is mentioned in one of the covenants of the deed of trust or mortgage.
6. Unpaid loan charges and renewal of loan charges, which include one or all of the following: title insurance charges, recording fee, reconveyance fee, notary fee, trustee's fee, charge for drawing papers, appraisal fees, and miscellaneous charges.
7. Unpaid renewal insurance premium.
8. Unpaid miscellaneous charges of any kind advanced by the lender.
9. Unpaid assessments, encumbrances, and liens and other such charges.
10. Loans criticized by bank examiners, usually classified as "critical," "problem," "nonconforming," or "possible loan loss."
11. Loans criticized by other supervisory and regulatory bodies.

The delinquent-loan collection and servicing division must be so organized that adequate control and follow-up of all such delinquencies is maintained at all times. The control records which must be maintained, and the procedures which must be followed in order to operate delinquent-loan servicing in a successful manner, will be described.

Functions of Delinquent-loan Collection and Servicing

The main functions of delinquent-loan collection and servicing are:

1. To restore all possible delinquent loans to good standing; that is, to bring them up to date in all respects. This work is called "rehabilitating," or "retrieving." It also means keeping the number of loans transferred to Other Real Estate at a minimum; that is, loans on which foreclosure has been completed and title to the property has been transferred to the name of the lender. Anything that can be done to make such transfers unnecessary will reduce loss exposure.

2. To prevent loans in good standing and delinquent loans from dropping down into the established delinquent-loan classifications. Loans thirty days delinquent are usually termed "normal delinquent loans," while "established delinquent loans" are those sixty days or more delinquent. Most loans which become fifteen to thirty days past due are promptly restored to good standing by the borrower on receipt of the first delinquency

notice. If the borrower fails to respond to the first delinquency notice, a more intensive follow-up for payment is initiated.

Such an intensive follow-up usually starts with a telephone call to the home of the borrower, or to the borrower at his place of business if there is no answer to the telephone calls to his home. If as a result of the telephone call the payment has been promised, the borrower's file is held on the collection officer's desk until payment has been received. In cases where the telephone contact cannot be made, a letter is written, and a telegram is sent to the borrower in case the letter is not answered. If these contacts are not successful, a personal call to the home of the borrower or to his place of business is made by a field representative.

3. To see that all unpaid taxes, loan advances, and miscellaneous unpaid charges are paid.

4. To have any breach in any of the covenants of the deed of trust or mortgage corrected.

5. To have all nonreducing loans put on a monthly reduction basis.

6. To maintain adequate information on any loan subject to criticism or comment by examiners.

7. To index all loans on which the principal balance is more than the permitted percentage of the appraisal value.

8. To keep a ready reference breakdown on loans by types of properties and by dollar amount.

9. To keep accurate records of changes in delinquency classifications so that increases or decreases in delinquencies can be analyzed. In order to obtain the net change the record should include loans that have been transferred to Other Real Estate during a given period.

Other functions of delinquent-loan collection and servicing include the following:

1. Maintenance of a weekly or monthly runoff record of all loans in the portfolio. This function in some companies is handled by the statistical division of the loan administration department.

2. Analysis of all new legislation which might affect delinquent loans in the portfolio. For example, the Soldiers' and Sailors' Civil Relief Act of 1940, as amended, the Servicemen's Readjustment Act of 1944, as amended, FHA and VA regulations, the state banking code, national bank legislation, or other legislation governing all mortgage lenders.

3. Maintenance of semiannual detailed reports covering interest accrual figures on a comparative basis.

4. Maintenance of detailed expense, profit, and loss reports covering all loans transferred to Other Real Estate.

5. Inspection of properties on which payments are delinquent.

6. Recommending all necessary foreclosure action.

7. Recommending all foreclosure cancellations.

8. Recommending all advertising for trustee's sale on loans under foreclosure where all efforts to reinstate the loan have failed.

9. Analysis of the operating costs and expenses of the delinquent-loan collection and servicing operations.

10. Maintenance of continuous follow-up on delinquent taxes.

11. Follow-up of all delinquent loans where the lender is acting as agent or correspondent. These comprise loans sold to others on which the lender handles the loan for a fee.

12. To maintain at all times friendly and courteous relations with the borrowers.

Some delinquent-loan collection and servicing divisions are subdivided, with one servicing officer and his staff handling FHA loans only, another VA loans, while another will handle the conventional loans. In such an operation all delinquent-loan collection and servicing procedures are under the supervision of the officer in charge of the entire delinquent-loan division. Some lenders place servicing officers in charge of delinquent loans, regardless of type, by alphabetical groupings of the loans, for example, A to L and M to Z.

Regardless of the form of operation, the objectives of delinquent-loan collection and servicing are to reduce delinquencies and the risks of loss and to modify the factors which contribute to the risks of loss.

Maintenance of a foolproof tickler system to ensure continuous follow-up of delinquencies is essential for effective delinquent-loan collection and servicing operations. In addition, lenders with large loan portfolios usually use a control or follow-up card for each loan which has become delinquent, or on which there is some other default. A digest of the loan and case history is recorded on each card. Delinquent notices sent to the VA or FHA, together with their acknowledgment receipt, can also be recorded on the card. These control cards are segregated according to type of loan. Some lenders use cards of different colors for each type, a practice that has proved to be of great assistance in follow-up work.

At the time the delinquent-loan ledger cards or other forms of ledger records are withdrawn for attention, it is the responsibility of the officer in charge of these operations to review such records in detail. He must decide the loans on which statements should be sent, letters written, telephone calls made, and he must decide whether the borrower should be invited into the office to discuss the delinquency or whether a field contact should be made at the home of the borrower. An able officer has the ability to analyze each case quickly and decide what course of action should be taken. This also applies to all delinquent loans in the categories previously mentioned which come before him for review.

One of the most important responsibilities of the officer in charge of delinquent-loan collection and servicing operations is the handling of loans on which foreclosure is to be completed. There is always the possibility that the lender will experience a loss of some amount, especially a loss of some of the accrued interest and carrying charges. Proper handling of these cases will usually result in many of the loans being reinstated without loss.

There is great diversity in laws governing the time within which a mortgagor may redeem his property after foreclosure. In some states the redemption period is only six weeks; in others it ranges from six weeks to two years. Efforts are being made to have the period made uniform in all the states.

Foreclosure action is seldom taken unless all other efforts to have the delinquent loan reinstated have failed. Some borrowers ignore requests for a reinstatement program, and the starting of foreclosure action causes the borrower to contact the lender and endeavor to work out some payment program which will bring the loan up to date. Most of these cases occur during a period of recession or depression. Foreclosure action is also started when a borrower has abandoned the property or other conditions develop which warrant foreclosure action by the lender in order to protect its interests.

Personalized Nature of the Collection System

It is the general practice of lenders to send a statement of payment past due when the first delinquency occurs. This statement gives in detail the amount of interest, installment, and loan trust funds past due. Most borrowers remit the amount delinquent on receipt of this notice. If any borrower fails to respond to the first delinquency notice, additional action by the lender becomes necessary.

The establishment of the collection system on a personalized basis has undoubtedly improved delinquent-loan collection and servicing operations and customer relations and has reduced delinquencies. Form letters have been eliminated by most lenders. Such letters have little value in remedying a chronic delinquency, and when they are used indiscriminately can cause needless offense. Instead of form letters, an effort should be made to treat each case on its own merits and fit the approach to the circumstances surrounding the individual situation. Where the borrower fails to respond to the delinquency notices or to a letter or telephone call, it is sometimes possible to arrange an interview at the lender's office. If this cannot be arranged, a personal call by a representative of the lender should be made at the home of the borrower. Improved mechanical operations by use of electronic equipment covering mailing of statements and delinquency notices permit collection officers more time to devote to decision-making problems of each delinquency.

Some departments may be small enough to enable the officer to follow all payments and immediately note every failure to pay according to schedule. In larger departments there must be complete coordination between the cashier and accounting division and the delinquent-loan collection and servicing division. On certain specified dates the accounting division should report to the delinquent-loan collection and servicing division all loans on which payments have not been made according to schedule. A better method appears to be the procedure in which the personnel check the ledger cards or other loan payment records and withdraw all delinquent loan records for follow-up and maintenance of the necessary records. In many companies the delinquent-loan collection and servicing division also makes up the first delinquency statement notice to the borrower. In addition, by having such a control in this division, an efficient tickler system can be maintained for intensive follow-up of each delinquent loan.

Credit File

In preparation for an interview with a borrower who calls at the office of the lender, the interviewing officer should have both the ledger card or other loan payment record and the loan folder before him. He should study all pertinent facts and the contents of the loan folder prior to the interview.

In the well-organized mortgage loan department such information should be in one place, which by some lenders is called the "credit file." Some lenders maintain the credit file separate from the loan folder itself, while others assemble the information in the loan folder. The latter procedure seems to be more efficient, as there is less danger of loss of information. The file should be maintained in complete detail for each loan and particularly for each delinquent loan. It should contain a summary sheet which lists data about the loan. In addition, the folder and ledger card or other loan payments record should show such details as the original loan agreement and any changes made subsequently, the interest and principal payment record by months, the yearly tax record, annual assessments, the original appraisal and any reappraisals, appraiser's comments on the property and neighborhood, the original loan setup, and the insurance coverage. Other contents of the folder should include:

1. Loan history sheets, which give in chronological order synopses of all interviews
2. Field reports covering personal contacts
3. Credit information about the borrower
4. Original copies of the appraisals
5. Copies of bank examiners' comments or criticisms, if any
6. Copies of criticisms of other supervisory or regulatory bodies
7. All other pertinent details

This file is the heart of the delinquent-loan collection and servicing program and must be kept up to date. If there is no recent property inspection report on file at time of delinquency, it is advisable to have an inspection of the property made immediately on delinquent loans on which a workout appears doubtful or the period of delinquency might be prolonged and also in case the indications are that the interview might be of a serious nature. Only after the interviewing officer has familiarized himself with the background of the loan is he in a position to conduct a satisfactory interview with the borrower.

Many large mortgage lenders supplement the loan folder and ledger-card record with individual loan cards on which all pertinent information concerning the loan is recorded in condensed form. These cards can be used for follow-up procedures; they can also be used to keep the control records covering delinquency notification in accordance with regulations of the FHA and the VA.

Each loan folder, ledger card, or other loan payment record and loan follow-up card should at all times be kept on a current basis so that, if the necessity arises, any officer other than the servicing officer can efficiently analyze any loan. Unless all information about a particular loan is a matter of record, no one except the servicing officer or someone in the delinquent-loan collection and servicing division to whom the loan has been assigned can handle the case properly without unnecessary delay in assembling data and in attemping to reconstruct the history of the loan. Therefore, the same complete and detailed records and files must be maintained whether one man, twenty, or more are servicing a loan portfolio.

Collection Interview

The approach which the servicing officer handling delinquent loans takes at the time of the interview depends entirely on the circumstances of each case. The handling of an interview covering the first default in payment is different from that covering a chronic delinquency or habitually late payer, and the handling of an interview dealing with a delinquency that occurs during the first six months of the loan is somewhat different from the handling of an interview covering a first default after an excellent five-year-payment program.

The basic reason for any delinquency can be very quickly ascertained by an able interviewer. He can easily get an accurate picture of the entire case and make a decision as to the remedy for reinstatement of the loan. Most borrowers are honest. When they default, it is generally because of mismanagement of their financial affairs or because of circumstances beyond their control, such as sickness or loss of employment. What is just another default to a servicing officer may be a tragedy to the borrower. A patient, friendly attitude will often help to cure the default. When this happens, the lender has merited the good will of the borrower, while a different treatment might have made the borrower become antagonistic and affected the good will and customer relations of the lender.

Servicing interviews are more successful when they are carried out in comparative privacy. It is not to be expected that people will care to talk freely about their personal affairs within hearing of other employees or customers. In a private interview the borrower is usually encouraged to talk frankly and should be made to feel that the lender wants to help him.

First Default in Payment

The first default in a payment of any nature is a danger signal and should be given immediate attention. The attitude and action taken by the servicing officer may help to correct the default and keep it from happening again. The length of time the loan has been on the books will make a difference in the manner of approach, but in any case the cause of default should be definitely determined, and a decision covering the action to be taken should be reached.

In large mortgage lending operations the procedure in handling the first default in payment is somewhat different from that outlined in the preceding paragraphs, as in the normal activity of the department hundreds of loans will become thirty days past due in a given month and will be restored to good standing upon receipt by the borrower of a statement of the delinquency or a letter or telephone call. The financial outlay that would be required to follow up such delinquent payments for a large operation would be unnecessarily burdensome. The contact regarding the first default in payment is usually made by sending a notice of the delinquency. Follow-up by letter, telephone, or visit to the home of the borrower is usually made after the loan has become delinquent one payment, and in some cases two payments. In all such cases the reason for the delinquency is ascertained, a complete history of the case is written, and a program for reinstatement is arranged either by full payment of the amount that is past due or by a program for additional payment each month until the loan is brought completely up to date. The underlying cause of the delinquency and the attitude of the borrower have a major bearing on the manner in which the collection efforts will be continued.

Reasons for Delinquencies

There are some borrowers, few in number, who use every means available to take advantage of any apparent leniency shown toward a delinquency or restoration program. This type of borrower does not make payments on schedule and does not keep promises regarding a payment program for reinstating the particular loan or loans. Reasons for nonpayment on almost any class of loan in such cases are usually the following:

1. Carelessness.
   a. Nonpayment due to oversight.
   b. Nonpayment due to neglect.
2. Improper handling of income.
   a. Income not on a sound budget basis.
   b. Overburdened with large installment payments.
   c. Maintaining an automobile at prohibitive expense based on income.
   d. Too many social obligations.
3. Marital difficulties. During the past few years there has been a large increase in the number of these cases.
4. Improper attitude toward obligations.
   a. Impressions that lender should always be willing to let payment be deferred for any reason whatsoever.
   b. No response to lender's request for cooperation.
   c. Unwillingness to endeavor to reinstate loan.
   d. Diversion of income to other interests.
   e. Resentment or ill will toward lender if not paying in accordance with terms of the note when requested to make proper payments.
   f. No payment ever made unless constantly demanded by the lender.
   g. In many cases foreclosure must be threatened or foreclosure started to get action.
5. Vacations.
   a. During the summer months payments on mortgage loans will show a decrease, and many loans will become delinquent because funds equal to two or three payments will be used by the borrower for vacation expenses. In some cases it will take the borrower several months to restore the loan in question to good standing.
6. Taxes.
   a. There is a marked decrease in loan payments during the time that the tax-installment payments on conventional loans are due. This is particularly true on conventional loans which are delinquent, including nonaccrual and loans under foreclosure, as well as on problem and nonconforming loans. Conventional loans in the process of being restored to good standing will be temporarily slowed up, and a careful and rigid follow-up is imperative in order to avoid having such loans fall into the hopeless class.
7. Dishonesty.
   a. Willful violation of trust.
   b. Falsification of income and expense statements covering income property.
   c. Falsification of facts covering any given situation.

The foregoing could be classified as "unwarranted delinquencies."

On the other hand, there are basic and fundamentally sound reasons why a certain percentage of even good loans will become delinquent or give trouble for either short or long periods.

Delinquencies and loss exposure occur most frequently during depressions or recessions, but loan troubles emerge at other times too. Inability or unwillingness to pay has been caused by one or more of the following conditions:

1. Unemployment of short or long duration due to strikes, depressions, economic conditions. Borrower probably on relief and receiving barely enough to eke out an existence.

2. Temporary illness, serious illness, or permanent disability. Heavy expense incurred during hospitalization may cause a loan to become badly delinquent.

3. Accidents. Same conditions prevail as in serious-illness cases or permanent disability.

4. Probate of estate. Because such cases require the services of an attorney and the legal procedures in many cases take several months, payments are not made. Where possible, the attorney will arrange to have such loans properly serviced. In other cases, the property will be sold and the loan paid off.

5. Financial distress of various kinds. Loss of money in a business venture, income or salary insufficient to service the loan properly, heavy obligations caused by divorce proceedings, death in family.

6. Borrower endeavoring to carry too many properties. Borrower property-poor, rents insufficient to service the loans properly, poor management (inability of borrower to operate properly).

7. Bankruptcies and suits of various kinds. Suits to quiet title, suits to clear title, composition agreements, court orders, bankruptcy.

8. On income properties. Vacancies caused by changes in conditions in certain districts, vacancies caused by poor condition of the building, heavy upkeep, and obsolete equipment.

9. On farm properties. Weather hazards (acts of God), crop failures, lack of finances, market conditions, inability of owner to operate properly.

The foregoing could be classified as "warranted delinquencies."

The failure to restore any given loan to good standing and the eventual foreclosure and transfer of the property to Other Real Estate must be due entirely to insurmountable conditions which it is not humanly possible for the borrower and the lender to adjust. It is the primary duty of the loan-servicing officer who supervises delinquent-loan collection and servicing operations to see that the number of such loans is kept at an absolute minimum at all times.

From an efficiency standpoint the most successful method of keeping the quality of the mortgage loan portfolio at the highest level is to maintain a constant supervision of the good loans to see that the borrower adheres to the terms of payment as specified in the note. As nearly all loans are now written on an amortized basis, the first sign of weakness in the loan, even though the interest is kept up to date, is:

1. Installment payments on conventional loans are not made.

2. Advance charges incurred when the loan was made or renewed remain unpaid.

3. Current taxes are allowed to become delinquent.

4. Regular payments start slowing up.

In delinquent-loan collection and servicing a control and follow-up of each delinquency must be established with the handling of each delinquency based on the circumstances covering each case. In many cases only a regular statement is necessary, while in others a personal letter, telephone call, visit at the home of the borrower, or office interview might be required. Failure of the borrower to cooperate in a reinstatement program might cause the lender to start foreclosure proceedings in order to force the borrower to take action to clear up the loan delinquency. The supervision and follow-up of a loan at the first indication of weakness will save many loans from becoming seriously delinquent.

The many reasons listed covering loan delinquencies clearly indicate the necessity for having able servicing officers who are students of human nature, fair in dealing with each borrower, diplomatic and understanding, and able to win the borrower's confidence, and who clearly analyze the history and merits of each case. The pay-up-or-else attitude is out—for good. A new public relations concept has taken its place. To the credit of the mortgage lending industry, the concept which calls for close borrower and lender relationship has been adopted by the lenders themselves.

Safety of Principal

The policy of mortgage lenders in converting capital funds and deposits into earning assets or in determining the proportion of these assets to be invested in mortgage loans is established by the board of directors or by a committee of the board. Generally no fixed program for the investment of funds is followed; instead the officials endeavor to analyze the needs of their company and the constantly changing character of the investment market so that the return will be as high as is consistent with the safety that must always be given first consideration.

To meet daily requirements banks keep cash in their vaults and maintain deposits with other banks and the Federal Reserve bank subject to withdrawal on demand. These are called "primary reserve funds." Life insurance companies, savings and loan associations, mortgage companies, etc., also keep these primary reserves.

In addition to the primary reserve institutional lenders invest a certain portion of their funds in short-term obligations, including United States government, state, and city bonds that have a high degree of liquidity but bring in relatively little income. United States Treasury bills or notes are also examples of this type of investment. These funds constitute the secondary reserve which is available for any unusual demand for cash or for seasonal requirements. The deposits of savings banks are, in the main, time deposits. There is less need for liquid reserves in these banks than in commercial banks. In addition to the primary and secondary reserves, the funds of institutional lenders are placed in loans and in various other forms of investment. While mortgages or deeds of trust do not qualify as a part of the reserve, they do constitute an acceptable invesment medium. It is from funds in the loan and investment accounts that the greater part of a mortgage lender's earnings are derived. When a mortgage loan has been made at a stipulated interest rate, the lender cannot increase this rate even though interest rates prevailing in the mortgage market should rise; but amortization payments regularly received on mortgage investments provide a continuous flow of funds that can be invested at whatever rates may happen to prevail at the time such funds become available.

After safety and liquidity have been considered, the deciding factor in the choice of an investment is the net yield or return obtainable.

The final objective of mortgage loan portfolio administration is to secure the performance of the mortgage contract in accordance with its terms. When this objective is realized, the lender is assured a fair return on its investment, the funds which were made available to the borrower are repaid, and the property which was pledged as security is kept in good condition.

It is the duty of the lender to protect the borrower and to assist him in any of his difficulties, and to make all possible adjustments that good judgment permits, but this ends whenever the safety of the principal of the loan is placed in jeopardy. When this condition arises, foreclosure action usually becomes necessary.

It is important to proceed promptly in taking foreclosure action. In the past some lenders, when pressing for loan payments or when starting foreclosure action, have been too concerned with the possibilty of unfavorable public relations. This is quite understandable, as friends and neighbors of the borrower may have knowledge of what is happening. However, it is well to remember that when strong action is called for, it should be taken regardless of any possibility of unfavorable reactions. If the loan has been properly serviced with full consideration and helpfulness extended to the borrower, the lender should have little concern over the possibility of ill will being created in such cases.

The entire operation of the delinquent-loan collection and servicing division should be geared to help maintain safety of principal, as it is loans in the delinquency categories on which nearly all losses are incurred.

Personality of Interviewer

The impression that the mortgage loan interviewing officer makes upon the person whose delinquent loan he must correct will have great influence upon his accomplishments. In almost any personal contact with a delinquent-loan borrower ill will can develop unless the interview is handled properly. This means that any person engaged in loan-servicing work should have a pleasant personality and be able promptly to win the confidence of the borrower. Loan interviewers must have support in all their endeavors. If they are wrong, the department head should correct the situation in a diplomatic manner. Cases of this nature are a rare exception today.

The borrower is bound to react to the attitude of the person to whom he is talking, and it is very important that the interviewer be very sympathetic and give complete attention to the customer. If the borrower does not like the interviewer, he does not like the lender. The officer who takes a superior attitude or tries to impress the borrower with his own ability has little chance of making a satisfactory deal. He should act naturally under all circumstances and take a humane and sympathetic interest in the borrower's problems. The problems of a borrower whose loan is delinquent are very real and very personal. In coming to the lender to discuss his problem he talks to a person, not to a department. He believes it is the officer who controls the answer to his problem, and he rightfully looks to no one else. The borrower knows more about his own problems than the interviewer does, and it is his duty to learn about them.

Personality of the Borrower

One of the most important points in effective delinquent-loan collection and servicing and customer relations is the ability of the interviewer to understand as completely as possible the personality of the borrower. If the borrower becomes disgruntled and dissatisfied, he must be handled very carefully and with great diplomacy. It is very important to know the type of person being contacted regarding a delinquency before too much pressure is used. In some cases people who are disagreeable may be the victims of circumstances which arouse the sympathy of the lender; on the other hand a very pleasant person may be an unreliable borrower.

If a delinquent borrower is steadily employed and has the ability to make payments but disregards delinquency notices and refuses to pay, the strongest approach is usually the best approach. It is very important to learn the borrower's character and reputation early, and action should be taken promptly to correct the delinquency. Many such loans are found in any delinquent-loan portfolio, and no valid reason for the delinquency is obtainable. The follow-up of such loans is an added cost to the delinquent-loan collection and servicing division, and this type of delinquency should be kept at a minimum at all times. If the borrower would like very much to pay up the delinquency but because of conditions beyond his control cannot make any payments for the time being, he deserves the sympathy, advice, and assistance of the lender.

Aids in Delinquent-loan Collection and Servicing

During the past several years mortgage financing has almost doubled in the dollar amount of loans, and this industy has expanded to reach into every city and hamlet in the country. Types of borrowers have increased to include those in every walk of life. The average age of borrowers has lowered rapidly. A large percentage of loans made in the past several years has been made to younger borrowers who never before had purchased homes or incurred obligations for the purchase of homes. The entire activity of mortgage lending has broadened, and as a result there is a new concept of lending which calls for even closer borrower-lender relations than in the past.

This has undoubtedly increased the problems of loan administration officers and at the same time has increased their responsibilities. One of the major aids to delinquent-loan collection and servicing of these new types of loans, which include veteran loans, is an immediate personal contact with the borrower at the time of the first serious delinquency. A diplomatic interview to explain the responsibilities of both the lender and the borrower will aid greatly in having the loan restored to good standing and kept current in the future. The need for sending a notice of delinquency promptly on all delinquent loans is of utmost importance. Also, after notice of delinquency has been mailed, a foolproof system of follow-up should be maintained in order that the checking of payments on all such loans can be maintained.

Delinquent loans should be handled on an individual and personal basis, and the follow-up covering the delinquency should always be based on the merits of each case. No two borrowers are alike, and the reasons for delinquency vary widely. This presents a continuous challenge to servicing officers to handle each delinquency and personality in an able manner.

Sending Default Notices

A notice of delinquency is usually sent ten days after the first default has occurred. In many cases a borrower will become and continue to be a one-payment delinquent and take no steps toward bringing the loan completely up to date, even though statements reporting the delinquency are mailed regularly each month. A record of each statement sent should be made on the ledger card or other loan payment record so that the servicing officer can very quickly tell how many previous notices have been sent without action being taken by the borrower to bring the loan up to date. Depending upon the circumstances surrounding each case, it might be necessary, after one or two notices have been mailed, to send a letter calling attention to the delinquency and asking that the loan be brought completely up to date, or in some cases a telephone call might be advisable, provided the borrower can be reached by telephone.

Delinquency notices are usually not sent on loans more than thirty days delinquent unless it is for comparison purposes at the request of the borrower, or as a reminder in cases where the borrower has promised to maintain a regular-payment porgram but has failed to do so. If the borrower does not pay the thirty-day delinquency and the loan becomes sixty days delinquent, it is necessary at this time, or in many cases much sooner than this, to have the delinquent borrower call at the lender's office to discuss the delinquency or to have a representative of the lender call at the home of the borrower. A personal contact usually will disclose the reason for the delinquency, and in most cases a repayment program can be arranged for reinstatement of the loan. In many of these cases the agreed-upon reinstatement program is not maintained, for delinquent borrowers sometimes make promises covering payments and then fail to keep their promises. A rigid follow-up of these cases must be maintained.

Getting the Borrower into the Office of the Lender

It is often difficult to get the borrower who is delinquent in his loan payments to come into the lender's office for an interview. From the viewpoint of the lender this is the best method of handling serious delinquencies, including loans under foreclosure, but many borrowers who are delinquent in payments are reluctant to call in person to discuss their problems.

By calling at the lender's office the borrower will meet the interviewing officer in person, and the loan file, ledger card, and other pertinent information covering the case are available. Besides, the interviewing officer with a background of years of experience in interviewing the delinquent borrowers is able to suggest the best method for working out a reinstatement program which will be satisfactory to both the lender and the borrower.

The loan file in such an event should be brought completely up to date, and if a reinstatement program is arranged, the lender should make certain by a rigid follow-up to see that the promised payment program is strictly adhered to.

Contacting the Borrower at the Home

The practice of calling on the borrower at home is now generally accepted by most lenders. It has been found that a field representative who has the ability to meet the borrower and win his confidence and obtain all the details concerning the delinquency is invaluable in reducing delinquencies. This procedure has been developed because of the difficulty of getting the delinquent borrower into the office of the lender for an interview. It is usually found that the borrower will be more frank in discussing his problems in his home than in the lender's office. If a reinstatement program is arranged, the representative who contacted the borrower should be charged with the responsibility of seeing that the program is maintained.

Objectives of Interview with the Borrower

When a borrower calls to discuss his loan delinquency, the loan ledger card or other loan payment record and folder are obtained, and a complete report is written covering the discussion. In all personal calls at the home of a borrower or his place of business, the field representative should write a brief digest containing the pertinent facts of the case. The interviewer should review with the borrower all phases of the present situation, study progress or lack of progress, and make helpful suggestions of various kinds. The lender is primarily interested in having the loan reinstated by one means or another, such as:

1. Payment of the entire delinquency
2. A payment program which will provide for current payments plus an additional amount each month which will bring the loan up to date as quickly as possible
3. An authorization to charge account monthly for interest and installment if borrower has bank account and delinquency is not large
4. An assignment of rents if the property is rented and if factors warrant such action

Contact by the lender at the home or office of the borrower should have the same objectives, and a complete report of the interview should be recorded on the field report. Many borrowers readily agree to one or the other of the above-mentioned methods of restoration, but go on further. Reasons for failure to comply with the restoration program are numerous, and statistics reveal that many borrowers will not adhere to the restoration program agreed upon.

There are many cases where a definite restoration program cannot be arranged. A very thorough investigation and rigid follow-up of such cases is imperative. Also, if it is an income property that is involved, the property must be inspected carefully at frequent intervals to see that it is being kept in good condition, and the monthly income and expense records must be analyzed.

Personal contact is one of the most important phases of a satisfactory servicing and rehabilitation program, and it is necessary that maximum possible benefit be obtained from the first contact, so that further calls will not be required unless they are absolutely necessary.

Detailed and complete reports of the interview must be written, also a record must be kept of action taken by the borrower after a program of payment has been made. This record, including a concise credit report of the borrower, proves of inestimable value to the state and national examiners, other supervisory authorities, and executive management.

Bank examiners and examiners for life insurance companies, savings and loan associations, and others are primarily interested in the standing of nonconforming, problem, and delinquent loans and the lender's program of rehabilitation of such loans in cooperation with the borrower.

Every effort should be made during the interviews with borrowers on delinquent loans to impress the borrower with the seriousness of the delinquency. An interview should always be conducted on the basis of complete cooperation and encouragement, but it should be stressed that the loan must be restored to good standing by some program of payment satisfactory to the lender.

In cases of income property an exact report of the income of the borrower and condition of the family and any special conditions should be recorded or brought up to date. A plan of payment should be arranged which will obviate the necessity of the lender's acquiring the property. Any additional security such as real property or chattels should be ascertained and included in the record.

After an interview, a delinquent loan should be further identified and explained by the following comments:

1. *Promised liquidation*—monthly reduction in delinquencies on a satisfactory payment schedule.

2. *Employment and welfare cases*—including part-time work and small income, also cases where the borrower is eligible to receive, or is receiving, assistance from some public agency which will permit payment of at least current interest.

3. *Slow workout cases*—where the borrower has no present or future prospect of a quick liquidation of the delinquency, but where the equity in the property, or its rental value, warrants the lender's carrying the loan for a given period.

4. *Suspense cases*—includes all loans where some set of conditions prevents immediate action. Probate, divorce, condemnation, clearing title, quieting title, future inheritance, or seasonal income (particularly in farm loans) are examples. Also loans on which payments are subject to court order, or a composition agreement has been made. It is understood that any cases in this classification are almost certain of an eventual liquidation.

5. *Hopeless loans*—eventual foreclosure and transfer to Other Real Estate loans where no possible solution is apparent. In some instances such loans are also restored to good standing.

In the interview, the confidence of the borrower must be won, and the lender's attitude should at all times be friendly and sympathetic. Above all, the interviewer must use diplomacy in order to avoid the creation of any ill will or resentment, as such an attitude by the borrower will not only be a detriment to the lender on this particular loan but possibly on others.

All possible facts which will prove of value in reaching a satisfactory solution to the problem should be recorded.

Inspections and Reappraisals

Whenever a personal call is made by the field representative at the home of the borrower, he should make a careful inspection of the property. A well-trained field representative will note the condition of the yard and whether or not the borrower is maintaining the property in good order, or whether it shows signs of neglect. He will also inspect the exterior of the house and especially the interior to see whether or not the borrower is keeping the house in a good, livable condition. He should note particularly the condition of the paint, floors, and ceilings. If the housekeeping is good and the children are clean and well cared for, the family will probably try their best to work out their difficulty in a reasonable length of time. If the upkeep of a house is not good, the prospect of escaping trouble with the loan is not good.

A personal call has many other advantages. The lady of the house is not apt to be on the defensive at home and in familiar surroundings. Being at ease, she will talk more freely, and much more information can be obtained. If the call is intelligently made, the general knowledge gained, combined with the information in the loan portfolio, together with the payment record, should enable the servicing officer to reach a fair and final decision as to how the case should be handled.

In addition to collecting interest and principal according to the terms of the contract, another essential part of the servicing is to make certain that each property in support of a loan is properly maintained. Proper maintenance protects the security of the loan, and inspection may reveal failure to keep the property in good condition. Inspection may uncover other important information which will be helpful in deciding the best collection

methods to pursue or indicate any changes which may be required in servicing policy. The need for property inspections is greatly increased if there
is any tendency toward default in payments.

If the inspection reveals any deterioration in the condition of the property,
it is imperative that the lender see to it that these conditions are corrected,
as in some cases a failure to maintain the property could prove as serious as
failure to make regular payments. In some of these cases it is necessary that
a reappraisal of the property be made by the appraiser in order to establish
its present value. This will determine the lender's actual security supporting
the loan and any possible loss in case of foreclosure. The general question
of making reappraisals, however, is usually a matter of policy, although it is
sometimes required by state regulations or statutes. On conventional loans
where the borrower has failed to maintain regular monthly reductions of
principal, bank examiners and other supervisory authorities sometimes request reappraisals. A reappraisal provides a statement of value, as distinguished from an inspection, which provides only a statement of the physical condition of the property. The reappraisal might create an inflexible
condition which must be faced at once, in case it shows a serious decrease in
the value of the property.

During a declining real estate market many loans which have been
properly made and properly serviced will exceed the legal ratio of the loan
and the appraisal when based on current reappraisal. To an experienced
mortgage man this will not be a matter of too great concern provided the
new value reflects only a general decline in the real estate values rather
than something detrimental to the individual property or the neighborhood.

An inspection which reflects only the physical condition of the property
will frequently be sufficient to alert the mortgagee to danger in that particular mortgage. Many lenders believe that periodic reappraisals should be
made on all loans in the portfolio. Examiners view such a practice with
approval.

A current appraisal of the property is needed in all cases where a foreclosure of the property is being completed. In addition to the lenders
appraisal value, the appraiser is usually requested in such cases to determine
the current market value of the property.

On delinquent loans the inspection report should be discussed with the
borrower if the condition of the property warrants it, but a reappraisal figure
should never be given to the borrower or discussed with him. Reappraisal
figures generally do not reflect the present market value of the property and,
if disclosed to the borrower, might cause misunderstanding.

Assembling File on Each Delinquent Loan

One of the most important procedures in handling delinquent loans is
the maintenance of an up-to-date folder or record of interviews which can

be kept separately or in the loan file. No interview should be made with a delinquent borrower unless the interviewing officer has information before him covering the history of the loan.

When a delinquency first occurs, the lender should start at once to accumulate information for the successful servicing of the loan. If this information is kept up to date, a complete record is accumulated covering correspondence, telephone calls, interviews, and any other items affecting the loan. By having this information available at all times, any officer or loan servicer may quickly become familiar with every phase of the activity on each delinquent loan. Knowledge of the conditions covering any delinquent loan should never be left to memory. A record should be kept and made available for use. This not only helps the lender but also the borrower.

Other Functions

Other functions of delinquent-loan collection and servicing operations are:
1. Follow-up on delinquent taxes
2. Changes in ownership of property securing mortgage loans
3. Fire losses
4. Foreclosures
5. Collecting unpaid advances
6. Servicing of loans sold to others which have become delinquent

Unpaid taxes should be reported by the head of the tax division or by a tax servicing agency to the servicing officer promptly. In many cases of tax delinquency, tax payments are made part of the borrower's monthly payments. The lender then advances the taxes when they become due.

On loans under foreclosure it is usually the practice of the lender to pay any delinquent taxes immediately, for unpaid taxes are a prior lien ahead of the loan on the property. As in all other phases of loan servicing, the degree of insistence covering the payment of delinquent taxes depends on a consideration of all the aspects of the loan, and action should be considered on an individual basis. Nonpayment of taxes constitutes a breach of the mortgage covenants, and as they are a prior legal claim, a rigid follow-up for the payment of taxes should be maintained.

In the follow-up of delinquent loans it is often found that the property has been sold and the loan assumed by a new owner. It is important from a servicing standpoint that the new property owner's name be known promptly and that he be interviewed and informed of his responsibilities regarding payments on the loan. It is advisable when having such an interview to find out the borrower's employment, income, and a brief history of his obligations. A retail credit report covering this new borrower should also be obtained.

Some lenders sell mortgage loans which they have originated. A great majority of such sales involve loans on which the properties are located some distance from the purchaser. The mortgagee that sells the loan assigns its rights in the mortgage to the purchaser by means of a legal instrument called an assignment, which is recorded in the same manner as the mortgage. The mortgagee that sells the loan usually continues to service it and as a remuneration for the servicing operation retains a portion of the interest collected.

When a fire occurs in a property on which the lender holds a mortgage, an inspection should be made as soon as possible in order to determine the extent of the damage and to form an estimate of the probable expense of restoring the property. By having an inspection made promptly the lender is in a position to judge the fairness of the adjustment made by the insurance company. When the loss is not extensive and the amount of the loss is very nominal, it is customary for a lender to permit the owner to make the necessary repairs without supervision. The duty of the servicing officer is to exercise essential control and assure restoration of the property so that the value of the collateral covering the mortgage loan is preserved.

Loan Administration

After a mortgage loan has been placed in the portfolio, supervision of the loan follows. This operation constitutes a cycle in which the funds of the lender are converted into mortgage loans, then converted into cash, which again becomes available for investment. A break in the cycle occurs when it is necessary to complete foreclosure on loans that are not paid in accordance with their terms, or where a serious default in one of the covenants of the deed of trust or mortgage has occurred.

No longer is it the generally accepted policy that once a mortgage loan is put on the books it can be forgotten. Lenders now recognize the fact that if a mortgage loan portfolio is to be maintained in sound condition, it must be constantly supervised.

Loan portfolio administration, as previously stated, may be described as the core of the loan administration program. It must operate efficiently if these functions are to be effectively performed. Customer relations in particular must at all times be given careful consideration, inasmuch as some borrowers have no contact with the lender except through the delinquent-loan collection and servicing division.

In the administration of delinquent loan operations the administrative officer in charge of the department should at all times be kept informed of the delinquent loans in the portfolio, of the trend of delinquencies, and of any changes in the condition of the portfolio which might require special attention. The administrative officer should approve all foreclosure action and the placing of any loan in the nonaccrual classification. In addition, operating procedures, as well as personnel problems and efficiency, should be reviewed periodically. Policies covering the handling of serious delinquency cases should also be discussed with the administrative officer. Unless he is continuously informed of operations, he will not be in a position to assist in the proper operation of the division.

Real Estate Management

Not an Actual Part of the Mortgage Loan Department

Although real estate management is not technically an actual division of most mortgage loan departments, it is a very closely allied operation. The exact position of the real estate management division in a mortgage loan department is shown by item 15 in Figure 1, Chapter 3, and is identified as Other Real Estate. This division is termed Owned Real Estate by some mortgage lenders, and by some others it is called the real estate management division. No matter what title is used the operational procedures and functions are very similar in all mortgage lending companies.

Functions of Real Estate Management

The major function of such a division is the handling of all properties on which foreclosure has been completed and title to the property has reverted to the lender. This is a major responsibility. When foreclosure of a mortgage loan has been completed, the loan which had existed on the property has been transferred from the mortgage loan portfolio to the real estate management division. The property is thereafter carried on the books of the lender as Owned Real Estate or Other Real Estate.

Inasmuch as there is no longer a loan on this property, the real estate management division functions as an entirely separate entity, but the manager or other officer in charge of the mortgage loan department has a great deal to do with the functions, policies, and procedures of that division. The chief appraiser of the mortgage loan department also is closely identified with this division in assisting in establishing property values, studying market prices, and in decisions regarding the ultimate disposal of the property. For example, his opinion is needed on an FHA loan on which foreclosure has been completed regarding the feasibility of holding the property for eventual sale or transferring title to the FHA and applying for debentures. This is also the case concerning certain VA loans on which foreclosure has been completed. In the case of VA loans, however, the VA reserves the right to bid on the property at the foreclosure sale and pay the lender the full amount of the loan plus reasonable foreclosure expenses.

Use of Real Estate Agents

In the disposal and management of properties on which foreclosure has been completed many lenders use real estate agents or brokers, while others perform all these functions within their own organizations. In the latter case all such lenders place such properties which are for sale in the hands of real estate brokers. It is quite obvious that real estate brokers and other real estate agents know more about selling properties and the market on properties than does the officer in charge of the real estate management division. When properties are placed in the hands of brokers or other agents for sale or rental, careful supervision must be maintained by the real estate management division.

Responsibilities of Management

There are numerous responsibilities involved in the management of this division, the most important of which are the following:

1. Supervision
2. Development of methods to be employed covering repair and rehabilitation of the premises
3. Establishing proper and fair rental prices and sales prices
4. Decisions as to whether to hold property for future sale or to sell as soon as title is obtained
5. Maintenance of detailed and accurate records covering costs, sales, profit and loss statements on each property, as well as records of expense of management of each particular property
6. Maintenance of complete records covering real estate brokers and agents in all areas served by the lender regarding ability, reputation, clientele, organization, and efficiency of such agencies

Activity of Real Estate Management Division

During the past several years the typical real estate management divisions have been comparatively inactive, because of widespread prosperity and a rising real estate market, and foreclosures have been comparatively few in number. This division is always very active when there are upheavals in the mortgage market or an increase in unemployment or when there is general depression as there was during the period from 1929 to 1933. As delinquencies and foreclosures increase, the activities of the real estate management division increase. It usually happens that a mortgage lender acquires most properties through foreclosure at the time of a depression or recession, when the market price for any type of property is likely to be very low.

Losses on Foreclosed Loans

Losses on some conventional loans on homes during the Great Depression of the early 1930s reached as high as 33 per cent of the loan balance, while on conventional loans on farms and other types of properties losses reached 50 per cent of the balance of the loan in many cases. In the event of another serious depression it is very likely that losses would never reach the percentage noted above, for nearly all loans of recent years have been written on an amortized basis.

Selling Properties Acquired by Foreclosure

When there are numerous foreclosures, a decision must be made regarding the right time to dispose of the individual property. Many lenders feel that the first loss is the smallest loss and dispose of such properties as quickly as possible. Other lenders carefully analyze the market and sell only when they are quite certain that the best price possible can be obtained. Selling such properties quickly without regard to market conditions might, of course, have a tendency to depress the market.

Other Real Estate, or Owned Real Estate

Mortgage lenders who do not maintain property management divisions covering properties in addition to those acquired by foreclosure usually identify the real estate management division as the Other Real Estate, or Owned Real Estate, division. The functions of such a division consist of three major operations, namely, (1) maintenance inspection and repair, (2) rentals, and (3) sales.

On foreclosed properties rehabilitation and renovation in practically all cases are necessary in order that the property may be in a presentable condition when offered for sale.

Use of Rental Agents

Most lenders in leasing or renting foreclosed properties utilize the services of competent rental agents. Such agents are able in most cases to obtain the highest rents that good tenants are willing to pay.

Establishing Selling Price of Foreclosed Properties

Prior to placing a foreclosed property on the market the selling price is usually agreed upon by the chief appraiser, the manager of the Other Real Estate division, the sales agent, and the manager of the mortgage loan department. Detailed records covering listings of such properties and selling prices must be maintained. In some instances a lender in selling such a property is requested to make a loan to the purchaser for a portion of the selling price.

Purchase Money Mortgage

If such a loan is made, the mortgage is known as a purchase money mortgage. Considerable confusion exists concerning this type of mortgage. Although it is a first mortgage, it definitely differs from the regular first mortgage made by a lender on conventional, VA, and FHA loans. This type of mortgage is used primarily in the sale of Owned Real Estate, or Other Real Estate, by institutional lenders. It covers the sale of property which has been acquired by the lender as a result of the completion of foreclosure proceedings. Although there are generally no legal restrictions as to loan-value ratio and on the term of such loans, the amount of the loan is usually for not more than 80 per cent of the appraisal of the property. Usually a one-year amortized loan renewable in four years is made to cover such transactions regardless of the type of property.

In the sale of such properties the lender gives careful consideration to the credit standing of the purchaser, and the amount of cash to be paid at the time of the sale is determined to some extent by these credit factors.

Purchase money mortgages are also used when an owner of a property sells to a buyer who can pay only a small part of the purchase price in cash. The individual owner in these transactions takes back a first mortgage for the difference between the cash paid and the purchase price of the property. No other mortgage is involved in such transactions.

SUMMARY

A delinquent loan is one on which any payment specified in the note, deed of trust, or mortgage is not made when due. A loan is also delinquent when the borrower fails to comply with any other covenant of the deed of trust or mortgage.

Interest earned and collected represents the major income from a mortgage investment. Consequently, all records in delinquent-loan collection and servicing operations are based primarily on the degrees of interest delinquencies.

Regardless of the size and type of the portfolio, collection difficulties and defaults will be encountered in either good or bad times.

The most important qualification of an officer handling delinquent loans and other defaults is the ability to make collections, have other defaults cured, and at the same time retain the good will of the delinquent borrower.

There are distinct types of delinquencies, including the chronic and irresponsible, as well as the delinquent who merits every consideration where nonpayment has been due to conditions beyond his control. The servicing officer's tact and judgment are tested by his ability to meet and solve each individual situation and condition effectively.

An effective delinquent-loan collection and servicing operation cannot be maintained unless there is a foolproof follow-up procedure, as well as complete information covering each delinquent borrower.

Other requirements which are necessary in the operation of effective delinquent-loan servicing include the maintenance of adequate records covering delinquencies in various categories, and reporting of delinquent loans to both the FHA and VA in accordance with their respective regulations.

Personal contact with delinquent borrowers is now recognized as a necessary part of effective delinquent-loan collection and servicing, as in the past few years the average age of borrowers has lowered and many such borrowers need guidance, encouragement, and understanding when circumstances arise which prevent them from making a payment of the loan for either short or long periods.

Mortgage lending now reaches into every city and hamlet of our nation. This growth itself has increased delinquent-loan collection and servicing activities.

The failure to restore any given loan to good standing and the completion of foreclosure action must be due entirely to insurmountable conditions which are not humanly possible for the borrower and the lender to adjust. It is the primary duty of the officer who supervises delinquent-loan collection and servicing operations to see that the number of such loans is kept at a minimum at all times.

Real estate management is not technically a division of the mortgage loan department but is closely allied with it. Many lenders identify this division as Other Real Estate, or Owned Real Estate, which covers the handling of properties on which foreclosure has been completed.

In the disposal as well as management of such properties most lenders use real estate brokers or real estate agents, while some perform all such duties within their own organization.

There are numerous responsibilities involved in the management of this division, the most important of which are the following: repair, renovation, and rehabilitation; rentals, leases, and sales; decisions regarding selling price and whether to hold or sell a certain property; maintenance of detailed records covering costs, sales, profit and loss, and expenses of management; listings of properties, brokers, and clientele.

Real estate management operations for foreclosed properties have been comparatively inactive during recent years, as we have been in a period of prosperity and a rising market. Foreclosure completions have been few in number. Most mortgage lenders acquire properties through foreclosure during a depression period such as the period from 1930 to 1935.

When there are numerous foreclosures, important decisions are required regarding the right time to dispose of a certain property and the proper selling price.

QUESTIONS

1. Explain how a loan becomes delinquent.
2. Name the three classifications used in servicing mortgage loans

3. Explain why the work of delinquent-loan collection and servicing in large companies is usually grouped by types of loans.
4. Describe the forces and circumstances which bring about the necessity for transferring a loan to Other Real Estate.
5. Name a major cause of an increase in loan delinquencies.
6. Why are unpaid taxes a lien prior to the mortgage loan?
7. Describe the most satisfactory way of handling an interview with the borrower.
8. During what periods of time is there likely to be a great deal of activity in Other Real Estate operations?
9. Explain how the credit cycle in mortgage financing is broken.
10. Name the reasons why the administrative officer in charge of the delinquent-loan collection and servicing division approves every foreclosure action.
11. Give reasons why it is important that the delinquent-loan collection and servicing division maintain an adequate tickler system for follow-up of delinquencies.
12. Explain why a lender's collection system, if established on a personalized basis, improves customer relations and reduces delinquencies.
13. Name four situations which would place a loan in the delinquent classification.
14. Name five unwarranted reasons for delinquents.
15. Explain in what manner reappraisals are required in some states.
16. Describe the basic property management operations.
17. Name twelve functions of the delinquent-loan collection and servicing division.
18. Explain the part that maintenance and repair play in Other Real Estate operations.
19. List the items which are usually shown on the ledger card.
20. Explain why it is important to ascertain the market value of a property prior to completion of the legal action necessary to place a property in Other Real Estate.
21. From a servicing standpoint describe the most successful method of keeping the quality of the mortgage loan portfolio at the highest possible level.
22. Explain the method by which a lender obtains debentures on a foreclosed FHA loan from the FHA.
23. Give reasons why a property which has been transferred to Other Real Estate is no longer a part of the mortgage loan portfolio.
24. Explain why nonpayment of taxes constitutes a breach of the mortgage covenants.
25. Give reasons why the method of handling an interview concerning the first default is different from the method of handling an interview concerning a chronic delinquency.
26. Explain the advantage of sending a representative of the delinquent-loan collection and servicing division to call on a borrower at his home regarding payments.
27. Name some of the categories in which delinquent loans are placed after an interview.
28. Give reasons why it is necessary in some delinquency cases to have the lender's appraiser make a reappraisal of the property.

29. Give the reasons why the field representative who makes a personal call at the home of a borrower delinquent in payments is required to inspect the property carefully.
30. Name the considerations which should govern the selection of an agent to handle rental, management, or sale of foreclosed properties.
31. List the major functions of real estate management.
32. Explain why the opinion of the chief appraiser is important in real estate management operations.
33. Give the reasons why the real estate management division is not identified as an actual part of the mortgage loan department.
34. Name the parties who usually set the selling price of a property on which foreclosure has been completed.
35. Explain why it is necessary to renovate, repair, and rehabilitate foreclosed properties.

ASSIGNMENTS

1. Study and describe the organization of the delinquent-loan collection and servicing department in a company of your selection, including all forms used.
2. Write a brief report covering the type of foreclosure proceedings ordinarily used in the state where you reside.
3. Draw up an agreement between the mortgage lender and an agent covering the duties, responsibilities, and limitations of both the agent and the lender, with respect to the rental, management, or sale of a foreclosed property.

BIBLIOGRAPHY AND SUGGESTED READING

Bryant, Willis R., "Effective Loan Servicing by Commercial Banks," address, Mortgage Bankers Association of America convention, Chicago, 1949.

Bryant, Willis R., "Today's Mortgage Servicing Opportunities and Responsibilities," lecture, Western Mortgage Banking Seminar, Stanford University, Stanford, Calif., Aug. 20, 1953.

Bryant, Willis R., "This Business of Making Mortgage Loans and Servicing Them," American Bankers Association, Savings and Mortgage Division, Workshop Conference, Fairmont Hotel, San Francisco, February, 1960.

DeHuszar, William I., *Mortgage Servicing*, McGraw-Hill Book Company, Inc., New York, 1954.

Downs, James C., *Principles of Real Estate Management*, National Association of Real Estate Boards, Institute of Real Estate Management, Chicago, 1950.

Home Mortgage Lending, chap. 12, American Institute of Banking, Section American Bankers Association, New York, 1953.

Pease, Robert H., and Homer V. Cherrington (eds.), *Mortgage Banking*, chaps. 15, 16, McGraw-Hill Book Company, Inc., New York, 1953.

Appendix A

Activities of Trade Associations, Institutes, Leagues, and Societies Related to Mortgage Lending

Importance of Trade Associations

In the mortgage lending industry and related industries, trade associations, leagues, institutes, and societies were formed many years ago. These have all played a major role in contributing to the growth and development of mortgage lending. Some of these improvements include operational procedures, education, construction of houses and other types of properties, appraisal standards, and loan-administration techniques. In fact every phase of mortgage lending owes it growth and improvement, in part, to these associations.

Activities and Objectives

The activities and objectives of each one of these various types of associations are briefly described in this appendix. It should be noted that in each case the activities are nationwide. There are both state and local chapters of each, and in some cases there are state and city associations which operate as independent associations. For example, the Mortgage Bankers Association of America has its headquarters office in Chicago, and the office of its general counsel in Washington, D.C. No other branch offices are maintained. However, there are many state associations, such as the Florida MBA, the Arizona MBA, the California MBA, and the Michigan MBA, which operate as independent associations. City associations include the Chicago MBA, the Seattle MBA, the Detroit MBA, the New York MBA, and many others. Each has as one of its objectives the improvement of every phase of mortgage lending and related activities.

The major associations, societies, institutes, and leagues are the following:
1. American Bankers Association, Savings and Mortgage Division
2. American Institute of Architects
3. American Institute of Banking, Section American Bankers Association
4. American Institute of Real Estate Appraisers
5. American Life Convention
6. American Savings and Loan Institute
7. American Society of Appraisers
8. Institute of Life Insurance
9. Life Insurance Association of America

10. Mortgage Bankers Association of America
11. National Association of Home Builders
12. National Association of Mutual Savings Banks
13. National Association of Real Estate Boards
14. National Savings and Loan League
15. Society of Residential Appraisers
16. United States Savings and Loan League

Students of mortgage lending and of related industries should carefully analyze the contents of this appendix and obtain descriptive materials from the respective headquarters offices of these associations. A knowledge of these basic activities and the objectives of these associations is valuable and necessary.

American Bankers Association, Savings and Mortgage Division

Over the past fifty years, the savings and mortgage division of the American Bankers Association has played an important role in promoting thrift and home-ownership. The vast accumulation of savings now owned by the citizens of the United States is due in large measure to the foresight of the division's founders fifty or more years ago and to the officers and committeemen who, through the years, have carried on the objectives of those founders.

Commercial Banks in the Savings Business

National banks, which were organized to serve the particular needs of commerce, were accepting savings deposits within thirty years of their establishment in 1863, and by 1896 savings departments were being organized.

The recognition of savings by banks which were members of the Federal Reserve System, through amendment to the Federal Reserve Act in 1917, testified their growing importance and led to a still greater volume. The division devoted more of its attention to mortgage lending and as a consequence attracted leading mortgage men who eventually became active in the division's work. By process of evolution, the division in 1948 became the savings and mortgage division. On December 31, 1960, the mortgage holdings of commercial and mutual savings banks totaled $55.7 billion, representing 40 and 74 per cent, respectively, of savings deposits.

Ninety per cent of all banks accept savings deposits to a large extent, and invest these deposits in mortgages. Hence the division develops means to make the savings and mortgage business more profitable to banks.

Through sponsorship of thrift education, banks do a great deal in formulating habits of thrift in both children and adults. The division works closely with school savings depositories.

The division's *Home Mortgage Loan Manual,* its *Human Side of Mortgage Loan Servicing,* and other publications on construction loans, merchandising mortgage credit, and mortgage lending generally enable a bank to attain a high degree of proficiency in this field.

Through the Committee on Real Estate Mortgages, all housing and mortgage legislation introduced in Congress is studied in order to enable the ABA to state its positions clearly before committees of Congress.

The headquarters office is located at 12 East 36 Street, New York 16, N.Y.

The American Institute of Architects

The American Institute of Architects is dedicated to the betterment of the profession of architecture as a vital social force concerned with the planning of human environment in the United States. It is a national professional organization whose membership includes registered architects throughout the nation. There are chapters of the AIA located throughout the United States. Each chapter functions as an autonomous unit in seeking solutions to problems of planning the physical environment of its community. Officers at both the local and national level are elected annually by membership vote.

The birth of the AIA followed the establishment of the American Medical Association by ten years. It preceded the formal organization of the nation's lawyers by twenty-one years. Like the other two great professional bodies, the AIA has maintained throughout its history a high code of professional standards and ethics which governs the practice of the profession and the relationship of the architect to his client. Today, at the urging of the AIA state registration laws require the architect to demonstrate his competence.

In the 1890s one of the AIA's earliest public contributions was its fight to restore to the nation the original concept of the national capital in Washington, D.C., as formed by Thomas Jefferson and L'Enfant. Few will remember, or even believe, that this national shrine had been desecrated to the point that a railroad station squatted at the foot of the Capitol building and railroad tracks ran across the Mall. Led by its president, Daniel E. Burnham, a renowned architect of his day, the AIA waged a determined fight and ultimately succeeded in having the original plan restored and the eyesores were removed. In the twentieth century, both the national organization and local chapters of AIA work perpetually to safeguard and restore the aesthetic, functional, and economic values to the community.

The headquarters for the national organization is housed at the famous Octagon House in Washington, D.C., which was occupied by President Madison after the White House had been burned in 1814. The AIA has restored the historic building to its former grace as one of the most beautiful structures in Washington.

American Institute of Banking, Section American Bankers Association

The American Institute of Banking was organized in 1900 as a result of requests by bank employees in various cities for a program of education that would enable them better to understand the work they were doing. The American Bankers Association assisted the American Institute of Bank Clerks, as it was first known, and in 1908 the name was changed to the American Institute of Banking. As a section of the American Bankers Association, the Institute receives a portion of the dues paid by each bank that is a member of the Association.

The Institute's general plan of operation has been to carry on its activities through local organizations of bankers called chapters. For bankers living in communities where the banking personnel is not sufficient to maintain the chapter form of organization, Institute courses are made available either through study groups or through individual correspondence enrollment direct with the national office.

Each chapter is an independent unit as far as its local government is concerned, within the limitations prescribed by the bylaws of the American Institute of Banking and by the regulations of the Executive Council. Yet all the chapters are bound together under the general principles of the Institute idea into a national organization that is unique among organizations in this country. More than 280 chapters, many of which have been in existence for over thirty-five years, are now carrying on Institute work.

Chapters that are located in the metropolitan centers, and therefore have a large membership, find it possible each year to offer the full program of the Institute and even to offer additional banking courses demanded by local circumstances. Chapters in less populous communities usually offer the courses in rotation.

The textbooks used in all courses have been prepared especially for the Institute. Each textbook is written by a distinguished author or authors from the academic or banking fields. Bankers, attorneys, and certified public accountants are asked to contribute to or appraise textbook manuscripts. Text manuscripts are edited by a professional editorial staff.

The text material supplied by the Institute *represents the minimum requirements for any course.* The instructor may contribute as much more as he thinks desirable.

Detailed information concerning chapter organization and operation may be obtained from the national office of the American Institute of Banking, 12 East 36th Street, New York 16, N.Y.

Home Mortgage Lending

The course in home mortgage lending is designed both for students whose experience in this specialized field is limited and for those with more background in the subject. The text first discusses the background of mortgage lending experience and sets forth the fundamentals of the mortgage lending business. The greater portion of the book is devoted to a practical consideration of mortgage lending activities; the loan application procedure; the inspection and appraisal of real estate; the determination of the credit standing of the borrower and his ability to comply with the terms of the mortgage; the closing of mortgage loans; the servicing of loans; and the special attention needed for delinquent loans. One chapter is devoted to the handling of FHA-insured loans and VA-guaranteed loans and another to the management of foreclosed real estate. The closing chapter outlines the limitations on mortgage investments and the control of mortgage lending operations.

The American Institute of Real Estate Appraisers

The American Institute of Real Estate Appraisers, of the National Association of Real Estate Boards, was organized in 1932. Its objectives are to award the professional M.A.I. to properly qualified appraisers of real property, to formulate and enforce Rules of Professional Conduct, to establish educational standards for the profession of real property appraising, to encourage standards in educational institutions for the career of real estate appraising, to cooperate with the National Association of Real Estate Boards and other organized groups in developing and conducting educational programs, to promote research, and to conduct meetings, seminars, conferences, educational courses, and conventions deemed helpful in realizing these objectives.

Through its quarterly publication, *The Appraisal Journal,* and the activities of its chapters, members exchange appraisal information and cooperate generally to improve operations and techniques.

Chapters meet monthly in most principal cities, and special meetings are also held from time to time.

The headquarters office of the Association is located at 36 South Wabash Avenue, Chicago 3, Ill.

American Life Convention

The American Life Convention, organized in 1906 as a nonprofit, voluntary trade association, is the eldest international association of life insurance companies. Its membership comprises legal reserve life companies domiciled in the United States, the District of Columbia, and three provinces of Canada. The organization deals with practically all problems affecting the interests of legal reserve life insurance companies and their policyholders.

Meetings

The American Life Convention holds an annual meeting regularly each year, usually during the second week in October. Regional meetings, varying in number from three to four, have been held in recent years, usually in the spring. The various sections of the American Life Convention likewise regularly hold annual meetings.

Regional meetings are usually held each spring, the number and locations of such meetings being determined by the executive committee.

The American Life Convention has made a contribution to the legislative welfare of the business through its long-standing policy in promoting a sympathetic public attitude toward the business itself.

General bulletins, legal bulletins, an insurance law digest, a joint premium manual, a valuation and policy-form manual, and a *Newsletter,* published twice monthly, are some of the publications distributed by this association.

Headquarters offices are located at 230 North Michigan Avenue, Chicago, Ill.

American Savings and Loan Institute

Organized in 1921, the Institute has been associated with the United States Savings and Loan League since 1929. The Institute is the educational and training organization of the business, providing educational opportunities for savings association personnel. It sponsors chapters and study clubs in over 100 cities, as well as offering home study courses through correspondence. The American Savings and Loan Institute has a total membership of over 14,000 savings association people. By providing standard textbooks for use in its courses, it assists various chapters throughout the country in developing their educational programs in accordance with Institute standards and in securing competent teachers. The Institute recognizes satisfactory performances of its students by granting an achievement award, a standard diploma, and a graduate diploma.

The American Savings and Loan Institute also sponsors an annual conference for members and various regional conferences for savings association personnel.

The accounting division conducts comprehensive research on accounting subjects and makes available office equipment, forms, and supplies to assist associations in their accounting responsibilities. All the profits resulting from the sale of supplies are used to expand the Institute's educational program.

Headquarters offices are located at 221 North LaSalle Street, Chicago 1, Ill.

American Society of Appraisers

The American Society of Appraisers was organized in 1951 when the American Society of Technical Appraisers and the Technical Valuation Society merged for the common purpose.

The objectives of the Society are:

The Society shall foster the spirit of fellowship among appraisers; promote the exchange of ideas and experiences among its members; cultivate the profession of appraising; establish and maintain standards of ethics and performance for the guidance of those of its members who are engaged in the determination of the value of property, tangible and intangible, of every kind, character and description; gain and retain for the members of the Society universal recognition as qualified, objective, unbiased appraisers and advisors of property values; establish for its members the status of expert witness before courts, administrative tribunals and agencies, and other governmental and municipal authorities; award a professional designation to qualified members of the Society; and to attain recognition of the profession of value determination in property economics by educational and governmental institutions and bodies.

The American Society of Appraisers published in 1955 the *Appraisal and Valuation Manual*. The manual has received wide acclaim. It contains a wide range of articles written by outstanding specialists in their respective fields.

The Society has chapters throughout the nation. The national headquarters office is located at 1028 Connecticut Avenue, N.W., Washington 6, D.C.

The Institute of Life Insurance

In 1939 the life insurance companies formed the Institute of Life Insurance to serve as a central source of information on life insurance and to act in a public relations capacity for the life insurance business.

Membership in the Institute is open to United States and Canadian legal reserve life insurance companies doing business in the United States. The membership of the Institute represents nearly 96 per cent of the total assets of life insurance companies operating in this country.

The board of the Institute of Life Insurance appoints from its twenty members not fewer than five, nor more than seven, who serve as an executive committee. Additionally, the board appoints the chairman and elects a president, who is the chief executive officer of the Institute.

The objectives of the Institute are (1) to provide the public with a clearer concept of life insurance and what it means to them in the social and economic development of the nation, and (2) to translate public attitudes to the life insurance companies, thereby enabling them to render a better and more effective service to the public.

Probably the best-known publication of the Institute is the *Life Insurance Fact Book,* of which some 140,000 copies are distributed yearly to newspapers, radio stations, libraries, publishers, teachers, magazine editors, and others who may be researching the subject of life insurance. Production of the *Life Insurance Fact Book* is a direct responsibility of the division of statistics and research, which also supplies statistical information for Institute publications and meets thousands of requests during the year from the public for specific facts about life insurance. It is of great value to all mortgage bankers throughout the nation as the statistics on mortgages are excellent.

The Institute conducts a nationwide public service advertising program in 805 daily and Sunday newspapers.

The headquarters office is located at 488 Madison Avenue, New York City.

The Life Insurance Association of America

This association was organized in December, 1906. For the first thirty-eight years of its existence it was known as "The Association of Life Insurance Presidents." In 1944 the name of the organization was changed to "Life Insurance Association of America."

The purpose of the Association is "to promote the welfare of policyholders and the interest of life insurance." It has undertaken large responsibilities over the years and has aligned its activities with the broadening scope of life insurance in our national economy.

The Association closely follows legislation covering both life insurance and accident and health insurance in all states, Congress, and the District of Columbia and takes action through its representatives in opposition to adverse measures or in seeking appropriate amendments.

A law library is maintained which affords source material for research in connection with the Association's activities relative to legislation, litigation, and general law problems.

The Association's headquarters are located at 488 Madison Avenue, New York City.

The Mortgage Bankers Association of America

The Mortgage Bankers Association of America is the national trade association representing the principal investor and lending interests in the field of mortgage financing. Its principal interests, as well as those of its members, are in the urban mortgage field.

In 1934, the FHA was created under provisions of the National Housing Act. The Mortgage Bankers Association, at the initiation of this new venture in government, was somewhat skeptical of long-range possibilities for the Federal government in the mortgage business. It did, however, approve the basic principles of longer-term loans, regular amortization of principal and interest, and other modern innovations which the FHA system has brought to the industry.

Membership is but one interesting facet of MBA's development. Originally, members were mostly from Middle Western states and the farm states because the organization was for farm lenders. Then, after it became the Mortgage Bankers Association with the emphasis on the city side of the business, expansion began all over the country. For many years, however, the bulk of the membership was still largely concentrated in the center section of the country. The first broadening of the roster was in the East and Seaboard states and then in the Far West.

Today, membership in MBA is unique in that it combines in one group all the principal lending and investor interests, except savings and loan associations, in the mortgage industry, including life insurance and title and trust companies, commercial and mutual savings banks, and mortgage loan correspondents. It is the only national organization devoted exclusively to mortgage lending and investing.

MBA has long devoted extensive research and study to providing better and more readily available mortgage financing by which more and more people within various income groups can acquire homes.

In 1948 the MBA Seminars were started which later became the MBA School of Mortgage Banking at both Stanford and Northwestern Universities.

The Association is now approaching its half-century anniversary of service to the mortgage industry.

Headquarters offices are located at 111 West Washington Street, Chicago, Ill.

The National Association of Home Builders

Home building is the newest and perhaps the least understood of America's great industries. Although housing has always been one of man's primary concerns, it is only in recent years that the building of homes has been recognized as one of the nation's basic industries.

Behind these enormous building activities is a unique organization, the National Association of Home Builders. It numbers over 40,000 members in all parts of the nation.

The Association of Home Builders was formed in 1943 to represent home builders in all sections of the country. It sought to merge common interests, work out common problems, and give collective representation for members. Within three years after its founding the original 700 members had increased to 11,000. The governing body of the Association is its board of directors. National officers are elected annually by the board of directors. The fundamental goal of the NAHB is constantly to improve American housing, to help its members produce a better product, and to make it easier for every family to acquire a home of its own. Activities of the Association, carried out by committees and its staff, range all the way from technical improvements in planning and construction to producing materials used by teachers in educational activities sponsored by this industry.

Headquarters offices are located at 1625 L Street, N.W., Washington, D.C.

National Association of Mutual Savings Banks

The first national gathering of mutual savings bankers was held in April, 1920. Recognizing the need for the cooperative effort on an industry-wide basis, a group of 300 saving bank officers and trustees met in Boston at that time and organized the National Association of Mutual Savings Banks.

The principal purposes for which the National Association of Mutual Savings Banks was organized over forty years ago were to bring about the effective cooperation of the mutual savings banks of the United States; to advance the interests of depositors of mutual savings banks; and to encourage thrift and savings among the people of the United States by the extension of the mutual savings bank system.

Considered by many as one of the most truly representative national trade organizations in the country, the Association's member banks have assets of 99.8 per cent of the entire savings bank industry.

The headquarters office is composed of separate divisions, dealing with problems of administration, research, public relations, and bank operations. In addition, there is a legal department, with headquarters in New York and in Washington. The staff of the National Association, together with general counsel, is responsible for holding committee meetings, preparing bulletins on subjects of current interest, disseminating up-to-the-minute information to the press, arranging industry-wide conferences, attending hearings before congressional groups, and generally keeping member banks advised of all matters affecting savings bank interests. The official magazine is the *Savings Bank Journal.*

For over 145 years, during which the mutual savings banks of the nation have maintained a record of service and stability unmatched in financial annals, they have been dedicated to a cause, which, far from having accomplished its purpose, is more than ever an indispensable cornerstone in our economy and social thrift. The opportunities for mutual savings banks in the coming years are unprecedented. Through the close cooperation of all member institutions and the state associations, which the National Association has enjoyed for many years, the system as a whole can look forward to even greater accomplishments than in the past.

Headquarters offices are located at 60 East 42d Street, New York, 17, N.Y.

National Association of Real Estate Boards

The Association has Real Estate Boards and realtor memberships throughout the nation. The objectives are to unite those engaged in the recognized branches of the real estate business, including brokerage, management, mortgage financing, appraising and land development, home building, and ownership of real estate, for the purpose of exerting effectively a combined influence upon matters affecting real estate interest.

The National Association of Real Estate Boards was actually founded in 1908. At that time it was known as the National Association of Real Estate Exchanges. The first NAREB publication, known as the *National Real Estate Journal,* was started in 1910. The name of the Association was changed to National Association of Real Estate Boards in 1915. The first national program of real estate education was started by NAREB in 1923. The first full professorship in real estate was established, and the masters degree in real estate was first authorized at the University of Michigan in 1926. The American Institute of Real Estate Appraisers was formed in 1923 with the designation M.A.I. The Institute of Real Estate Management was formed in 1934, and the Home Builders Institute was formed in 1940.

The first case study in real estate appraisal was given by AIREA in cooperation with the University of Chicago in 1925.

Headquarters offices are located at 36 South Wabash Avenue, Chicago 3, Ill.

National Savings and Loan League

The National Savings and Loan League is a trade association having as its members over 600 large and progressive-type savings and loan associations throughout the country. It was formed in 1943 to provide intelligent and progressive leadership at the Federal government level for the savings and loan business.

In addition to a series of general publications relating to such matters as accounting, statistics, taxation, business reports, legal reports, etc., the National Savings and Loan League is small enough to render special services whenever called upon to do so.

The executive offices are located at 18th and M Streets, N.W., Washington 6, D.C.

Society of Residential Appraisers

The Society of Residential Appraisers is an international professional organization of specialists in residential property valuation. Organized in 1935, its aim is to promote higher standards of residential property valuation. Through its monthly publications, research bulletins, and activities of Society chapters in 107 cities in the United States and Canada, members study techniques and problems of appraising residential property, exchange appraisal information, and cooperate generally to raise the standard of appraising.

As of January, 1961, Society membership included 2,950 senior members in 820 cities plus 10,300 associate members who are directly concerned with residential property valuation. Both classifications of membership are bound by a code of ethics, copies of which are available upon request.

Society membership represents both full-time professional appraisers and others having general need for appraisal information but primarily men identified with real estate and building businesses, savings and loan associations, life insurance companies, commercial and mutual savings banks, mortgage banking firms, and government agencies.

High standards of professional conduct have been established. Understanding of valuation concepts and procedures has been expanded. Appraisal facts of both national and local nature are continuously disseminated.

The headquarters offices are located at 7 South Dearborn Street, Chicago, Ill.

United States Savings and Loan League

April, 1956, marked the 125th anniversary of the savings and loan business. By 1890 the savings and loan business was nationwide, and today it is one of the fastest-growing segments of the nation's financial system. The business specializes in thrift and homeownership. The United States Savings and Loan League is the service organization for the savings and loan business. It exists to assist in promoting thrift; to encourage private investment in the purchase of homes; to devise and secure safe methods of conducting the business of savings associations and cooperative banks; and to improve the statutes and regulations affecting the business. The United States Savings and Loan League was formed in 1892.

It is the medium by which members, large or small, can exchange experience and knowledge, thus elevating the standards and services of individual institutions and the business as a whole.

Of great assistance and value to all mortgage lenders is the *Savings and Loan Fact Book*, published yearly. This book contains a wide range of essential information on savings, home building, and savings and loan operations.

Closely associated with the League is the American Savings and Loan Institute, which has been described.

The headquarters office of the League is located at 221 North LaSalle Street, Chicago, Ill.

Appendix B

Basic Provisions of Housing Acts[1]

National Housing Act: June 27, 1934, Public Law 479, 73d Congress

This act created the Federal Housing Administration with authority to insure long-term mortgage loans made by private lending institutions on homes and to insure lenders against loss on loans financing home alterations, repair, and improvements. The act also authorized establishment of national mortgage associations to provide a secondary market for home mortgages. The Federal National Mortgage Association was later established by the Reconstruction Finance Corporation. It created Federal Savings and Loan Insurance Corporation to insure up to $5,000, for any individual, savings invested in savings and loan associations.

Reconstruction Finance Corporation Act: January 31, 1935, Public Law 1, 74th Congress

The act was amended to authorize the RFC to subscribe for or make loans upon the nonassessable stock of any national mortgage association organized under Title III of the National Housing Act and of any mortgage loan company or other similar financial institution whose principal business is that of making loans upon real estate mortgages. Pursuant to this authority, the RFC organized the RFC Mortgage Company to make mortgage loans on urban income-producing properties when credit was not otherwise available at reasonable rates.

Emergency Relief Appropriation Act of 1935: April 8, 1935, Public Resolution 11, 74th Congress

Appropriations for public works, including $450 million for housing. (WPA and Bureau of Labor Statistics in Department of Labor undertook cooperative construction pattern survey to aid public-works planning, housing projects included. WPA and Department of Commerce undertook first extensive real property inventory of urban housing conducted in 203 urban areas. Reports also included data on occupancy, condition, value, and mortgage status.)

[1] For a more complete coverage of this subject, see *Federal Housing Programs,* Washington; see also *Summary of the Evolution of Housing Activities in the Federal Government,* Housing and Home Finance Agency, Washington.

Bankhead-Jones Farm Tenant Act: July 22, 1937, Public Law 210, 75th Congress

This act authorized the Secretary of Agriculture to make forty-year, 3 per cent loans to farm tenants, laborers, and sharecroppers to finance the purchase of farms and to make repairs and improvements (including housing) and five-year 3 per cent loans for minor improvements and repairs and for the refinancing of existing indebtedness.

United States Housing Act of 1937: September 1, 1937, Public Law 412, 75th Congress

The act created the U.S. Housing Authority (originally in the Department of Interior) to provide loans and annual contributions to local public housing agencies for low-rent housing and slum-clearance projects.

National Housing Act of 1938: February 3, 1938, Public Law 424, 75th Congress

This act liberalized insurance of mortgages on new, moderate-cost homes and provided insurance of mortgages on rental housing projects built by private corporations and on farm homes.

President's Reorganization Plan No. 1: June 7, 1939, Public Resolution 20, 76th Congress

The plan was made effective on July 1, 1939. It established the Federal Loan Agency and Federal Works Agency to coordinate and supervise various other agencies, including those with housing functions. The RFC Mortgage Company, Federal National Mortgage Association, Federal Home Loan Bank Board, Home Owners' Loan Corporation, Federal Savings and Loan Insurance Corporation, and Federal Housing Administration were placed in the Federal Loan Agency. The U.S. Housing Authority was transferred to the Federal Works Agency.

Amendment of Home Owner's Loan Act of 1933: August 11, 1939, Public Law 381, 76th Congress

The act was amended to permit extension of authorization of home loans refinanced by HOLC from fifteen to twenty-five years. It authorized the Bureau of the Census, in connection with the 1940 census, to obtain data on the characteristics of the nation's housing supply and occupancy. This became the first census on housing.

Amendment to the United States Housing Act of 1937: June 28, 1940, Public Law 671, 76th Congress

The amendment was made to authorize the use of its loan and subsidy provisions and the projects provided under the act for housing defense and war workers during the period of emergency. It authorized priorities in deliveries of materials for national defense.

Second Supplemental National Defense Appropriations Act: September 9, 1940, Public Law 781, 76th Congress

This act appropriated $100 million to the President for defense housing erected by War and Navy Departments.

Lanham Act: October 14, 1940, Public Law 849, 76th Congress

As subsequently amended, this act became the basic war-housing law under which, and related laws, 945,000 public war-housing accommodations were provided, including the veterans' emergency housing built after World War II.

Soldiers and Sailors Civil Relief Act of 1940: October 17, 1940, Public Law 861, 76th Congress

This act provided relief to servicemen with respect to mortgages and other obligations.

Defense Housing Amendment (Title VI) to National Housing Act: March 28, 1941, Public Law 24, 77th Congress

The amendment authorized more liberal mortgage insurance to builders providing new homes in critical defense areas.

Emergency Price Control Act of 1942: January 30, 1942, Public Law 421, 77th Congress

The act authorized rent control, among other provisions.

Establishment of National Housing Agency: February 24, 1942, Executive Order No. 9070, President

This order transferred to the National Housing Agency responsibility for substantially all nonfarm housing programs of the Federal government (except housing located on military or naval reservations or bases). The Federal Home Loan Bank Administration, Federal Housing Administration, and the Federal Public Housing Authority became constituent agencies of National Housing Agency.

Servicemen's Readjustment Act of 1944: June 22, 1944, Public Law 346, 78th Congress

The act authorized among other things the guaranty and, later, insurance by the Veterans' Administration of GI loans to veterans to purchase, build, or improve homes.

Amendment to Servicemen's Readjustment Act: December 28, 1945, Public Law 268, 79th Congress

Major amendments to loan guaranty provisions of the Servicemen's Readjustment Act: Guaranty limit raised to $4,000 for real estate loans. "Reasonable value" of the property substituted as a criterion of eligibility in place of the previous limitation of "reasonable normal value." The maximum maturity for home loans was raised from twenty to twenty-five years. The guaranty was made automatic in the case of loans made by supervised lenders. The act authorized guaranty of loans to refinance delinquent indebtedness and also provided a system of loan insurance whereby the lender is reimbursed for losses up to 15 per cent of the aggregate amount of insured loans.

Veterans Emergency Housing Act of 1946: May 22, 1946, Public Law 388, 79th Congress

This act established the Office of the Housing Expediter on a statutory basis and reaffirmed the powers granted to the Expediter by Executive Order No. 9686. It strengthened the powers of the Expediter to establish ceiling prices and rents for new housing and to allocate or establish priorities for the delivery of materials or facilities for housing. The RFC was authorized to make premium payments to producers of building materials and to guarantee markets for new-type building materials and prefabricated houses. The FHA Title VI mortgage insurance program was amended and extended. Veterans were granted preference in the sale or rental of new housing.

Extension of RFC: August 7, 1946, Public Law 656, 79th Congress

The life and powers of the RFC were extended through June 30, 1947, authorizing, among other things, the RFC to provide a secondary market for loans guaranteed or insured under the Servicemen's Readjustment Act of 1944.

Farmers' Home Administration Act of 1946: August 14, 1946, Public Law 731, 79th Congress

This act created the Farmers' Home Administration in the Department of Agriculture and transferred to it the functions of the Farm Security Administration. It amended the Bankhead-Jones Farm Tenant Act to include, among other things, veterans' preference in direct loans to finance the purchase, enlargement, or improvement of farms and the insurance of loans made by private lending institutions for the same purposes.

Housing and Rent Act of 1947: June 30, 1947, Public Law 129, 80th Congress

The act repealed the Veterans Emergency Housing Act but extended certain provisions, with revisions. It extended Title VI mortgage insurance by the FHA and authorized insurance of loans to finance the manufacture of prefabricated houses. It required veterans' preference in sale and rental of new housing and authorized the Housing Expediter to require permits for construction of amusement and recreation facilities. It also extended rent control, with administration in the Office of the Housing Expediter.

RFC Extension Act: June 30, 1947, Public Law 132, 80th Congress

This extension eliminated authority of the Reconstruction Finance Corporation to provide a secondary market for mortgages guaranteed or insured under the Servicemen's Readjustment Act of 1944. It also provided for the transfer of all assets and liabilities of the RFC Mortgage Company to the RFC. The RFC Mortgage Company was dissolved on April 8, 1948.

Act Terminating Certain War Powers: July 25, 1947, Public Law 239, 80th Congress

The act started the two-year period provided under the Lanham Act for the removal of temporary war and veterans' housing; it also started the ten-year period during which applications for guaranties and insurance of home loans under Servicemen's Readjustment Act of 1944 could be made.

Reorganization Plan No. 3: July 27, 1947, Reorganization Plan No. 3, 80th Congress

The plan established the Housing and Home Finance Agency to succeed the National Housing Agency and to coordinate and supervise the functions of three constituent agencies—the Federal Home Loan Bank Board, Federal Housing Administration, and Public Housing Administration—and to perform other housing functions. It established the National Housing Council with representation also from several other agencies concerned with housing to promote the most effective use of Federal housing functions and activities.

Amendment to United States Housing Act of 1937: July 31, 1947, Public Law 301, 80th Congress

The act was amended to permit local housing agencies to exceed statutory cost limitations if they provided the difference between limitations and actual construction costs. It also prohibited eviction of overincome tenants from low-rent public housing if eviction would result in undue hardship.

Housing and Rent Act of 1948: March 30, 1948, Public Law 464, 80th Congress

The act extended rent control and veterans' preference in new housing to April 1, 1949. It also extended prohibition against eviction of overincome tenants from low-rent public housing.

FNMA Secondary Market Operation: July 1, 1948, Public Law 864, 80th Congress

Secondary market authorization of the Federal National Mortgage Association was extended to include GI-guaranteed or insured home and farm loans, but limited all purchases to certain GI and FHA loans (restricted to sales housing) executed after April 30, 1948. The law authorized FHA insurance of 95 per cent mortgages on veterans' cooperative housing under Title II of the National Housing Act. It also provided an incontestability clause for VA-guaranteed loans.

Housing Act of 1948: August 10, 1948, Public Law 901, 80th Congress

The act authorized the study and encouragement of modernized and standardized building codes and of standardized measurements of housing materials and parts; revised FHA mortgage insurance with liberalized provisions for insured mortgages on lower-priced sales housing, moderate-rental housing, and cooperative housing;

authorized RFC loans, and broadened FHA insurance of minimum yield on debt-free moderate rental housing; liberalized secondary market provisions of Public Law 864, 80th Congress, particularly to permit purchase of FHA-insured rental housing mortgages; eliminated restriction on removal of overincome tenants of low-rent public housing projects; authorized the VA to increase interest rate for GI loans up to 4½ per cent with the approval of the Secretary of the Treasury.

Housing and Rent Act of 1949: March 30, 1949, 81st Congress

This act amended the Housing and Rent Act of 1947, extended rent control and veterans' preference in new housing through June 30, 1950, and extended the Section 608 FHA mortgage insurance authorization on rental housing to June 30, 1949.

Housing and Rent Act of 1950: June 23, 1950, Public Law 534, 81st Congress

The act extended rent control until December 31, 1950. It also continued veterans' preference in new housing completed after June 30, 1947, until June 30, 1951. Significant among the provisions of the Housing Acts of 1948, 1949, and 1950, were the following:

1. The FNMA was empowered to borrow funds from the United States Treasury as they were needed to pay for mortgages purchased over-the-counter or under commitment contracts.

2. A plan by FHA of yield insurance guaranteeing 2¾ per cent net to investors in rental housing.

3. Permission to construct 810,000 public housing units in a six-year period and authorization of loans and grants for slum clearance.

4. Allocation of $150 million for housing and educational institutions.

5. Appropriation of $300 million for housing and educational institutions.

6. Termination of authority in October, 1950, to make Section 505 (a) loans, which left only the VA 501 loans at 4 per cent interest rate (the 4¼ per cent FHA interest rate became effective in March, 1950, when the rate was reduced from 4½ per cent).

7. Further liberalization of terms for FHA loans.

The Defense Housing and Community Facilities and Services Act of 1951: September 1, 1951, Public Law 139, 82d Congress

Congress passed this act lowering down payments required on VA- and FHA-financed homes. Under continuous pressure from Congress and from builders and others, the Federal Reserve Board, upon recommendation by, and with the concurrence of, the VA and FHA, further relaxed its Regulation X with a new schedule of low down payments, particularly on houses selling at $10,000 or less. This was made effective as of June 11, 1952.

The Housing Act of 1952: July 14, 1952, Public Law 531, 82d Congress

This act increased FHA insurance authorization by $400 million covering defense, military, and disaster housing.

The amount of commitments by FHMA which can be outstanding to purchase defense and disaster mortgages was increased by $900 million. Federal savings and loan associations were authorized to purchase loans secured by first liens on improved real estate which are insured by FHA or guaranteed by VA without regard to the 50-mile area restriction.

The Housing Act of 1953: June 30, 1953, Public Law 94, 83d Congress

This act increased FHA mortgage insurance authorization to $3.4 billion, extended maturity on low-cost homes to thirty years, and increased permissible interest rates up to 5 per cent on sales housing. It also extended Title IX authorization providing defense housing programmed by HHFA as needed for military housing or defense workers in critical defense housing areas.

The Housing Act of 1954: August 2, 1954, Public Law 560, 83d Congress

The Housing Act of 1954 was signed by the President on August 2, 1954. The new law lifted the maximum mortgage amount for new construction of FHA loans under Section 203 for owner occupancy to $20,000 for a one- to two-family structure. The loan-to-value ratio and maturity terms were liberalized considerably by the act. Loans on one- to four-family dwellings could be made up to 95 per cent of value and 75 per cent of the remainder. These ratios applied to all cases where improvements were built under FHA inspection and covered owner-occupants. A 90 per cent: 75 per cent ratio applied to any improvements on one- to four-family dwellings not built under FHA inspection. Compared with the no-down-payment, thirty-year loans then being purchased by certain insurance companies and mutual savings banks, these new FHA loans found a ready acceptance by institutional buyers in the secondary market as well as by primary lenders. Of great interest to many states was the authorization of the open-end clause in mortgages or deeds of trust securing loans insured by FHA. Thus, additional advances would be made under the original instrument for the purpose of repairs and improvements. The chartering of the new FNMA was authorized, and the liquidation of the old corporation had the following beneficial effects:

1. Greatly reduced the amount of Federal funds formerly used to support an artificially low interest rate

2. Would eventually result in the transfer of FNMA to private ownership via the requirement that sellers of mortgages to this agency must purchase nonrefundable capital stock of the new FNMA in the amount of 3 per cent of their sales to the association

The Housing Act of 1955: August 2, 1955, Public Law 345, 84th Congress

After weeks of controversy Congress passed the Housing Act of 1955 on August 2, 1955, and it was signed by the President on August 11, 1955. The principal provisions of the act covered the following:

1. Increase of FHA mortgage insurance authorization by $3.4 billion

2. Substitution of "estimated replacement cost" for "estimated value" as the basis for FHA appraisal of cooperatives and urban renewal housing program

3. Authorization of 45,000 additional public housing units during the year 1955–1956; all restrictions tying construction of these units in with urban renewal programs were removed

4. Independent administrative status for the Federal Home Loan Bank Board

The Housing Act of 1956: August 7, 1956, Public Law 1020, 84th Congress

This act was signed by the President on August 7, 1956. The principal provisions of the act covered the following:

1. A fixed interest-rate provision was written into FHA Title I. It provided for a maximum discount of 5 per cent per year for the remainder.

2. Insured loans on houses more than one-year old at the time of application may be on the terms as new construction.

3. To assist in providing housing for borrowers over sixty years old, down payments may be made by a third party on mortgages insured under Section 203.

4. In the FNMA secondary market operations the stock purchase requirement was set up to vary up or down for 2 per cent of the mortgages sold, except that the requirements may not be less than 1 per cent.

5. Federal savings and loan associations were authorized to make uninsured repair and modernization loans up to $3,500.

The Housing Act of 1957: July 12, 1957, Public Law 85-104, 85th Congress

On the last day legally available for an expression of approval or veto, July 31, the President signed the Housing Act of 1957, which became Public Law 85-104 of the 85th Congress. This act had been passed on July 12, 1957.

Some of the more important provisions of the act were the following:

1. Amended Section 203 (b) (2) of the National Housing Act to permit FHA to insure mortgages in an increased amount including approved service charges and appraisal and inspection fees

2. Permitted builders to get loans up to 85 per cent of the amounts allowable for homeowners

3. Amended Section 203 (b) of the National Housing Act to set the amount of FNMA stock subscription at not more than 2 per cent or less than 1 per cent of the outstanding amount of mortgages sold to FNMA

4. Increased the authority of the United States Treasury to buy FNMA stock by $65 million

5. Authorized the United States Treasury to buy FNMA obligations issued under its secondary market operation up to $2.5 billion instead of the previous limit of $1.35 billion

The Housing Act of 1958: April 1, 1958, Public Law 85-364, 85th Congress

The 1958 Emergency Housing Act, Public Law 85-364, 85th Congress, was signed by the President on April 1, 1958. It is known as Senator Sparkman's Emergency Housing Bill. It increased the maximum loan-to-value ratio on FHA 203 and FHA 220 loans to 97 per cent of the first $13,500 of value or replacement cost.

It increased from $450 million to $950 million the FNMA special assistance fund. It authorized an additional $25 million to FNMA for the purchase of military housing mortgages insured under Section 803 and $25 million for the purchase of mortgages at research centers under Section 809. It increased the 4 per cent interest rate to 4½ per cent, the rate ceiling on FHA Section 803 military housing mortgages.

It amended Section 305 of the National Housing Act by creating a new FNMA special assistance category, with a revolving fund of $1 million for the purchase of VA and FHA Title II mortgage loans on new construction where the loan does not exceed $13,000. It amended Section 500 (b) to permit interest rate to be adjusted by the Administrator with the approval of the Secretary of the Treasury up to a ceiling of 4¾ per cent, provided that the rate established is at least ½ per cent below the rate on FHA 203 loans. It repealed Section 605 of the Housing Act of 1957 which authorized the FHA Commissioner and the VA Administrator to regulate discounts on FHA-insured and VA-guaranteed loans.

The Housing Act of 1959: September 23, 1959, Public Law 86-372, 86th Congress

This act was signed by the President on September 23, 1959. Two previous bills had been vetoed. Some of the basic provisions of this act were the following:

1. It raised FHA residential property insurance to maximum loan limits: to $22,500 on one-family homes, $25,000 for two-family homes, with no change in three- and four-family homes.

2. It lowered down payments to 3 per cent on the first $13,000, 10 per cent on $13,500 to $18,500, and 30 per cent over $18,000.

3. The new FHA interest-rate ceiling, Section 203, on one- to four-family homes was made 5¾ per cent. The former ceiling was 5¼ per cent.

4. It made the following changes in Title III covering FNMA operations:

   a. The mortgage limit on FNMA purchases of mortgages in secondary market operations was raised from $15,000 to $20,000.

   b. The provision contained in the special assistance program permitting FNMA to make purchases at par was extended in hardship cases to cover all commitments that had been made prior to the expiration date (August 27, 1958) but not yet delivered.

   c. $25 million was authorized for FNMA purchases of Section 213, $12.5 million for consumer cooperatives, and $12.5 million for builder-sponsored cooperatives.

Housing Legislation during 1960

No housing act was passed by Congress during the year 1960, but the following housing amendments were passed:

1. To extend FHA Title I insurance program for one year and remove the dollar limitation on the authorization of that program; to provide an increase in the college-housing loan authorization and increase the limitation on other educational facilities; to increase the limitation on housing for nurses and interns; and to increase the revolving fund for public facility loans.

2. Congressional action was completed when both houses adopted the conference report on H.R. 10960, which contains the following amendments of interest to HHFA: providing Federal income tax relief to FNMA stockholders and extending

to real estate investment trusts the same type of tax treatment which is accorded regular investment companies.

The National Housing Act of 1961: June, 28, 1962, Public Law 87–70, 87th Congress

Title I: New Housing Programs

Section 101: Housing for moderate income and displaced families

This section amends Section 221 of the National Housing Act. For a newly purchased structure, the down payment must be at least 3 per cent of the acquisition cost, including closing costs. The maximum maturity is thirty-five years but may be raised to forty years at FHA's discretion.

Section 104: This is the "condominium" section, under which the FHA is authorized to insure a mortgage covering family units in a multi-family structure and an undivided interest in the common areas and facilities of the structure.

Title II: Housing for Elderly and Low-income Families

Section 201: Housing for the elderly—direct loans

Eligible mortgagors are to include consumer cooperatives and public agencies not receiving Federal financial aid under the public housing statute.

Title III: Urban Renewal and Planning

Section 301: Federal aid for small communities, etc.

This section raises the ratio of the Federal grant to total expenditure on a renewal project front two-thirds to three-fourths in any community of 50,000 population or less.

Section 306: Sale of urban renewal land for housing for moderate-income families

With the approval of the HHFA Administrator, land in an urban renewal area may be sold to a public body or to a nonprofit or limited-dividend corporation or cooperative.

Title IV: College Housing

Section 401: The loan authorization for college housing is raised by $300 million on July 1 of each year of the years 1961 through 1964. The sum allocable to hospitals is raised $30 million on July 1 of each year, 1961 through 1964.

Title V: Community Facilities

Section 501: The scope of the program is expanded to include grants for mass transportation facilities and equipment committed before December 31, 1961.

Title VI: Amendments to the National Housing Act

Section 601: FNMA special assistance authorization

The FNMA special assistance authorization is increased by $750 million to a total of $1.7 billion.

Section 602: Limitation of mortgage amount

Mortgages insured under Sections 809 and 810 and under Section

213 in urban renewal areas are exempted from the $17,500 ceiling on mortgages eligible for FNMA purchase.

Section 603: FNMA lending authority

Under this section FNMA is authorized to make short-term loans on the security of FHA and VA mortgages.

Section 605: The maximum loan schedule for insured mortgages is changed to provide for 97 per cent up to the first $15,000 of appraised value, 90 per cent of the value between $15,000 and $20,000, and 75 per cent of the value above $20,000 up to a maximum mortgage amount of $25,000 for a single-family house and $27,500 for a two-family house. The maximum maturity for loans under Section 203 prior to construction is raised to thirty-five years; it remains thirty years for other loans.

Section 610: Nursing homes

The maximum loan-to-value ratio for nursing homes financed under FHA's Section 212 is raised from 75 to 90 per cent of value.

Title VIII: Home Owners Act of 1933

This section authorizes Federal savings and loan associations to make the new-type FHA-insured home-improvement loans.

Section 902: Federal Reserve Act

National banks are authorized to make the new-type FHA home-improvement loans even though they may not be secured by first liens.

Section 903: Voluntary Home Mortgage Credit Program

This section extends VHMCP for four years.

Appendix C

State Legal Limitations Covering Mortgage Loans by Life Insurance Companies

State	Official State Legislature or Senate number	Loan-to-value ratio, per cent	Limitation as to realty to be mortgaged
Alabama	Act. 438, L. 1943	80	None
Alaska	Sec. 42-1-22	50	None
Arizona	Art. 9, Ch. 64, L. 54	66⅔	None
Arkansas	L. 1961, Act. 466, H. 488	75	None
California	A. 1859, L. 1959	75	Single family
Colorado	H.B. 174, L. 1961	75	None
Connecticut	S.B. 1132, 10/1/61	75	None
Delaware	Sec. 706 PP5, Delaware Code	75	Residential only
District of Columbia	H.R. 7145, Public Law 86-329	75	None
Florida	H.B. 1626	75	Two family
Georgia	H. 115, 56-1022	75	None
Hawaii	181-281, R.I. 1955	75	Single family
Idaho	41-627(2), L. 1951	75	Single family
Illinois	H. 863, L. 1959	75	None
Indiana	Laws 1935, Ch. 162, amended 1961	75	Single family
Iowa	H. 39, L. 1959	75	None
Kansas	S.B. 182, L. 1959	66⅔	None
Kentucky	S.B. 198, L. 1960	75	Single family
Louisiana	Act 145	75	None
Maine	No statutes		
Maryland	C.H. 216, L. 1959	75	Single family
Massachusetts	S.B. 229, L. 1960	75	None
Michigan	Statute 24-1942	75	Single family
Minnesota	S.F. 732	75	None
Mississippi	S. 1729, L. 1958	66⅔	None
Missouri	House Bill 202	75	None
Montana	Passed 1961	75	Two family
Nebraska	L.B. 690, L. 1959	75	None
Nevada	Statutes, 1960	66⅔	In Nevada
New Hampshire	L. 1955, L. 1957	80	Four family

State Legal Limitations Covering Mortgage Loans
by Life Insurance Companies (Continued)

State	Official State Legislature or Senate number	Loan-to-value ratio, per cent	Limitation as to realty to be mortgaged
New Jersey.........	R.S. 1937	75	None
New Mexico........	Sec. 58-4-7(E)	65	None
New York..........	L. 1959	75	Single family
North Carolina......	H. 193, L. 1959	75	None
North Dakota.......	Passed February, 1961	75	None
Ohio..............	S. 399, L. 1959	75	Single family
Oklahoma..........	Title 36, Sec. 172	60	None
Oregon............	738.255, 1961	80	None
Pennsylvania.......	H. 1172	75	None
Rhode Island.......	No general law		
South Carolina......	Code L 37-49, amended 1962	75	None
South Dakota.......	Sec. 31-140(1)	50	None
Tennessee..........	Passed 1961, Tennessee Code	75	None
Texas..............	S-377, H. 391, L. 1959	75	None
Utah..............	31-13-13 Code, Ann. 1953	75	Single family
Vermont...........	Act. 153, S. 59, 1945	80	One or two family
Virginia...........	Ch. 273, Virginia Laws 1960	75	Single family
Washington........	48.13.120 R.C.	75	Single family
West Virginia.......	Sec. 3428	66⅔	None
Wisconsin..........	Sec. 206.34, Statutes 1959	66⅔	None
Wyoming..........	52-1006, C.S. 1945, L. 1957	75	Single family

SOURCES: Mortgage Bankers Association of America, Education and Research Division, and mortgage banking firms.

Glossary of Terms Most Frequently Used in Mortgage Lending[1,2]

Abstract of Title. A written history of the title transaction or conditions which affect the title to a designated parcel of land from the original source of title to the present, and consisting of a summary of all the instruments disclosed by the records setting forth their material parts.

Acceleration clause. A clause in a deed of trust or mortgage which accelerates or hastens the time when the debt becomes due; for example, most deeds of trust or mortgages contain a provision that the note shall become due immediately upon the sale or transfer of title of the land or upon failure to pay an installment of principal or interest.

Acceptance. Agreement by drawee of negotiable paper to pay.

Acknowledgment. A formal declaration before a duly authorized officer by a person who has executed an instrument that such execution is his act and deed.

Acquittance. A written document which releases a person from paying a debt or performing a contractual obligation.

Administrator. A person appointed by the probate or surrogate court, or by the registrar of wills, to settle the estate of an intestate decedent. Title to property of a decedent vests in said decedent's heirs and/or devisees named in his will, subject to administration of such decedent's estate. The administrator after his appointment has merely the power to take under his control all property of decedent and administer it according to law and under the direction of the probate or surrogate court.

Ad valorem. Latin for "according to value." Used in connection with real estate taxation.

Affirmation. A solemn declaration, made by a person whose religious beliefs prohibit him from taking an oath.

Affidavit. A statement or declaration reduced to writing and sworn or affirmed to before an officer who has authority to administer an oath or affirmation.

Agency. The business of one entrusted to another.

[1] Acknowledgment is gratefully made to *Cyclopedic Law Dictionary,* published by Callaghan and Company, Chicago, for assistance with respect to certain legal definitions used in this Glossary.

[2] Acknowledgment is gratefully made to *Bouvier's Law Dictionary,* published by J. B. Lippincott Company, Philadelphia, for assistance with respect to certain legal definitions used in this Glossary.

395

Alias. An assumed name; also known as. From the Latin *alias dictus,* "otherwise called."

Amenity income property. That property which contributes satisfaction rather than money income to its owner.

Amortization. The gradual reduction of a debt by means of periodic payments sufficient to pay principal and thereby liquidate the debt.

Appraisal. The act of placing an estimate of value on real property and the process of preparing such an estimate.

Assessed valuation. The valuation placed upon real or personal property for purposes of taxation.

Assessment. A charge made against property by the state, county, cities, and authorized districts.

Assignee. One to whom property or rights to, or an interest in, property has been assigned.

Assignment. A transfer of any present or future interest in property, real or personal.

Attachment. A seizure of a defendant's property as security for any judgment plaintiff may recover in the pending action.

Attest. To witness or testify, that is, to affirm that a document is true or genuine.

Attorney in fact. One who is legally appointed by another to transact any business for him, in other words, a legal agent.

Bankrupt. Any person, firm, or corporation unable to pay his or their debts and whose assets become liable to administration under bankruptcy law for the protection of creditors.

Beneficiary. The person designated to receive the income from a trust estate, or from a trust deed.

Bequeath. To give by will; make a bequest of property.

Bequest. The act of bequeathing.

Borrower. One who receives funds, with the expressed or implied intention of repaying the loan in full, or giving the equivalent.

Breach. Violation of a legal obligation.

Broker. One who for a commission or fee brings parties together and assists in negotiating contracts between them. In real estate transactions the broker usually brings together the buyer and the seller and the mortgage lender.

Builder. One who assembles building materials in order to fabricate, erect, or construct, or who oversees building operations.

Category. Any comprehensive classification or description of things.

Caveat. Let him beware. In real estate transactions, it is a formal warning against the performance of certain acts.

Caveat emptor. Let the buyer beware.

Certificate of Claim. Certificate by the lender that a loan made under Section 501, 502, 503, 505, or 507 of the Servicemen's Readjustment Act of 1944 is in default and requesting that the VA make good the guaranty. This statement is made on Form VA 4-1874. A Certificate of Claim is also used where foreclosure has been completed and lender applies for FHA debentures. In the latter case the Certificate of Claim comprises fees for advertising, notice of default charges, fees for recording, service charges covering delinquent payments, late charges covering delinquent payments, amounts expended for repairs, revenue stamps, travel expenses (if any), title insurance premium, trustee's fee, interest figured from date interest on the loan first became delinquent to the date notice of default was filed, and interest from date of filing notice of default to date of acceptance of title by the FHA. (This interest is computed at rate on loan less rate carried in the debentures.)

Chattel mortgage. A mortgage on personal property.

Clinic. Originally a medical term meaning a group of specialists who worked together on the same patients, each doing only his specialty. A more recent meaning is any group of specialists who cooperate to solve a problem of common interest, such as mortgage lending problems.

Cloud on title. A proceeding or instrument such as a deed, or deed of trust, or mortgage, or a tax or assessment, judgment, or decrees which, if valid, would impair the title to land.

Coinsurance. An agreement between the insurance company and the insured whereby the insured agrees to insure up to full replacement value of the property and the company agrees to charge a reduced premium.

Coinsurance clause. A clause in an insurance policy which expects the policyholder to carry insurance to some named percentage of the value of the property covered. In return for this the policyholder benefits through a reduction in rate.

Collateral. Stocks, bonds, evidence of deposit, and other marketable properties which a borrower pledges as security for a loan. In mortgage lending, the collateral is the specific real property which the borrower pledges as security.

Commitment. A pledge or engagement; a contract involving financial responsibility or a contingent financial obligation to be performed in the future; a promise by a lender to make a specific loan to a prospective borrower.

Condemnation. The lawful taking of private property for public use. The owner must be given a fair price, and the property must be acquired only for some special need. The right of the state or its political subdivisions to condemn property is called the "right of eminent domain."

Condition of sale contract. The instrument containing the terms upon which the vendor of property by auction proposes to sell it.

Conditional sale contract. A contract for the sale of property, the property to be delivered to the buyer, the seller to retain, however, the title thereof until the conditions of the contract have been fulfilled.

Constant rate. Used either in purchase-leaseback transactions or in mortgage financing which involves a level payment mortgage and includes both interest and principal payments. For example, a $1 million deal at 6½ per cent interest for twenty years would be a constant rate of 8.95 per cent of the loan amount or purchase price.

Construction loan. A loan which is made to finance the actual construction of improvements on land. It is the practice to divide the loan into four or five equal parts, or disbursements, which are paid as the construction progresses.

Contract. An agreement between two or more parties to do or not to do a particular thing.

Contractor. Generally speaking, a person who undertakes an agreement to do a particular thing. In the building industry the contractor is the party who contracts to construct the edifice or improve or alter it in some way.

Contractual savings. Require fixed payments at fixed intervals, such as home-loan and installment payments.

Conveyance. The transfer of the title to land from one person or class of persons to another.

Court of equity. A court in which suits based on equitable rights may be brought.

Covenant. An agreement between two or more persons, entered into by deed, whereby one of the parties promises the performance or nonperformance of certain acts, or that a given state of things does or shall or does not or shall not exist.

Credit. The ability to borrow on the opinion conceived by the lender that he will be repaid.

Cubic foot. The number of cubic feet in a building, which is ascertained by multiplying the width by the depth by the mean height.

Curtail schedule. A listing of the amounts by which the principal sum of an obligation is to be reduced by partial payments and of the dates when each payment will become payable.

Debentures. Form of payment made by the FHA to mortgage lenders upon completion of foreclosure and transfer of title to FHA.

Debt. A sum of money due by certain and express agreement.

Deed. An instrument in writing under seal, duly executed and delivered, containing a transfer, a bargain, or contract, usually in conveying the title to real property from one party to another. There are two general types of deed—the quitclaim and the warranty. Under the quitclaim deed the seller conveys property to the purchaser, the title being only as good as the title held by the seller, who conveys all claim, interest, or right to the property as far as his own title is concerned. Under a warranty deed the seller also conveys all claim, right, and title to the property, but also warrants the title to be clear subject only to such matters as may be shown in the deed. The warranty is recognized by law as the subject for future restitution of loss to the purchaser if any defects in the title are conveyed by the seller. A seal is not required in some states; the term "grant deed" is used in place of "warranty deed" in some states.

Deed of trust. A conveyance of the title land to a trustee as collateral security for the payment of a debt with the condition that the trustee shall reconvey the title upon the payment of the debt, and with power of the trustee to sell the land and pay the debt in the event of a default on the part of the debtor.

Deed restrictions. Limitations placed in a deed limiting or restricting the use of the land.

Default. The nonperformance of a duty, whether arising under a contract or otherwise.

Deficiency judgment. A personal judgment against any person liable for the debt secured by a mortgage or deed of trust and being the amount remaining due to the mortgagee or beneficiary after foreclosure.

Demand mortgage. A mortgage which is payable on demand by the holder of the evidence of the debt.

Demise. A transfer or conveyance of rights or estate.

Depreciation. The loss of value for any reason of land or improvements. It may be physical deterioration due to wear, pests, and ravages of time, or obsolescence, a term which applies when property loses due to other influences, such as change of styles or change of character of neighborhood.

Devise. A gift of real property to another by a person's last will and testament.

Direct-reduction mortgage. A mortgage which directs that all payments have to be used for the reduction of the outstanding balance of principal.

Disbursements. See *Construction loan.*

Dwelling unit. The living quarters occupied, or intended for occupancy, by a household.

Easement. A right or interest in the land of another which entitles the holder thereof to some use, privilege, or benefit, such as to place pole lines, pipeline, roads thereon or travel over.

Eminent domain. The inherent right of a sovereign power to appropriate all or any part of the private property within its borders for a necessary use by the public, with or without the consent of the owner, by making reasonable payment to such owner.

Encroachment. An unlawful extension of one's right upon the land of another.

Encumbrance. A claim or lien upon an estate.

Escalator clause. Gives the lender the right to increase the interest rate on the loan at any time after a specified date.

Escrow. Securities, instruments, or other property deposited by two or more persons with a third person, to be delivered on a certain contingency, or the happening of a certain event; when used in the expression "in escrow," the state of being so held. The subject matter of the transaction is the escrow; the terms with which it is deposited with the third person constitute the escrow agreement; and the third person is the escrow agent.

Estate. The degree, quantity, nature, and extent of interest which a person has in real property.

Equity. Value in excess of a mortgage or deed of trust or value of an interest in a contract of sale. (See also *Court of equity.*)

Equity of redemption. A right which the mortgagor (borrower) of an estate has of redeeming it, after it has been forfeited by law by the nonpayment, at the time appointed, of the money secured by the mortgage to be paid by paying the amount of the debt, interest, and costs.

Escheat. The lapsing or reverting of land to the state.

Execution. A writ issued in the name of the people, under the seal of the court, and subscribed by the clerk, or issued by a justice of the peace directed to a sheriff, constable, marshall, or commissioner appointed by the court, to enforce a judgment against the property or person of a judgment debtor.

Executor. One to whom another person commits by his last will the execution of that will and testament.

Extended coverage. Insurance agreed to, and paid for, by the insured which covers fire, lightning, windstorm, hail, aircraft damage, vehicle damage, riot, explosion, and smoke damage.

Factor. An agent. One who transacts business for another. One specially employed to receive goods from a principal and sell them for a compensation.

Federal Home Loan Banks.[3] A system of eleven regional banks established by the Home Loan Bank Act of 1932 to provide certain facilities for savings and loan associations and like institutions, mutual savings banks, and life insurance companies in connection with their home mortgage lending activites, on conditon that they become members of the system.

Federal National Mortgage Association. An association which was organized by the RFC on February 10, 1938, under provisions of the National Housing Act. At one time grouped with other agencies to form the Federal Loan Agency, it was later transferred to the Department of Commerce in 1942, and September 7, 1950, under Reorganization Plan 22, was made a part of the HHFA. Over a period of years it was authorized to purchase or to commit for purchase FHA and VA loans totaling $3.65 billion. Funds for mortgage purchases were obtained by FNMA by borrowing from the United States Treasury. On July 31, 1953, FNMA owned loans with balances of over $2.5 billion with additional commitments to purchase $5 billion more loans. The new FNMA chartered under the Housing Act of 1954 started its activity with funds provided by government subscription of $93 million of preferred stock available from accumulated funds of the former FNMA. The rechartered FNMA, among its several duties, will manage and liquidate the former FNMA portfolio. Under the present setup, sellers of mortgages to this agency must purchase nonrefundable (but transferable) capital stock of the new FNMA in an amount of 3 per cent of their sales to that corporation. The new FNMA is authorized to sell debentures up to ten times the amount of its capital and surplus. It may purchase FHA and VA mortgages at market prices only. Hence it is prohibited from paying more for loans than the existing market price.[4]

Federal Reserve banks.[5] Reserve banks were created by, and operate under, the Federal Reserve System. Each Federal Reserve bank has nine directors, in three classes as follows:

Class A—Three directors: chosen by and representing the stockholder member banks.

Class B—Three directors: These directors must be actively engaged in their district in commerce, agriculture, or industrial pursuit and should be businessmen in their own field.

Class C—Three directors: chosen by the Board of Governors of the Federal Reserve System.

No Class B or C director may be an officer, director, employee, or stockholder of any bank. No Senator or Representative to Congress may be a member of the Board of Governors of the Federal Reserve System nor a director of a Federal Reserve bank. The capital stock of each Federal Reserve bank is divided into shares of $100 each, all of which is owned by member banks. The capital stock is dependent upon the number of member banks that each Federal Reserve bank has as its stockholders and the size of the member banks.

---

[3] See *The Federal Home Loan Bank System,* Federal Home Loan Bank, Washington, 1952.

[4] See *Background and History of the Federal National Mortgage Association,* Oct. 31, 1959.

[5] See *The Federal Reserve System: Purposes and Functions,* Board of Governors of the Federal Reserve System, Washington, 1954.

The twelve Federal Reserve districts with their respective cities and branches are as follows:

District	Reserve city	Branches
1	Boston	None
2	New York	Buffalo
3	Philadelphia	None
4	Cleveland	Cincinnati
		Pittsburgh
5	Richmond	Baltimore
		Charlotte
6	Atlanta	Birmingham
		Jacksonville
		Nashville
7	Chicago	Detroit
8	St. Louis	Little Rock
		Louisville
		Memphis
9	Minneapolis	Helena
10	Kansas City	Denver
		Oklahoma City
		Omaha
11	Dallas	El Paso
		Houston
		San Antonio
12	San Francisco	Los Angeles
		Portland
		Salt Lake City
		Seattle

Federal Savings and Loan Insurance Corporation. Created by Congress and approved by the President on June 27, 1934, insures the savings of each individual or group in an insured institution up to $10,000. It operates under the supervision of the Federal Home Loan Bank Board.

Fee. A reward or wages given to one for the execution of his office, or for professional services, as those of a counselor or physician or mortgage lender.

Fee simple. An absolute fee; a fee without limitation as to any restrictions or any particular class of heirs.

Fiduciary. One who holds a thing in trust for another, such as a trustee.

Fire insurance. A contract whereby, for an agreed premium, one party undertakes to compensate the other for loss on a specific subject by reason of fire.

First mortgage. A mortgage that is a first lien on the property pledged as security.

Foreclosure. The legal process by which a mortgagor of real or personal property, or other owner of a property subject to a lien, is deprived of his interest therein. The usual modern method is sale of the property by court proceedings or outside of court.

Freehold estate. An estate of freehold is one which is to endure for an uncertain period which must, or at least may, last during the life of some person.

Garnishee. An attachment of assets in the possession of a third person.

Grant. A generic term applicable to all transfers of real property.

Grantee. He to whom a grant is made.

Grantor. He by whom a grant is made. The seller of real property, i.e., the grantor in a deed gives up title.

Grid. Chart of weights and grades used in rating the borrower risk, the property, and the neighborhood.

Hazard insurance. A contract whereby, for an agreed premium, one party undertakes to compensate the other for loss on a specific subject by specified hazards, such as acts of God or war.

Homestead estate. The rights of record of the head of a family or household in real estate, owned and occupied as a home, which are exempt from seizure by creditors.

Household. See *Dwelling unit.*

Hypothecate. To pledge a thing without delivering the possession of it to the pledgee. To pledge to a creditor in security for some debt or demand, but without transfer of title or delivery of possession.

Income. The money return received by the owner for the use of his property by a renter, salary and wages, commissions and royalties, etc.

Income property. That property which produces a money income rather than yielding satisfaction to the owner.

Incumbrance. Any right to, or interest in, land which may subsist in third persons, to the diminution of value of the estate or tenant, but consistently with the passing of the fee.

Institutional lender. A mortgage lender that invests its own funds in mortgages and carries a majority of such loans in its own portfolio, i.e., mutual savings banks, life insurance companies, commercial banks, savings and loan associations. Although individuals hold mortgage loans and service them, they are not generally classified as institutional lenders.

Instrument. A document or writing which gives formal expression to a legal act or agreement, for the purpose of creating, securing, modifying, or terminating a right; a writing executed and delivered as the evidence of an act or agreement.

Interviewer. One who elicits information from another.

Intestate. Without having a valid will.

Irrevocable. Which cannot be revoked or recalled.

Junior mortgage. A lien that is subsequent to the claims of the holder of a prior mortgage.

Justified price. The price which an informed and prudent buyer would be warranted in paying. May or may not coincide with the market price.

Late charge. Penalty permitted by both FHA and VA covering any monthly payment not made by the fifteenth of the month in which payment is due. FHA permits 2 per cent of monthly payment, while the VA permits 4 per cent of the monthly payment. Some lenders exact a late charge for delinquencies on installments of conventional loans.

Lease. A species of contract for the possession and profits of lands and tenements either for life or for a certain period of time, or during the pleasure of the parties. (Tenements in such cases means estate or interest.)

Leasehold. The estate held by virtue of a lease.

Legal description. A description of a parcel of land sufficient to identify the property.

Legatee. One to whom a legacy is bequeathed.

Lessee. A tenant under a lease.

Lessor. One who leases.

Level-payment mortgage. One that provides for the payment of a like sum at periodic intervals during its term, part of the payment being credited to interest for the time involved and the balance of the payment being used to amortize the principal.

Levy. To raise, for example, to levy or raise a tax or an assessment; or to seize, for example, levy an execution, to raise money for the payment of a judgment.

Lien. A hold or claim which one person has upon the property of another as a security for some debt or charge.

Liquidity. A term referring to that condition of an individual or business, a high percentage of the assets of which can be quickly converted into cash without involving any considerable loss by accepting sacrifice prices.

Lis pendens. Notice of suit pending.

Loan. The letting out, or renting, of a certain sum of money by a lender to a borrower to be repaid with or without interest.

Loan-closing charges. A term applied to those charges which arise out of the final closing of a loan and the compliance with all the instructions of the mortgagor and mortgagee.

Loan trust funds. In connection with FHA and VA loans, the accumulation of funds to take care of taxes, fire insurance, and FHA premiums as they become due and payable.

Loan-value ratio. The relationship between the amount of the loan and the appraised value of the property usually expressed as a percentage.

Locked mortgages. A conventional loan on a security other than a home loan in which additional installment payments or full pay-off of the loan are prohibited for a specified number of years.

Mechanic's lien. A claim created by statutory law in most states, existing in favor of mechanics or other persons who have performed work or furnished materials in and for the erection or repair of a building. A mechanic's lien attaches to the land as well as to the building.

Merchantable title. One which a court of equity considers to be so clear that it will force its acceptance by a purchaser.

Moderator. One who restrains or regulates. The presiding officer of a meeting.

Moratorium. A period during which an obligor has a legal right to delay meeting an obligation, especially such a period granted in an emergency as to debt or generally by a moratory law.

Mortgage. A contract by which specific property is hypothecated for the performance of an act without the necessity of a change of possessions.

Mortgage insurance premium. The price paid by the borrower for insurance under FHA loans, furnished by the Federal government in favor of the lender, insuring payment of the loan in event of default by the borrower after foreclosure.

Mortgage note. A negotiable promissory note secured by a mortgage on certain specific real estate.

Mortgage pattern. The lending policy of an institution or investor regarding loans secured by real property.

Mortgage portfolio. The aggregate of mortgage loans held by the lender.

Mortgage risk. The hazard of loss of principal and/or interest in the loaning of funds secured by a mortgage.

Mortgagee. The lending party under the terms of a mortgage.

Mortgagor. The borrowing party who pledges property.

Mutual Mortgage Insurance Fund. A fund (established under the National Housing Act) into which all mortgage insurance premiums and other specified revenue of the FHA are paid from which losses are met.

Mutual Mortgage Insurance system. A plan (established by the National Housing Act and administered by the FHA) for insuring lending institutions against hazards in connection with mortgage loans.

Negotiable note. A note which may be transferred from one person to another in the course of business, and which entitles the last holder to collect the sums due.

Net income. That part of the gross income which remains after the deduction of all charges or costs.

Net worth. The equity of the owners in the business, i.e., the net assets determined by subtracting all liabilities from the value of the assets.

Net yield. The yield of certain property, real or otherwise, clear of all charges and deductions; that part of the gross yield which remains after the deductions of all charges or costs.

Open-end mortgage. Mortgage, or deed of trust, written so as to secure and permit Additional Advances on the original loan.

Operative builder. A builder for his own account who erects houses for sale to others at an expected profit; a speculative builder.

Option. The right, acquired for a consideration, to buy or sell something at a fixed price within a specified time.

Other Real Estate. Real estate owned by a lender usually acquired by foreclosure of deeds of trust or mortgages.

Package mortgage. A mortgage or deed of trust including certain items which are technically chattels, such as stoves, refrigerators, washing machines, and garbage-disposal units.

Panel. A group of men gathered together to discuss questions of mutual interest.

Party wall. A wall built along a lot line, in which adjoining owners have a mutual interest.

Percentage lease. A lease which provides for a rental based upon the amount of business done by the tenant.

Personal property. Estate or property which is not real property, consisting of things temporary or movable—chattels.

Plat. A map showing dimensions of a piece of real estate based upon the legal description.

Power of attorney. An instrument in writing whereby one person, the principal, authorizes another, the attorney in fact, to act for him. The powers are determined by the express terms of the instrument itself; they are not implied, except in so far as may be necessary to carry out the powers expressly granted.

Prepayment penalty. Penalty for the payment of a debt before it actually becomes due.

Price. The consideration in money given for the purchase of a thing.

Promissory note. A note bearing evidence of debt and transferrable by endorsement.

Property mortgage. A mortgage on the right and interest which one has in lands and chattels to the exclusion of other persons.

Purchase money mortgage. A first mortgage, but one which definitely differs from the regular first mortgage made by a lender on conventional, VA, and FHA loans. This type of mortgage is used primarily in the sale of Owned Real Estate, or Other Real Estate, by institutional lenders. It covers the sale of property which has been acquired by the lender as a result of the completion of foreclosure proceedings. Although there are generally no legal restrictions as to loan ratio and on the term of such loans, the amount of the loan is usually for not more than 80 per cent of the appraisal of the property. Usually a one-year amortized loan renewable in four years is made to cover such transactions regardless of the type of property. In the sale of such properties the lender gives careful consideration to the credit standing of the purchaser, and the amount of cash to be paid at the time the sale is determined to some extent by these credit factors. Purchase money mortgages are also used when an owner of a property sells to a buyer who can only pay a small part of the purchase price in cash. The individual owner in these transactions takes back a first mortgage for the difference between the cash paid and the purchase price of the property. No other mortgage is involved in such transactions.

Quitclaim deed. A deed of release. An instrument by which all right, title, or interest which one person has in or to an estate held by himself or another is released or relinquished to another.

Rate. A public valuation or assessment of every man's estate; or the ascertaining of how much tax everyone shall pay.

Rating. Grade; classification. A credit rating is a letter or number used by a mercantile or other agency in reports and credit-rating books to denote the ability and disposition of various businesses to meet their financial obligations.

Real estate owned. All real estate owned by a lender other than that carried as Other Real Estate.

Real property. Land and generally whatever is erected on, or growing upon, or affixed to, land.

Realtor. A real estate broker who is an active member of a member board of the National Association of Real Estate Boards, and as such an affiliate member of the National Association, who is subject to its rules and regulations, who observes its standards of conduct, and is entitled to its benefits.

Reconstruction Finance Corporation. A Federal government financed corporation, created by the Reconstruction Finance Corporation Act, approved January 22, 1932. The general purpose of the laws creating this corporation was to stop deflation in agriculture and industry and thus increase employment by the restoration of men to their normal jobs. This corporation is no longer in existence.

Reconveyance. To convey back or to the former owner. An expression generally used in California referring to a release of deed of trust.

Refunding. The process of refinancing a debt which cannot conveniently be paid when due.

Rental value. The estimated amount of rent which could be obtained for the use and occupancy of a property.

Replevin. The return to, or recovery by, a person of goods or chattels wrongfully taken or detained.

Reproduction cost. The sum of money which would be required to reproduce a building less an allowance for depreciation of that building.

Reserve. This term has a number of technical meanings. In banking it most frequently refers to the legal reserve which banks must maintain on deposit with the Federal Reserve System. The Federal Reserve System Board of Governors has the power to raise and lower reserve rates, within statutory limits, to control the supply of credit.

Reversionary clause. A clause which provides that any violations of restrictions will cause title to the property to revert to the party who imposed the restriction or to his nominee.

Right of redemption. The right of the owner to reclaim title to his property if he pays the debt to the mortgagee within a stipulated period of time after fore-closure.

Right of way. Authority to use the lands of another for ingress and egress.

Risk analysis. The analysis of the risks involved in a given undertaking; usually prepared prior to embarking on the undertaking.

Risk rating. A process by which the various risks usually divided as to (1) neighborhood, (2) property, (3) the mortgagor, and (4) the mortgage pattern are evaluated. Usually the system employs the use of grids to develop precise and relative figures for the purpose of determining the over-all soundness of the loan.

Risks. In insurance, those causes against loss from which the insurer is to be pro-tected by virtue of the contract for insurance.

Sales agreement. An agreement by which one of two contracting parties, called seller, gives a thing and passes the title to it, in exchange for a certain price in current money to the other party, who is called the buyer, or purchaser, who on his part agrees to pay such price.

Satisfaction. Settlement of a claim or demand; payment.

Secondary financing. A loan secured by a second mortgage or deed of trust on real property.

Security. Something given, deposited, or pledged to make secure the fulfillment of an obligation or the payment of a debt.

Service charge. A fee which is charged by a bank against a depositor for services rendered in the bookkeeping of the depositor's account.

Servicing. The collection of payments of interest and principal, and trust fund items such as fire insurance, taxes, etc., on a note by the borrower in accordance with the terms of the note. Servicing by the lender also consists of operational procedures covering accounting, bookkeeping, insurance, tax records, loan-payment follow-up, delinquent-loan follow-up, and loan analysis.

Setback. The distance from a lot line which by law, regulation, or restriction in the deed must be left open; the linear distance between the lot line and the build-ings or building line.

Shiftability. A quality that renders an investment exchangeable in the market with little if any variation in price.

Special assessment. A special charge against real estate such as a street assessment or sewer assessment for installation of public improvements from which the property benefits.

Square-foot cost. The result, in dollars, of dividing the cost of the improvements by the number of square feet of floor therein. (See also *Cubic foot.*)

Subordination. The act of a creditor acknowledging in writing that the debt due him from a debtor shall be inferior to the debt due another creditor from the same debtor.

Subpoena. A writ commanding the person designated in it to attend court under a penalty for failure.

Subrogation. The substitution of another person in the place of the creditor, to whose rights he succeeds in relation to the debt.

Surety. One legally liable on default of another.

Teller. One who receives payments of any nature to apply on a mortgage loan, including pay-offs, which are tendered in person by the borrower at the office of the lender. Makes entry of payment in passbook, or issues other type of receipt used by lender. Balances receipts and disbursements at end of each day in accordance with accounting procedure of lender.

Term. The period or duration of a note, acceptance, time draft, bill of exchange or bond; synonymous with tenor and usance.

Termites. Antlike creatures which infest lumber. They gnaw tunnels in it and breed. There are two types, namely, the subterranean type which works between the ground under buildings and the structure above, the floor, the sills, and the studding. The other, a flying variety, lodges in the roof or walls.

Term mortgage. One having a specific term, usually not over a five-year maturity, during which interest is paid but the principal is not reduced.

Title. The means whereby the owner of lands has the just possession of his property.

Title theory and lien theory. Some states in the nation, known as "title-theory states," have the view that a mortgage gives the mortgagee some sort of legal title to the land. Other states, called "lien-theory states," have the view that the mortgage has merely a lien to secure the debt.

Torrens Certificate. A certificate issued by a public authority, known as register of titles, establishing title in an indicated owner. Used when title to property is registered under the Torrens system.

Trust deed. An agreement in writing conveying property from the owner to a trustee for the accomplishment of the objectives set forth in the agreement. Trust deeds are generally used in many states rather than mortgages to secure loans on real property.

Trustee. A person, real or juristic, holding property in trust. (See *Fiduciary.*)

Unencumbered property. Property that is free and clear of any assessments, liens, easements, or encumbrances of any kind.

United States government marketable securities. This market is the basic bond market of the nation. It is the price trend in this market which vitally affects the price trends in all other bond markets and the markets for corporate securities and municipal bonds. It is through its operations primarily in United States Treasury bills that the Federal Reserve System (our central bank) operates to add to or cut down on the supply of money in the nation. It is through the operations in this market that the Federal Reserve System influences trends of interest rates.

United States government nonmarketable securities. These are mostly the familiar savings bonds. They cannot be traded or transferred. Savings bonds are not sold but are redeemed.

United States Treasury bills. Regular issue of bills have a maturity of ninety-one days and are almost the equivalent of cash.

United States Treasury bonds. These are, by accepted definition, securities that when sold have a maturity of more than five years. A bond with a term of five to ten years is called a medium-term bond; a bond with a maturity of over ten years is called a long-term bond.

United States Treasury certificates. These are securities issued with a maturity of not more than one year.

United States Treasury notes. These are securities issued with a maturity of not less than one year nor more than five years.

Valuation. The act of establishing the value of real property. (See *Appraisal.*)

Vendee. The person to whom a thing is sold.

Vendor. Seller.

Waiver. The relinquishment of a right or refusal to accept a right.

Warrant. A covenant whereby the grantor of an estate and his heirs are bound to warrant and defend the title. (See also *Deed.*)

Waste. Willful damage to property.

Weight. Form of valuation for the portion of the rating of the borrower, property, and neighborhood.

Without recourse. When a person endorses a note in such a manner that he does not guarantee its payment to future holders, he endorses the note *without recourse.*

Zoning. A legislative process by which restrictions are placed upon the use to which real property may be put.

Index